"To have such a comprehensive res[...] from such a range of authors is like [...] hard to find such a compendium. Like the slow turning of a large diamond, this book displays the many facets of the wonder of Christian worship."

—**Lester Ruth**, Duke Divinity School

"Who is the God worshiped by ordinary churchgoers, and how is that God related to the Holy Mystery studied by biblical scholars and theologians? This book attempts to bridge the gap between these two worlds, inviting worshipers to reflect more deeply on familiar acts such as prayer, singing, sacraments, and proclamation, and to consider how their embodied acts cohere with what we say we believe. Worship leaders from a wide variety of backgrounds will benefit from this solid body of work by both senior and emerging scholars in the fields of biblical studies and systematic, historical, missional, and liturgical theologies."

—**Martha Moore-Keish**, Columbia Theological Seminary

"'Christians tend to *experience* worship more than *think* about it.' This provocative phrase introduces readers into a thoughtful exploration of how fundamental Christian doctrines sustain, shape, and are expressed in liturgical practices and vice versa. Written by leading scholars and practitioners, clearly organized, profound but accessible, and ecumenically sensitive, *Theological Foundations of Worship* is an essential guide for those seeking to gain a deeper understanding of the multifaceted connections between what we believe and what we do in corporate worship."

—**María Eugenia Cornou**, Calvin Institute of Christian Worship

"In a pain-full world, worshipers crave the immediacy of a direct experience of God in worship—to feel whole. The desire to *feel* something instantly each time we gather, however, often takes priority over the need to *reflect* intentionally on the meaning of worship. The diverse perspectives in this volume's depths offer an opportunity to reconnect feeling and reflecting with doing. Place this book beside your prayer book, your devotional guide, your hymn book, your favorite sacred video clips, or your spiritual playlist of songs, and let them talk with each other. You will *feel* more deeply and *worship* more fully."

—**C. Michael Hawn**, Perkins School of Theology, Southern Methodist University (emeritus)

Theological Foundations of Worship

Worship Foundations

*How Theology, History, and Culture
Inform Our Worship Practice*

Series Editors: Melanie C. Ross and Mark A. Lamport

Theological Foundations of Worship

Biblical, Systematic, and Practical Perspectives

Edited by
Khalia J. Williams and Mark A. Lamport

Introductions by
NICHOLAS WOLTERSTORFF and N. T. WRIGHT

Baker Academic
a division of Baker Publishing Group
Grand Rapids, Michigan

© 2021 Khalia J. Williams and Mark A. Lamport

Published by Baker Academic
a division of Baker Publishing Group
PO Box 6287, Grand Rapids, MI 49516–6287
www.bakeracademic.com

Printed in the United States of America

Library of Congress Cataloging-in-Publication Data

Names: Williams, Khalia J., editor. | Lamport, Mark A., editor. | Wolterstorff, Nicholas, writer of introduction. | Wright, N. T. (Nicholas Thomas), writer of introduction.

Title: Theological foundations of worship : biblical, systematic, and practical perspectives / edited by Khalia J. Williams and Mark A. Lamport ; introductions by Nicholas Wolterstorff and N. T. Wright.

Description: Grand Rapids, Michigan : Baker Academic, a division of Baker Publishing Group, [2021] | Series: Worship foundations : how theology, history, and culture inform our worship practice | Includes bibliographical references and index.

Identifiers: LCCN 2020049531 | ISBN 9781540962515 (paperback) | ISBN 9781540964366 (casebound)

Subjects: LCSH: Worship.

Classification: LCC BV10.3 .T44 2021 | DDC 264—dc23

LC record available at https://lccn.loc.gov/2020049531

21 22 23 24 25 26 27   7 6 5 4 3 2 1

Contents

Preface

Khalia J. Williams and Mark A. Lamport

Three concepts occupy our minds and motivate us to explore theological considerations of worship in this book.

First, Christians tend to *experience* worship more than *think* about it. Believers treasure comfort with familiar patterns of worship, acts of ritual, and behaviors of movement and inherently resist contemplation of comprehensive or coherent theology of worship. To some degree, our human nature prompts us to coast when we can and push aside the difficult process of analysis. Understandable, yes, but those who are charged with worship and ministry leadership should have an intentional connection of what they profess to believe (theoretically) and what they plan and perform (practically) as worship. After all, God's very being and action drive us to seek God, demand that we imitate God, and compel us to praise God. And, as Ron Highfield rightly deduces, "We cannot know God without passion, longing, seeking, following, and praising. To know him is to praise him, for he is most worthy of praise."[1]

Experiences in Christian worship simultaneously reveal the profundity of our waywardness and the magnificence of God's being. Illuminations, therefore, that emerge from worshipful encounters are part of our Christian formation—the first part to recognize our lack; the second part to will personal reform; and the third part to act, and in doing so, to be reshaped individually and corporately. As Don Saliers, architect of fifteen books on

1. Ron Highfield, *Great Is the Lord: Theology for the Praise of God* (Grand Rapids: Eerdmans, 2008), 201–2.

the relationship of theology and worship as well as the author of chapter 4 in this book, points out, "In worship, people are characterized, given their life and their fundamental location and orientation in the world."[2] As the church worships, faith is incubated, and the believer's place in the world is more clearly understood. As Debra Murphy observes, "In corporate worship the lives of Christians are formed and transformed, Christian identity is conferred and nurtured."[3]

But Nicholas Wolterstorff, from whom you will soon hear in the series introduction to follow, is concerned that all too often biblical and theological doctrines have been displaced, discarded, or forgotten in favor of therapeutic, relational, or managerial knowledge drawn less from the canonical Scriptures than from the canon of contemporary popular culture.[4]

Jim Wellman, one of the editorial advisory members for this series and the author of chapter 16 on secularism and worship, points to the prevalence of "megachurches" as evidence of this shift in focus. He argues that worship in megachurches is designed to touch, create, and respond to a set of six desires in human beings: welcome, a "wow" moment, a charismatic figure, invitation for deliverance, invitation to purpose, and small-group community. This is a perfect function of French sociologist Émile Durkheim's social dualism of personal fulfillment and social connection, says Wellman; this dualism is always swinging back and forth and is very hard to maintain, but megachurches do it with great artistry.[5]

Second, God is worthy of worship, and this task induces the church's identity. Wolterstorff and Wellman call upon us to reconsider the nature of worship and its connection to theology. Christian theology is about the God we worship; correspondingly, the way we worship should actually reflect our theological beliefs. Russian Orthodox theologian Alexander Schmemann proclaims: "Worship is the life of the Church, the public act which eternally actualizes the nature of the Church as the body of Christ."[6] Swiss Reformed theologian J.-J. von Allmen unveils this DNA structural, formative process:

2. Don Saliers, "Liturgy and Ethics: Some New Beginnings," in *Liturgy and the Moral Self: Humanity at Full Stretch Before God*, ed. E. Bryon Anderson and Bruce Morrill (Collegeville, MN: Liturgical Press, 1998), 17.

3. Debra Dean Murphy, *Teaching That Transforms: Worship as the Heart of Christian Education* (Grand Rapids: Brazos, 2004), 16.

4. Nicholas Wolterstorff, *The God We Worship: An Exploration of Liturgical Theology* (Grand Rapids: Eerdmans, 2015).

5. James Wellman Jr., Katie Corcoran, and Kate Stockly, *High on God: How Megachurches Won the Heart of America* (Oxford: Oxford University Press, 2020).

6. Alexander Schmemann, *Introduction to Liturgical Theology* (Crestwood, NY: St. Vladimir's Seminary Press, 1966), 12.

"By its worship, the Church becomes itself, becomes conscious of itself, and confesses itself as a distinct entity."[7]

Therefore, our worship contains theology in code, to translate what is expressed by the language of its worship—its structures, its ceremonies, its texts, and its spirit—into the language of theology. To worship is to pay reverence and to honor God for God's worth. Worship is a mode of acknowledging who God is and the greatness of what God has done, is doing, and will do. In other words, the unsurpassable excellence of God.

Why then, laments Wolterstorff, do some alternative, contemporary liturgies strip so many things out? Why is there no confession of sins? Why no intercessions? Why no readings of Scripture? Why no sense of the majesty of God?[8]

Wolterstorff further affirms God as worthy of worship, as one who is vulnerable, as one who participates in mutual address, as one who listens, as one who hears favorably, and as one who speaks. God, he says, "does not only stoop down to listen to us, to hear us, and to speak to us; God stoops down to dwell and work within us in the person of Jesus Christ through the action of the Holy Spirit."[9]

Third, there is a prevailing—albeit misconceived—idea that worship is music and music is worship. Admittedly, definitions of worship are not easily offered; in this series we see it from a holistic view inclusive of music, preaching, prayer, art, liturgy, service, sacraments, initiation, and so on. In addition, we recognize the liberative and restorative role music has held in worship for certain cultural contexts, especially within marginalized communities. At the same time, we note that in some worship settings, music has become the very definition of worship; it is where the planning and theological processes start and stop. Paul Westermeyer, longtime professor of church music at Luther Seminary, observes that some theological schools have largely abandoned an integrated theological study of Christian music.[10] This historical omission, he conjectures, may have led to the prevailing idea of worship misconceived as primarily music. James Hastings Nichols gets at this when he points out that eighteenth- and nineteenth-century evangelical revivals had an overriding concern for conversion. Sermons were designed to convert the unconverted, and Sunday worship left its liturgical moorings. Serious Christians went to midweek services to praise and commune with

7. J.-J. von Allmen, *Worship: Its Theology and Practice*, trans. Harold Knight and W. Fletcher Fleet (London: Lutterworth, 1968), 42.

8. Wolterstorff, *The God We Worship*, 23–24.

9. Wolterstorff, *The God We Worship*, 161.

10. Personal email communication with the editor (June 18, 2018).

God, and congregational "sung praise" at the presumably primary service on Sunday was silenced. That turned worship toward religious entertainment. As that turn was filtered through the American economy, conversion became less important (or was forgotten or misconceived), while the marketing of God gained control—concerns for numbers and bottom lines took precedence, and music became a primary means to persuade people to come to church. Voilà: worship is the way you market a product called Christianity, and music is its primary sales tool.

Worship is experienced as a normalized function of Christian bodies, whether they be Orthodox, Roman Catholic, Anglican, mainline or evangelical Protestant, Pentecostal or independent; yet now the assumptions that drive worship are less considered by clergy and laity.

When the church reflects on its worship, possibilities for corrective measure, where necessary, are more likely. For example, quadrants of the global church, primarily the Western church, have in some respects drifted away from worship as a community endeavor to that of individually negotiated experiences, which values "my" relationship with God over that of "our" shared relationship together. As a further cautionary tale, wrong-headed emphases that laud personal success and even economic prosperity may sometimes trump an orthodox rendering of the church-in-worship.

Concept of the Book and the Series

To address these three preliminary concepts and others, we are motivated, in this book and in this series, to attempt a reconciliation of the differences between the God studied by theologians and the God worshiped by churchgoers on Sunday. Such reconciliation seems imperative, to say the least. Worship is one of the central functions—if not *the* central function—of the church along with mission, service, education, justice, and compassion. Since worship occupies a prime focus of Christianity, a renewed sense of awareness of one's theological presuppositions must be maintained to ensure authenticity in worship. We invite the reader's vigorous interaction with Martyn Percy's "Epilogue" (after chap. 17 below), designed to assist each reader in mapping out their own personal theology of worship. This was a subject of interest in the 1960s with Vatican II; that also is when Protestant communities increasingly attempted to address matters of inculturation. Of late, increased cultural issues have come to dominate and drive much of the reflection on worship.

Therefore, this Worship Foundations textbook series is designed to explore accessible yet focused themes in the academic domain of practical theology/

liturgical studies and arises from an observable dearth in the literature on theological, historical, sociological, and biblical foundations for the practice of authentic worship. Our intention is that Orthodox, Catholic, Anglican, Pentecostals, independents, and various sectors of all Protestant stripes could resonate with the theological themes and language herein. These books will present scholarship on the history of, and updated reports on, the practices of engaging worship across the breath of the Christian tradition.

Most introductory textbooks on Christian worship are organized around themes. Consider three of the most widely used books currently on the market: James F. White's *Introduction to Christian Worship* (Abingdon, 2001), Juliette Day and Benjamin Gordon-Taylor's *The Study of Liturgy and Worship* (Liturgical Press, 2013), and Ruth C. Duck's *Worship for the Whole People of God* (Westminster John Knox, 2013). Each of these books has specific strengths (e.g., Duck's volume emphasizes African American, Korean, and Latinx contributions). However, there is also considerable overlap between the volumes. These books include chapters on prayer, music, space, time (liturgical calendar), preaching, baptism, and the Eucharist.

This organizational structure—one that privileges lectionary readings, liturgical seasons (Advent, Epiphany, Lent, Pentecost, etc.) and assumes weekly celebration of the Eucharist—makes logical sense to students who come from High Church traditions. However, students from free-church backgrounds—as are many who identify with evangelical tendencies—approach the study of Christian worship with different questions and expectations. This book is intended to be accessible to an evangelical audience as well (in addition to other theological orientations) by offering a biblical and theological orientation and by highlighting themes not discussed in competing works: for example, in chapters on creation, pneumatology, sanctification, and mission.

Because of the prevalence of worship across the world, we argue that the heuristic pragmatism of the topic demands a more comprehensive treatment as opposed to only disparate individual titles. The Worship Foundations series is a synchronic study presenting and celebrating the state of contemporary worship and the various faith traditions and unique practices. It is also a diachronic study remembering and rehearsing the historical evolution of Christian worship in the global arena. Such study is particularly timely because of the approaching third millennium of the church beginning in 2033.

Series Introduction

Nicholas Wolterstorff

Professor of Philosophy Emeritus, Yale University

This first volume of the series Worship Foundations offers essays on the theological foundations of worship; the next volume offers essays on the various historical traditions of worship. In each case, it is Christian communal worship of God that the writers have in mind. In this introduction to the first book in the series, let us reflect on the practice itself, Christian communal worship of God, and conclude by asking, Who are the agents of such worship? A continuation of this introduction will appear in the next volume of the series.

In what follows, I employ a term that almost all writers on these matters use: "liturgy." In the introduction to the second volume, I will discuss, in some detail, just what it is that we are referring to when we speak of "liturgy." But I judge that no confusion or obscurity will result from using the term while postponing that discussion. A worship service is an enactment of a liturgy. And the agents in a worship service are liturgical agents.

What Are We Doing When We Worship God?

What is worship? My *Merriam-Webster's Collegiate Dictionary* (11th ed.) tells me that our word "worship" comes from the Middle English "worshipe," meaning "reverence paid to a divine being." It says that the Middle English "worshipe" comes, in turn, from the Old English "weorthscipe," which is a combination of the term "weorth," meaning worth or worthy, with the suffix "-scipe," which means the state of something. The term "worship" in present-day English remains true to its etymological origins: to worship God is to pay reverence to God for God's worth. It is a mode of acknowledging God's worthiness: the excellence of who God is and the greatness of what God has done, what God is doing, and what God will do. In Christian worship, we acknowledge the *distinctive and unsurpassable* excellence of God.

There are other ways of acknowledging God's distinctive excellence—for example, by obeying God's injunction to love our neighbors as ourselves and by participating in God's cause of bringing about justice. But these ways of acknowledging God's excellence are not worship of God. Why not? What is distinctive of worship as a mode of acknowledging God's excellence?

What is fundamentally distinctive, I would say, is the *orientation* that characterizes worship. In our everyday lives we are oriented toward our tasks, toward our fellow human beings, toward what they do and make, toward the natural world. In worshiping God, we turn around and orient ourselves toward God. We turn away from attending to the heavenly bodies, away from attending to our neighbor, and so forth, in order to attend directly to God. We face God. In worship, our acknowledgment of God's excellence is *Godward* in its orientation.

We are close to identifying the species of acknowledging God's excellence that is worship of God, but we are not quite there yet. What's missing, I would say, is what I will call a certain *attitudinal stance* toward God. In the absence of that distinct attitudinal stance, Godward acknowledgment of God's distinctive excellence is not yet worship of God.

By the term "attitudinal stance," I do not mean a feeling or emotion. The stance may include a feeling or emotion, but it is not to be identified with either of those. An attitudinal stance toward someone is a way of regarding that person. Regarding someone with admiration is an example of an attitudinal stance toward that person; regarding someone with disdain is another example.

The English term "adoration" seems to me to best capture the attitudinal stance of the worshiper toward God; our worship of God is our adoration of God. To adore something is to be drawn to it on account of its worth, to be gripped by it for its excellence. We speak of adoring some person, some work of art, some scene in nature.

Adoration has different content depending on the object of adoration and on how the adoring person understands that object; adoration of a painting by Vincent van Gogh is different in its content from, say, adoration of some mathematical proof. So let us dig inside the Christian adoration of God so as to identify some of its content.

Our adoration of God, for God's distinctive and unsurpassable excellence, incorporates being in *awe* of God for God's excellence. In the Orthodox liturgy, after the bread and wine have been brought into the sanctuary and the Eucharist proper is about to begin, the priest says, "Let us stand reverently; let us stand in awe."

The content of our adoration of God includes more than awe, however. One can be in awe of something without worshiping it. The destruction wreaked by a tornado evokes awe but not adoration. In our adoration of God, what more is there than awe?

My dictionary's description of the etymology of our word "worship" suggests that beyond awe there is *reverence*. "In reverence, let us stand before the Lord." Reverence is not the same as awe; nobody reveres the awesome power of a tornado.

Without now making any claim to exhaustiveness, I suggest that the adoration definitive of Christian worship has yet a third component: *gratitude*. One would need to be dull indeed not to notice the prominence of gratitude to God in Christian worship.

Let me pull things together. I suggest that Christian worship of God is a specific mode of Godward acknowledgment of God's distinctive and unsurpassable excellence. Specifically, it is that mode of such acknowledgment whose attitudinal stance toward God is awed, reverential, and grateful adoration. Christians do not assemble and engage in ritual actions to placate God, they do not assemble to keep themselves in God's good graces, they do not assemble to keep their ledgers on the positive side—or if they do assemble for such reasons, what they are doing is profoundly wrong. They assemble to worship God. Facing God, they acknowledge God's distinctive and unsurpassable greatness in a stance of awed, reverential, and grateful adoration.

No one presently writing about Christian worship would say that Christians assemble to placate God, to keep themselves in God's good graces, to keep their ledgers on the positive side, or anything else of the sort. What one does find is that a good many writers, instead of focusing on the thing itself—namely, worship of God—focus instead on one or another *function* of worship. Some focus on the *formative* effect on those who worship, virtually ignoring the thing itself, the worship of God. And some focus on the *expressive* function of worship—we express our feelings, our convictions, our commitments—and virtually ignore the thing itself, the worship of God.

Common though these functional understandings are, they distract us from the worship of God. If we are formed by worship, it is by engaging in the activities of worshiping God that we are formed. We express our "religious affections," as Jonathan Edwards called them, by engaging in the activities of worshiping God. The worship of God is basic. Its formative and expressive functions, though important, are secondary. When we focus on the functions of worship, human beings displace God as the focus of our attention.

We Worship God with Our Bodies

A fundamental feature of Christian communal worship is that we worship God with our bodies—with our minds too, of course, yet indeed with our bodies. It is by using our vocal cords to utter words and sing hymns that we praise God; it is by using our ears to listen that we apprehend what God says to us in the reading of Scripture and in the preaching of the sermon; it is by kneeling and bowing that we humble ourselves before God as we say our petitions. Elsewhere I have employed so-called speech-act theory to explore, in depth, how this works: how it is that by making certain sounds with my vocal cords I do that quite different thing of praising God.[1]

Of course, not everyone can speak or sing, not everyone can listen, not everyone can kneel or bow. But everybody who participates in Christian worship can perform, and does perform, at least some of these bodily activities. Everyone who participates in any way worships God with their own body. Nobody worships as if they had no body, as if they were disembodied.

It is not only by worshiping God with our bodies that we incorporate the physical world into our worship. We also do so by employing material things and substances in our performance of liturgical actions: water, bread, wine, crosses, candles, fire, Bibles, hymnals, liturgical texts, in some traditions also incense, in some traditions also icons, likewise on and on. We worship God not only with our bodies but also with water, with fire, with bread, with wine. We do not leave the physical world behind when we assemble to worship God; we bring it with us in order to incorporate it within our worship, thereby bestowing upon it a dignity it had not previously known.

Who Are the Liturgical Agents?

Who are the agents in Christian communal worship? The answer seems obvious: all those who have assembled for worship, the people and those who lead

---

1. See chapter 4 in my book *Acting Liturgically* (Oxford: Oxford University Press, 2018).

them. To us this answer seems obvious, but to many in previous centuries it would have seemed not obvious but false.

In late medieval Western Christianity, it was commonly thought that liturgy is the work of the clergy; they are the liturgical agents. With the exception of Easter, when laypeople were expected to receive the bread of the Eucharist, laypeople were to use attendance at a liturgical enactment as the occasion for private devotions that were, ideally, related in some way to what was going on in the liturgy. Books were published giving guidance for such devotions. In his fascinating book *The Stripping of the Altars: Traditional Religion in England, c. 1400–c. 1580*, Eamon Duffy writes:

> The pious lay person at Mass was urged to internalize [by vividly imagining the events of Christ's life and death] the external actions of the priest and ministers. The early sixteenth-century treatise *Meditatyons for goostely exercyse, In the tyme of the mass* interprets the gestures and movements of the priest in terms of the events of Maundy Thursday and Good Friday, and urges the layman to "Call to your remembrance and Imprinte Inwardly In your heart by holy meditation, the holl processe of the passion, frome the Mandy unto the point of christs deeth." The effect of this sort of guidance was to encourage the development of representational [i.e., symbolic] elements in the liturgy and to set the laity looking for these elements.[2]

It was typical of participants in the so-called Liturgical Movement of the early twentieth century, and of writers influenced by them, to claim that in classical and Koine Greek the term *leitourgia* referred to *actions of the people*[3] and then to use that etymological claim to make the polemical point that liturgy is not what the clergy alone do but what the people do along with their leaders. An indication of the success of the Liturgical Movement on this point is that it now seems obvious to us that not just the clergy but also *the people* are liturgical agents. Liturgy is not just what clergy do.

But are the people and those who lead them the only liturgical agents? We could ask what the term "the people" means in this question. Does it refer to the individual persons, or does it refer to a collective entity, the people? Is it just individual persons who praise God together, or is it also the collective entity—the people—praising God? Important though that question is, let it

---

2. Eamon Duffy, *The Stripping of the Altars* (New Haven: Yale University Press, 1992), 19.

3. I understand it to be the view of all Greek scholars that this is not what *leitourgia* meant in classical and Koine Greek. The term referred not to action *of* the people but to an action *for* the people. A *leitourgia* was the contribution by a well-to-do person to some public project—the building of a ship, for example. Andrew Carnegie's funding of libraries across the United States was his *leitourgia*—his liturgy.

pass. However we understand the reference of the term "the people," are the people and those who lead them the only liturgical agents?

They are not. Along with many others, I hold that God is also a liturgical agent. When we address God in praise, thanksgiving, confession, and so forth, God listens. By the reading of Scripture and the preaching of the sermon, God speaks to us. By the celebrant offering us the bread and wine of the Eucharist, Christ offers himself to us. And if God blesses what we are doing, the Spirit is active among us. The role of God as liturgical agent is discussed in considerable detail in several of the essays in this volume.

Introduction

N. T. Wright

Research Professor of New Testament and Early Christianity,
St. Mary's College, University of St. Andrews/Senior
Research Fellow, Wycliffe Hall, University of Oxford

Finding myself paired with Nick Wolterstorff in this volume—he introducing the series and I introducing this first book within it—takes me back to the summer of 1988, when Nick and I were both teaching summer courses at Regent College, Vancouver. We were staying down the hall from each other in a faculty residence and frequently met to discuss what we were doing. Among other topics was the fact that the students taking his course and the students taking my course (in the same time period, so there was no overlap of students) were comparing notes and coming to the conclusion that we were saying quite similar things.

This was initially puzzling. My course was a historical study of Jesus in his first-century context, a foretaste of my 1996 book *Jesus and the Victory of God*.[1] Nick's course was titled Liturgy and Justice. What could such different topics have in common? Reflecting on that now, over a quarter of a century later, I think we were both part of a larger movement of thought. The present series of books is a later fruit of that movement. So now, rather than weary the reader by "introducing" the present essays one by one—they can do that for themselves—we may profitably reflect on the significant change that has

1. N. T. Wright, *Jesus and the Victory of God*, Christian Origins and the Question of God 2 (London: SPCK; Minneapolis: Fortress, 1996).

come over much of Western Christianity in the last generation, with the new interest in liturgy as a fascinating and important marker.

With hindsight we can see that the evangelical movements of the middle and late twentieth century were heavily influenced by forms of Platonism. The eventual goal was that the "soul" should leave "earth" and go to "heaven." What mattered in the present was therefore to turn away from the things of earth and cultivate the life of heaven, starting with the initial act of justifying faith. This should not then be compromised by any adding of "works," since that would be taking back with a Pelagian left hand what had just been given away by an Augustinian right hand. All this was heard within a Platonic world. The much-revered C. S. Lewis himself, though often pointing toward a more Jewish vision of renewed creation, allowed his alter ego in the children's stories to murmur that the Narnian experience was "all in Plato."[2]

Thus, when it came to Jesus and the New Testament, we knew in advance what ought to be said: Jesus was the divine Son of God. No doubt he was a human being, but that really wasn't the point (this remains a problem in systematic theology to this day). Any attempt to locate Jesus in his actual historical setting was suspect; the attacks of "historical criticism" had to be kept at arm's length. This often led to a suspicion of the task and discipline of "history" itself—and with that, to a wariness about consulting, as historical waymarks, the Jewish writings of the period. Were they not concentrating on earthly things and advocating "works"? In my own research, then and subsequently, I was firmly rejecting this whole approach. The Word, after all, became *flesh*.

Likewise, when it came to issues of justice, locally or globally, the strongly Platonic streak of evangelical Christianity urged people to resist any engagement or involvement. These were "worldly" issues, and we should leave them to the politicians and social workers. Our task was to save souls for eternity, not to oil the wheels of a machine that would one day fall over a cliff. This regularly meant supporting the status quo, or at least discouraging people from questioning it. This was what Nick was challenging, as he has continued to do.

The same approach showed up, finally, in liturgy. The rejection of apparently High Church practices—processions, robes, incense, chanted Psalms, not to mention genuflection and crossing of oneself—had several cultural roots, not least the folk memories of sixteenth-century Protestant martyrs and, in Britain and thence in America, the sense that the Reformation had successfully freed the country from the pope's foreign rule. This was, again,

2. C. S. Lewis, *The Last Battle*, The Chronicles of Narnia, book 7 (London: The Bodley Head, Random House, 1956), 759.

coupled with the suggestion that any kind of organized liturgy was a covert form of "works," and since Protestants always suspected Roman Catholics on that front, there was all the more reason to deconstruct the liturgy and its attendant practices. The second half of the twentieth century thus saw more and more evangelical churches, even in mainline denominations like my own, shedding the last vestiges of formal liturgy, replacing the organ with a rock group, and exchanging the robed choir for sound technicians and video projectors. Somehow these didn't count as "works" in the same sense. The charismatic renewal has sometimes, no doubt accidentally, added to this an impression that any "prepared" or printed liturgy was by definition a restriction of Spirit-led freedom, though as that movement comes of age, there are welcome signs of a serious return to liturgical responsibility. But in these ways the cult of "spontaneity," a major feature of secular culture at the time, smuggled itself into unwitting churches under cover of a basically Platonic spirituality. Again, Nick's work on liturgy has refused to accept this movement and has charted a quite different course.

The analogy between what I was doing with Jesus in his historical context and what Nick Wolterstorff was doing with justice and with liturgy should thus be clear. We were both trying to roll back the tide of Platonism and re-establish the truth that God the Creator could be believed in and honored by bodies, history, communities, and even rituals. After all, even the most free of free churches have "rituals." Nobody suggests, I think, that the "freedom of the Spirit" in worship might be compromised because the guitarist needs to practice those chord sequences in advance. And to suppose that God the Creator was indifferent to injustice—that he was not appalled at racist policies in South Africa or the Southern states, or at the wickedness of corrupt tyrants or warlords—meant turning a blind eye not just to the Old Testament but also to the teaching of Jesus himself. (But then, the actual teaching of Jesus never featured large in evangelical circles, since one knew in advance that his real concern, supposedly backed up by a truncated reading of Paul, must have been to save souls for heaven.)

Cultural changes never take place overnight, and many churches still display the confusions I have listed, and more besides. The reason for this is fairly clear (as I have argued in more detail in my 2019 book *History and Eschatology: Jesus and the Promise of Natural Theology*).[3] In the eighteenth and nineteenth centuries, the Western world as a whole absorbed a reborn Epicureanism. God was pushed upstairs, and the world below continued under its own

---

3. N. T. Wright, *History and Eschatology: Jesus and the Promise of Natural Theology* (London: SPCK; Waco: Baylor University Press, 2019).

steam—in politics, history, economics, science, ethics, and other spheres too. (The idea that this secularism is a new thing, the result of scientific inquiry, is a mere smokescreen: the appeal to ancient Epicureanism is clear throughout the movement.) Things that the churches had done before—including education, medicine, and the care of the poor—were taken over by the state, leaving the church to save souls and teach people to pray to the now-distant God. *And the churches have, by and large, gone along for the ride*, accepting a diminished role and not noticing, for instance, that things commanded and modeled in the New Testament, like speaking God's truth to the powers of the world (think of Jesus addressing Pilate in John 18 and 19!), were being taken over by other agencies, in that case the journalists. The churches' retreat into Platonism, in other words, has been an understandable though highly regrettable reaction to modern Epicureanism. No matter if God is in a far-off "heaven"; we have "souls" that can get in touch with him there and finally escape to join him in his distant paradise.

But Platonism remains deeply unsatisfactory for any serious Christian, for any reader of Scripture. The Bible from Genesis to Revelation insists upon the goodness of creation and upon the solid promise that the Creator God will put creation to rights at last. This essentially Jewish vision was what lay behind Jesus's announcement, the key to his whole public career, that God's kingdom was coming "on earth as in heaven" (cf. Matt. 6:9–10) albeit through the unexpected means of his own messianic death, resurrection, and ascension. This is what Paul meant when he declared in his most famous letter that the good news of Jesus unveiled to the world the faithfulness of God—God the Creator, God the covenant-keeper. This result, not in an *escape from* the present creation, groaning in travail as it is, but in the *redemption of* that creation itself, something much Western Protestantism had never really thought through.

Once we grasp this Jewish vision of the gospel and discern the many ways in which it supplies the proper answer to the Epicureanism of Western culture, many lines of thought open up, including the kind of historical study of the New Testament that I have undertaken and the work for justice, both in theory and in practice, that Nick Wolterstorff has been doing. Between those two, history and justice, we find liturgy: the point at which, and means by which, the body of Christ here on earth joins with the whole company of angels and archangels in heaven, in anticipation *not* of a supposed ultimate time when we shall leave earth and go to join that heavenly host, but of the promised time when "all things in heaven and on earth" will be united in the Messiah himself (cf. Eph. 1:10), when the "new heaven and new earth" (Rev. 21:1) will be not two things but one, because God will be "all in all" (1 Cor. 15:28). All things *will be* put right (justice); all things *have* in principle *been* put right in Jesus, the Messiah and Lord (history); the church celebrates all that *will be* (justice) in advance by gladly rehearsing the story of what *has been* put right in Jesus (liturgy).

Christian liturgy—as the essays in this book explain from many angles— must therefore be formed, and where necessary re-formed, on the principle of *inaugurated eschatology*. By that I mean that in Jesus, as Israel's Messiah, the Creator God has launched his sovereign and saving rule on earth as in heaven. The goal is to bring all things in both spheres into one; the means to this is sketched in the Sermon on the Mount. The church's task in the present is to live by heaven's joy amid earth's continuing sorrow; to celebrate heaven's sovereignty in the face of earth's tyrannies and anarchies; to invoke heaven's healing love on the world, which is suffering from the sickness unto death. Every act of Christian worship, from the solitary Christian kneeling down in a private room to the vast cathedral congregation singing its heart out, is an anticipation of that eventual joy, that sovereignty, that healing love. It is a temple moment, when heaven and earth are held together, with image-bearing humans standing dangerously in the middle. It is a Sabbath moment, when the age to come arrives mysteriously in the present as we anticipate God's completion of the new creation.

What is more, every act of worship joins the present-day church with genera- tions long gone. This is why the historical study of liturgy matters so much. It isn't just that we can learn from our elders and (often) betters. It is that their worship remains part of the whole worship of God's Christ-shaped, Spirit- filled people, in which we also partake. We have a responsibility the other way too: so to worship in the present that those who come after us may be able to share with us while also bringing their own new and particular gifts to the table.

That is another reason why serious reflection on liturgy, such as we find in this book ably edited by Khalia Williams and Mark Lamport, matters so much for the Protestant and evangelical traditions at this present time. In many contemporary churches, the puzzling rejection not only of the great hymns but even of the Psalms themselves, along with many great prayers, means that a generation may be growing up seriously impoverished. My hope and prayer for this book is that it will help our churches to explore, delight in, learn from, and reinhabit the best of the past, and in particular to understand and appreciate what good liturgy is and why it matters. It is time, and more than time, to put away our Platonic prejudices and to embrace, in worship as in so many other ways, the good news that in Jesus the life of heaven has come to earth and that in the Spirit that heaven-and-earth life is ours as well, anticipating and thus sustaining our hope for God's completion of what was launched through Jesus. May this book be a means, under God, of that celebration and that hope.

PART 1

Biblical Practices of Worship

Exegetical and Biblical Theology

— 1 —

Old Testament and Worship

Andrew E. Hill

The Bible records the story of "salvation history," God's progressive plan of redemption that culminates in the Christ event: the life, death, burial, resurrection, and ascension of Jesus the Messiah. The ultimate destination of God's story is worship, the worship by his people Israel (Isa. 43:7), the worship by his church (1 Pet. 2:4–5), and the worship by the nations (Ps. 86:9). Worship is "the human response to God."[1] According to Robert Webber, "worship does God's story"; that is, worship is a narrative that tells the story of God's redemptive activity in history.[2] The basic plotline of the biblical story may be outlined as follows:

1. Daniel I. Block, *For the Glory of God* (Grand Rapids: Baker Academic, 2014), 23. Robert E. Webber's definition of worship in its broadest sense as "a meeting between God and His people" found in *Worship Old and New* (Grand Rapids: Zondervan, 1982), 11, is helpful to the discussion of Old Testament worship, especially since the tabernacle was also known as the "tent of meeting" (Exod. 27:21; 28:43). This chapter assumes a progressive or developing monotheism for the Hebrew people from Abraham to the time of Moses (cf. Block, *For the Glory of God*, 35–37). A nascent trinitarian understanding of the One God is also assumed, given the "plurality" of God revealed in the Old Testament (with references to the Creator God, the Spirit of God [Gen. 1:1–2; cf. Isa. 63:10–11], and the angel of the LORD, who receives worship [Exod. 3:2–4; Judg. 6:21–22; 13:20]).

2. Robert E. Webber, "Worship Does God's Story," in *Ancient Future Worship* (Grand Rapids: Baker Books, 2008), 29–40.

Triune God of the Bible
↓
Creation→ Fall ↓→ ←Judgment→ ←Redemption→ Re-creation
[. . . . . Covenants . . . .][3]

Old Testament Worship and the Primeval Prologue: Genesis 1–11

The early chapters of Genesis portray humanity in a direct relationship with God as Creator. This immediate and ongoing experience of God's divine Presence emphasizes worship in the form of intimate fellowship with the Creator (cf. Gen. 3:8) and in the form of service to God in priestly management of their garden environment (2:15).[4] This human propensity for worship is rooted in the nature of persons created in God's image (the *imago Dei*), the image (essence) and likeness (nature) of God (1:26–27).[5] Significantly, God's creation of woman as the fitting complement to man (2:20–24) "completes the preparation of the image of God and emphasizes an equal share in fulfilling God's will on earth, specifically, worshiping and serving the LORD, ruling and having dominion over the earth, and producing life—not just physical life but eternal and spiritual life."[6] The fall of humanity was both "paradise lost" and "worship lost." Our ancestral parents were overcome by the temptation to become "like God" (3:5). The mystery of divine testing and an explanation for the probationary experience of humanity in the garden aside, God delights in loving obedience from his human creatures, not forced submission.[7] The rest of the biblical narrative tells the story of God's relentless and gracious pursuit of humanity, to restore the worship we once knew in the intimacy of his divine Presence.

---

3. Central to this redemptive plan is the "offspring theology" announced in Gen. 3:15—the promise of a child who will overcome the enemy of humanity and set all things right. The means by which God redeems fallen creation is in the reestablishment of relationship with humanity through a series of covenant enactments. These covenants begin with Adam (though the term "covenant" is not found in Gen. 1–2; cf. Hosea 6:7), Noah and his family (Gen. 9), continue with Abraham and Sarah (Gen. 12; 15; 17), are extended to the Israelite nation through Moses at Mount Sinai (esp. Exod. 19–24), are expanded to include kingship through the line of David (2 Sam. 7), are consolidated and universalized in the new covenant proclaimed by Jeremiah (Jer. 31), and find fulfillment in the New Covenant realized in the Christ event (Luke 22).

4. See Allen P. Ross, *Recalling the Hope of Glory: Biblical Worship from the Garden to the New Creation* (Grand Rapids: Kregel, 2006), 106, on Adam and Eve as archetypical Levites.

5. On the relational nature of the *imago Dei*, see Jeremy S. Begbie, *Voicing Creation's Praise: Towards a Theology of the Arts* (Edinburgh: T&T Clark, 1991), 150–51, 181–82.

6. Ross, *Recalling the Hope of Glory*, 107.

7. Worship is an act of the will as well as an emotional response of the heart to God. Note the repeated imperatives to love God and obey his commands in the Mosaic Law (e.g., Deut. 6:4–5; 10:12; 11:1).

After the fall, humanity responded to God in worship in various ways: presenting tribute offerings (Gen. 4:1–5), calling on the name of the Lord in prayer (4:26), living an obedient life before God (5:22, 24; 6:9), offering sacrifices of thanksgiving (8:20–22); accepting God's post-flood covenant to fulfill the earlier creation mandates to populate the earth (9:18–19; cf. 1:28). Although the origins of proper worship of God after the fall are unclear, it is likely that God revealed liturgical forms by which reverent awe might be appropriately expressed.[8]

Two of the worship accounts in Genesis 1–11 are especially instructive for biblically informed worship. The first, the presentation of tribute offerings by Cain and Abel (4:1–5), places emphasis on the heart and attitude of the worshiper, not the type or quality of offering given. As Daniel Block observes, Cain responded in anger to God's rejection of his offering, not in humility and remorse.[9] His anger led to the murder of his brother and lying to God (4:5–9). In retrospect, the New Testament indicates that Abel's offering was accepted because God deemed him to be righteous (Heb. 11:4).

The second account, the post-flood worship of Noah, also contributes to the biblical understanding of post-fall and post-flood worship. Our basic definition of worship is seen in Noah's response to God's deliverance with thanksgiving, symbolized in ritual sacrifice (Gen. 8:20). The mysterious but consistent interplay of God's work of judgment and redemption is situated in covenant relationship (Gen. 9). A series of God-initiated covenant relationships with humanity will undergird his redemptive story (cf. Gen. 12:1–3). Noah's altar building and presentation of clean animals as burnt offerings foreshadows one of the core rituals for worshiping God in the patriarchal and Mosaic eras of Israelite history (Gen. 8:20–22; cf. 15:9–11; Exod. 20:24–26).

Old Testament Worship during the Patriarchal Period (2000–1400 BC)

Progressive revelation in the Old Testament (i.e., the gradual self-disclosure of God to his people) implies a progressive understanding and practice of worship as well. The variety of terms for worship used in the Old Testament reveal the multifaceted character of Hebrew worship and indirectly speak to its developmental aspects.[10]

8. Block, *For the Glory of God*, 59.
9. Block, *For the Glory of God*, 61.
10. One word for worship is often translated "seek, inquire" (Heb. *dāraš*; Pss. 24:6; 69:32 [33 in MT]; Isa. 11:10), indicating that genuine worship is a quest for God—not out of duty, but freely and earnestly in gratitude for God's goodness (Pss. 27:4, 8–9; 63:1–4). Worship is to revere, venerate, and fear God with a sense of awe and respect (Heb. *yārēʾ*). The righteous do fear the Lord because of who he is as a unique, holy, just, loving, and merciful God; and for what he does

The developmental nature of Hebrew worship is also evidenced at times in the worship responses of the patriarchs to specific events of divine revelation. For instance, altar building was a key element of patriarchal worship. These altars often marked site-specific places of theophanies and were associated with acts of ritual sacrifice and prayer (Gen. 12:8; 26:25; 35:7; cf. Exod. 20:24–26). In addition, altar building sometimes precipitated a change in place name as a result of divine intervention and a dramatic word from God (e.g., "Adonay-Yireh [The LORD Will Provide]," Gen. 22:14; El-Bethel, ["God of Bethel"], 35:7). The numerous names ascribed to God through the biblical narrative were another way the Hebrew patriarchs and matriarchs came to know the character, attributes, personality, and purposes of their God.[11]

The worship by Abram and Sarai was divinely initiated: their worship of God occurred as he revealed who he is in word and deed. And that worship was divinely motivated: their worship was the human response to divine self-disclosure (notably in theophany). We learn that "the LORD said to Abram, 'Leave'" (Gen. 12:1), and "Abram left" (12:4). His response of obedience was an act of worship, another illustration of the basic definition of worship selected to frame this study.[12]

During this era significant developments in worship include covenant-renewal ceremonies (Gen. 15:8–21; 35:11–15); the rite of circumcision as a sign of covenant obedience (17:9–14); prayer (praise and thanksgiving, 12:8; 13:4); intercession (18:22–23) and petition (24:12); altar building (e.g., 12:7, 8; 13:18; 22:9); the setting up of stone pillars and pouring of libations as a drink offering (28:18, 22; 35:14); taking of vows (31:13); sacrificial offerings of animals and foodstuffs (31:54; 46:1); pilgrimage to sites of theophany (35:1); tithing and a cultic meal of bread and wine (14:17–24).

The Joseph story supplies a definition of divine providence: God's overruling for good (Gen. 50:20). This theological truth will inform the prayers

---

as Creator, Covenant Maker, and Israel's Redeemer (Lev. 19:32; Ps. 27:1; Hab. 3:2). Worship is also "work" (Heb. 'ābad) in the sense of performing a service to God (Exod. 3:12; Isa. 19:21, 23). The "loyal service" of worship includes obedience to the commandments of God (Deut. 10:12, 20). Drawing near to God (Heb. nāgaš; qārab) is another aspect of Old Testament worship, implying the observance of appropriate protocol and proper rites of purification (Exod. 19:22; 20:21; Lev. 9:6–7; Num. 4:19; Jer. 30:21). These worship-related terms indicate that God is approachable and desires to have a meaningful relationship with his people (Deut. 4:7). For a catalog of Old Testament worship-related terms, see "Old Testament Vocabulary of Worship," in *The Complete Library of Christian Worship*, ed. Robert E. Webber (Nashville: StarSong, 1993), 1:3–9.

11. On the importance of the divine names and titles of God in the Old Testament for worship, see Andrew E. Hill, *Enter His Courts with Praise!* (Grand Rapids: Baker, 1996), 280–83.

12. God's promise to bless the nations through Abraham and Sarah was tied to a specific piece of real estate (Gen. 12:1–3). The divine placement of Israel in the land of Canaan, or Palestine, thus at the crossroads of the ancient trade routes, facilitated the Hebrews' role as the light of God's revelation to the nations (cf. Isa. 49:6; 51:4; 60:2–3).

of God's faithful, especially prayers of lament, petition, and intercession in times of crisis (cf. Pss. 33:18–22; 44:23–26 [24–27 MT]; 73; Lam. 3:19–27; Hab. 3:1–19).

Abram's encounter with Melchizedek, the priest and king of Salem, is an important episode in God's redemptive story (Gen. 14:17–20). Abram and Melchizedek have the "Most High God" in common. He blesses Abram, suggesting his own primacy. The psalmist references the priesthood of Melchizedek in the context of Davidic kingship. On the basis of the Melchizedek story, the book of Hebrews develops the theology of the greater priesthood of Jesus the Messiah (Heb. 4:14–5:10; 7:1–28). Ralph Martin observes that "at this early offering of thankful worship to Yahweh, the basic elements of Israel's worship form were present. From [Israel's] nomadic beginnings, [its] worship included theophanies, promises of the land, the practice of marking important places with an altar, the figure of a high priest, and a cultic celebration using bread and wine."[13]

The story of Abraham's "binding" of Isaac (Gen. 22) is an example of the interface of culture and revelation. The mystery of testing and providing in God's redemptive dealings with fallen humanity, including the introduction of the divine name Adonay-Yireh, "The LORD Will Provide," is emphasized (v. 14). The story dramatizes a theological truth by means of an object lesson and teaches that the ultimate purpose in worship is the glory of God. The memorializing of a foundational theological principle through story, in this case God's disapproval of human sacrifice, affirms the principle of "substitution" in sacrificial worship (cf. Lev. 18:21; Deut. 12:31; 18:10).

Old Testament Worship during the Mosaic Period (1400–1000 BC)

The miraculous deliverance from Egypt and the covenantal experience at Mount Sinai are known as the formative period of Israelite religion. The exodus from Egypt is the major redemptive event of the Old Testament and the prototype of Christ's atoning work (cf. John 1:29; 1 Cor. 5:7). The character of worship as spiritual warfare is clearly portrayed in the exodus event, when God brought judgment on the Egyptian gods (cf. Exod. 12:12; 15:3; 18:11).

One striking feature of the Hebrew exodus narrative is the revelation of the divine name YHWH to Moses prior to his ministry as Israel's deliverer (Exod. 3:14). The ineffable name YHWH, the "I AM," embodies several aspects of God's nature and character, including holiness, transcendence,

13. Ralph P. Martin, "Worship," in *International Bible Encyclopedia: Revised*, ed. G. W. Bromiley (Grand Rapids: Eerdmans, 1988), 4:1118.

immanence, provision, and eternality (see God's "self-characterization" in Exod. 34:6–7).[14]

Central to the Sinai covenant experience is the conflict between the ideology of Israelite monotheism and the pervasive polytheism of the ancient biblical world, with its attendant idolatry (cf. Exod. 20:2–7). On the plains of Moab, Moses led the Israelites in an important renewal of the covenant law that reinforces this "One-ness" or "Only-ness" of God and provides the baseline for the Shema, the core prayer and creed of later Judaism (Deut. 6:4).[15]

The covenant ratified at Mount Sinai served as a charter and legitimized and standardized the institutions of Hebrew religion. Specifically, the covenant was the foundation for the sacrificial system, the Sabbath, the tabernacle, the priesthood, the liturgical calendar (bringing redemptive rhythm and a sense of holiness to time), and also for the moral, civil, and ceremonial law designed to reshape Hebrew society and religion after the pattern of God's holiness. God's desire to live among his people in a portable tent-sanctuary (Exod. 25:8) lays the foundation for the "Immanuel theology" (Isa. 7–8; Matt. 1:23). This "God with us" theology will ultimately be realized in the incarnation of Jesus the Messiah and the gifting of the indwelling Holy Spirit to the Christian(s) (1 Cor. 3:16; 6:19).[16]

The Passover became the defining festival of Hebrew religion; it was observed by a memorial meal and perpetuated through a catechism (Exod. 12–13). The Passover festival celebrates the exodus from Egypt as the supreme act of divine judgment and deliverance in Hebrew history (Exod. 6:6; 15:13; Deut. 7:8; 13:5). The exodus event exalted the God of the covenant, YHWH, who redeemed Israel (Ps. 77:12–20 [13–21]). It stood as a perpetual reminder to successive generations that redemption inevitably leads to the worship of YHWH (Exod. 15:18).[17]

14. On the theological significance of the name YHWH (LORD), see Block, *For the Glory of God*, 36–38. The Thirteen Attributes of God in later Judaism are extracted from this passage (Exod. 34:6–7); cf. Hayim H. Donin, *To Be a Jew* (New York: Basic Books, 1991), 22. The communication of divine revelation through theophany (i.e., a visible and/or audible manifestation of God) permeates the exodus event: "the angel of the LORD" (Exod. 3:2); other angelic beings (23:20); miracle (8:16–19); flame in a bush (3:2); fire, smoke, thunder, and lightning at Mount Sinai (19:18–20); vision/dream (Num. 12:6–8); voice (Exod. 24:1); cloud of glory (16:10); cloud of guidance/pillar of fire (40:34–38); and meeting with God "face-to-face" (33:11, 20–23) are recorded in the narrative.

15. The Shema is expressed in three passages from the Torah of Moses (Deut. 6:4–9; 11:13–21; Num. 15:37–41). On the Shema as the "Great Commandment" of later Judaism, see Hill, *Enter His Courts with Praise!*, 110, 119.

16. For treatment of "Immanuel Theology," see Andrew E. Hill, *1 & 2 Chronicles*, NIV Application Commentary (Grand Rapids: Zondervan, 2003), 246–47.

17. For fuller discussions of the exodus event as the formative stage of Hebrew worship, see Ross, *Recalling the Hope of Glory*, 169–208; Vernon M. Whaley, *Called to Worship: From the Dawn of Creation to the Final Amen* (Nashville: Thomas Nelson, 2009), 55–68.

The Mosaic covenant enacted at Mount Sinai applied the principle of God's holiness to all of life for Israel (Exod. 19:6; Lev. 11:44). In addition to the holiness of God, other key theological principles, underscored by the instructions for the tabernacle and the officiating priesthood, include substitutionary sacrifice, mediation of worship through the priesthood, the giving of the tithes and offerings, the need for preparation in worship, and the tension between divine immanence and transcendence (cf. Isa. 57:15; Gal. 3:24). The concepts of sacred space, the value of visual theology by way of symbolism and aesthetics, are introduced in the decor, furnishings, and architecture of the tabernacle (cf. Exod. 25–40). Israelite worship was carefully prescribed and highly detailed: God was his own worship leader!

Old Testament Worship during the Hebrew Conquest and Settlement Period

Conflicting loyalties were the issue for the Israelites during the settlement period under Joshua and beyond. Joshua's charge to Israel, "Choose this day whom you will serve," challenged the people to covenant obedience under the rule of YHWH (Josh. 24:15). Life in Canaan tested the Israelites' loyalty to YHWH, their Deliverer and Provider. Agricultural fertility was essential to survival, and the question centered on who could provide the water resources needed for sustaining human and animal life in a land depending on rainfall. Many of the Hebrews chose to serve the Baals, the "local deities" supposedly responsible for rainfall and fertility, instead of the Lord God. Preferring idolatry and the attendant immorality, the Hebrews languished through repeated downward spirals of social violence, religious apostasy, and foreign oppression (Judg. 2:10–19). YHWH, ever faithful, delivered his people through a series of judges empowered by the Lord's Spirit in response to Israel's repentance (e.g., Othniel, Judg. 3:10; Samson, 14:19).

Old Testament First Temple Worship (966–587 BC)

The transition from theocracy to monarchy was as revolutionary for Hebrew religion as it was for Hebrew politics. Chief among the several religious issues raised by Israelite kingship was the notion of God's "residency" among his people. The tabernacle theology of Moses respected God as one who was both "resident" and "nomad," in that his sanctuary was portable. The Jerusalem temple theology that originated with kings David and Solomon restricted God's "residency" to a permanent site. This had implications for "taming" God and opened the door to potential abuses as leaders fostered the idea of the divine Presence in Jerusalem, protecting the material world that the Israelites claimed.[18]

A related tension for worship during the monarchic era was the role of king as a religious functionary and thus the relationship between the institution of kingship rooted in Judah (Gen. 49:10–11) and the priesthood rooted in Levi (Deut. 33:8–11). King Saul was rejected by God due, in part, to his usurpation of priestly duties (1 Sam. 13; cf. 15). By contrast, fugitive David received holy bread from the priests at Nob (1 Sam. 21:1–9). As king, David organized the procession bringing the ark of the covenant into Jerusalem and wore the Levitical ephod for that event (2 Sam. 6:12–14; 1 Chron. 15:27). The story of Melchizedek—the Canaanite priest of Salem who shared a cultic meal with Abram, received a tithe from Abram, and blessed him—foreshadows the eventual merging of the offices of priest and king in a single messianic figure (cf. Ps. 110; Heb. 4:14–7:28).

Once installed as king over all Israel, David transferred the ark of the covenant from the house of Abinadab in Kiriath Jearim (where it had resided for twenty years) to Jerusalem (2 Sam. 6:1–19; 1 Chron. 15–16).[19] This was a "national" event, as David gathered all Israel in Jerusalem (1 Chron. 15:3, 25, 28). He was prominent among all the priests, Levites, and Levitical musicians in leading the joyful processional (1 Chron. 16:1–27). The Chronicler is careful to note that David and all Israel brought the ark up into Jerusalem (1 Chron. 15:28). David's orchestration of the all-Israel event demonstrated his loyalties both to the God of Israel and the nation of Israel as the people of God. Situating the ark of the covenant in Jerusalem also served to legitimate David's rule under God's authority and made the city the political and religious center of his newly founded kingdom.

David's innovative move to house the ark of the covenant in a special tent established in Jerusalem also had implications for forging a unified Hebrew people (1 Chron. 15:1–2; 16:1). The tabernacle of Lord was stationed in Gibeon (about 5.5 miles north-northwest of Jerusalem) during the reigns of David and Solomon (1 Chron. 16:39). During this transitional period, before the building of Solomon's temple, the Levitical priesthood was divided into two cohorts, with one serving at the Jerusalem tent housing the ark, and the other serving at the tabernacle in Gibeon (1 Chron. 16:37–42).

Also important to the development of Hebrew religion during the monarchic period were the ideas and attendant ritual practices related to sin and

18. Cf. Ross, *Recalling the Hope of Glory*, 321; and Block, *For the Glory of God*, 71, on Jeremiah's condemnation of temple worship.

19. See Mark J. Boda, *After God's Own Heart: The Gospel according to David* (Phillipsburg, NJ: P&R, 2007), 104–5, on this new phase of Hebrew worship founded by David.

repentance (2 Sam. 12–13; Pss. 32; 51); the need for preparation in worship is seen in the "entrance psalms" (Pss. 15; 24) and in the development of musical guilds and the role of choral and instrumental music in temple worship under the auspices of King David (1 Chron. 25). The reorganization of the Levitical priesthood (1 Chron. 23–24; 26) and the reemergence of the importance of religious symbol, notably in the ark of the covenant, was showcased in the satellite worship center established by David and brought an entirely new dimension to Hebrew worship (1 Chron. 15–16; cf. 2 Chron. 7:12). Further distinctives were regarding obedience to God's directives as ranking higher than ritual sacrifice (1 Sam. 15:10–31) and guarding against the religious syncretism, idolatry, and false religions of other surrounding people groups (1 Kings 3:1–2; 11:1–13).

David's role as the organizer of the musical guilds and his presumed leadership in the development of the Psalter for the music of the temple liturgy comes as no surprise (1 Chron. 6:31–32; 25:1–31). He is credited with writing nearly half the songs in the Psalms. David even commissioned the writing of psalms for special occasions, like the return of the ark of God to Jerusalem (1 Chron. 16:7; cf. 13:8). Singing some psalms was also part of the temple dedication (Ps. 30), Sabbath worship (Ps. 92), temple worship (2 Chron. 29:28, 30; Ps. 100:2; Amos 8:3), and other special festivals (Isa. 30:29). The technical notes preserved the Psalter's superscripts regarding musical scores and instrumentation further demonstrate the use of the Psalms as the hymnbook of the temple.[20]

The Old Testament gives considerable attention to the elaborate preparations for the Jerusalem temple made by King David as "general contractor," and the construction of the extravagant worship space by his son and successor, King Solomon (1 Chron. 22–29). The Jerusalem temple was the focal point of Hebrew worship, housing the divine Presence and serving as the very footstool of the God of Israel in his rule over the entirety of his creation (1 Chron. 28:2; cf. Pss. 99:5; 132:7). The temple was both a worship center for ritual sacrifice (2 Chron. 7:12) and a house of prayer (1 Kings 8; Isa. 56:7; Matt. 21:13). Increasingly, the temple was associated with prayer, especially by Hebrews displaced or dispersed by the Assyrian and Babylonian exiles. The theology of prayer voiced in Solomon's prayer of dedication for the temple took on new meaning for the Hebrew diaspora (1 Kings 8:33–34, 52–53).

---

20. The literature on the Psalms is vast. See Hill, *Enter His Courts with Praise!*, 193–210; Tremper Longman, *Psalms: An Introduction and Commentary*, Tyndale Old Testament Commentaries (Downers Grove, IL: InterVarsity, 2014), 15–16. On the five books of the Psalms understood as a cantata highlighting the Davidic covenant, see Andrew E. Hill and John H. Walton, *A Survey of the Old Testament*, 3rd ed. (Grand Rapids: Zondervan, 2009), 427–28.

The Prophetic Response to Kingship

The Old Testament prophets served God and the people of Israel (and the nations) as the "conscience" of the Hebrew monarchy and as "warriors" in the cosmic battle between true and false worship (cf. 1 Kings 18:17). The prophet was the voice of the transcendent and Holy Other in promoting the knowledge of God (Hosea 6:3). As ardent iconoclasts, the prophets were also boldly challenging corrupt leadership in Hebrew political and religious life (Amos 5:21–22). They were the voice of the Hebrew quest for the "ideal" life, calling people to repentance (Isa. 1:16–18) and proclaiming a Torah-based life that practiced the love of God and neighbor (Deut. 6:4; Lev. 19:18, 33–34). The twin themes of the prophetic message focused on the restoration of proper worship (cf. Isa. 57; 58) and a lifestyle of social justice (Mic. 6:8).

Old Testament Worship and the Babylonian Exile (605-587 BC)[21]

The series of Babylonian invasions of Judah, culminating in the sack of Jerusalem in 587 BC and the subsequent deportation of tens of thousands of Hebrews to Mesopotamia, profoundly impacted the religious life of Israel (2 Kings 24:10–17; 25:1–26; 2 Chron. 36:15–20).[22] The political institution of kingship and the religious institution of the temple were overthrown and dissolved. Through continued covenant violations, the Hebrews earned the Lord's curse for disobedience and as a result forfeited the land of promise (Lev. 26; Deut. 28). The unthinkable had happened. What had seemed impossible to the Hebrews was now reality. The Lord had indeed scorned his altar, disowned and abandoned his personal sanctuary, and delivered his own people to the enemy (Lam. 2:7).

However, neither the loss of the temple nor the relocation of the Hebrew captives to Babylonia caused the worship of the Lord to cease. The Babylonian diaspora meant that the worship of God was now disconnected from the land of covenant promise. The focus of Hebrew religion shifted from the temple-based rituals of sacrificial worship to the nonsacrificial aspects

21. This section calculates the chronology of the Hebrew exile in Babylonia from the captivity of Daniel in 605 BC, recognizing the further deportations of Hebrews in the subsequent Babylonian invasions of Judah in 597 (2 Kings 24:10–17) and 587 BC (2 Kings 25; 2 Chron. 36; Jer. 39); cf. Iain Provan, V. Philips Long, and Tremper Longman III, *A Biblical History of Israel* (Louisville: Westminster John Knox, 2003), 279–80.

22. The Assyrian captivity of the Northern Kingdom's Israelites as a result of the Syro-Ephraimite war (734–32 BC) and the Assyrian sack of Samaria in 722 BC cannot be overlooked (cf. 2 Kings 15; 16:5–9; 17; 2 Chron. 28:5–21; Isa. 7–9). Several thousands of Hebrews were deported to Mesopotamia in the aftermath of those conflicts.

of worship. If the books of Lamentations and Psalms are any indication, the corporate worship of the First Temple period gave way to a greater emphasis on individual worship and personal piety, highlighting repentance and confession, lament, prayer, and praise, especially in song and hymn (cf. Pss. 137; 149; 150; Lam. 3:19–27).

The prophetic voices of the day reinforced this more personalized approach to worship with their teaching about individual responsibility before God for sin and repentance (Jer. 31:27–30; Ezek. 18:1–20). Daniel offers insight into the personal spirituality of the diaspora Jewish communities, with his discipline of praying three times each day while facing Jerusalem (Dan. 6:10; cf. Ps. 55:17). The experience of personal worship in the diaspora brought new meaning to Psalm 141:1–2 for Hebrew captives, sending up prayers to God like the incense offering of the temple ritual.

The destruction of the first temple altered worship leadership as well. The Levitical priesthood no longer mediated worship for the Hebrew people. For their part, the priests became pastor-teachers during the exilic period, offering instruction in Torah and perhaps leading worship for house assemblies (cf. Ezek. 33:30–32). Jewish tradition finds the roots of the synagogue in the gathering of the elders at Ezekiel's home during the Babylonian exile (Ezek. 8:1; 9:6; 14:1). The references are too cryptic to warrant definitive conclusions. By the time of Ezra and Nehemiah, these "officials and elders" certainly did constitute the civil and religious power structures of postexilic Jerusalem (Ezra 6:7–14; 10:8).

The reference to "hanging up the harps" in Babylonian exile is often cited as evidence for the disuse of instrumental music in Second Temple and later synagogue Judaism (cf. Ps. 137:1–5). How long it took for the Hebrews to abandon musical instrumentation in worship is unclear, and so are the degree and the geographical extent to which that may have happened. Texts like Nehemiah 12:27–28; Ezekiel 33:32; and Psalms 149; 150 suggest the use of instrumental music during the postexilic period in continuity with earlier Hebrew worship.[23]

The Babylonian exile corrected a corrupt theology of "sacred place" in Hebrew religion: some leaders misunderstood and at times sought to manipulate God (claiming that existence of the physical structure of the Jerusalem temple guaranteed the blessing and security of the divine Presence; cf. Jer. 7). Ezekiel's visions of God's abandonment of the Jerusalem temple were sobering reminders that God was not tethered to a building made with hands

---

23. Cf. Harold M. Best and David K. Huttar, "Music in Israelite Worship," in Webber, *Christian Worship*, 1:229.

(Ezek. 1; 10; 43:1–12; cf. 1 Kings 8:27). Finally, the new-covenant promises of Jeremiah and Ezekiel had dramatic implications for the future development of Hebrew worship in the prophesied age of the messiah (cf. Jer. 31; Ezek. 34; 37).

Old Testament Second Temple Worship (515-350 BC)[24]

God commissioned the prophets Haggai and Zechariah to rally the people to rebuild the Jerusalem temple after the return from Babylonian exile. Their overlapping ministries were dated to 520–518 BC (Hag. 1:1; Zech. 1:1). Haggai and Zechariah had complementary ministries. Haggai called the people to rebuild God's temple (Hag. 1:8), and Zechariah called the people to rebuild the temple of their heart so they might offer proper worship to God (Zech. 1:3; 8:3, 8–9, 18–23). The people responded in obedience, and the second temple was completed in 515 BC (Ezra 5:1–2; 6:13–18).

Second Temple Jewish worship emphasized prayer, in keeping with the prayer focus associated with Solomon's temple (1 Kings 8:27–30). Prayers (at times accompanied by fasting) included petition and intercession (Ezra 8:21–23; Neh. 1:4–11), repentance and penitence in the context of covenant renewal and worship (Ezra 9:5–15; Neh. 9:16–37), and praise and thanksgiving for God's presence and work (Neh. 9:1–15; cf. 12:27–30).[25] Equally important, the worship leaders, the priests and Levites, were ceremonially cleansed for temple service (Neh. 12:27–30; 13:6–13; Zech. 3:3–10; Mal. 2:1–9). The arrival of Ezra in Jerusalem (458 BC) redefined the role of scribe in Israel. As a priest-scribe he became the model for a later class of religious professionals whose sole task was the study and exposition of the Hebrew Scriptures (Ezra 7:10).[26]

The composition of the book of Psalms spans as many as ten centuries, from the ancient song of Moses (Ps. 90) to postexilic sung prayers of praise and thanksgiving (Ps. 146). The Psalter may have been edited into its final form by priests and Levitical musicians around the time the second temple was dedicated (Ezra 6:13–18). Or perhaps that happened later, when the rebuilt walls of Jerusalem were dedicated in the time of Nehemiah (Neh. 12:27–43).

24. The second temple and the worship conducted there remained in place until the destruction of Jerusalem by the Romans in AD 70, during the First Jewish War (AD 67–73). This chapter assumes that the Hebrew Bible (Old Testament) was fully formed before the conquest of Syria-Palestine by Alexander the Great and the Greeks in 332 BC.

25. On prayer in the postexilic prophets Haggai, Zechariah, and Malachi, see Andrew E. Hill, "Prayer in the Minor Prophets (The Book of the Twelve)," in *Praying with Ancient Israel*, ed. P. G. Camp and T. Longman III (Abilene, TX: Abilene Christian University Press, 2015), 69–86.

26. See Graham H. Twelftree, "Scribes," in *IVP Dictionary of Jesus and the Gospels*, ed. J. B. Green, S. McKnight, and I. H. Marshall (Downers Grove, IL: InterVarsity, 1992), 732–35.

The poetry of the Psalms features an array of subgenres, including hymns, songs of praise and thanksgiving, storytelling or history psalms, lament, wisdom, imprecatory, royal, Torah, and messianic psalms (as seen through the lens of Christ's resurrection and eventually the New Testament).[27] Whether in temple, synagogue, or church, the sung prayers of the Psalms have been a staple of corporate worship, personal prayer, and spiritual formation for the people of God for thirty centuries.[28]

Rebuilding the altar of burnt offering before construction of the second temple enabled the returned Israelites to restore the worship centered around ritual sacrifices; they also renewed the keeping of the Hebrew festival calendar (Ezra 3:1–6; 6:19–22; cf. Exod. 23:14–19). The religious reforms of the restoration community by Ezra and Nehemiah prioritized Sabbath observance, keeping the Sabbath day holy, as God had commanded (Neh. 13:15–22; cf. Exod. 20:8–11; 23:10–13).

The public reading of the Torah of Moses as part of a covenant renewal is described as an act of worship (Neh. 8:5–6). The Levites' instruction in Aramaic, accompanying the reading of God's law in Hebrew, was done in such a way that the people had a clear understanding of what was being read, fulfilling one of their priestly functions (Neh. 8:7–8; cf. Deut. 33:10; 2 Chron. 17:7–9). Such early Jewish concern for helping the people of God understand the Scriptures is instructive. This event provides precedent for the Septuagint (LXX), the translation of the Hebrew Bible into Greek, some two centuries later.[29]

The postexilic prophets cast a vision for eschatological worship, in keeping with their exilic and pre-exilic predecessors. Haggai, Zechariah, and Malachi all refer to "the day of the LORD." Their prophecies include tribute from the nations flowing to the Jerusalem temple (Hag. 2:7), peace among the nations and security for Israel in the presence of God (Hag. 2:9; Zech. 2:11; 14:11), the nations' joining Israel as the people of God and making annual pilgrimage to Jerusalem to worship the Lord Almighty as King (Zech. 2:10–12; 14:16–19), removal of the stumbling block of idolatry and false worship (Zech. 5:5–11), global expression of glory for the God of Israel (Zech. 8:20–22; 14:16–19; cf. Mal. 1:11, 14), pervasive holiness unto the Lord that will characterize this

27. See Bernard W. Anderson, *Out of the Depths: The Psalms Speak for Us Today*, rev. ed. (Louisville: Westminster John Knox, 2001).

28. Cf. William L. Holladay, *The Psalms through Three Thousand Years* (Minneapolis: Fortress, 1993).

29. See Karen H. Jobes and Moisés Silva, *Invitation to the Septuagint* (Grand Rapids: Baker Academic, 2000). The Pentecost event birthing the church is foreshadowed: the diverse crowd of people gathered in Jerusalem were amazed that they heard the Galileans speaking in their own native language (Acts 2:1–11).

eschatological day (Zech. 14:20–22), and ultimately the vindication of the righteous and the judgment of evildoers (Mal. 3:17–18).

Between the Testaments

Craig Bartholomew and Michael Goheen rightly remind us that the movement from the Old Testament to the New Testament was not a giant leap across a chasm of "silent centuries." Rather, there was an "interlude," a period of transition, an interval of time for pause and reflection between the first and second testaments.[30] The intertestamental era is such a bridge, or segue, from the old covenant to the new covenant—from Malachi to Matthew.

We learn about this era of history from Jewish religious literature of that time, especially a collection of books known in Protestant Christian circles as the Apocrypha. For the Orthodox Church and the Roman Catholic Church, this literature is considered deuterocanonical, a second canon. In these traditions the books are appended to or interspersed within the Old Testament.[31] Apart from the canonical debate of the limits or expansiveness of the Old Testament, the literature reminds us there was still a people of God worshiping during this "interlude."

The books of the Apocrypha reference an array of worship responses. We find mentions of pilgrimages to Jerusalem and festival worship (Tob. 1:6; 5:14); prayer (Sir. 7:14; 28:2); repentance and confession, including fasting (Jdt. 4:10–14); music and singing, including praise hymns and new psalmody (1 Macc. 4:24, 54; Sir. 50:18–21); temple worship (Jdt. 16:16–18; 1 Esd. 5:50–53); and Sabbath keeping (2 Macc. 8:27). The Apocrypha recognizes that personal devotion to God is rooted in obedience to the Torah of Moses and is essential for proper worship (4 Macc. 5:24). The fear of the Lord (Sir. 1:11–20; 7:29–31) and a right heart are also accorded prominence in the worship of God (Sir. 1:12; 21:6; 38:10).

One apocryphal book important for biblical worship studies is Tobit. This anonymous Jewish literary work was probably written between 200 and 170 BC. The book is usually classified as a moralizing short story. Tobit offers a window into Jewish daily life and religion just before the New Testament era.[32] Personal spirituality in Tobit is rooted in the fear of the Lord (4:21; 14:2, 6) and is demonstrated by three distinct religious practices: prayer, sometimes

---

30. Craig G. Bartholomew and Michael W. Goheen, *The Drama of Scripture*, 2nd ed. (Grand Rapids: Baker Academic, 2014), 119.

31. See David A. deSilva, *Introducing the Apocrypha* (Grand Rapids: Baker Academic, 2002), 15–41.

32. See the introduction to "Tobit" in deSilva, *Introducing the Apocrypha*, 63–84.

combined with fasting, and almsgiving (4:5–11; 12:8–15). In fact, these three acts of piety became known as the "three pillars" of Judaism in later Jewish religious practice.[33] Jesus's teaching in the Sermon on the Mount (Matt. 5:1–7:29) offers theological commentary on the three pillars of Judaism: almsgiving, prayer, and fasting (Matt. 6:1–18). Jesus's instruction on these spiritual practices serves as one bridge between the worship of the intertestamental era and the New Testament.

Practical Implications for Worship

- The basis for Hebrew worship in the Old Testament is God himself, "the Holy One of Israel" (Ps. 89:18), the God of Abraham, Isaac, and Jacob (Exod. 3:15). God is both the "object" of worship and the "subject" of worship. God receives the worship of humanity because he is supreme among the gods, is sovereign ruler of the cosmos, and graciously established covenant relationship with his people (cf. Ps. 95).[34] God is the subject of worship, which celebrates God's activity in history as Creator and Redeemer, Provider and Sustainer, Sanctifier and Enabler.[35]

- Worship is a narrative, centered in the exodus event of the Old Testament and the Christ event of the New Testament—the redemptive work of God across the Testaments. The grand story of God's salvation history is designed to bring a story-shaped liturgy to worship as outlined in Scripture, enacted in Israel, and refocused in the New Testament church.[36]

- Worship is a whole-person response to God (Deut. 6:4–5; 11:13), a lifestyle of loving obedience and loyal service in gratitude for God's mercies: this is true worship (Rom. 12:1–2 NIV).[37] Worship is an action verb; it

33. The idea of almsgiving, prayer, and fasting as the three pillars of Jewish piety in later Judaism is an adaptation of the Jewish tradition that the world rests on three pillars: the knowledge of the Torah, the worship of God, and works of charity (deeds of lovingkindness to others); cf. George F. Moore, *Judaism in the First Centuries of the Christian Era* (New York: Schocken Books, 1971), 1:35; 2:162–79.

34. Block, *For the Glory of God*, 29–53.

35. Marva Dawn, *Reaching Out without Dumbing Down* (Grand Rapids: Eerdmans, 1995), 76; cf. Block, *For the Glory of God*, 55–80.

36. See Robbie F. Castleman, *Story-Shaped Worship* (Downers Grove, IL: InterVarsity, 2013), 14. Note the value of the liturgical calendar in organizing and informing story-shaped worship, whether the festival calendar of ancient Israel or the Christian year developed during the early centuries of church history. Cf. Robert E. Webber, *Ancient-Future Time: Forming Spirituality through the Christian Year* (Grand Rapids: Baker Books, 2004).

37. Cf. Daniel I. Block, "Toward a Holistic, Biblical Understanding of Worship," in *For the Glory of God*, 1–27.

tells and enacts the Christ event in celebration of Jesus the Messiah.[38] This type of worship is distilled in offerings of sacrifices of praise to God and sacrifices of doing good for others (Heb. 13:15–16). God still looks at the heart of the worshiper, not at outward appearances and ritual forms (1 Sam. 16:7; Ps. 51:16–17; Isa. 57:15; 66:2).

- At one level, worship is spiritual warfare. God's redemptive work defeats the enemy, Satan, and all the powers of sin and death (Rev. 20:7–15). In the Old Testament this is seen in the judgment brought against the gods of ancient Egypt and Canaan (cf. Exod. 12:12; 18:11; 1 Kings 18:36–40). In the New Testament this is recognized in the death, burial, resurrection, and ascension of Jesus the Messiah—Christ the victor over sin and death (cf. 1 Cor. 15:50–57). Walter Brueggemann concurs, declaring that worship is spiritual warfare: "The act of praise is indeed world-making for the community which takes the act of worship as serious and realistic. . . . Worship is not only constitutive, but inevitably polemical. Praise [of Christ] insists [that] not only is this the true world, but that other worlds are false. . . . The church sings praises not only toward God but against the gods."[39]

- Worship that is transparent and genuine makes a place for the use of the psalms in the liturgy. These prayers of the people of God still have currency for the doxology of the church. Not only praise and thanksgiving but also lament, the honest doubts and righteous complaints of the faithful. The "lament" must not be confused with the "lamentation." The lamentation is an expression of grief over a calamity that is not reversible (e.g., a funeral dirge). The lament is an appeal to God's compassion to intervene and change a desperate situation. The lament may be an individual or community prayer, and each has a distinctive structure. Laments are praise offered in a "minor key" in the confidence that God is faithful and in anticipation of a new lease on life.[40]

- Worship is covenantal. A covenant creates relationships. The lovingkindness of God (Heb. ḥesed), a core attribute of his identity (Exod. 34:6–7), is made tangible in his declaration "I will be your God" (promise), and "you will be my people" (obligation) (Jer. 7:23 NIV; cf. Exod.

---

38. Robert E. Webber, *Worship Is a Verb* (Peabody, MA: Hendrickson, 1995), 43–64.

39. Walter Brueggemann, *Israel's Praise: Doxology against Idolatry and Ideology* (Philadelphia: Fortress, 1988), 26–27.

40. Anderson, *Out of the Depths*, 60; see further Walter Brueggemann, "The Costly Loss of Lament," in *The Psalms and the Life of Faith*, ed. Patrick D. Miller (Minneapolis: Fortress, 1995), 98–111; John D. Witvliet, *The Biblical Psalms in Christian Worship* (Grand Rapids: Eerdmans, 2007), 70–71, 80–81.

6:7). The people of Israel received a new identity as God's chosen people, holy nation, and kingdom of priests through God's covenant initiative (Exod. 19:5–6). The Sinai covenant is regulated by the law of love (Deut. 6:5; 11:1). Likewise, the new covenant in Christ (Luke 22:13–23) established a unique relational identity for Jesus's followers as children of God (John 1:12–13), sons and daughters of the Father, the Lord Almighty (2 Cor. 6:17; cf. Gal. 4:6–7). This new and better covenant is also regulated by the law of love: the love of God with our whole being, and the love of neighbor as ourselves (cf. Matt. 22:34–40).[41]

All this, and more, informs the New Testament understanding of the Old Testament as preparatory history for the coming of Jesus the Messiah (Gal. 3:24). The Old Testament is also a worship primer, a shadow of the good things to come in Christ (Heb. 10:1). The First Testament is preparation for the worship of God in Spirit and truth (John 4:23–24). God is Spirit, to whom his people offer worship energized, informed, and enabled by the Holy Spirit (1 Cor. 2:9–16; 12:3). God is worshiped in truth, the truth that "Jesus is Lord" (Acts 2:36; 1 Cor. 12:3; Phil. 2:11). This is the foundational Christian tenet, the mystery of Jesus the Messiah as fully human and fully divine, the very Son of God (cf. 2 Tim. 2:8; Rev. 22:16). So come, worship the Lord with gladness! (Ps. 100:2).

For Further Reading

Block, Daniel I. *For the Glory of God: Recovering a Biblical Theology of Worship.* Grand Rapids: Baker Academic, 2014.

Brueggemann, Walter. *Worship in Ancient Israel.* Nashville: Abingdon, 2005.

Castleman, Robbie F. *Story-Shaped Worship.* Downers Grove, IL: InterVarsity, 2013.

Hill, Andrew E. *Enter His Courts with Praise!* 1993. Reprint, Grand Rapids: Baker, 1996.

Ross, Allen P. *Recalling the Hope of Glory: Biblical Worship from the Garden to the New Creation.* Grand Rapids: Kregel, 2006.

Whaley, Vernon M. *Called to Worship: From the Dawn of Creation to the Final Amen.* Nashville: Thomas Nelson, 2009.

41. See Scot McKnight, *The Jesus Creed: Loving God, Loving Others*, anniv. ed. (Brewster, MA: Paraclete, 2019).

— 2 —

New Testament and Worship

Pheme Perkins

In a World Full of Gods

In the first century, people were immersed in worship events ranging from the tokens worn by children to ward off disease to being part of a crowd of spectators watching processions and ritual dramas that celebrated special festivals in honor of a city's patron deities. Individuals who traveled to a famous temple or healing shrine often left behind inscriptions, votive offerings, or just graffiti scratched on a cult statue's base or wall. These told others of the ways in which that god or goddess had reached out to help the worshiper. Less dramatic perhaps, but part of everyday life, people could recognize the local spaces marked as places for communicating with a deity, such as a statue, altar with an inscription, a sacred grove or spring, or the protective spirits of the household and honored near the hearth. For the wealthier homes in the Roman world, paintings and mosaics reminded viewers of famous mythological stories or depicted rites from some of the fashionable, newer religious imports, such as worship of the goddess Isis, from Egypt.[1]

1. Valerie M. Warrior, *Roman Religion* (Cambridge: Cambridge University Press, 2006); Jörg Rüpke and David Richardson, *Pantheon: A New History of Roman Religion*, trans. D. M. B. Richardson (Princeton: Princeton University Press, 2018), 1–19, 226–33, 258–59; Larry W. Hurtado, *At the Origins of Christian Worship: The Context and Character of Earliest Christian Devotion* (Grand Rapids: Eerdmans, 1999), 3–28; Risto Uro, "Ritual and the Rise of the

So the real challenge for the new "Christ believers"—who have "turned to God from idols to serve a living and true God, and to wait for his Son from heaven, whom he raised from the dead" (1 Thess. 1:9–10 NIV)—is to determine how they can worship a God who has no anchor in the visible world of deities and worshipers. This chapter maintains that as the apostle Paul spread the good news that God was calling all humanity to salvation in Christ, Paul saw the Christian community as "the body of Christ" and enlivened by the Spirit.

Jews who lived in the territory of Galilee, Samaria, and Judea were protected from a physical and social world in which gods, goddesses, lesser divinities, and their devotees all clamored for attention. Coins were minted without divine images. Galileans had clay oil lamps from Judea rather than cheaper ones produced from molds with pagan religious symbols.[2] Herod the Great avoided any such images on buildings in Jewish territory, but Caesarea, his new seaport opening to the world of maritime trade, included a dramatically positioned temple honoring the divine Augustus.[3] Unlike the other gods, Israel's God had only one sacred place for the typical forms of worship, which involved sacrificial offerings and had ritual specialists.

From Temples to House Churches

Jews dispersed throughout the world, as well as those who lived in Palestine outside Jerusalem, gathered on the Sabbath for prayer, reading of the Mosaic Torah, and reflection on it. Those gatherings are a different form of worship and distinct from the liturgical forms associated with temples. The Greek term for the gathered community, "synagogue," could also be used for the building in which they met. First-century synagogues had more in common with what many Christians refer to as the "church hall" than with the sanctuary, which serves as the formal worship space. Synagogues were not "sacred spaces" with priests or other religious specialists comparable to what the temples had.[4]

Similarly, the earliest Christians did not worship in special buildings. They used the houses or workshop spaces in which some members of the

Early Christian Movement," in *The Early Christian World*, ed. Philip Esler, 2nd ed. (London: Routledge, 2017), 431–35.

2. Jodi Magness, *Stone and Dung, Oil and Spit: Jewish Daily Life in the Time of Jesus* (Grand Rapids: Eerdmans, 2011), 65.

3. Jodi Magness, *The Archaeology of the Holy Land: From the Destruction of Solomon's Temple to the Muslim Conquest* (Cambridge: Cambridge University Press, 2012), 170–81.

4. Anders Runesson, "Synagogues," in *T&T Clark Encyclopedia of Second Temple Judaism*, ed. Daniel M. Gurtner and Loren T. Stuckenbruck (London: T&T Clark, 2020), 2:766–72.

group lived (e.g., Acts 20:7–8). As a result, there are no traces in the archaeo-logical record for tracking early Christian presence in cities like Corinth or Rome or Jerusalem. We rely on Paul's letters for glimpses of how the first believers worshiped. They gathered regularly for prayer, reading from Scripture, a shared meal, and, on occasion, listening to a letter from the apostle himself (Col. 4:16). Paul typically begins his letters with a thanks-giving or blessing section that expresses his continued heartfelt prayer for the recipients (e.g., Rom. 1:7–12; 1 Cor. 1:4–9; Eph. 1:15–18; Phil. 1:3–11; Col. 1:3–10; 1 Thess. 1:2–7). He also acknowledges or requests prayers from those churches as he endures the imprisonments and hardships of spreading the gospel (e.g., Rom. 15:30–32; 2 Cor. 1:11; Eph. 6:20; Phil. 1:19; 1 Thess. 5:25). By weaving these fledgling house-church communities together in a tapestry of letters, hospitality to visitors, and ongoing prayers of thanks-giving to God, Paul has translated the shared ethnic and religious identity of Jews into a genuinely new, global identity of the people whom God is calling to be his own in Christ.[5] So as the local church gathers to pray, praise God, hear the news of salvation, and encourage each other in holiness of life (cf. 1 Thess. 5:16–25), they are at the heart of God's plan for the entire human race.

Christians today use the word "church" for both a building and the com-munity that gathers there for prayer, Scripture reading, and other group activi-ties. Sometimes signs outside a building indicate that more than one Christian denomination uses that space. Often locals will still refer to the building with the denomination of its original builders even though it provides wor-ship and gathering space for more than one group. In some cities a "church building" may even be home for those who follow a religious tradition other than Christianity. Perhaps we should return to the New Testament practice of using "church" for the believing community.

Churches and Other Private Associations

The New Testament does not provide enough detail to construct an order of worship for these first-century communities. Some scholars confidently appeal to historically problematic statements about first-century Jewish synagogue worship for templates to reconstruct Christian worship. In addition, these small communities of non-Jewish believers had no ties to Jewish synagogues. To supplement the sparse details in the New Testament, other scholars turn to archaeological evidence for the many private associations of tradespeople or

5. Robert Jewett, *Romans*, Hermeneia (Minneapolis: Fortress, 2007), 79–91, 109–16, 713–23.

devotees of specific deities. Membership lists, association rules, and religious calendars are known from numerous inscriptions.[6]

Association regulations could explain Paul's approaches to behavior among believers in 1 Corinthians. Some groups expelled individuals for breeches of prescribed conduct (as in 1 Cor. 5:1–5). Certain inscriptions listing association members include erasures: public testimony to expulsion and a mark of social dishonor to the person in question. The celebratory meals of religious associations were fairly sparse. They were not the sort of luxurious banqueting by the wealthy elite, as familiar from Roman art and literature.[7] Rules for provisions to be provided to each associate point to a quite modest fare of bread, wine, and some other accompanying food like sardines. Groups that met in spaces with wall paintings or floor mosaics depicting lavish banquets may have imagined themselves sharing such luxury. Paul lashes out at the Corinthians for inebriated overconsumption by wealthier members while the poor were left with little (1 Cor. 11:20–22, 33–34). Evidently they did not have more formal rules for equitable distribution of food.[8]

Collection of funds due from members of religious associations required accounting. Officials had to prove trustworthy in spending for the meals and other associated cultic activities, such as honorific crowns and paying funeral expenses for deceased members. We do not know how New Testament churches managed the day-to-day economics of belonging to an association. But this evidence belies any naive assumptions about wealthy patrons or everyone chipping in for a meal "potluck" style. Some of Paul's assurances about the collection for the poor in Jerusalem match reassurances about trustworthy management of funds in association texts (e.g., 2 Cor. 8:6–24; 9:1–5).[9] But the apostle urges his churches to look well beyond their own membership rolls. His network of trans-local ties forged by letters and prayer enlisted a culturally unusual step of supporting the poor in Jerusalem, a distant city with whom the local congregation had no personal or ethnic ties. That collection may have been facilitated at their weekly gathering for worship (1 Cor. 16:1–4), a practice still observed in churches today.[10]

6. John S. Kloppenborg, *Christ's Associations: Connecting and Belonging in the Ancient City* (New Haven: Yale University Press, 2019).

7. Katherine M. D. Dunbabin, *The Roman Banquet: Images of Conviviality* (Cambridge: Cambridge University Press, 2003), 50–55, 92–94.

8. Kloppenborg, *Christ's Associations*, 149–50.

9. Kloppenborg, *Christ's Associations*, 262–63.

10. Joseph A. Fitzmyer, *First Corinthians*, Anchor Bible 32 (New Haven: Yale University Press, 2008), 614.

Led by the Spirit

Formal rules for the selection of officers with designated terms of service are the norm in other religious associations. Those in charge made sure members participated in the group's official meals, conducted themselves properly toward others in the group, or paid fines levied on those who failed to meet their obligations. As Paul tries to sort out problems in Corinth, we have no glimpses of such an official presiding over worship. None of the generic Spirit-inspired roles listed in 1 Corinthians 12:4–11 match the categories of association leaders. The qualifications proposed for individuals who were to supervise churches after the apostle's death in 1 Timothy 3:1–7 (*episkopoi*, "bishops") match the requirements for moral character and financial responsibility in community officials, but they make no reference to supervising worship.[11] When 1 Timothy 2:1–2 enjoins "supplications, prayers, intercessions, and thanksgivings" for all, including rulers, to ensure the peaceful, socially approved life for members, one would expect such prayers to be offered by a leader on behalf of the assembled community.[12] First Timothy 5:17–22 comes closer to formal rules of governance in stipulating payment for those elders who work at preaching and teaching along with rules for handling accusations of misconduct against an elder. The instructions that the apostle extended to Timothy concerning public teaching include reading of Scripture (1 Tim. 4:13), which also suggests activities that occurred as part of the community's gathering for worship.[13]

Only some of those in the Corinthian church would have had enough literacy and familiarity with the Jewish traditions to read and interpret them for non-Jewish converts. If such input had not been a regular part of their gatherings, it would be hard to see how a Christ association of Gentiles would have become familiar with the passages to which Paul refers in his letters or how they could be reminded to apply the Israelite story to themselves: "These things happened to them to serve as an example, and they were written down to instruct us, on whom the ends of the ages have come" (1 Cor. 10:11).[14] Paul's approach to these stories suggests that when we read the Old Testament in worship, it should not be as Israelite history of no significance to Christians. Instead, our preaching and reflection should unfold God's Word for believers today.

For the Corinthian assembly, Paul discussed assorted instances of what he considered to be dishonorable or disruptive behavior by women prophesying

---

11. I. Howard Marshall, *The Pastoral Epistles* (Edinburgh: T&T Clark, 1999), 52–57, 170–81.
12. Marshall, *Pastoral Epistles*, 418–24.
13. Marshall, *Pastoral Epistles*, 562–63.
14. Fitzmyer, *First Corinthians*, 387–88.

without customary head covering (1 Cor. 11:2–16), allegedly contrary to traditions Paul had handed on, and the predilection for speaking in tongues as a form of praying in the Spirit. Without someone to interpret speaking in tongues, such expression fails the test of building up the community: "What should be done then, my friends? When you come together, each one has a hymn, a lesson, a revelation, a tongue, or an interpretation. Let all things be done for building up" (1 Cor. 14:26). Paul also appeals to the negative impression outsiders would get from the chaos of such a worship service (1 Cor. 14:21–25).[15]

Instead of rules and penalties, Paul turns to a familiar political metaphor for the state as a body that can only function if its diverse parts are guided by the head. When individual parts turn on each other or claim to be the body, it is destroyed (e.g., Seneca, *On Anger* 2.31.7; Dio Chrysostom, *Discourses* 33.44; 34.32). A fable used to quell the restless populace by the Roman senator Menenius (Livy, *History* 2.32.7–33.1) imagines disaster if teeth, mouth, and hands fail to provide food for the belly.[16] Shakespeare's Menenius lashes out at leaders representing the mob of commoners:

> The senators of Rome are this good belly,
> And you the mutinous members; for examine
> Their counsels and their cares, digest things rightly
> Toughing the weal o' the common, you shall find
> No public benefit which you receive
> But it proceeds or comes from them to you
> And no way for yourselves. What do you think,
> You, the great toe of this assembly?
>
> (*Coriolanus* 1.1, lines 146–53)

For Paul, the Spirit-inspired harmony of all those baptized into the body of Christ does not allow for political, social, or ethnic divisions (1 Cor. 12:12–26). Nor are the diverse roles within the community indications that the Spirit inspires distinct gifts in order to honor some over others. But it is the principle of the Spirit to build up the body of Christ. On that basis Paul insists that, within the assembly for worship, prophetic speech should take priority over those praying in tongues: "For those who speak in a tongue do not speak to people but to God . . . since they are speaking mysteries in the Spirit. On the other hand, those who prophesy speak to other people for their upbuilding and encouragement and consolation" (1 Cor. 14:2–3).

15. Fitzmyer, *First Corinthians*, 521–27.
16. Jewett, *Romans*, 743–44.

Whether the restrictions on women teaching or having authority over men (1 Tim. 2:12; also 1 Cor. 14:33b–36) mean that women could not lead worship, the primary setting for prayer and instruction, remains hotly debated among Christians today.[17] Those who have women as ordained ministers treat the prohibitions as antiquated. The primary purpose was to exclude women from the quasi-civic role of presiding at meetings and disciplining persons who violated association bylaws and ethical standards. Evidence for women's roles in mixed-gender associations remains ambiguous. Women named on the membership lists of mixed-gender associations are not in bylaws that designate responsibilities of officeholders. Patrons, whether male or female, who provided assembly space or funds for meals or other cultic materials typically have no involvement in the group's activities. So designation of a woman as the patron does not permit one to infer that she supervised its activities, led prayers or other cultic actions, or even attended meals.[18]

Celebrating the Lord's Supper

The building blocks of Christian worship are all mentioned in Paul's letters. Worshipers addressed God with psalms, hymns, praise, thanksgiving, petitions, and blessings. They listened to Scripture and words exhorting them to live holy lives as persons reborn through baptism. Some exhortation included the Spirit-inspired words of Christian prophets. By mid-second century the extended forms of praise, petitions, Scripture reading, and instruction preceded the remembrance of Jesus's final meal with his disciples (Justin Martyr, *Apology* 65.1–66.3; 67.1–7).[19] However, the normal pattern for such dining in the first century would have a group sharing the meal prior to the extended verbal actions of singing, reading, and instruction (see John 13–17).[20]

Paul reprimands believers in Corinth by recalling the foundation story for their meal before discussing Spirit-inspired prayer:

> When you come together, it is not really to eat the Lord's supper. For when the time comes to eat, each of you goes ahead with your own supper, and one goes

17. Fitzmyer, *First Corinthians*, 528–33; Marshall, *Pastoral Epistles*, 452–60.

18. Kloppenborg, *Christ's Associations*, 86, 190–96, 203.

19. Paul F. Bradshaw, *Early Christian Worship: A Basic Introduction to Ideas and Practices*, 2nd ed. (Collegeville, MN: Liturgical Press, 2010), 47–48; Maxwell E. Johnson, "Worship, Practice and Belief," in Esler, *Early Christian World*, 411–13; David Aune, "Worship, Early Christian," in *The Anchor Bible Dictionary*, ed. D. N. Freedman, vol. 6, *Si–Z* (New York: Doubleday, 1992), 985.

20. Marianne Meye Thompson, *John* (Louisville: Westminster John Knox, 2015), 279–81, 293.

hungry and another becomes drunk. What! Do you not have homes to eat and drink in? Or do you show contempt for the church of God and humiliate those who have nothing? . . . For I received from the Lord what I also handed on to you, that the Lord Jesus on the night on when he was betrayed took a loaf of bread, and when he had given thanks, he broke it and said, "This is my body that is for you. Do this in remembrance of me." And in the same way he took the cup also, after supper, saying, "This cup is the new covenant in my blood. Do this, as often as you drink it, in remembrance of me." For as often as you eat this bread and drink this cup, you proclaim the Lord's death until he comes. Whoever, therefore, eats the bread or drinks the cup of the Lord in an unworthy manner will be answerable for the body and blood of the Lord. (1 Cor. 11:20–27)

Paul's version of Jesus's words fits the template used in Luke 22:19–20, though Luke also has an initial cup blessed before the loaf (Luke 22:17–18), with anticipation of a future beyond Jesus's death. Jesus will rejoin believers in the banquet of God's kingdom (cf. Mark 14:25).[21]

These words are not yet the fixed ritual for consecrating bread and wine that they later became. Our earliest recorded eucharistic prayer does not use them (*Didache* 9.1–4, ca. AD 90). *Didache* 10.7 instructs that the prophets may offer the thanksgiving with whatever words they wish.[22] (According to Justin, the presider prays over the elements to the best of his ability, *First Apology* 67.5.)

The formal prayer in *Didache* 9.4 compares the broken bread of the Eucharist to bread scattered on the mountains and then gathered to become one in God's kingdom. This conviction that worshipers are united with others everywhere makes Christ believers different from an association honoring any other deity. Paul's preferred image for the unity of believers, the church as "body of Christ," applies across the spectrum of their relationships. To become "answerable for the body and blood of the Lord" does not mean failure to recognize the ritual change in bread and wine, but protests social divisions between community members at the meal that initiates their worship gathering.[23] Paul instructs believers to wait until all have arrived and to eat something at home if hungry; this advice leaves us in the dark about how

---

21. Andrew B. McGowan, "'Is There a Liturgical Text in this Gospel?': The Institution Narratives and Their Early Interpretive Communities," *Journal of Biblical Literature* 118 (1999): 73–87; McGowan, *Ancient Christian Worship: Early Church Practices in Social, Historical, and Theological Perspective* (Grand Rapids: Baker Academic, 2014), 23–43; McGowan, "The Myth of the 'Lord's Supper': Paul's Eucharistic Meal Terminology and Its Ancient Reception," *Catholic Biblical Quarterly* 77 (2015): 503–21.

22. Aune, "Worship," 976–77; Valeriy A. Alikin, *The Earliest History of the Christian Gathering: Origin, Development and Content of the Christian Gathering in the First to Third Centuries,* Supplements to Vigiliae Christianae 102 (Leiden: Brill, 2010), 108–12.

23. Fitzmyer, *First Corinthians,* 445–46.

bread and wine for the weekly gathering were provided. Was someone in charge of collecting a fixed amount from each member, as in some groups? Were some wealthier Christians providing both the household space and the food, with perhaps extra for themselves and friends? We cannot tell.

Participation in this one "body of Christ" establishes a religious boundary between Christians and the world of gods surrounding them.[24] Faced with some who attended "meals" honoring other gods or goddesses, Paul warns against sharing the cup and table of demons (1 Cor. 10:14–22).[25] The shared bread united worshipers in the one body of Christ: "The bread that we break, is it not a sharing in the body of Christ? Because there is one bread, we who are many are one body, for we all partake of the one bread. Consider the people of Israel; are not those who eat the sacrifices partners in the altar? . . . You cannot partake of the table of the Lord and the table of demons. Or are we provoking the Lord to jealousy?" (1 Cor. 10:16–18, 21–22). The individuals whom Paul has in his sights possibly continued to be members of another association connected with their occupation, family, or ethnic origin. Dining on meat from an animal sacrifice would have been a much rarer event than the weekly gathering of Christ believers, so occasions for joining another deity's "table" may have been quite rare.[26] Also, for any group that had its membership incised in stone rather than recorded in a ledger, to disassociate would mean the public disgrace of having one's name chiseled out.[27] No wonder Paul pulls out all the rhetorical stops here.

Churches today have widely differing positions on inviting those who are not full members in good standing to receive bread and wine (or grape juice) at their celebration of the Lord's Supper. Unless everyone in the congregation knows what to expect, worship leaders need to give some guidance. Some churches follow a rule as old as *Didache* 9.5, including any baptized Christian. Some offer an open invitation to any visitors who feel so moved. Others from churches that require full membership for participation present a more hospitable face by inviting any who wanted to receive a blessing to come forward for that.

Persevere in Prayer, Always Giving Thanks

The New Testament suggests a shift from an evening meal followed by prayer and teaching; we have evidence that in Bithynia by AD 110, hymns, prayers,

24. Uro, "Ritual," 436.
25. Fitzmyer, *First Corinthians*, 393–94.
26. Kloppenborg, *Christ's Associations*, 214, 226–27.
27. Kloppenborg, *Christ's Associations*, 131–34.

and verbal instruction could be distinct from the meal. Pliny reported to the emperor Trajan that some accused Christians "were accustomed to assemble at dawn on a fixed day to sing a hymn to Christ as to God, and to bind themselves by an oath, not for the commission of some crime, but to avoid acts of theft, brigandage, and adultery, not to break their word, and not to withhold money deposited with them when asked for it. When these rites were completed it was their custom to depart, and then to [re]assemble [in the evening] to take food, which was however common and harmless" (Pliny the Younger, *Letters* 10.96).[28]

Assembling without a meal to celebrate Christ in hymns, offer prayers to God, receive some instruction, and renew commitment to a life of holiness may already be occurring in the first century. In Paul's letters the lists that encourage Christians to see themselves always praying suggest that possibility.[29]

1 Thess. 5:16-18	Phil. 4:4-6	Col. 3:16-17	Eph. 5:19-20	Rom. 12:12
Rejoice always,	Rejoice in the Lord always;	With gratitude in your hearts	Be filled with the Spirit,	Rejoice in hope,
pray without ceasing,	. . . in everything by prayer and supplication	sing psalms, hymns, and spiritual songs,	as you sing psalms and hymns and spiritual songs among your-selves, . . .	
			making melody to the Lord in your hearts,	be patient in suffering,
give thanks in all circumstances.	with thanks-giving let your requests be made known.	. . . giving thanks to God, the Father, through [Christ]. . . .	giving thanks to God the Father at all times and for everything in the name of our Lord Jesus Christ.	persevere in prayer.

Whether they are gathered as a community to worship God or praying individually, joy and thanksgiving should be the melody for Christian prayer. Believers celebrate the goodness of God's saving presence. Perhaps that rejoicing does not seem remarkable, but every letter adopts this approach in a context of suffering that could have destroyed the fledgling churches. The Thessalonians have weathered a storm of local persecution (1 Thess. 3:1–10).

28. Pliny the Younger, *Complete Letters*, trans. P. G. Walsh (Oxford: Oxford University Press, 2006), 278.

29. Jerome H. Neyrey, *Give God the Glory: Ancient Prayer and Worship in Cultural Perspective* (Grand Rapids: Eerdmans, 2007), 12–13.

Philippians, Colossians, and Ephesians all reflect situations in which Paul himself was imprisoned and facing execution. Paul is aware of how fragile the network of small churches is, yet he remains full of joy and confidence (cf. Phil. 1:19–20; Col. 1:24–30).[30]

Whether selecting psalms from the Scripture or composing new psalms and hymns for their own use, Christians do not adopt poems of lament or abandonment by God. The infancy narratives in Luke's Gospel provide compositions in which familiar biblical phrases were used in hymns celebrating the coming of salvation through Jesus. Each was adopted as a concluding prayer for the daily celebration of the canonical hours in monasteries and religious communities, the Benedictus for morning prayer (Luke 1:68–79), the Magnificat for evening prayer (Luke 1:46–55), and the Nunc Dimittis for night prayer (Luke 2:29–32).[31]

The glimpses of the first generation of believers at prayer that Luke presents in the Acts of the Apostles draw on the framework of Pauline letters.[32] So it is hardly a surprise to find Paul and Silas praying and praising God though confined under the harsh conditions a prison had to offer (Acts 16:25). But in this dramatic reconstruction of imprisonment in Philippi, Paul's confidence is instantly confirmed. They have gained the attention of the other prisoners. Though freed by an earthquake, no prisoners escape. Instead the jailer, who would have taken his life, is baptized. Subsequently the apostles are let go with apologies from civic officials for mistreating a Roman citizen. This is a vivid narrative that has some historical problems.[33] Luke provides several variations on the template of prayer associated with divine rescue (Acts 4:23–31; 12:5–12; 27:35–36). Similar glimpses of believers gathered in prayer thus picture an ideal to which Christians should aspire (Acts 1:14; 2:42–47; 13:2; 20:7–12), though scrubbed of some tensions evident in the Epistles.

Competitive claims to higher status for a special gift of the Spirit, as for speaking in tongues or prophesying, are mentioned by Paul in 1 Corinthians. In addition, tensions over food endangered the common meal in Rome (Rom. 14:1–4),[34] and in preferred seating for the wealthy coupled with contempt for

30. John Reumann, *Philippians*, Anchor Yale Bible Reference Library 33B (New Haven: Yale University Press, 2008), 104–6, 150, 242; Robert Wilson, *Colossians and Philemon* (London: T&T Clark, 2005), 110; Scot McKnight, *The Letter to the Colossians* (Grand Rapids: Eerdmans, 2018), 118–19.

31. Joseph A. Fitzmyer, *The Gospel according to Luke I–IX*, Anchor Bible 28 (Garden City, NY: Doubleday, 1981), 356–61, 374–79, 422.

32. Richard I. Pervo, *Acts*, Hermeneia (Minneapolis: Fortress, 2009), 12–14.

33. Pervo, *Acts*, 400–415.

34. Jewett, *Romans*, 833–44.

the poor undermined Jesus's teaching about God's kingdom (James 2:1–7).[35] Tempering the ideal snapshots with notes of reality reminds us that gathering in worship has always been a work in progress. We are always short of the people whom God calls us to be and thus short of the celebratory banquet of the kingdom (Mark 14:25).

Looking to the Heavens

Paul is not referring to believers as "the body of Christ" simply to calm down fractious social relationships in Corinth. Being part of this body is expressed in the group's two core rituals: The baptism by which believers were incorporated into the body reflects participation in the saving event of Christ's death and resurrection (Rom. 6:3–11).[36] And the founding story of the church is associated with their meal gatherings, as they commemorate the body of the Son of God, who gave his life for them. Writing to a church in Rome that was not part of his network, Paul can summarize their ethical life as the body of Christ in which many Spirit-inspired gifts contribute to the whole: "We are members of one another" (Rom. 12:3–8).[37]

More dramatic expressions of "the body of Christ" shift from local house-church assemblies to the cosmic stage. The earliest hymnic expressions of salvation achieved through Christ thus present his resurrection as exaltation to the right hand of God. All the heavenly powers worship this glorious figure (Phil. 2:6–11).[38] Believers belong to a body that has Christ as its head (Col. 1:15–20; Eph. 1:20–23).[39] Christians were not just dreaming of some far distant realm. They mirror this reality whenever they are worshiping Christ. This pattern may have been adapted from first-century Jews who saw their communal prayers as joined with worship that angelic powers were continuously offering before God's throne.

Fragmentary scrolls that incorporate liturgical writings found at Qumran provide first-century Jewish examples. Songs of the Sabbath Sacrifice (4Q400) refer to the blessings and praises of various orders of angelic priests and conclude with a figure in high-priestly apparel positioned near the divine throne chariot. The Words of the Luminaries (4Q504) suggest supplication

35. Dale C. Allison, *James*, International Critical Commentary (London: Bloomsbury T&T Clark, 2013), 379, 396–405.

36. Jewett, *Romans*, 396–402.

37. Jewett, *Romans*, 739–47.

38. Reumann, *Philippians*, 354–57, 372–74.

39. Wilson, *Colossians and Philemon*, 144–57; Ernest Best, *Ephesians* (Edinburgh: T&T Clark, 1998), 157–96.

for each day of the week in prayers that survey the story of salvation from Adam onward. These communal prayers are asking God for both physical deliverance and spiritual strengthening. Their Sabbath prayer appears to focus on praising God for creation.[40]

Revelation provides the most dramatic descriptions of heavenly worship in the New Testament. As the heavenly Son of Man with such liturgical accoutrements as lampstands to represent the churches, the risen Lord is fully identified as divine (Rev. 1:9–20). The praises of the heavenly beings alternate between God, enthroned as the Creator (4:8–11), and the sacrificed Lamb, with seven horns and eyes representing the spirits of God sent throughout the world (5:9–11). A doxology sung by every creature honors both God and Christ (5:13–14).[41] Neither the phrases spoken by the heavenly powers in Revelation nor these hymns to Christ as Lord and Savior were the words of the "psalms, hymns, and spiritual songs" used in first-century churches. These passages were composed or adapted by each author to focus attention on key transition points in a narrative or letter. But the "Holy, holy, holy," which Revelation 4:8 took from Isaiah 6:3, will be incorporated into the eucharistic prayers of Christians everywhere by the fourth century AD.

How significant is the practice of imagining Christian worship as echoes of an entire universe that sings hymns honoring God as Creator and Christ as Redeemer? In the small first-century house-church assemblies, which could not point to any earthly temples or dramatic public rituals or even small inscribed altars to command attention, they pushed back against everything others thought religion required.[42] Others might ask, "So *where* is your god?" Their reply pointed to the heavenly sanctuary (cf. Heb. 9:11–14; John 4:21–24). However, Paul cautions against seeking experiences of transport into the angelic ranks, as some believers did. Our task in this world remains anchored to the love of God expressed in Christ crucified. The apostle refuses to speak of his own heavenly visions (2 Cor. 12:1–7) and warns against those who hope some form of bodily discipline will aid devotees in entering "worship of angels" (Col. 2:16–19).[43] He suggests that such persons have actually lost

40. James R. Davila, *Liturgical Works* (Grand Rapids: Eerdmans, 2000), 83–90, 209–11, 239–41; Noam Mizrahi, "Songs of the Sabbath Sacrifice," in Gurtner and Stuckenbruck, *Second Temple Judaism*, 1:512–15; Daniel E. Falk, "Words of the Luminaries," in Gurtner and Stuckenbruck, *Second Temple Judaism*, 1:547–48.
41. David E. Aune, *Revelation 1–5*, Word Biblical Commentary 52 (Dallas: Word, 1997), 303–38; Craig R. Koester, *Revelation*, Anchor Yale Bible Reference Library 38A (New Haven: Yale University Press, 2014), 126–30.
42. Hurtado, *Christian Worship*, 49–51.
43. Wilson, *Colossians and Philemon*, 49–54, 98–114, 145; McKnight, *Colossians*, 220.

the nerves and ligaments connecting them to the head of the body, Christ, now enthroned in heaven (3:1–2).

On the one hand, our worship should acknowledge the big picture of creation and salvation. Perhaps this worship can even recover some sense of the Jewish Sabbath prayers that celebrate God as Creator. For Christians, the body of Christ in its cosmic sense is God's new creation and still in the process of being born (Rom. 8:9–30). So the reason for worship goes beyond whatever individual needs or feelings we each carry with us. Even the smallest congregation participates in a hymn-singing universe. On the other hand, our worship remains anchored in this life, which still hopes for the coming of God's reign. Paul cautions the Corinthians against enthused prophets and speakers in tongues or efforts to experience angelic worship; thus, he indicates that worship is not be a dramatic production, transporting believers from this world into imagined heavens.

Practical Implications for Worship

In Matthew 6:1–18, Jesus declares an even more striking indictment of the first-century presumption that honoring gods is fittingly expressed in dramatic public gestures.[44] Here the Greek word "hypocrite" refers to an orator or actor, someone playing a role. Giving alms, fasting, and prayer are essential to piety, but not, Jesus warns, if a worshiper is acting it out for others to approve (cf. Luke 18:9–14). In Matthew 6:7–8 Jesus introduces the Lord's Prayer by mocking the long formulas that non-Jews use to try to compel attention from their deities. Israel's God is merciful and compassionate, knowing what his children need. So the actual prayer in Matthew 6:9–13, which Christians were reciting three times a day by the end of the first century (*Didache* 8.2–3), does not require special experts or rituals. Anyone can learn it.

God pays attention to the heart, not the external production. In the Lord's Prayer, repentance or change of heart requires forgiving others just as we ask God to do for us. Matthew 6:14–15 repeats that condition lest familiarity with the prayer would cause readers to miss that point. James 5:13–16 expands a ritual of anointing by the elders, confession of sin, and prayer over the sick to a communal acknowledgment of sin. Such cautions remind worshipers that they are not yet among the saints in heaven. Humility fostered by this ritual does not require those external dramas that Jesus questioned. Instead, it reaches out to everyone with sympathetic compassion.

44. Ulrich Luz, *Matthew 1–7*, trans. James E. Crouch (Minneapolis: Fortress, 2007), 299–304.

The New Testament does not provide a video guide or even a short hand-book for Christian worship. By tracking the small details in its pages, with some help from the remains of other first-century religious groups, we can see that gathering to worship with others was essential to being in Christ. Worship involved everyone as part of that body filled with the Spirit. It was not modeled on the elaborate festivals and productions created by profession-als at pagan temples in the cities. In late antiquity, as Christianity grew in numbers and sociopolitical importance, its public worship was transformed by adopting features of civic religious ritual. After the first two centuries, cathedrals started to appear, and gradually some rather sizeable churches were established.

Our glimpses of worship in the New Testament provide encouragement for all the local churches around the globe who might feel too small, lack clergy, or face persecution. They are just as much the body of Christ as a packed cathedral. What matters is believers gathered to praise God, to remember and celebrate salvation in Christ, to support the suffering, and look forward with hope and joy to God's kingdom. Pray always!

For Further Reading

Aune, David E. "Worship, Early Christian." In vol. 6, *Si-Z*, of *The Anchor Bible Dictionary*, edited by David Noel Freedman, 973–89. New York: Doubleday, 1992.

Bradshaw, Paul F. *Early Christian Worship: A Basic Introduction to Ideas and Practices.* 2nd ed. Collegeville, MN: Liturgical Press, 2010.

Esler, Philip, ed. *The Early Christian World*. 2nd ed. London: Routledge, 2017.

Hurtado, Larry W. *At the Origins of Christian Worship*. Grand Rapids: Eerdmans, 1999.

Kloppenborg, John S. *Christ's Associations: Connecting and Belonging in the Ancient City*. New Haven: Yale University Press, 2019.

McGowan, Andrew. *Ancient Christian Worship: Early Church Practices in Social, Historical, and Theological Perspective*. Grand Rapids: Baker Academic, 2014.

Pecklers, Keith F. *Liturgy: The Illustrated History*. Mahwah, NJ: Paulist Press, 2012.

PART 2

Theological Principles of Worship

Systematic and Historical Theology

— 3 —

Creation and Worship

W. David O. Taylor

All creatures are aflame with the present glory of the Lord.

—Jürgen Moltmann, *The Source of Life*

Some people read books in order to find God. But the very appearance of God's creation is a great book. Look above you! Look below you! Take note! Read!

—Augustine, *The City of God*

What is the relation between God's creation and the worship by God's people? That's the question that this chapter aims to answer. At a general level, the question involves an investigation of the relevant biblical data, a study of theological convictions and confessions that inform how we think about the topic, and finally, an examination of the ways that our respective traditions have tied the creaturely things of heaven and earth to the practice of corporate worship.

Specific questions that may profitably be asked include these: How is the Father already at work in the physical world, gracing it to accomplish its God-given ends in our liturgical spaces? How are the bodies of human beings, made in the image of God, caught up in the bodily life of the resurrected Jesus via our acts of prayer and proclamation? In our liturgies, how is the Spirit at work in the things of color, stone, wood, metal, and wind? And how does the labor of human hands enable the faithful to participate in creation's ongoing worship of its Maker?

This chapter proposes that our confession of God as triune offers us a compelling vision for the way creation and worship might be related, whatever our denominational context. In support of this argument, first, this chapter looks at a biblical line of thought. Second, it proposes a theological vision that reckons seriously with the work of Father, Son, and Spirit in creation. Third, it offers a few practical examples for practitioners tasked with the responsibility of leading God's people in worship.

The following affirmations are far from exhaustive. But my hope is that they will serve, on the one hand, to establish a theological grammar for how we think about the link between creation and worship, and on the other hand, to support our personal efforts in our local contexts.

A Biblical Perspective on Creation and Worship

When Holy Scripture is read through a temple theology, we contend that it is possible to perceive a richly dynamic relationship between the "work" of creation and "work" of worship. Faithful worship, on this view, is oriented simultaneously backward historically, to the original creation; and forward eschatologically, to the new creation; while always linked figuratively upward, to the "kingdom of heaven," the domain of God's perfect rule. From this viewpoint creation plays a significant role in the church's worship precisely because it is God's unswerving pleasure to establish worship "on earth as it is in heaven."

The Temple Theology of Holy Scripture

Three lines of imagery—cosmological, horticultural, and architectural—are repeatedly brought together by the biblical authors to describe the place of the temple, the place that betokens both the presence and the order of God in fullness.[1] Here I contend that a temple theology persuasively describes the mind of the apostolic church and as such reinforces the integral relation between worship and creation.

1. Cf. Nicholas Perrin, *Jesus the Temple* (Grand Rapids: Baker Academic, 2010), 67.

The Garden as Sanctuary

We begin with the garden. "The garden of Eden," Gordon Wenham writes, "is not viewed by the author of Genesis simply as a piece of Mesopotamian farmland, but as an archetypal sanctuary."[2] The garden, in other words, is the primordial temple. The linguistic parallels between Genesis and Israel's worship bear noting. God's command to Adam to "till and keep" the garden, for example, is the same language used in Exodus 3:12 and Numbers 28:2 to describe sacrificial offerings. Thus, if Eden functions like a kind of sanctuary, then Adam appears as a kind of priest, offering the things of creation to the Creator on behalf of the cosmos, and conversely, offering the things of the Creator to his fellow creatures in God's name.[3]

The cherubim that guard the east entrance to the garden, to use another example, evoke the cherubim of Solomon's temple, who guard the entrance to the inner sanctuary (1 Kings 6:23–28; see also Exod. 25:18–25; 1 Kings 6:29). God clothes Adam and Eve in a manner similar to the way that Moses clothes the priests (Exod. 28:40–41; Lev. 8:13).[4] And the water in the garden brings to mind the great river that flows out of the new Jerusalem temple to sweeten the Dead Sea. Thus the garden, as a microcosm of "the heavens and the earth," represents the house of God, a place of ordered flourishing under the personal rule of Yahweh.

The Tabernacle and Temple as Edenic Sanctuaries

With the introduction of the tabernacle and Solomonic temple, the presence of God now occupies a specific place.[5] The world in its fullness represented the dwelling of God; now, after the distortion of creation that resulted from sin, the divine Presence is concentrated, but not diminished. Yet the prophets hope that the whole earth will again "be filled with the knowledge of the glory of [God]" (Hab. 2:14). In short, the Jerusalem temple, as a symbolized miniature cosmos, represents a liturgical meeting point of the primal creation and the final creation.[6]

2. Gordon J. Wenham, "Sanctuary Symbolism in the Garden of Eden Story," in *Proceedings of the 9th World Congress of Jewish Studies* 9 (1986): 399; Jon D. Levenson adds: "Like temples, [gardens] are walled off from quotidian reality, with all its instability and irregularity and the threats these pose, and thus they readily convey an intimation of immortality." *Resurrection and the Restoration of Israel: The Ultimate Victory of the God of Life* (New Haven: Yale University Press, 2006), 86–87.

3. Wenham, "Sanctuary Symbolism," 401.

4. Peter Enns, *The Evolution of Adam: What the Bible Does and Doesn't Say about Human Beings* (Grand Rapids: Brazos, 2012), 73, argues that Israel's temple informs Israel's narrative of the creation story, not the other way around.

5. Jon Levenson, "The Temple and the World," *Journal of Religion* 64, no. 3 (1984): 297.

6. Cf. Allen P. Ross, *Recalling the Hope of Glory: Biblical Worship from the Garden to the New Creation* (Grand Rapids: Kregel, 2006), parts 2–4; G. K. Beale, "Cosmic Symbolism of Temples in the

The Prophetic Vision of a New Temple

With Ezekiel 33–48 we discover a theological halfway point between Israel's temple and the vision of St. John the Divine. In both narratives there is a visionary transport of the prophet to a high mountain, the sight of a new world with Jerusalem at its center, the presence of the glory of God in the city, a heavenly interpreter with a measuring rod, and the presence of the river of life.[7] Looking forward to the new Eden, then, the prophet's vision anticipates the renewal of the whole creation, from quark to quasar, which the words of Revelation 21:1–3 make fully clear.[8]

The Enfleshed New Temple

With the New Testament, the idea of the temple is profoundly reconfigured.[9] In John's Gospel, Jesus is presented as the new temple, the one who personifies the presence of God par excellence (John 2:19, 21). Recalling the Genesis story, God in Christ becomes ambulatory again, tabernacling "among us" (John 1:14). Jesus henceforth is the singular "place" of God on earth, the temple that now redefines all other places. He is the one in whom, through whom, and by whom all true worship will occur.

While Jesus is recognized as the true temple only in his resurrected state, it is with the descent of the Spirit at Pentecost that the church discovers *itself* as the temple (1 Cor. 3:16–17).[10] And though the temple's center of gravity, as it were, remains in the "heavenly realm," where Christ is seated at the right hand of the Father, temple life irrupts on earth through the Spirit-possessed

Old Testament," in *The Temple and the Church's Mission*, New Studies in Biblical Theology (Downers Grove, IL: IVP Academic), 29–80; Craig G. Bartholomew, *Where Mortals Dwell: A Christian View of Place for Today* (Grand Rapids: Baker Academic, 2011), chap. 4; T. D. Alexander, *From Paradise to the Promised Land: An Introduction to the Pentateuch* (Grand Rapids: Baker Academic, 2002).

7. Daniel I. Block, *The Book of Ezekiel: Chapters 25–48* (Grand Rapids: Eerdmans, 1998), 502–3. Discrepancies do exist, but the parallels are sufficiently strong to warrant a legitimate comparison. Cf. Joel 3 [4 MT]:17–18; Zech. 14:5b–11; John 7:38; Rev. 22:1–2.

8. Susan Niditch, "Ezekiel 40–48 in a Visionary Context," *Catholic Bible Quarterly* 48, no. 2 (1986): 208–24.

9. Joel B. Green puts the point incisively: "Given the respect assigned earlier to the Jerusalem temple and particularly to its sanctuary as the *axis mundi*—the meeting place between the heavenly and the earthly, the divine and the human—this appearance of divine glory is remarkable. God's glory, normally associated with the temple, is now manifest on a farm! At the birth of his son, God has compromised (in a proleptic way) the socioreligious importance of the temple as the culture center of the world of Israel." *The Gospel of Luke*, New International Commentary on the New Testament (Grand Rapids: Eerdmans, 1997), 131.

10. On the intertextual as well as socioreligious tension that opens up between the Jerusalem temple and the new *naos* (sanctuary) oriented around Jesus, as it is played out in the book of Acts, see Perrin, *Jesus the Temple*, 64–66.

church.[11] Rather wondrously, finally, the faithful discover that their own individual bodies are a kind of temple. In a comment on 1 Corinthians 6:19–20, N. T. Wright remarks, "It is, for Paul, a matter of transferring the holy worship of Israel from the Jerusalem Temple to the bodies of individual members of the church, even in Corinth—especially in Corinth! Once more, the Spirit has taken the place of the Shekinah."[12]

The New Temple and the New Creation

The restoration of the cosmos begins, then, in Christ, in his resurrected humanity, and extends outward by the Spirit through the church to encompass, as John of Patmos envisions it, a new heaven and a new earth (Rev. 21:1). The presence and good order of God, symbolized in the language of temple, now extends, one could say, to infinity and beyond.

In sum, while the New Testament employs the category of temple in largely figurative rather than literalistic manner, these various temples remain in thoroughly physical things: physical bodies, physical spaces, physical actions, physical worlds.[13] Whatever contrasts are at play, the creaturely shape of public worship is never regarded as problematic per se. What the New Testament finds problematic instead is corrupt minds, false imaginations, idolatrous hearts, forgetful memories, and warped passions.[14]

The primary theological language of the New Testament, then, is of "heaven on earth," and the promised inheritance of the saints is neither a flight to "the heavens" nor a flight away from earth, as in popular Christian imagination, but rather worship that takes place in a renewed creation, under the perfect rule of God.[15] Put in specifically liturgical terms, there is no place on earth "which cannot be a witness of the presence of Christ and a prelude to the restoration of the Cosmos."[16]

11. See G. K. Beale, "The Descent of the Eschatological Temple in the Form of the Spirit at Pentecost," *Tyndale Bulletin* 56 (2005): 73–102.

12. N. T. Wright, "Worship and the Spirit in the New Testament," in *The Spirit in Worship—Worship in the Spirit*, ed. Teresa Berger and Bryan D. Spinks (Collegeville, MN: Liturgical Press, 2009), 13–14.

13. Cf. John W. Cooper, *Body, Soul, and Life Everlasting: Biblical Anthropology and the Monism-Dualism Debate* (Grand Rapids: Eerdmans, 2000).

14. For detailed commentary on this issue, see, e.g., David Peterson, *Engaging with God: A Biblical Theology of Worship* (Grand Rapids: Eerdmans, 1992); Edith M. Humphrey, *Grand Entrance: Worship on Earth as in Heaven* (Grand Rapids: Brazos, 2011), esp. "'That Your Prayers Not Be Hindered': Avoiding Pitfalls in Corporate Worship."

15. Cf. Wright, "Worship and the Spirit," 21.

16. J.-J. von Allmen, "A Short Theology of the Place of Worship," *Studia Liturgica* 3, no. 3 (1964): 156. Adds Frank Senn: "This is precisely the eschatological dimension of the Christian liturgy that its celebrants exercise the priestly vocation of the redeemed world and thereby

With this biblical perspective in place, we turn to more specific theological concerns.

A Theological Perspective on Creation and Worship

Creation, from top to bottom, is an expression of the pleasure and grace of God. Karl Barth remarks that it is the Christian's duty "to love and praise the created order, because, as is made manifest in Jesus Christ, it is so mysteriously well-pleasing to God."[17] This is the first lesson in a distinctly trinitarian theology of creation. To love creation is a way for us to participate fully in *God's* pleasure in creation.[18]

In concrete terms, to take pleasure in the texture of fabrics, in the possibilities of metallic materials, in the logic of wood-carved utensils, or in the patterns of sound and sinew and scent—all such is to take pleasure in the Word made flesh, the one through whom creation has its being. Because Christ stands at the center of the cosmic order, moreover, the created realm can be properly regarded as the beloved world of God and a source of near-infinite delight for human beings.

In the context of corporate worship, the church takes the stuff of creation and makes something of it: song from wind, dance from motion, architecture from stone, poetry from language, paint from pigments. The church does so not only to make sense of its life before God in praise but also because the making of things—chairs and chalices, pulpits and bell towers—is a way for the people of God to take pleasure in God's beloved creation.

We do so on the conviction that creation is the gift of a gracious God.[19] In light of such grace, we *get to*, we do not just *need to*. We *need to* make clothes to protect ourselves against the elements, but we *get to* make cassocks and paisley ties. We *need to* build shelters, but we *get to* build cathedrals and meetinghouses. We *need to* give glory to God because our lives depend on it, but we *get to* do so with a wealth of sensory goods: pipe organs and balalaikas, syncopated jazz and resplendent cantatas, somber chants and whimsical songs.

---

enact life in the new creation." *New Creation: A Liturgical Worldview* (Minneapolis: Fortress, 2000), 62.

17. Karl Barth, *Church Dogmatics*, vol. III/1, trans. J. W. Edwards, O. Bussey, and Harold Knight (Edinburgh: T&T Clark, 1958), 346.

18. Cf. Jeremy S. Begbie, *Resounding Truth: Christian Wisdom in the World of Music* (Grand Rapids: Baker Academic, 2007), 189.

19. Barth, *Church Dogmatics* III/1, 44.

Creation Is a Gift of God and the Context for Culture Making

The Father makes a world; while wholly dependent on him, this cosmos is also endowed with its own integrity, its own way of being. He places human beings in it to draw out its riches and potentialities in care-filled ways.[20] They do so in Christ's name, in whom creation discovers its true end. They do so also by the Spirit's power, through which creation accomplishes its divinely ordained purposes. The calling of worship leaders, on this understanding, is to give loving attention to creation and to make something of it.[21]

In practical terms, how might our words of welcome become an expression of our priestly calling to welcome the blessing of God in our lives? How might our sermons give evidence of our primordial call to name the world rightly? How might our practices of eating and drinking make a direct connection to our call to steward the earth in ethically responsible ways? How might our acts of reconciliation bear witness to our interdependent identity as creatures made in the image of a Divine Communion? And finally, how might we reflect our culture-making God in our own culture-making activities: our Shaker furniture, our illuminated Bibles, our mystery plays, our processional dances, and our digital projections.[22]

Creation Is Marred by Sin but Not Robbed of Its Grace

In Genesis 3 we see that God's creation goes terribly wrong. But only in Christ do we see that creation is not simply caught up in forces of entropy; it is also caught up in forces of sin and death. Through human disobedience, sin enters the world and disfigures the world. Because of sin, creation is marred and the human creature becomes alienated from God, curved in on itself, and at odds with the rest of creation. Work becomes sweat and toil; death becomes "the last enemy"; evil deforms the human creature, and an economy of scarcity, rather than an economy of abundance, marks the human experience.

20. Ellen F. Davis notes that "a sanctuary has a kind of creative capacity of its own." "The Tabernacle Is Not a Storehouse: Building Sacred Spaces," *Sewanee Theological Review* 49 (2006): 306.

21. Calvin Seerveld, *Rainbows for the Fallen World: Aesthetic Life and Artistic Task* (Toronto: Tuppence, 1980), 24–25. Roger Hazelton states, "Creation does not happen all at once, nor is it entirely one complete and single act; God calls, forms, distinguishes, and names the multifarious world. Indeed, the more carefully we read and ponder the story told in Genesis, the more creation seems to take on the characteristics of a work of art." *A Theological Approach to Art* (Nashville: Abingdon, 1967), 53.

22. Cf. Andy Crouch, *Culture Making: Recovering Our Creative Calling* (Downers Grove, IL: InterVarsity, 2013), 101–17.

As it relates to worship, the near-infinite possibility for misuse of creation in idolatrous or self-indulgent ways becomes an ever-present danger. What is required is the initiative of God to heal us. In Christ's own initiative, then, to become "flesh from his flesh," we discover not only the comprehensive corruption of the human creature but also its destiny to be hale, holy, and capable, yet again, of intimate fellowship with the Father by the Spirit.[23] And because Christ is the true Worshiper, as Hebrews 12 describes him, broken but beloved human beings join the praise of the Firstborn of all creation and discover thereby their own true voices of praise.

The Church's Praise Is Correlative to Creation's Praise

To draw the above comments in the direction of the church's worship, I suggest that the church's praise subsists integrally in creation's praise. Worship occurs in and through creation because it is God's continual pleasure to call forth praise in all his works, at all liturgical times, and in all liturgical places.[24] God does so, not as an unfortunate requirement, but as a way to honor our human creatureliness, which belongs to this marvelous theater of God's glory, as John Calvin once called it.[25]

Job 12:7–10 says,

> But now ask the beasts, and let them teach you;
> and the birds of the heavens, and let them tell you.
> Or speak to the earth, and let it teach you;
> and let the fish of the sea declare to you. (NASB)

This means, among other things, that while human praise may be unique, it is not isolated worship. We join in and with creation's praise.[26] So when we sing our praises to God, we "join in with the ecstatic praise continually being offered up to the Lord by trees and flowers, sunshine and rain, angels, dragons, and snakes, as well as monarchs and generals of the world (Pss. 104; 148:7–10)."[27]

23. Gordon Lathrop, *Holy Ground: A Liturgical Cosmology* (Minneapolis: Augsburg Fortress, 2003), 45.

24. Cf. John Calvin, *Institutes of the Christian Religion* (1559), 2 vols., ed. John T. McNeill, trans. Ford Lewis Battles (Philadelphia: Westminster, 1960), 1.5.9.

25. Geoffrey Wainwright, *For Our Salvation: Two Approaches to the Work of Christ* (Grand Rapids: Eerdmans, 1997), 11.

26. Augustine says it this way: "Some people read books in order to find God. But the very appearance of God's creation is a great book. Look above you! Look below you! Take note! Read!" Cited in Karlfried Froehlich, "'Take Up and Read': Basics of Augustine's Biblical Interpretation," *Interpretation* 58 (2004): 5–16.

27. Calvin Seerveld, *Voicing God's Psalms* (Grand Rapids: Eerdmans, 2005), 141.

The purpose of creation in worship, on this view, is not to "get out of the way" but rather to serve the purposes of worship *through* creaturely ways. The purpose of creation, more specifically, is to train the faithful to taste and see that the Lord is indeed good *in* and *through* the very physical elements of baptism and Communion, the fleshy things that mark our acts of foot washing and laying on of hands, the material things that accompany our rituals of marrying and burying.

The Holy Spirit and the Worship by Creation

In the Nicene Creed the church confesses its faith in the Third Person of the Trinity, "the Lord and Giver of life." By this confession, the church affirms that the Spirit is the one who animates creation, upholds it, and brings it to perfection. In faith, the church affirms that the Spirit mends the human creature, conforming it by grace, through faith, to the life of God in Christ. In faith, the church affirms that the Spirit orders creation and all that lies within it.

This confession is crucial because it directly informs how we relate creation and worship. We can, for example, undoubtedly affirm that the Spirit is the God of order, not of chaos. But we can also affirm that a Spirit-constituted order will be an irrepressibly dynamic order, yielding new configurations of liturgical life and prompting praise through a host of creaturely ways, which in turn bear witness to the final vision of worship that arises from every tongue, tribe, and nation of the earth (Rev. 7:9).

On this view, the church is freed to welcome a broad range of culturally particular experiences of order: for example, in the syncopated gospel music of CeCe Winans,[28] the rhythmic pattern of Shakespearean sonnets, the liturgical poetry of Malcolm Guite,[29] the symphonic "singing in the Spirit" of Latino Pentecostals in southern California,[30] or the Renaissance polyphonic choral works of *Stile Antico*.[31]

While Christians have no business taking sin any less seriously than Christ himself takes it, Christians likewise have no business taking the power of the Spirit less seriously than Christ himself does. Though our experiences of the physical creation in worship may distract or distort our worship of God,

28. See http://www.cecewinans.com.

29. Malcolm Guite, *Sounding the Seasons: Seventy Sonnets for the Christian Year* (Norwich, UK: Canterbury, 2012).

30. See Juan Martinez, "Varieties of Latino Pentecostals, and other Protestants, in Los Angeles," August 15, 2012, https://crcc.usc.edu/report/the-latino-church-next/varieties-of-latino-pentecostals-and-other-protestants-in-los-angeles/.

31. See https://www.stileantico.co.uk/about.

our human weakness does not have the last word; the Holy Spirit does. With confidence in the effective work of the Spirit, we thus are freed to taste and touch, see and smell, hear and harken to the goodness of God's creation in our worship of God.

The Whole Person in Corporate Worship

The fundamental thrust of the New Testament is to understand the "spiritual" work of God as the work of the Holy Spirit to conform our whole humanity to the life of Christ. This is a comprehensive reality; no sphere of life is left untouched by the Spirit-ual work of God. This includes bodies, hearts, minds, wills, and so on; in worship our whole humanity gets to be sanctified.

Practically speaking, just as distinctively Christian worship ought to make space for spontaneous expressions of prayer and praise, as a way for our bodies both to be led by the movements of the heart and mind and, in turn, to lead the movements of the heart and mind, worship also ought to make space for ritualized and symbolic expression. A ritualized form of physical expression involves repeated activities that are performed for the good of our physical bodies, regardless of temperament or the feelings of the moment.

In both these ways worship invites our whole selves to "put on Christ" and to get a "feel for the Spirit." This is also a way to remind ourselves, in particular, that we perceive our physical bodies rightly, not by doing whatever we wish with them but by being gathered *in* our own bodies, *as* one body, *around* Christ's body.[32]

Triune Worship Is Physically Mediated Worship

The worship that the Father seeks, to borrow the language of John 4:23–24, is worship that is physically mediated rather than disembodied.[33] When Jesus tells the woman at the well that "a time is coming and has now come when the true worshipers will worship the Father in the Spirit and in truth" (NIV), his point is not to draw attention to her ability to be truthful or sincere in her

32. Cf. "A Trinitarian Theology of the Physical Body," chap. 7 in W. David O. Taylor, *The Theater of God's Glory: Calvin, Creation, and the Liturgical Arts* (Grand Rapids: Eerdmans, 2017).

33. Two traditions characterize the interpretation of this text: one tradition argues that John 4 points to the inner life of the individual worshiper, and another believes the text is best understood as a description of the activity of the Triune God to make faithful worship possible in this new "time," inaugurated by the coming of Christ and the descent of the Spirit. Cf. Taylor, *Theater of God's Glory*, chap. 8, "The 'Simple' Worship of God," and chap. 9, "The Trinitarian Space of Worship."

worship, as if true worship depended on our human abilities. His point is to underscore the work of the Triune God to enable true worship, what Christ and the Spirit who come from "above" make possible in this "new hour."[34]

Worship that the Spirit makes possible, as John's Gospel sees it, is made tangible in the new community that Christ gathers to himself: in their speech, their actions, their bodies, and the physical media that liturgically symbolize the new life in Christ.[35] John's Gospel points us therefore to worship, where creation plays an indispensable role: narratively through the story it tells (e.g., in foot washing) and dramatically through the story it enacts (by way of, e.g., eucharistic gatherings).[36]

Put more boldly, in John we discover no disparagement of physical space, no so-called sacred space, no alleged secular space.[37] We instead discover space that has been reconfigured by the presence of the Second and Third Persons of the Trinity. To worship in this Trinity-saturated space, then, is both a fulfillment of the prophetic word and a foretaste of the new creation. It means that every created thing, from bodies to buildings, from feasts to fasts, can become a vehicle for the grace and glory of God.

Practical Implications for Worship

How might such a biblical and theological vision for worship and creation be enacted in our common liturgical life? Allow me to suggest a range of ways; while not comprehensive, these ways may inspire other possibilities in our personal contexts.

One way to embody this vision is to seek opportunities for *our worship to bear witness to the specific geographic place in which we live.* Examples of this include the use of limestone, which is native to central Texas, in the building of First Evangelical Free Church in Austin, Texas; or the use of adobe clay to build the San Francisco de Asis mission church in Ranchos de Taos in New Mexico; or the use of woods that are indigenous to the Ozark-St. Francis National Forest in the Thorncrown Chapel in Eureka Springs, Arkansas.

34. Cf. R. G. Gruenler, *The Trinity in the Gospel of John: A Thematic Commentary on the Fourth Gospel* (Grand Rapids: Baker, 1986).

35. The Scriptures include numerous examples of material objects that—both accompanied by and apart from faith—mediate the power and presence of God. These include the tabernacle altar, Moses's rod, Elijah's mantle, Elisha's bones, Paul's handkerchief, and Jesus's own robe.

36. Cf. Wright, "Worship and the Spirit," 23.

37. Cf. H. Wayne Johnson, "John 4:19–24: Exegetical Implications for Worship and Place," unpublished paper presented at ETS, Baltimore, MD, in November 2013, https://www.dropbox .com/s/h4il69vuog82ue2/Johnson%20John%204.19-24%20ETS.pdf?dl=0.

Another way that a place of worship might bear witness to creation is through *the creative use of windows*. Leaders at Duke Divinity School made a deliberate choice to keep the windowpanes in Goodson Chapel clear rather than colored during renovations in 2005. This was done to remind people that, when they gathered for worship, God's world lay near at hand. The piney woods that surround the chapel re-present, to those who worship, a display of God's glory in creation.[38] And while clear-paned windows could be seen as merely a way to let sunlight into a space, for Duke Divinity School they represent an opportunity to receive the ministry of color characteristic of the changing of the seasons in nature.[39]

A more modest but perhaps more doable option is to choose *to display local wildflowers in locations throughout the church*, such as in the foyer or on the eucharistic table, rather than buying flowers that may have traveled a great distance or that involve an unnecessary and costly expense.

In this vein, a church may choose to *plant trees and bushes that are local to the region and that would thrive naturally*, rather than require an inordinate expense in upkeep. A church community could explore the biodiversity in their immediate region to discover what kinds of plant life grow there. They might learn about the birds that are most common to the ecology of the area and plant flowers that would attract them naturally. In doing so, a congregation might find itself frequently praising God for the unique wonder of their own environment.[40]

To enjoy a more direct experience of nature, *a congregation may wish to begin its Palm Sunday procession outside* (weather permitting and if the space is viable). In fourth-century Jerusalem, a procession of Christians moved through the city streets during major holy days, testifying thereby of the expansive scope of God's reign on earth.[41] Beginning one's processions

---

38. In email correspondence (March 16, 2018), Susan Pendleton Jones, who served as chair of the committee that oversaw the construction of the chapel, wrote:
> The tree-line fits perfectly with the placement of the windows above the chancel area but actually doesn't extend much beyond them on either side. On the northern apse side (opposite the organ) there are no (or maybe few) trees, but when seated you mainly see the sky. When standing, you see the Duke LSRC [Levine Science Research Center] building off in the distance, which gave us the sense of combining both the beauty of nature in worship (as you look outside toward the chancel) with the realities of the everyday world, symbolized by a generic classroom building out the baptismal apse side windows.

39. Susan Jones, email correspondence, March 16, 2018.

40. Mark Torgerson, in his book *Greening Spaces for Worship and Ministry: Congregations, Their Buildings, and Creation Care* (Herndon, VA: Alban Institute, 2012), includes many helpful possibilities along these lines.

41. Lester Ruth, Carrie Steenwyk, and John D. Witvliet, *Walking Where Jesus Walked: Worship in Fourth-Century Jerusalem* (Grand Rapids: Eerdmans, 2010), 23–24. This might also

outdoors may be a way for a congregation to experience something similar: a joyful taste of the elements in memory of Christ's triumphal entry into Jerusalem and in anticipation of Christ's final victory in the presence of all creation (Rev. 5).

A community may choose to celebrate the Feast of St. Francis with its blessing of animals. A congregation might invite all pet owners to gather in an outdoor space on October 4 for a lively gathering of creatures. Among other things, a pastor might read the Collect Prayer for St. Francis that includes this line: "We thank you for giving us these pets who bring us joy. As you take care of us, so also we ask your help that we might take care of those who trust us to look after them."[42]

One might also read a prayer for God's good earth. The Anglican Book of Common Prayer includes the following prayer for Knowledge of God's Creation:

> Almighty and everlasting God, you made the universe with all its marvelous order, its atoms, worlds, and galaxies, and the infinite complexity of living creatures: Grant that, as we probe the mysteries of your creation, we may come to know you more truly, and more surely fulfill our role in your eternal purpose; in the name of Jesus Christ our Lord. *Amen.*[43]

In a similar vein, one might read one of the psalms of creation (e.g., Pss. 8; 19; 148) in a fresh version, such as the English priest Jim Cotter's translation of Psalm 8:

> When I look at the heavens, even the work of your fingers,
> the moon and the stars majestic in their courses—
> the eagle riding the air, the dolphin ploughing the sea,
> the gazelle leaping the wind, the sheep grazing the fells—
> who are we human beings that you keep us in mind,
> children, women, and men that you care so much for us?[44]

---

describe the experience of Christians during the Feast of Fools, Children's Festival, and the Dance of Death.

42. See https://episcopalchurch.org/files/st_francis_day_resources.pdf.

43. See https://www.bcponline.org/Misc/Prayers.html#40.

44. Jim Cotter, *Psalms for a Pilgrim People* (Harrisburg, PA: Morehouse, 1998), 13. The psalms would also tell us to look up: to see how big the cosmos is and how small we are, and how good it is that we are small but glory-crowned. They would tell us to look down: to see our hands and feet that have been made to till and to tend creation in love. And they would tell us to look around us: to see the lilies of the field and the birds of the air, and the moss and the rocks and the rivers as well, how they neither worry nor uselessly toil but rather invite us to delight in a gracious Creator.

A new call to worship could be based on Psalm 24:1. It might go something like this:

> The earth is the Lord's, and all that is in it,
> *The world, and those who live in it.*
>
> Our bodies are the Lord's, and every part of them,
> *Our hands and feet, our heads and hearts, our skin and bone and*
> *   breath.*
>
> This place is the Lord's, and all that belongs to it,
> *Our doors and windows, our crosses and chairs, our books and*
> *   screens, all things great and small.*
>
> This land is the Lord's, and all that comes with it,
> *The flora and fauna, the soil and water, the buildings and parks, the*
> *   people and pets, what's mine and yours and ours together.*
>
> Oh come, let us worship and bow down;
> *Let us kneel before the Lord, our Maker!*
>
> For he is our God, and we are the people of his pasture,
> *And the sheep of his hand.*
>
> Amen.

The arts, of course, can fittingly serve these purposes too. One example of this is a 48 × 96–inch banner that artist James B. Janknegt painted for Eastertide in 2005; it was for Hope Chapel in Austin, Texas, and titled "Make All Things New." As one commentator describes it, "Janknegt's painting shows the risen Christ standing triumphantly over the pit of death and under the blessing hand of God, sweeping up the things of earth into a whirlpool of color. Birds, balls, and bicycles; musical instruments and charcoal grills; plants and houses, pets and people, mowers and swing sets—all are on their way to the new Jerusalem. Also present in the cosmic swirl are a loaf of bread and a glass of wine, symbols of God's broken body and spilt blood, the activators of the new covenant."[45]

Carrying the elements of Communion from the back of a worship space to the front might be a way to symbolize the interrelationship between the labor of Christ and the labor of human hands bringing the fruits of the earth, transformed into something new through an act of culture-making (grapes to

---

45. Victoria Emily Jones, "A Sweeping Vision of All Things Made New," April 21, 2016, https://artandtheology.org/2016/04/21/a-sweeping-vision-of-all-things-made-new/. Janknegt's painting can be seen on the artist's website: http://bcartfarm.com/wfs13.html.

wine, wheat to bread) to the table of God. At his table, God in turn offers the labor of Christ on the cross to the people so that the Spirit might transform them to become living emblems of the body and blood of Jesus in the world.[46]

Our physical bodies play a central role in tying the work of creation to the work of worship. When Christians open their hands to receive the minister's benediction, for instance, it is a way for them to perceive how all of life involves an openhanded reception of God's blessing. When a multiethnic community holds hands during the passing of the peace, it is a way for their bodies to signify the reconciliation that ought to characterize their whole lives. In doing these things a congregation gains *bodily knowledge* of the body of Christ. Or when a person lays hands on the sick in body and in heart, it is a way to underscore the immediate physical presence of Christ, who frequently heals through touch.

However we move our bodies in worship, it is with our bodies that we join all of creation's praise and, in our respective liturgical contexts, thereby discover the ways in which we might cling to God and release to God, stretch out to God and retreat from God, turn and return to God, fall before and rise again in faith before a God who reaches out to us in grace and turns our tentative gestures of faith into full-fledged movements of love and adoration.[47]

So much more could be included in this list of practical suggestions. Songs of creation care, such as "From Smallest Seed: The A Rocha Project Volume 1," could be sung.[48] A program could be started to recycle old church bulletins and worship programs. A congregation might hold hands during the Lord's Prayer to signify the bound-togetherness of the *imago Dei.* And feasting and fasting could take place throughout the year, to celebrate God's abundance and to commemorate God's sacrificial love, all for the sake of generosity to our neighbors in need.

Conclusion

In the end, when creation is viewed under a trinitarian light, I maintain that the church at worship is looking not at an escape from creation but rather at the preservation, healing, and liberation of creation so that it might become what

46. This is what Church of the Servant in Grand Rapids, Michigan, does every Sunday at worship: https://www.churchoftheservantcrc.org.

47. This is a point I develop more fully in *Glimpses of the New Creation: Worship and the Formative Power of the Arts* (Grand Rapids: Eerdmans, 2019), chap. 9, "Worship and the Kinetic Arts."

48. See A Rocha Arts, "From Smallest Seed: The A Rocha Project Volume 1," September 2, 2014, https://arochaarts.bandcamp.com/album/from-smallest-seed-the-a-rocha-project-volume-1.

the Father has eternally purposed for it. Rather than being regarded as accommodations to human weakness, all creaturely things in worship can be things that fittingly symbolize the church's worship in light of the resurrection.[49]

Instead of being perceived as concessions to corporeal life this side of the eschaton, they can be regarded as physical media that remain commensurate with our God-blessed creaturely condition and that function as foretastes of the age to come. On this reckoning the whole of the cosmos fittingly serves the work of God, in the public praise of God, as a portrait of God's glory in and through creation. And by God's grace the church at worship opens fresh eyes and begins to see that the earth is in fact our home, a home that God is in the business of renewing daily in anticipation of the renewal of the whole earth.

For Further Reading

Beale, Gregory K. *The Temple and the Church's Mission: A Biblical Theology of the Dwelling Place of God*. Downers Grove, IL: InterVarsity, 2004.

Lathrop, Gordon. *Holy Ground: A Liturgical Cosmology*. Minneapolis: Augsburg Fortress, 2003.

Moo, Douglas J., and Jonathan A. Moo. *Creation Care: A Biblical Theology of the Natural World*. Grand Rapids: Zondervan, 2018.

Taylor, W. David O. *Glimpses of the New Creation: Worship and the Formative Power of the Arts*. Grand Rapids: Eerdmans, 2019.

———. *The Theater of God's Glory: Calvin, Creation, and the Liturgical Arts*. Grand Rapids: Eerdmans, 2017.

Torgerson, Mark. *Greening Spaces for Worship and Ministry: Congregations, Their Buildings, and Creation Care*. Herndon, VA: Alban Institute, 2012.

49. Cf. Taylor, *Glimpses of the New Creation*, chap. 3, "The Theological Meanings of Art in Worship."

— 4 —

God and Worship

Don E. Saliers

How can we speak of God? This question yields several others: How *ought* we to speak of God? How do we come to knowledge of God? What is a "doctrine of God" for? How does worship shape and express our concept of God? This cluster of questions is one way into thinking about the nature of worship as relating to the divine. This inquiry is more than an attempt to formulate theories about divinity. Rather, this chapter attempts to frame the relationship between the human activity of worship and theology as *reflective thinking about the God who is worshiped* (our *logos* in relation to *Theos*). In this sense, what follows provides a basic approach to *liturgical theology*. Not all worship is "liturgical," yet communities of worship, no matter how free of set texts and ritual actions, show repeated patterns in how God is addressed as well as how God is seen and heard. Although worship can certainly be expressed in private (personal) devotion, my focus will be principally on communal (public) worship of a gathered assembly. While not all worship is explicitly prayer, we shall consider prayer (in all its modes) as the heart of the matter for Jewish, Muslim, and Christian worship. Thus praise, lament, petition, confession, adoration, testifying, and contemplation are all fundamental aspects of worship together and worship alone. How God is imaged and encountered in each of these modes varies among traditions. We will return to the question of how particular theologies emerge from the action of communal prayer.

Philosophical Approaches to God and Worship

There is a long tradition of thinking about God quite apart from the practices of worship and prayer. Philosophers and religious thinkers have reasoned about divinity for centuries. They have conceived of God as the ultimate origin of reality, as the source of all power and movement, as the greatest being, or as "Being-Itself" and thus beyond all categories. At the same time, specific religious traditions have given various names to their gods; some traditions refrain from any direct speaking of the unutterable nature of divinity. Here one thinks of the Jewish tradition of not pronouncing the true name of God, or of mystical traditions in which silence before the unutterable reality of God prevails. Whether or not we have knowledge of God is a matter of continuing debate. This generates philosophical questions about human knowledge and the nature of reality.

Philosophical theology and philosophy of religion characteristically are not concerned with worship as primary language about God. Rather, classical views of the divine have proceeded by reasoning from human existence and a general theory of reality (metaphysics). In these approaches, the concept of God is essentially contested and determined by various philosophical views about the nature of reality. How God is depicted depends upon how the world and the whole cosmos is described. In this sense, philosophical views tend to include God as a matter of speculation, not of prayer or worship.

The question "Is there a god?" arises when we wonder about causes and explanations of the nature of the world. "God" becomes an object of reasoning from the appearance of things.

Yet such reflection is not by "reason alone," to echo Immanuel Kant's famous treatise *Religion within the Limits of Reason Alone.* "God" is an object of speculative reasoning. For most philosophical traditions, the concept of God is resolutely part of questions about the nature of reality itself. How does the idea of God relate to what we perceive to be things in the world of time and space? Here the debate about divinity is often expressed around the terms "transcendence" and "infinity." God is beyond all finite things and transcends every specific thing in the world. Such a concept of God, arrived at by human reasoning, does not appear to be a matter of what we normally call "worship." This raises the question of what we mean by the term. We will return to this in due time. Notions of transcendence and the infinite are essential to worship of God; such notions are also found in some other religious traditions.

Meditation and Arguments for the Existence and Worship of God

The famous arguments for the existence of God in theologians such as Anselm (AD 1033–1109) and Thomas Aquinas (1225–74) are themselves grounded in meditation about the world. Anselm articulates his famous arguments in his treatise *Proslogium*, the original title of which was *Faith Seeking Understanding*. The opening chapter is devoted to awakening the human mind to the contemplation of God. Anselm's "ontological" arguments for God's existence are grounded in the search for intellectual understanding of God. Here we note that Anselm's audience is principally Christian persons of faith seeking a rational basis for belief in God. He issues his famous formula, *Fides quaerens intellectum* (faith seeking understanding), but the notion of worship is not overtly noted within his discourse. His arguments are purely rational. Yet the opening of the *Proslogium* is itself a call to meditation, indeed, to a form of contemplative prayer. We will return to this point. For now, we may note that for Anselm—and for Aquinas who follows—to think of the very term "God" seems at least to require a contemplative disposition. Even philosophical views of God may thus require a sense of awe or wonderment at the universe. This leaves an opening to consider the relationship between praying and thinking, between the human activity of worship and the task of reasoning about God.

Theology as Coming to Understand the One Addressed in Prayer

Suppose we claim that theology is a way of understanding the One who is addressed in prayer. This clearly involves human reasoning. Such a mode of reflection and reasoning is more complex than knowing by reason alone, as is clear, for example, in mathematics. Prayer is dialogue, a communion involving a relationship between those who pray and the divinity to whom the prayer and worship are addressed. This means that the thinking must exhibit something of the nature of that relationality with God in the very way it regards its subject. We might say that there is a distinctive "religious" character to such reasoning in contrast to purely detached knowledge. Simply put, theology as language about God must respect its "subject" while yet having a critical logic. Bernard of Clairvaux once said, "It is not disputation, but sanctity which comprehends if the incomprehensible can, after a certain fashion, be understood at all."[1] He was contrasting speculative theological debates with

---

1. Bernard of Clairvaux, *De consideratione* 5.30, cited by J. Leclercq, *The Love of Learning and the Desire for God*, trans. C. Misrahi, 3rd ed. (New York: Fordham University Press, 1982), 164.

the practice of holy living shaped by prayer and liturgical participation. From this point of view, if we are to understand anything about God, it will be because of the dynamics and the forms of worship. One could say that faith seeks theological understanding through worship.

Two classical terms are indispensable to this approach to theology: "apophatic" and "kataphatic." The apophatic tradition, influenced by Platonic philosophy, thinks of God by way of negation. Such forms of thought emphasize the divine transcendence. In essence, God is beyond the limits of human reason and language. This "negative theology" is contrasted with, yet also paired with, kataphatic expressions, "positive theology." Thinking about God uses specific images and descriptions. For most Protestants and many Western Christian traditions, this is the dominant understanding of theological discourse. Characteristically, it involves accepting primary biblical images and descriptions as making direct truth claims. However, a permanent tension remains in understanding relations between worship and any doctrine or teachings about God. In acknowledging the gap between liturgy and the divine subject of liturgy, both these approaches are required. Thinking theologically about worship and thinking liturgically about the divine requires us to deal with analogies, metaphors, and forms of description that both reveal and hide. In other words, the apophatic and kataphatic features of these contrasting forms of reflection are needed to do justice to the revelatory power of language about God. God cannot be reduced to our language about God.

We are again faced with the fundamental question of all Christian theology: How can God, who is beyond all human knowing, become known and worshiped under the finite conditions of creation? The Eastern Orthodox churches have stressed that God is *uncreated*, in contrast to all created things, including "heaven and earth." Without the possibility of apophatic thinking, the very mystery of God can easily be theologically diminished. In Søren Kierkegaard's terms, there is an "infinite qualitative distinction"[2] between God and creation. Yet without kataphatic thinking, prayer and worship of God would remain utterly silent, at least with respect to human language.

Toward an Understanding of Worship and Language about God

I propose the following key points as an outline of relations between prayer, worship, and theology:

2. Søren Kierkegaard, *Training in Christianity and the Edifying Discourse which "Accompanied" It*, trans. Walter Lowrie (Oxford: Oxford University Press, 1941), 139.

1. What we believe about God and the world is shaped by how we worship and what we pray. In the study of various forms of prayer—whether liturgical or free-church, using written texts and spontaneous expressions—we discover an "operational theology." Sometimes the theology is explicit, as in a prayer book. One example is found in the Prayer of General Thanksgiving. The worshiping community gives thanks to God for "creation, preservation, and all the blessings of this life." That prayer comes to focus in the phrase "but above all for thine inestimable love in the redemption of the world by our Lord Jesus Christ; for the means of grace, and for the hope of glory."[3] Praying this prayer to God forms a vision of the world and human life by addressing God in the mode of thanksgiving. Here the picture of God is christological.

2. The communal act of praying and proclamation (which can also be devotional) opens the world to us as a created and redeemed order of reality. The movements of prayer and worship are constitutive elements in "believing God." Here we see a living relationship, a reciprocity, between truth claims about God and the act of addressing God in a community of faith. It is not that we must first formulate a "doctrine" of God and then apply the doctrine in prayer and worship. The act of worship is not the same as applying a theory. Rather, the community's life of worship is both a generative practice born in a tradition and an interrogation of what has been stated as teaching or doctrine.

3. The theological task is to think prayerfully about the world and human existence and to worship thoughtfully out of our tradition and life experience. Believing is much more akin to trusting and loving than it is to mental efforts to state and defend a truth. Here Christians may think of Paul's statement to the Corinthians: "I will pray with the spirit, but I will pray with the mind also; I will sing praise with the spirit, but I will sing praise with the mind also" (1 Cor. 14:15).

4. Various modes of Christian prayer show a kind of "grammar" of God and God's attributes in relation to self and world. Praising, confessing, lamenting, interceding, and petitioning are all self-involving. Worship has to do with how we are affected by reading the world as the "arena of God's glory," the theater of the divine agency.[4] At the same time

3. This excerpt from the Book of Common Prayer can be viewed at https://contemplative gardener.com/morning-thanksgiving/.

4. This phrase from John Calvin is cited in Susan E. Schreiner, *The Theater of His Glory: Nature and the Natural Order in the Thought of John Calvin* (Grand Rapids: Baker Books, 1991), 17. For more, see Belden C. Lane, *Ravished by Beauty: The Surprising Legacy of Reformed Spirituality* (Oxford Scholarship Online, 2011), https://=/doi.org/10.1093/acprof:oso/9780199755080.001.0001.

worship involves bringing our unfolding human experience before God: suffering, rejoicing, seeking, and finding wonder and awe. One way of putting this is to say that worship as ongoing prayer is a sustaining activity of acknowledging the divine in all circumstances.

5. The Lord's Prayer as an act of worship is a major clue for the Christian community. In offering this prayer, we both follow a norm and experientially receive a pattern of life and teaching from Jesus Christ as the giver of the prayer. The petitions of this prayer cover a primary range of God's attributes: holiness, intentional will, a realm of inclusion—coupled with requests for God to satisfy human needs: for food, forgiveness, and final courage and belonging. These bear directly upon how we are understanding the world and God's relationship to the world through God's self-giving in the Word made flesh.

6. Theology is a way of understanding the mystery of God addressed in prayer. Understanding and reasoning is involved. Worshiping this way is the condition for faith seeking understanding. It involves listening as well as speaking, receiving as well as offering. If we are to formulate a doctrine of God, it will require thinking that is shaped by the very mystery it seeks to fathom. God, while an "object" of knowing, is always beyond any formulation of human knowing. It requires speaking of God as the One who knows us. Therefore, whatever language we have, the reality of God is beyond our words. This is the indelible truth of the "apophatic" element in all theology.

7. At the same time, human beings pray and worship out of received traditions of practice and thought. Just as any reading of Sacred Scripture inherits ways of reading and interpretation, so ways of worship and prayer inherit a history of practices. These are always embedded and embodied in cultural forms: music, language, gesture, images, and particular ritual actions. In this way, all worship of God depends upon the kataphatic resources of a tradition. Even in spontaneous, Spirit-led forms of worship and prayer there are inherited patterns of speech and bodily behavior. Yet these cultural forms and inherited forms of interpretation are, in authentic worship, offered as signs of access and reception of divine power. This is the fundamental paradox of worship: human means become the mediation of divine agency.

8. This peculiarity of prayer and worship opens the mystery of "transcendence" and "immanence" in theological reasoning. We begin by conceiving transcendence as vertical and immanence as horizontal, but we soon discover that the deeper we enter the reality of prayer and the

life of worship, the more these terms also refer to the inner immanence of the divine life. This is especially true of theological reflection on the "immanent Trinity" in Christianity and on the intrinsic holiness of God in Jewish and Islamic traditions. Authentic, non-idolatrous worship reveals a depth and richness never fully exhausted in our categories.

9. It is useful to point to the ancient songs known as the psalms. These texts have constituted Psalms, a primary book of prayer for Judaism and Christianity. They have shaped the images at the heart of the liturgical traditions in both. It is helpful to regard these psalms as both affirmations and interrogations of God and human worshipers. The praise of God is not simply about human experience; it is also part of the exchange of addressing and being addressed by the divine Word. The psalms can be understood in practice as a giving over to what Rowan Williams calls the "dispassion of religious language." This is a "suspension of the ordinary categories of "rational" speech. It also is a decentering of the human mind as the measure of all things."[5] In praise, "God is truthfully spoken of by learning to speak of the world in a certain way, and of the self in a certain way, by giving over what is said to the pattern of creation and redemption, a pattern moving through loss and disorder to life."[6]

Worship Over Time and the Changing Images of God

Worship over time alters our images of God. This does not mean that the divine nature or essence is changed. Some theologians, especially "process theologians," have proposed that God changes or progresses over time. It is not necessary to claim that the divine essence changes because our perception of the divine changes.[7] Here we focus on how human beings come to picture God differently over time, in their individual religious experience. This is equally true of specific traditions within Christianity. For example, the Protestant Reformation brought to light new conceptions of God's grace as well as the relationship between God in church and society. In other words, our religious

5. Rowan Williams, *On Christian Theology* (Malden, MA: Blackwell, 1999), 12–13.

6. Williams, *On Christian Theology*, 13.

7. Biblical accounts of God's relationship to Israel and to various human events is depicted as changing. God is said to have repented of anger and wrath. One of the most poignant passages is found in Hosea 11, where God says, "How can I give you up, Ephraim? How can I hand you over, O Israel? . . . My heart recoils within me" (11:8). In passages like these, one may find justification for saying that God changes the divine mind. Here it is useful to distinguish the "being of God" from the divine interaction in specific relationships to the world.

images are always responding to historical and social changes in the church. In this way "believing" in God's nature and attributes is intimately related to practices in worship and devotion. Of course, new dimensions of our images and conceptions of God are also influenced by changing theologies over time. This is dramatically illustrated in the Roman Catholic tradition following dramatic differences on specific teachings between Vatican Councils I and II. Still, it is a matter of debate whether new theological interpretations imply that the divine nature has changed. One way of addressing this issue is to observe that, over time, Jewish and Christian theologies grow and mature on specific understandings of God.

Considering these points, we return to the fundamental question of the relationship between human language and reasoning (theology) and the mystery of God in Godself. It is the glory of the apophatic tradition to remind us that all human reasoning and language cannot fully comprehend what we mean by the word "God." In the larger Christian tradition, most theologians have claimed that our conceptions of the divine are not regarded as identical to the transcendent reality of God. In the same way, all liturgies are not to be regarded as completely adequate to God's own self. This is the contrast between human religiousness (worship patterns and practices) and the divine life itself. The ancient prophets warned against making human rituals substitutes for worship of the living God (e.g., Isa. 45; Jer. 7; Amos 4).

The Inevitable Religious and Theological Problem: Idolatry

There remains, however, another crucial issue. Any reflection on the relationships between worship practices and our concept of God must come to terms with idolatry. A simple definition of idolatry is "the worship of false gods." In the history of actual religious practices, a more complex story emerges. The ongoing history of a religious tradition might be thought of as the never-ending struggle to distinguish "true" and "false" gods. In Jewish and Christian Scriptures, the ancient prophets are especially intent on marking what constitutes idolatry and warning against it. The first and second Mosaic commandments both reveal prohibitions. The children of Israel are not to worship other gods, which are found behind "idolatrous" behavior. "You shall not have any other gods before me" (cf. Deut. 5:7) and "You shall not make for yourself an idol . . . in the form of anything that is in heaven above, or that is on the earth beneath, . . . [and] shall not bow down to them or worship them" (5:8). The *religious* problem is with the practice and its consequences, disobedience and sin. The *theological* problem is found in distinguishing between false gods and the one true God. These are obviously interrelated. The complexity here results from the contrast between worshiping faithfully and worshiping with idolatrous tendencies. One example is a sincere Christian intention to worship God mixed with profound loyalties to one's country—a phenomenon observed not only in the Nazi era but also in problematic claims of God's favoring any nation-state over another.

A more formal definition involves offering devotion to a finite object as though it possesses infinite worth. Paul Tillich proposed that idolatry is placing our "ultimate concern" in that which is a finite reality in the world. Human beings, he thought, were capable of placing their sense of ultimate trust in that which is ultimate.[8] The religious problem of misplaced faith and trust involves the theological issue of identifying and acknowledging the nature of the living God of Israel, who is revealed in Jesus. Worship is the site of this struggle. What constitutes true prayer to the true God? Some believers and traditions will claim this is not a problem at all. This claim is found in various forms of fundamentalism, yet I contend that this double-edged problem is intrinsic to the very nature of worship. Can faithful worship include matters of doubt and unfaith within itself? In turn, this reveals a distinction between the enacted forms of worship and the mystery and reality of God in Godself. The history of Christian worship is, in one sense, a continuing tension between God and the human desire to worship God. This is why religious practice must always include confession of sin. Idolatrous tendencies are always possible because worship is always culturally embodied, even in traditions that deny this temptation. We might also note that the psalms are continually wrestling with this problem. "Create in me a clean heart, O God," prays David in Psalm 51:10. The tendency to idolatry is always present. Worship wrestles with the need to embody its own self-critique. Doxology requires lament and confession over human idolatries of all kinds: the worship of wealth, power, luxury, spiritual superiority, and so on.

Practical Implications for Worship

At the same time, worship is dependent upon a disposition of gratitude, thanksgiving, and blessing. The ancient Jewish berakah form of prayerful blessing is foundational to both Jewish and Christian worship patterns. "Blessed and praised are you, Holy God, for you have created all things." This form of prayer names what God has done in nature and history as a

8. See Paul Tillich, *Systematic Theology* (Chicago: University of Chicago Press, 1951), vol. 1, chaps. 2–3.

way of praising and worshiping God. Even in traditions that purport to be nonliturgical, we find the worshipers' intention to praise God by naming divine attributes and actions. Worship of God begins and ends in praise. This is the foundational element of acknowledging the difference between Creator and creature. Without awe, wonder, and humility, our language about God remains empty.

One way to express the nature of worship is to regard worship as a continuing practice of remembering. I think of the language of worship, in all its modes of prayer, as the language of the human heart at full stretch before God and neighbor. This echoes the ancient "Shema, Israel" of Deuteronomy 6:4–5, the call to remember God and to worship. "You shall love the LORD your God with all your heart, and with all your soul, and with all your might." This love for God infuses meaning into the "second . . . commandment" accented in the New Testament: "Love your neighbor as yourself" (e.g., Mark 12:31).

By "at full stretch" we mean that praying to and worshiping God is more than words. This requires the whole mind, the whole heart, and the whole will to be made vulnerable in the presence of the Divine. Worship thus is a willing openness of our whole life—not just our intellect, but also our whole body and human subjectivity itself. The Christian theological claim is this: because Jesus Christ as the Word made flesh is fully human as well as fully divine, prayer in his name will involve all our relationships in the world.

Therefore, worship is a pattern of life, a form of being alive to God and neighbor. There are specific liturgies and ways of praying that are part of the long history of religious faith. Each tradition has its distinctive languages, symbols, and actions. True worship (and here we must speak in fear and trembling) leads to a way of living that stands in praise and vulnerability of heart before the mystery of God's self-giving. This implies that the community of faith and all individual worshipers continue in maturation of their understanding of God. Learning to remember and to tell the truth about ourselves and our world is crucial. Without an ongoing conversation with God through specific stories, images, and communal practices, the "living memory" will remain as intellectual faith only. This is why a faith that dares to pray and worship shows a passion for God.

If it is not to be faithless or idolatrous, praying and worshiping confront us with a difficult truth. I have always found this warning from Miguel de Unamuno sobering: "Those who say that they believe in God and yet neither love nor fear Him, do not in fact believe in Him but in those who have taught them that God exists. . . . Those who believe that they believe in God, but without any passion in their heart, without anguish of mind, without uncertainty, without doubt, . . . even in their consolation, believe only in the

God-Idea, not in God Himself."[9] This warning is not intended to dismiss or diminish the necessity of prayer and worship. Quite the contrary, this reminds us that God is not simply a matter of right language or even of "right belief." In its original meaning "orthodoxy" signifies "right praise." To offer life at full stretch to God, as we noted earlier, means that we bring our hopes and fears, our sorrows and our joys, our laments and our deepest love, all these to the praise of God. All this is not so much about us as it is our petition that God will remember the world. Worship and prayer do not make God present. Rather, the divine life reveals itself to those assembled in biblical memory with gratitude and awe. The reality and presence of God is given in, with, and through the mystery proclaimed and celebrated as the Word in creation and made flesh in human history.

What does this imply for the worshiping life of the Christian churches here and now? First, we notice that the language we use (in preaching, praying, reading, and singing) depends greatly upon the nonverbal dimensions of life together. How we participate in the self-communication of God requires that we pay attention to the revelatory qualities of what we see, hear, touch, taste, and ritualize. Words can fail and become cliché without attention to what faithful form of life is being lived. Signs of love, courage, humility, and hope appear as we come to understand God's relationship to the world and to the church at worship. Does worship both form and express an ever-growing depth of faith over time? Our liturgies are about Christ's liturgy: hospitality, blessing, healing, feeding and being fed, consoling and admonishing, forgiving, supporting, and acting in the mercy of God.

Reconceiving the whole of a specific worship service as the ongoing prayer of Christ in the world sheds light on the relationships between the particular elements of worship and how we live in the world. This leads not to rigid formulas or to prescribed uniformity in a cultural style or a single tradition. Rather, what we have begun to explore in this chapter leads to a set of pastoral/ theological questions about communal worship. Cultural influences currently both change and challenge the patterns we may have inherited. If worship is "God-centered" and not "we-centered," we must ask how the ministries and

---

9. Miguel de Unamuno, *Tragic Sense of Life* (New York: Cosimo, 2005), 57–58. Instead, the reality and presence of God comes in and through the mystery proclaimed and celebrated in solidarity with human history and the whole created order. The language about God in worship and prayer depends upon all the nonverbal dimensions of life. To say and mean "I love you" or "I promise you" implies gestures, intentions, and signs of receptivity; so does the language we employ in worship. The language of love, of doubt, of courage, and of trust finds its true grounding in the "life practices"—in the loving, the struggling, and the trusting. In this way all the modes of prayer and the patterns of worship shape and express human existence before God and neighbor.

dynamics of care in our congregations become visible, audible, and palpable in our assemblies. For what and for whom do we pray? What do we lament? What do we give thanks for? Does our singing and our celebrating the Lord's Supper and baptism give us a taste of the kingdom of God?

I conclude with six interrelated questions for local congregations. These are for both the clergy and the laity—for all who lead and for all who participate in the ongoing prayer of the church:

1. Does our common worship form and express our human lives in *awe and wonder* over time, in response to God's Word?

2. Does our common worship form and express our lives in *gratitude and hospitality*, as we find these attested in the whole of Scripture?

3. Does our common worship form and express our lives in *delight and surprise*? Here we pay attention to how qualities of worship enable us daily to perceive being "surprised by joy," as C. S. Lewis remarked.[10]

4. Does our common worship form and express our lives in *truth-telling*? Here I suggest that we see the relationship between *lament, confession,* and *witnessing.* Worship must sound the truths about our suffering world, about our own complicities, and about how God actually comes to human beings in mercy and healing.

5. Does our common worship form and express our lives over time in *love and compassion* and mutual respect and care? The church must continually learn to be a community of intercession in prayer and in action. God remembers the poor, the forgotten, the oppressed, the outcast. So too, the community that is faithful to the Word of God also remembers them.

6. Finally, though not exhaustively, does our common worship form and express our lives in *hope*? The God of the prophets and the incarnation in Jesus of Nazareth always favors the "new creation," a world of justice, reconciliation, and peace. This is not simply hope for what we want, but the hope for what God intends for all of creation. This is why all worship is finally oriented to the eschatological promises of God. This is why we continually pray the words of the Lord's Prayer: "Thy kingdom come. Thy will be done on earth . . . as it is in heaven."

These questions are intended to be pastoral and practical, to aid in planning and preparing for and celebrating authentic worship of God. At the same

10. C. S. Lewis, *Surprised by Joy: The Shape of My Early Life* (London: G. Bles, 1955).

time, these are ultimately theological questions about the nature of God and how God comes to us and to the world.

For Further Reading

Barth, Karl. *Evangelical Theology: An Introduction*. Translated by Grover Foley. New York: Holt, Rinehart & Winston, 1963.

Farley, Wendy. *The Thirst of God: Contemplating God's Love with Three Women Mystics*. Louisville: Westminster John Knox, 2015.

Lathrop, Gordon W. *Holy Things: A Liturgical Theology*. Minneapolis: Fortress, 1993.

Ross, Melanie C. *Evangelical versus Liturgical? Defying a Dichotomy*. Grand Rapids: Eerdmans, 2014.

Saliers, Don E. *Worship as Theology: Foretaste of Glory Divine*. Nashville: Abingdon, 1994.

Wainwright, Geoffrey. *Doxology: The Praise of God in Worship, Doctrine, and Life*. New York: Oxford University Press, 1980.

5

Humanity and Worship

Ronald T. Michener

Therefore, I urge you, brothers and sisters, in view of God's mercy, to offer your bodies as a living sacrifice, holy and pleasing to God—this is your true and proper worship.

—Paul, Romans 12:1 NIV

"We are what we eat" is only partially true. What we eat also displays what and who we are. Similarly, our beliefs shape our worship, but our worship also shapes our beliefs. That is, our embodied practices, what James K. A. Smith calls our daily "liturgies," shape our understanding of reality.[1] What we do and think in worship reflects what Charles Taylor calls our social imaginaries.[2] Worship must not be reduced to the merely cognitive. It is not simply thinking a certain way about God or expressing one's reflections about God. It includes this, but it is more. It involves thinking and doing. Worship is about human beings orienting themselves toward God,

1. James K. A. Smith, *You Are What You Love: The Spiritual Power of Habit* (Grand Rapids: Brazos, 2016), 120–48. See his fuller development of this in his Cultural Liturgies trilogy (Grand Rapids: Baker Academic): *Desiring the Kingdom: Worship, Worldview, and Cultural Formation* (2009); *Imagining the Kingdom: How Worship Works* (2013); and *Awaiting the King: Reforming Public Theology* (2017).

2. Charles Taylor, *Modern Social Imaginaries* (Durham, NC: Duke University Press, 2004), 23–30.

acknowledging his transcendent magnificence and indwelling presence. This orientation requires the human being to acknowledge personal vulnerabilities, weaknesses, and inadequacies before God, who is the Creator and Sustainer of all humanity and all creation. Creaturely humility precedes worship of the Creator. As the saying goes, "God is God, and we are not." Worship, then, is integrally linked to our theological anthropology. As we will see, how we view and practice our humanity will impact our views and practices of worship.

Theological Overview: Humanity

Human Beings Created in the Image of God

One of the first things we must do to position humanity theologically is to affirm that humans are created in the image of God. Understanding and describing what precisely this means is not an easy task and is widely debated among theologians. To address the theme of this chapter, "Humanity and Worship," we briefly consider some of the significant theological issues pertaining to theological anthropology and the *imago Dei*. Before we can meaningfully discuss worship as it pertains to humanity, we must have a general idea of what is entailed by "humanity" itself. Since this book is explicitly theological in orientation, with this chapter's focus on how theological perspectives on humanity relate to worship, it is fitting to begin with a theological understanding of what it means to be human. It is no surprise that there are various understandings and debates in this regard. We cannot begin to address all the issues or settle all the debates; they are much too wide and deep to discuss in one chapter, much less in a preliminary section of a chapter. Entire books address this topic and do not resolve everything. With that said, we must put in-depth analyses of the thorny questions aside to address our task at hand. Nevertheless, we will at least mention several significant issues in theological anthropology to raise awareness of such matters when considering the meaning and practice of worship as human beings.

As humans created in the image or likeness of God, we are inherently spiritual beings.[3] That is, we cannot be reduced to mere physicality. At the same time, we are embodied spiritual beings; our bodies are a necessary but not a sufficient condition for us to be human spiritual beings. We are flesh-and-blood creatures animated by God: that is what makes us spiritual beings. In this sense, the human being is only properly functioning when oriented toward God and

3. For purposes of reflection on theological anthropology, "image" and "likeless" are regarded as synonymous. See Stanley J. Grenz, *Theology for the Community of God* (Carlisle, UK: Paternoster, 1994), 229 and 229n73.

reflecting God incarnate, Jesus Christ.[4] But what more specifically constitutes being created in the image of God? The biblical references to the *imago Dei* are quite minimal. The key verses lie in the creation narrative in Genesis 1:26–27. A few other explicit references appear in the Bible (e.g., Gen. 5:1–3; 9:6; 1 Cor. 11:7; James 3:9). Again, a number of opinions have been expressed on the nature of the *imago Dei*.[5] Marc Cortez identifies four broad historical-theological perspectives that include the structural, functional, relational, and multifaceted views.[6] Structural perspectives affirm that the *imago Dei* is a structural part of being human, especially with respect to human rational capacities. A functional view submits that the *imago Dei* lies in what humans do rather than what they intrinsically are as human beings. The relational view holds that the *imago Dei* lies in the relational aspects of humanity, whether this be sexual relationships or humans in other aspects of community engagement. The final perspective, summarized by Cortez, is the multifaceted view. This view suggests, as the name implies, that the *imago Dei* cannot be reduced to one of the above perspectives, but it involves various aspects of being and practicing our humanity.[7]

Stanley J. Grenz suggests four aspects to a multifaceted view of the *imago Dei*. The first is that humans have a "special standing before God." We have received God's love and commands, and we have been given the "responsibility" to reflect God to all creation. Second, the *imago Dei* indicates that human beings have a "special fellowship" with God and need God for "ultimate fulfillment." Third, the *imago Dei* is an "eschatological reality." That is, humanity's telos is found in God's ultimate plan, which is manifested in the revelation of Jesus Christ, in whom we are called to participate. Fourth, the *imago Dei* is integrally linked to community.[8] This is the critical key for Grenz: "This design is that we participate together with others in the community of the followers of Christ. Thereby we together reflect the divine life itself, which life is present among us through the Holy Spirit, who is the dynamic of the triune God."[9]

---

4. See Marc Cortez, *Theological Anthropology: A Guide for the Perplexed* (London: T&T Clark, 2010), 5–6.

5. For a thorough, contemporary investigation into the *imago Dei* from theological and biblical perspectives, see J. Richard Middleton, *The Liberating Image: The* Imago Dei *in Genesis 1* (Grand Rapids: Brazos, 2005).

6. Cortez, *Theological Anthropology*, 18–24. Cf. also Cornelis van der Kooi and Gijsbert van der Brink, *Christian Dogmatics* (Grand Rapids: Eerdmans, 2017), 260–66.

7. Cortez, *Theological Anthropology*, 18–29. Richard Middleton points out that the substantialist perspective of image (that which Cortez describes as "structural") was the majority understanding until the Reformation, when an alternative view was sought to blend the substantialist understanding of the image with a "dynamic, relational notion of the image as ethical conformity or obedient response to God." *Liberating Image*, 22.

8. Grenz, *Theology for the Community*, 230–32.

9. Grenz, *Theology for the Community*, 233.

Human Beings as Fallen and Broken

To this point, we have emphasized that human beings are embodied spiritual beings created in the image of God and entrusted by God to reflect God to creation. However, human beings are fallen, weak, and broken creatures due to their own sinfulness and rebellion against God; they are finite creatures who suffer from the effects of a broken creation in which they dwell.[10] One may argue that such fallenness is not an inherent part of primordial humanity, yet it remains the unavoidable condition in which humans as image bearers are situated. At the same time, this situated, broken indwelling in the world is also undergoing redemption, transformation, and renewal because of Christ, the perfect example of embodying and reflecting the *imago Dei*. Thus N. T. Wright insightfully highlights this restorative vocation of humanity with respect to creation:

> Creation, it seems, was not a tableau, a static scene. It was designed as a project, created in order to go somewhere. The creator has a future in mind for it; and Human—this strange creature, full of mystery and glory—is the means by which the creator is going to take his project forward. The garden, and all the living creatures, plants and animals, within it, are designed to become what they were meant to be through the work of God's image-bearing creatures in their midst. The point of the project is that the garden be extended, colonizing the rest of creation; and Human is the creature put in charge of that plan. Human is thus a kind of midway creature: reflecting God into the world, and reflecting the world back to God. That is the basis for the "truly human" vocation.[11]

With this broad framework in mind for our theological anthropology, how then does our humanity, and the way we understand what it means to be human, relate to our practice of worship? To this question we now turn.

Intersection: How Humanity Correlates with Worship Practice

Worship Is Integral to Humanity

Nicholas Wolterstorff submits: "Worshipping God is not just a good thing for human beings in general, and for the church in particular, to do; it is something we ought to do, something that is due God. Failure to do so is to wrong God. But obviously it is not something that we human beings do inevitably, unavoidably, ineluctably; God has created us free to worship or not to worship

10. This may include both natural and moral evils.
11. N. T. Wright, *After You Believe: Why Christian Character Matters* (Sydney: HarperCollins, 2010), 74–75.

God."[12] Wolterstorff is certainly correct in saying that worship is something we ought to do, and if we do not worship, we violate God; yet I would suggest taking this a step further: If we do not worship, we not only violate God but we also violate what it means to be essentially human. Worship, as Alexander Schmemann asserts, "is the essential act" for human beings, "which both 'posits' [their] humanity and fulfills it."[13]

Theologically speaking, worship is that which all humanity longs for in God, since it is in worship where our humanity thrives and flourishes. If this ultimate longing goes unpracticed, our authentic humanity is compromised. Again, to cite N. T. Wright: "There is such a thing as forgetting what it really means to be genuinely human. It is dangerously possible to start reflecting gods other than the true God in whose image we were made. But the other gods are not life-giving. To worship them, and to reflect their image, is to court death: the eventual utter destruction of all that it means to be truly human."[14] In this sense, the issue is not as much whether we worship, but what or whom we worship. This is implicit in the monolatry of ancient Israel. The assumption among the Israelites was not monotheism (which came later at Mount Sinai) but monolatry, that the God of the Israelites was the only one worthy of their worship among other gods that had also had influence. James K. A. Smith's recent work argues that humans are affective beings that indeed worship through their everyday liturgical practices, whether for good or ill.[15] In fact, it is impossible not to worship "because we can't not love *something* as ultimate."[16] It is important to keep this broader understanding of worship in mind, but for purposes of this chapter, when we refer to "worship," we will be referring specifically to the rightful, proper worship of the God of Scripture. Hence, for those committed to Christ, worship must flow from their position as redeemed human beings, created in God's image, to reflect the character of Christ to the world.

Worship is not something reserved for "saints." It is not about good, religious folk singing hymns and saying their prayers. We have often mistakenly portrayed worship as something reserved for the holier-than-thou characters

12. Nicholas Wolterstorff, *The God We Worship: An Exploration of Liturgical Theology* (Grand Rapids: Eerdmans, 2015), 163–64.

13. Alexander Schmemann, *For the Life of the World* (Crestwood, NY: St. Vladimir's Seminary Press, 1973), 118.

14. N. T. Wright, *Following Jesus: Biblical Reflections on Discipleship* (London: SPCK, 1994), 79.

15. Smith, *Desiring the Kingdom*, 122–23. Smith makes this point, interpreting Calvin's *sensus divinitatis* as humankind's propensity to worship. Cf. also Smith, *You Are What You Love*, 22–25.

16. Smith, *You Are What You Love*, 23.

dressed in white robes. Nothing could be further from the truth. Worship is for broken, needy, sin-struck human beings. It is for those who willingly acknowledge their weakness as human beings before God and before each other. The brokenness of humanity has ruptured relationships of the self from God, the self from its human authenticity, and the self from others. Human beings "recover their identity," as Wolfhart Pannenberg asserts, "through reintegration into the community," where "they recover a freedom which they neither possess nor can exercise for themselves in isolation, but which they possess only as recognized members of the shared world."[17] This "shared world" is what is known as "culture."[18] Pannenberg draws upon Johan Huizinga's notion of play with respect to understanding culture. Play is observed in all forms of life in human communities, religious and otherwise. He elaborates: "The subject of play has turned us from individuals and their concern with identity (although this theme itself is located within the horizon of the social relations of individuals) to the life-world which individuals share. In play, human beings put into practice that being-outside-themselves to which their exocentricity destines them. The process begins with the symbolic games of children and finds its completion in worship."[19]

Humanity, Bodies, and Worship

In order to speak of humanity in worship requires us to speak of human bodies in worship. Unfortunately, the human body vis-à-vis spirituality has been given a bad reputation. The body is seen as the cause of human corruption, lust, and illicit pleasures. We have sometimes mistakenly confused Paul's notion of the "flesh" (that which is directed away from God and bad for humanity) with "spirit" (everything that is God-directed and good for humanity). This confusion often invades our perspectives on what it means to be embodied as human beings and, more specifically, what it means to worship as embodied human beings. As Marcia Mount Shoop submits: "Body talk tends to focus mostly on lessons of control and moderation. The connection and complexities of the body as a spiritual entity receive little thematic treatment and even less embodied practice."[20] The body is seen as that which

17. Wolfhart Pannenberg, *Anthropology in Theological Perspective* (New York: T&T Clark, 1985), 312.

18. Pannenberg, *Anthropology in Theological Perspective*, 314.

19. Pannenberg, *Anthropology in Theological Perspective*, 338. Pannenberg draws from Johan Huizinga, *Homo Ludens: A Study of the Play-Element in Culture*, trans. R. F. C. Hull (London: Routledge & Kegan Paul, 1949).

20. Marcia W. Mount Shoop, *Let the Bones Dance: Embodiment and the Body of Christ* (Louisville: Westminster John Knox, 2010), 3.

requires ultimate control, creating a "disembodied ethos" in our worshiping communities that "encourages an unbalanced intellectualism."[21] Worship then becomes the practice to get beyond the body to reach what is ultimately real because the body is related to sin. When particular bodies in the corporate body of Christ become "disjointed" in this way, it is "surely an offense in an incarnational faith."[22] Warren S. Brown and Brad D. Strawn also address the danger of disembodiment in worship. They insist that if worship becomes primarily about individual experiences and one's internal, personal spirituality, as if the self is separated from our complete embodied personhood, then it becomes disconnected from the corporate body of Christ.[23]

The keen insights of Shoop, Brown, and Strawn do not minimize the place of the rational mind in worship but rather address the imbalance between thought, imagination, and embodiment. Recognizing this imbalance, we equally affirm that mind and body are mutually interactive within the inclusive whole of a human being. Hence, we suggest a holistic theological anthropology, where human beings are embodied spiritual beings that think, move, feel, love, imagine, and worship; all these are interactive without one aspect necessarily preceding the other. Simon Chan's *Liturgical Theology* also sees history affirming "that *lex orandi* and *lex credendi* sustain a dialectical relationship with each other: liturgy shapes doctrine and doctrine shapes liturgy."[24] Similarly, we may say that worship practices stem from what we think, and what we think also stems from our practices.

Different Approaches in Understanding Humanity in Worship

Diversity in Worship among Individual Embodied Beings

Worshiping bodies, human beings that worship, are broken beings—perhaps emotionally broken or physically broken, or a combination of both. Most human beings worship as hurting human beings. Yet human beings do demonstrate happiness or joy in life. The broken, hurting, or joyful human being may express the self with emotional exuberance or in solemnity and sorrow. One's worshipful expressions will be shaped by one's situation in

21. Shoop, *Let the Bones Dance*, 4.
22. Shoop, *Let the Bones Dance*, 4.
23. Warren S. Brown and Brad D. Strawn, *The Physical Nature of Christian Life: Neuroscience, Psychology, and the Church* (Cambridge: Cambridge University Press, 2012), 148.
24. Simon Chan, *Liturgical Theology: The Church as Worshiping Community* (Downers Grove, IL: IVP Academic, 2006), 49, emphasis original. Or, as Chan says a few pages later: "Right belief and right practice (*orthopraxis*) can only come from right worship, and vice versa" (52). See also Brown and Strawn, *Physical Nature of Christian Life*, 152.

life and may vary significantly from person to person. Within the worshiping body of Christ, there must be a recognition of diversity of human bodies and various manifestations of the conditions of that diversified embodiment (joy, pain, brokenness, etc., as mentioned above) experienced by individual human beings.

Diversity in Worship among Corporate Diverse Bodies

As our various conditions in life's journey affect our manner of worship, so too our denominational backgrounds and religious subcultures also influence our worship styles or visual displays of worship. Yet with the vast diversity of worship styles among diverse bodies of believers, all are embedded in patterns of liturgical worship practices. As Smith puts it:

> All Christian worship—whether Anglican or Anabaptist, Pentecostal or Presbyterian—is liturgical in the sense that it is governed by norms, draws on a tradition, includes bodily rituals or routines, and involves formative practices. For instance, though Pentecostal worship is often considered to be the antithesis of liturgy, it actually includes many of the same elements: charismatic worship is very embodied (hands raised in praise, kneeling at the altar in prayer, laying on hands in hope, etc.); it has a common, unwritten routine, . . . and these practices of Pentecostal worship are deeply formative, shaping our imagination to relate to the world in a unique way.[25]

Some churches are more charismatic, emotional, and physically exuberant than others; some are more solemn and reserved. But a solemn and reserved style does not mean that physical activity is absent. Worship includes mind and body: whether or not one raises hands for worship, most liturgies still require standing and sitting at various intervals during a church service, not to mention using one's voice for singing, reading Scripture, or saying public prayers. It is not that one particular way or tradition is better than another for worship, even though some may be more oriented toward movement of hands and limbs than others.[26] Whatever tradition one is a part of, it is important that one takes a posture of hospitality toward other traditions and is intentional about learning from those who differ from one's perspectives and practices. Further, one must not denigrate the importance of the physical body in the act of worship—whether the body is engaged in a more subdued or more

---

25. Smith, *Desiring the Kingdom*, 152.

26. For different perspectives on worship practices among various Protestant persuasions, see Paul A. Basden, ed., *Exploring the Worship Spectrum: Six Views* (Grand Rapids: Zondervan, 2004).

animated fashion. A priority must be concern for the local and worldwide body of believers, as well as the larger body of Christ, for the sake of unity in community. We turn to this more explicitly in the next section.

Concern for the Community

Worship Is Relational and Respectful

As human beings, we are essentially relational. Worship is a relational turning toward God and a relational activity *in community* toward God. As such, it means that bodies are expressing themselves to God in verbal praises and singing, moving, acting, and reacting together. Whatever this looks like, it must involve respect for the other and respect for different preferences in movement, expression, words, emotions, and so forth. Worship is not simply about "me and God," blocking those around me out of mind. Worship is indeed an expression of the body, but it is more about the corporate body of Christ as embodied human beings in community than it is about individual, autonomous bodies in worship. Smith affirms this: "The goal of worship is not a private re-fueling, but a public disturbance—to create subversive ambassadors of the coming King."[27] Of course, admitting this "public disturbance" of sorts reminds us that human movement always requires courtesy and respect for those around us. In manifesting such respect, humility complements worship.

In this way, worship is subversive by running against the grain of modern (or postmodern, for that matter) selfish egoism. This is keenly expressed by Wright:

> All of this life of worship is something to be learned. Communities can grow into liturgy and the sacraments, and can take delight in discovering that these things can become, as it were, habits of the community's heart as well as of the individual's. Shared worship is part of what it means when we compare Christianity to a team sport. It is together that we are God's people, not as isolated individuals. That being-togetherness does not, of course, mean uniformity. What counts is precisely the coming together of people who are quite unlike one another in everything.[28]

Whenever and however people gather, differences will abound. The church is called to be a community where vast national, cultural, socioeconomic, and racial differences are joining in one body to manifest Christ's call to unity

27. James K. A. Smith, *The Devil Reads Derrida: And Other Essays on the University, the Church, Politics, and the Arts* (Grand Rapids: Eerdmans, 2009), 77.
28. Wright, *After You Believe*, 223.

and reconciliation to the world. This, like any type of virtuous activity, takes intentional, regular, disciplined practice and humility. Intentional worship with such heterogeneous communities displays subversion to xenophobia, racism, economic partiality, and any form of elitism.[29] Worship displays, in community, not the turn toward the power of empire and exclusion, but the weakness of the cross and the inclusive invitation into the resurrection power of God's renewal of all creation.

Worship Is Local, Historical, and Proleptic

Community-centered worship is both locally particular and historically rooted. That is, worship is to be focused on the specific local community in worship together, yet also on the broader, historical community of faith through the ages. In our local church contexts, we are proclaiming "the story of Israel and Jesus in the service of the Word and we enact the story at the Lord's Table. Like Israel, we rehearse God's mighty deeds of salvation and offer thankful praise and worship to God[,] who saves us."[30] When we worship by proclaiming psalms and hymns, reciting the Lord's Prayer and creeds, we are identifying ourselves, uniting ourselves to all Christians who have, are, and will be professing faith and exalting the one, holy, triune God of the ages.[31] In this broad array of expressions of worship, the local Christian community is bound together in the story of God's creation and redemption of his people and creation, in the past and present. But the Christian community is also rehearsing gratefulness to God, proleptically, for the renewal and restoration of humanity with each other and all of creation in the eschaton. In this regard, worship also plays a vital missional role. Christians who "participate in Christ through worship are each time shaped in the image of the new humanity and reminded of their public role as witnesses to and ministers of the world's reconciliation with God."[32] In

29. Adam Hearlson makes the following provocative insight in this regard: "Subversion has been a part of Christian worship since its inception. In the Roman catacombs, the earliest Christian art is full of subversive images—the underground walls are adorned with women and slaves serving Communion, secret symbols of Christian fidelity, and symbols critical of the Roman empire. Worship as a subversive art is both an act of resistance and an act of creativity." *The Holy No: Worship as a Subversive Act* (Grand Rapids: Eerdmans, 2018), under chap. 1, "The Way of Subversion."

30. Robert E. Webber, *Ancient-Future Faith: Rethinking Evangelicalism for a Postmodern World* (Grand Rapids: Baker, 1999), 102.

31. See Glenn Packiam, *Discover the Mystery of Faith: How Worship Shapes Believing* (Colorado Springs: David C. Cook, 2013), under chap. 4, "Retelling the Story." Cf. also, Webber, *Ancient-Future Faith*, 104.

32. Jens Zimmermann, *Incarnational Humanism: A Philosophy of Culture for the Church in the World* (Downers Grove, IL: IVP Academic, 2012), 15.

summary, worship is both a local and broadly communal endeavor that is essential to *being* human. Human beings flourish in community-centered practices of gratitude and adoration to God that are embedded in the narrative of God's work in creation through humanity and through all time.

Practical Implications for Worship

We have seen that worship is integral to being human; it is embodied, diverse, and relational. With these above reflections in mind, what are some "practicable" implications for worship? The applications are numerous, several of which are already expressed above. Nonetheless, I will conclude with three brief related themes that may be of further help in this regard: habitual (or ritual) practices, embodied applications, and intentional acts towards the "other."

Habitual Practice of Worship

In an age where new and fresh always seems better, there is often little place for the priority of repetition. Protestants may be especially suspicious toward repetition in worship, since repetition seems like mere tradition and thoughtless action drained of authentic personal faith. Such a perspective, however, is greatly misinformed and simply incorrect. Indeed, a danger of repetition may be mentally disengaged activity. But there is much about bodily repetition that breeds virtue and consistency. The key is linking the virtuous repetition with an engaged mind and body. In our regular habits of worship, we consistently rehearse the story of God's gracious creating and redeeming work through his people throughout history. Worship is not only a practice; it also takes practice and discipline. Byron Anderson puts this well: "Yes, repetition and ritual breed familiarity, but it is the familiarity of the inhabited place, of the indwelling heart. It is just this familiarity that is required for our ability to take the music into the depths of our being. Through ongoing practice, through the ritual patterns of Christian worship, we come over time to take into ourselves, to make our own, the grammar and narrative of the Christian life."[33]

Liturgical, habitual practice is significant and critical for worship because it corporately shapes our bodies and minds toward a Christian imagination and "dispositions" that do not yield "habituation to secular liturgies,"[34] which are

---

33. E. Byron Anderson, "Worship: Schooling in the Tradition of Jesus," *Theology Today* 66, no. 1 (2009): 21–32, esp. 31.

34. Smith, *Imagining the Kingdom*, 183. See also his entire section on "Redeeming Repetition: On Habituation," 181–86.

"antithetical to the Christian faith."[35] Proper worship is like regular exercise; it builds patterns into one's life in the context of the faith community, patterns oriented Godward and outward, rather than resting inward on personal experience. This is where embodied worship and ethics consistently work together in a repetitive, interchangeable circle of activity and practice. As with any skill—musical, sports, or otherwise—it requires doing the skill to obtain the skill. As Douglas Davies wisely insists: "Just as musicians become musicians through performance, sports people such through playing and actors through acting, so Christians become Christian through worship, ethics and the life of faith in mundane events."[36] In this constant, habitual orientation and reorientation through worship, it provides us with the focused moral strength to manifest Christ's love to the world.[37] Habits are human, and habitual, practiced worship nurtures our humanity as we focus ourselves beyond ourselves and in community toward God.

Embodied Worship Applied and Misapplied

As we have maintained, worship is essential to our humanity, a humanity that is thoroughly embodied and relational, created in the image of God. Embodiment is not reduced to mere personal or individual embodiment, however, but is about the individual embodied within the larger body of Christ. This does not negate the individual person but situates the person within the context by which each, as an individual, flourishes in the fullness of being human. Being human means nurturing that humanity in the context of and relationship with others.

With this in mind, worship practices will vary among diverse human beings. For some, acts of worship will be more demonstrative; others may be more reserved. But some sort of bodily action and community participation would seem to follow, so that worship is not reduced to rational reflection or personal feeling.[38] Embodied worship properly applied, however, will not promote autonomous experiences for the sake of the individual, but the bringing together of individuals for the sake of the larger body. Unfortunately, some contemporary worship or "praise" songs seem to promote a "me and God" or "me and Jesus" mentality.[39] Some seem to express intimate love for Jesus or are

---

35. Anderson, "Worship," 31.

36. Douglas J. Davies, *Anthropology and Theology* (London: Bloomsbury Academic, 2002), 42.

37. Jeffrey P. Bishop, "Body Work and the Work of the Body," *Journal of Moral Theology* 2, no. 1 (2013): 113–31. Bishop remarks: "The act of bowing the head and reorienting the body reorients desire and the will for action in the world" (130).

38. Brown and Strawn, *Physical Nature of Christian Life*, 152.

39. See Brown and Strawn, *Physical Nature of Christian Life*, 149.

about falling in love with Jesus.[40] Indeed, we are to love Jesus, the Christ, but we are not "in love" with Jesus. Loving God or Jesus is quite different from the notion of the sexually laden, romantic metaphor of "falling in love." In my view, this is a misapplication of embodiment in worship.

Recognizing the Other in the Worshiping Community

If worship is communal and relational, how do we attend to and respect the disabled among us? Michelle Voss Roberts says, "People with disabilities continue to find themselves shut out of worship spaces because of able-bodied and able-minded norms. Christian congregations remain segregated by race and social class."[41] This, then, raises a concrete question: How can we embrace disabled people among us, bringing them into the community so that they may embrace inclusion instead of exclusion? Without minimizing the conditions of those disabled (bodily or mentally) or severely ill who require significant help from others for their daily grooming and basic functioning, let us remember that we are all "deeply dependent on the labor and attentions of others, as well as the vehicles, tools, and appliances that facilitate our existence. Human engagement with the world is prosthetic in nature."[42] Mobile phones, tablets, and portable computers have become external appendages on which we depend for our daily functioning in the world.[43] Here the point is not to make value judgments on the appropriate or inappropriate nature of technology for meaningful human contact. This may go either way, depending on its use. Rather, it is to emphasize our utter reliance upon many factors for our daily routines and needs. We count on other people and resources apart from ourselves for virtually everything we do.

Of course, the "other" among us is not simply the one who may not function in the same way as we do physically or mentally, but also includes those who may be radically (or not so radically) different racially or culturally. Each person must be considered as "together with" and not "less than" within each local community of worship, as well as in the corporate body of Christ

---

40. I do not wish to mention specific choruses or songwriters in this regard since this may come across as vindictive and would not promote constructive dialogue.

41. Michelle Voss Roberts, *Body Parts: A Theological Anthropology* (Minneapolis: Fortress, 2017), xliii.

42. Roberts, *Body Parts*, 115. Brown and Strawn comment that "Identifying ourselves as a part of the disability scene is an important part of acknowledging our dependence." *Physical Nature of Christian Life*, 153–54. For their insights in this regard, they draw upon Alistair McIntyre's work *Dependent Rational Animals: Why Human Beings Need the Virtues* (Chicago: Open Court, 1999).

43. See Roberts, *Body Parts*, 114.

throughout the world. This may sound idealistic if left at that. But the idealism becomes realism with daily, intentional, hospitable activity, beginning with simple gestures: smiles, handshakes, conversation, recognition, acts of forgiveness and charity, and regular demonstrations of kindness and gratefulness for the other in our midst.

Conclusion

These three practice-centered applications of humanity and worship—habit, embodied action, and recognizing the other—are overlapping and interrelated. Perhaps the primary embodied practice that expresses these three aspects in an exceptional manner is found in the Eucharist, or Lord's Supper.

Partaking of the Lord's Supper is a habitual, participative celebration that embeds the body of Christ in the past, present, and future. In its regularity, we rehearse the gospel of Jesus's presence with us in community through the Holy Spirit; we remember the bread he provides for us both in terms of our daily food and his embodied, physical life. We remember his lifeblood shed for us through the wine. We remember together by celebrating together, also allowing our memories to turn toward the future when Christ will restore and renew all creation. This regular habit of worship in Communion shapes our imaginations. God then works through us to reshape the imagination of those in the world.

Further, the Lord's Supper speaks clearly of embodiment and the recognition of the other: the incarnate body of Jesus and the body of Christ, the church. It is a physically engaged practice without partiality, where all in Christ are called to participate and share together what the Lord has provided—male and female, rich and poor, sick and healthy, abled and disabled, all races, all nations, all peoples of any kind. It is about bodies cooperating physically and mentally as the bread and wine are served. This may require an assortment of bodily movements, from reaching out to receive the elements, walking up to the table, or kneeling while being served. In any case, it is a communal, embodied engagement in worship that clearly displays the vulnerability of our humanity.[44] This is lucidly expressed by Michelle Voss Roberts: "The body parts remembered in the Eucharist are, above all, vulnerable, and Christ's vulnerability is the vulnerability shared by all bodies. The crucifixion and resurrection of Christ implicate every organ of sensation and action. Hands and feet pierced and immobilized. . . . This particular body, broken, opens

---

44. Brown and Strawn, *Physical Nature of Christian Life*, 151. Also see Roberts, *Body Parts*, 120–21.

to the other. Jesus Christ represents the divine presence within all vulnerable bodies created in the *imago Dei*."[45] In this habitual, embodied, vulnerable, and impartial worship at the Lord's Supper, we have an exemplary model of worship and *being* human, not as disparate functions, but as two united in purpose. Worship is thoroughly and robustly human, and being human it is about being human in community, the body of Christ, to reflect the image of God.

For Further Reading

Brown, Warren S., and Brad D. Strawn. *The Physical Nature of Christian Life: Neuroscience, Psychology, and the Church*. Cambridge: Cambridge University Press, 2012.

Chan, Simon. *Liturgical Theology: The Church as Worshiping Community*. Downers Grove, IL: IVP Academic, 2006.

Davies, Douglas J. *Anthropology and Theology*. London: Bloomsbury Academic, 2002.

Hearlson, Adam. *The Holy No: Worship as a Subversive Act*. Grand Rapids: Eerdmans, 2018.

Shoop, Marcia W. Mount. *Let the Bones Dance: Embodiment and the Body of Christ*. Louisville: Westminster John Knox, 2010.

Smith, James K. A. *Desiring the Kingdom: Worship, Worldview, and Cultural Formation*. Cultural Liturgies 1. Grand Rapids: Baker Academic, 2009.

———. *Imagining the Kingdom: How Worship Works*. Cultural Liturgies 2. Grand Rapids: Baker Academic, 2013.

Wright, N. T. *After You Believe: Why Christian Character Matters*. New York: HarperCollins, 2010.

45. Roberts, *Body Parts*, 122.

— 6 —

Christology and Worship

Bruce T. Morrill

Theological Overview

Christology is the effort to bring theological understanding to the Christian belief in the divinity and humanity of Christ Jesus. In this sense, theology reflects upon the experience of believers and, as such, is one step removed from the immediate experience of practiced faith. Across the range of Christian communities, the church has abundant experiences of Christ's presence and action in their lives, including engagement with Sacred Scripture, prayer, liturgy, and worship, as well as moral and ethical life in church and society. Historically, there has been a wide variety of expressions for the fundamental belief in Jesus as Lord. None of these experiences and shared traditions have developed in isolation from the way Christians in given times and places have understood their world, their place in it, and perhaps most importantly, what it means to be human.

The fundamental question of Christology, then, is this: What does it mean to profess that Jesus Christ is Lord? That profession was the basic creedal statement of the earliest believers in Christ, most likely even before the term "Christian" had been coined. Over the past century academic theologians have been availing themselves of contemporary biblical studies, critical scholarship of Christian history and ideas, and philosophical and social-scientific anthropology, aiming to construct more adequate interpretations of the salvific significance of Christ Jesus. Increasing attention is being given to the contexts of particular Christian communities, along ethnic, geographic, gender, or other lines of inquiry, in order to articulate how those believers' circumstances, their "world," meets the vision of the new world revealed in Christ.

A more in-depth exploration might proceed by surveying the varieties of Christologies emerging in our time. The present chapter, however, has the specific mandate of relating Christology to the ways of Christian worship, past and present, identifying how communities have brought understandings of Christ and his salvation to their liturgies, sacramental rites, and various services of worship. In turn, worship practices have also, at times primarily, shaped theological teaching about the person and mission of Christ.

Christology centered on the mission of the eternal Word (Greek *Logos*) of God taking flesh (becoming incarnate), as attested in the Prologue of John's Gospel, has been the predominant way of understanding and worshiping Christ Jesus as Son of God and Savior from ancient Christianity to the present. When it comes to the way Christians—Orthodox, Catholic, Protestant, evangelical—worship God, the "classical" doctrine is what to this day, albeit with variations, shapes the imaginations and prayers of assembled believers; the symbols and rituals comprise the traditions across the churches. First let us briefly examine the origins of this Logos Christology in those early church centuries, then we can move on to a basic synopsis of the story of God, humanity, Christ, and salvation that this type of Christology tells. All this seems essential for us to better understand why and how Christian churches have gone about divine worship as they have.

Classical Logos Christology

Logos Christology emerged through the first seven centuries of Christianity to become the orthodox—that is, correctly worshiping and properly believing—standard for the churches, East and West. In the culture of that day, Neoplatonic and Stoic philosophies comprised their theoretical frameworks for understanding the human being, the world's existence, and what could and could not be said about God in relation to the biblical deposit of the faith. Repeatedly the bishops across the entire church needed to meet in councils to resolve vociferous disputes over the right belief in God as Father, Son, and Spirit, as well as in the divinity and humanity of the Son, Christ Jesus. The intricacies of the trinitarian and christological debates and resolutions are notoriously complex. If one wonders why the arguments could be so divisive and run so long, the important thing to recognize is that Christology has always been about soteriology (*sōtēr*, "savior," the Greek root for "salvation"). This means identifying what is so troubled about humanity and the world as to need Christ Jesus and then understanding the deliverance that he brings.

Rather than attempt a generalized synopsis of what became classical Christology, it may be better to provide a brief study of the soteriological Christology of Athanasius, a fourth-century bishop of Alexandria, Egypt. Athanasius's *On the Incarnation of the Word* presents a narrative of the human predicament in relation to God and creation in terms that have been carried through and influenced how Christians tell the story of salvation and orient their worship of God in Christ over centuries and across continents. The enduring categories include incarnation, death and resurrection, atonement, participation—all in the framework of God who is Father, Son/Word/ Logos, and Holy Spirit.

As with all patristic Christology, Athanasius's anthropology is individualistic in the sense that it focuses on the nature of the individual human person, comprised of body and soul, and the free exercise of human will. Each human being, nonetheless, participates in a shared human condition within and inseparable from a wider cosmic field, wherein ruling powers, visible and invisible, set the parameters of what humans may do with their wills, minds, and bodies. In all inner and outer aspects of the person, human beings are active members and thus participants in larger entities that exist in metaphysical spheres—that is, on levels of existence above and yet pervading and influencing the physical world. Such a basic philosophical perception of the world and how humans participate in it aligns readily with orthodox Christian belief that the God who creates us is the same God who saves or redeems us. Sacramental worship, especially baptism and Eucharist, comprises the essential way believers enter participation—body and soul—in the very life for and through which God has created and seeks to unite with us.

For all the metaphysical complexity substantiating classical Christology, still the only way Athanasius (and any Christian) can share the gospel message is by means of telling a story. The bodily nature of human existence requires narration, an account that speaks from and to our experience within time and space. In connecting the divine and human in his explanation of salvation in Christ, Athanasius situates the story in the social experience of power in his world, with kings and dominions. It does not take much effort to recognize resonance with kingdom imagery in both the Old Testament, including Adam's being entrusted with dominion over all creatures, and the New—the parables of Jesus, Paul's contrast between living in Adam's or Christ's domain (Romans), the Lamb's universal rule (Revelation).

In the context of a strongly hierarchical world, Athanasius frames the Word of God's incarnation in terms of Christ establishing a protective and thriving dominion:

> And like as when a great king has entered into some large city and taken up his abode in one of the houses there, such city is at all events held worthy of high honour, nor does any enemy or bandit any longer descend upon it and subject it; but on the contrary, it is thought entitled to all care, because of the king's having taken up his residence in a single house there; so, too, has it been with the Monarch of all. For now that He has come to our realm, and taken up his abode in one body among His peers, henceforth the whole conspiracy of the enemy against [humankind] is checked, and the corruption of death which before was prevailing against them is done away. For the [human race] had gone to ruin, had not the Lord and Saviour of all, the Son of God, come among us to meet the end of death.[1]

This story of the great king conveys a crucial aspect of Athanasius's Christology and soteriology: The salvation of humanity comes from the Son of God's decision to condescend and take on a body like our own, endowing humanity with a status that withstands death. But caution: status does not imply that the Christian's part in salvation is static or passive in relation to the thoroughly divine work of Christ—rather, the contrary. And here the notion of participation comes into play.

Earlier in his text, Athanasius explains the intimate connection between the incarnation of the Word of God and the creation of humanity through God's eternal Word. The biblical reference obviously is John 1:1–5, but Athanasius, in a move typical of the patristic authors, also exploits the first creation story in Genesis, whereby God makes humankind in God's image and likeness (1:26). God created people "after His own image, giving them a portion even of the power of His own Word; so that having as it were a kind of reflection of the Word, and being made rational, they might be able to abide ever in blessedness."[2] Human rationality includes the exercise of the will, which God knew could vacillate between good and evil, and so God gave humanity "grace" and "the law" in the garden. Humanity needed these, for upon the exercise of their will rested humanity's fate. Created "out of nothing," says Athanasius, humanity was naturally bound to corrupt and vanish. God, however, took pity on humanity. What would prevent such corruption (death)

---

1. Athanasius, *On the Incarnation of the Word* 9.3–4, in *Select Writings and Letters of Athanasius, Bishop of Alexandria*, ed. A. Robertson, vol. 4 of *Nicene and Post-Nicene Fathers*, Second Series (Oxford: Parker, 1892; many reprints and online), 37.

2. Athanasius, *On the Incarnation* 3.3 (p. 37).

was knowledge of the One who created humanity. Such knowledge—such a "partaking of the Word"—would enable humans to "live henceforth as God."[3]

Here Athanasius lays out an anthropology wherein humans are created to enjoy the divine life and escape death's corruption by the grace of participating in the Word, steadfast in good behavior. With the human being having made the bad choice, however, death becomes not only the natural power over humanity but also "the threat of the Deity."[4] Death came to have a legal hold over humans, for God (recall the image of the just ruler) had to condemn humans in their disobedience. Yet God could not abandon humanity, these "creatures once made rational, and having partaken of the Word."[5] Humanity's original participation in the image and likeness of God—the Word of God—is the reason for God's taking pity again on humans, a pity in the face not only of their natural corruption (returning to nothingness) but also their subjection to King Death's sinful dominion.

Just as the Word of God is the one through whom humans were originally created out of nothing in God's image, so also the Word is the only one who can again create humanity after the divine image. This requires the defeat of death's hold over humanity, yet also, crucially, the reorienting of humanity's idolatrous vision. Once humanity had willfully broken from their participation in the Word, they fixed their vision sinfully on created reality, seeking to create their own happiness therein—a hopeless venture amid all that ultimately passes away. Such is the outcome of giving oneself over to the force, the dominion, of death.

Given humanity's double predicament of sin and death, the divine Son had to accomplish two "works of love; first, in putting away death from us and renewing us again; secondly, being unseen and invisible, in manifesting and making Himself known by His works to be the Word of the Father, and the Ruler and King of the universe."[6] Athanasius lists those two deeds in order of importance, not chronology. That second type of work Christ did through his mission of teaching and healing, whereby he could "persuade" people to recognize his divine identity in his human actions. This was a matter of turning humanity's idolatrous vision back to the Word. One might wonder, however, how people could do that since they were still in death's hold. The question points toward why Athanasius considers "the nature of the death of [Christ's] body" to be "the sum of our faith."[7]

3. Athanasius, *On the Incarnation* 3.4–5 (p. 38).
4. Athanasius, *On the Incarnation* 3.5 (p. 38).
5. Athanasius, *On the Incarnation* 6.4 (p. 39).
6. Athanasius, *On the Incarnation* 16.5 (p. 45).
7. Athanasius, *On the Incarnation* 19.3 (p. 46).

The purpose of Christ's death was to bear humanity's curse, constituting his death as a perfect sacrifice for sin and release from debt, freeing for life in the resurrected body. Christ could not die by infirmity because his body was the Word's body, life its very self, incapable of corruption; rather, he received the death of humans so as to "assure all of us of His having effected the blotting out of corruption."[8] Christ's resurrected body become the source and proof of the resurrection secured for all. Believers now participate in that redeemed life, with Christ's sovereign power evident in the inspiring character of the martyrs, in the continence of virgins and young men, and in warlike people becoming peaceable "when they come over to the school of Christ."[9]

Despite whatever degree of alienation late-modern Christians might experience from such a heavily mythological and hagiographic delivery of the Christian message, we might nonetheless hear in Athanasius's writings a dynamic, if not passionate, proclamation of the life-giving love that God, in Christ, exercises not only for but also among and through humanity.[10] The exercise of our human wills is not merely an individual, let alone private, matter but instead is shared in social life, evidenced in bodies placed on the line and for the good of the entire human race.

How shall we conceive of such divine power in human bodily existence? Athanasius, again typically for patristic soteriology, explains in terms of deification. When Athanasius famously concludes, "For he was made [human] that we might be made God,"[11] the shape such deification (participation in God's Word) takes is in practice of the virtues. To speak of participation in the divine life, of deification, is not to claim for humans the very nature of God, is not to claim that humans become gods (although, alas, cultures to our present day bestow godlike status on some of their own). No, deification encapsulates the revelation of what God is doing precisely in the humanity of humans. Elsewhere Athanasius writes: "For we all, partaking of the Same [Word], become one body, having the one Lord in ourselves . . . [we] become distantly as He is in the Father; distantly not in place but in nature."[12] The

8. Athanasius, *On the Incarnation* 22.4 (p. 48).
9. Athanasius, *On the Incarnation* 51.6 (p. 64).
10. Swedish Lutheran theologian Gustaf Aulén argues for the "classical account" of Christ's death as atonement that, situated in a larger trinitarian soteriology, gives priority to God's saving initiative while also asserting the incarnate Son's death and resurrection as empowering the baptized for participation in the mystery of divine love for the life of the world. See Gustaf Aulén, *Christus Victor: An Historical Study of the Three Main Types of the Idea of Atonement*, trans. A. G. Hebert (New York: MacMillan, 1977), 1–15, 143–59.
11. Athanasius, *On the Incarnation* 54.3 (p. 62).
12. Athanasius, "Four Discourses against the Arians: Discourse III" 22, in *Select Writings and Letters*, 406.

distance is bridged in terms resonant with Johannine tradition (see 1 John 3:24; 4:13): "Reasonably are we, as having the Spirit, considered to be in God, and this is God in us. . . . By the participation of the Spirit we are knit into the Godhead."[13] The Spirit, sharing in the same nature as God the Father and the Son, is able to divinize believers.

Baptism establishes one's participation in the divine life, endowing believers with the Spirit of God and, thereby, the grace for living the virtues. The Christian thus receives the means to strive against the mutability of the passions, against inconsistent uses of reason and will that hinder a good way of life, life in God. The other evil from which Christ has saved humanity is corruption—that is, mortality. Participation in the sacrament of the Eucharist is the Christian's assurance of being subject to neither death's dominion nor its ultimate claim; instead, the Christian will be raised to immortality. Patristic literature is replete with this theme of immortality and immutability. With death comprising the dominion characterized by mutability of mind (the struggle to practice the virtues) and body (the uncontrollable changes wrought by both external-environmental, societal, and interpersonal causes, plus intrinsic bodily changes and decline), the promise of immortality in Christ's dominion likewise reveals the power of the Spirit, who raised Christ from death, as now working in the baptized—in body, mind, and spirit. A subsequent bishop in the Alexandrian line, Cyril, taught of the sanctifying power of the Eucharist—the life-giving flesh of the divine Word, the risen and ascended Christ—as communicants' participation in the life that abolished death's total threat to them.[14]

Correlations between Classical Christology and Worship: East and West

Eastern Worship and Theology

Logos Christology, along the basic lines of Athanasius's work, took hold and proliferated, with variations in philosophical details requiring several major councils (mentioned above) in its classical period, from the fourth through seventh centuries. During that same period, the quite elaborate liturgical rites of the Eastern churches (Egypt, Syria, Cappadocia, Greece) solidified into forms that those churches celebrate to this day. In the earliest centuries the way

13. Athanasius, "Four Discourses" 25 (pp. 406–7).
14. "So we approach the mystical gifts and are sanctified, becoming partakers of the holy flesh and the honorable blood of Christ the Saviour of us all. . . . For being by nature, as God, life, when he had become one with his own flesh, he made it life-giving." Cyril of Alexandria, "The Third Letter of Cyril to Nestorius," in *Christology of the Later Fathers*, ed. Edward R. Hardy, The Library of Christian Classics: Ichthus Edition (Philadelphia: Westminster, 1954), 352.

Christian churches worshiped, especially how they baptized and celebrated the Eucharist, informed the arguments that developed into orthodox teaching about Christ; but the direction of influence basically reversed in those ensuing centuries. The unambiguous affirmation of Christ Jesus's divinity as the Word Incarnate—conqueror of sin and death, now ascended to the Father's right hand and ruler over all dominions of the cosmos—grounds Eastern Orthodox worship in both space and time.

Orthodox church interiors are laid out to convey movement between heaven and earth. The image of Christ *Pantokratōr* (Ruler of All), painted on the ceiling, looms over the sanctuary, while icons of biblical and later holy men and women line the ceiling and walls, drawing believers into participation with the saints, exemplars in faith and virtue, before the altar of the heavenly banquet. Assembling on Sunday shapes believers' experience of time.[15] The Day of the Resurrection is not only the first day of the week in the present order of creation but also the Eighth Day of creation, the start of God's fashioning new heavens and a new earth through the power of the same Spirit who, with the Word, creates and sustains existence and who, moreover, raised the human body of the Word from death (Rom. 8). Celebration of the Divine Liturgy each Sunday is sacramental, bodily revelation of and sharing in the unseen God, with the eternal Word speaking through proclamation of Sacred Scripture and the offering of the gifts of bread and wine that, through prayer in the power of the Spirit, become Christ's redeeming body and blood for communion in him. Throughout the liturgy, Almighty God is implored, and thereby encountered and affirmed, as merciful, compassionate, and forgiving, the giver of graces through covenant histories and now by participation in the eternal covenant in Christ.

Western Traditions

Eastern Orthodoxy practices the faith as based in Scripture and tradition, with an understanding of the latter as having reached its completion in the Seventh Ecumenical Council in the eighth century. Western European Christianity, on the other hand, also bases belief and worship on Scripture and tradition, yet it has seen continued development in theological tradition right through the second millennium.

In the medieval West, the Logos model provided the framework for Christology and worship; however, the convergence of theology's academic relocation, elements of feudal culture, and evolution in penitential ritual led

---

15. See Alexander Schmemann, *For the Life of the World: Sacraments and Orthodoxy*, rev. ed. (Crestwood, NY: St. Vladimir's Seminary Press, 1982), 47–66.

to modified interpretations of why and how Christ's death, in particular, achieved humanity's salvation.[16] A key figure was Anselm, a learned Norman monk who served as archbishop of Canterbury from the late eleventh to the early twelfth century. In working out his rational explanation for why God the Son became man, Anselm was responding to incredulity over belief that the eternal, immutable God could undergo the suffering and death depicted in increasingly graphic detail in crucifixes and paintings. Another image influential to his thought was the satisfaction that a penitent was required to make for sacramental absolution of sins. Yet most basic to Anselm's argument was the feudal notion of honor, whereby offenses against a person of high rank could be propitiated only by an act or offering of equal or greater rank. Only in that way could proper social order be restored. Anselm applied this scenario to humanity's disobedience toward God, the predicament being the inability of mortal creatures to make satisfaction for offense against the One greater than all creation. God takes the salvific initiative through the incarnation of the Son, whose consistent life of righteousness and truth leads to his freely dying, capably making satisfaction to the Divinity, thus to the credit of indebted humanity. Through the incarnate Word, God restored the cosmic order.

That incarnation and propitiatory death proved to be the loci of Anselm's christological soteriology is a characteristic that would only burgeon through the medieval and Reformation periods. In ways drawing upon and even exceeding Anselm, the thirteenth-century professor Thomas Aquinas explained Christ's death as making satisfaction for humanity's sins, expanding interpretation of the redemptive passion in terms of the merit that Christ (the incarnate Word) attained for his humanity and for all the members of his body (the church). But Aquinas also explained Christ's loving and free offer of his divine-human life unto death as a sacrifice both appeasing God and uniting humanity in fellowship with God. Unfortunately, later scholastic and popular theologies (in preaching and penance) lost the free and loving divine priority in the Son's mission for humanity by emphasizing, even exclusively, the need to placate a God utterly offended by human sins. By the end of the Middle Ages, images of resurrection, so difficult to conceive and sustain, had long receded, while all-too-human demonstrations of anger, vengeful justice, and hierarchical penal systems could shape the story of Christ's death as heroic substitutionary torture and execution, the gruesome

16. For this section I have relied upon and refer the reader, for further expert details, to Robin Ryan, *Jesus and Salvation: Soundings in the Christian Tradition and Contemporary Theology* (Collegeville, MN: Liturgical Press, 2015), 71–100.

measures of which were necessary to expiate the innumerable sins of a justly condemned humanity.

Sacramental rites in the medieval period contributed to the salvation-by-the-expiatory-death-of-Christ theology. A religion focused on sacrifice for sin, not surprisingly, thought of Christ in terms of a priestly intermediary, uniting and reconciling God and humanity. Such Christology, in turn, provided an allegorical narrative through which people interpreted their witnessing the central act of worship performed by the hierarchical priesthood, the holy sacrifice of the Mass. From the early Middle Ages forward, the Christology of the eternal divine Word become flesh took ritual symbolic (sacramental) focus in the wafer of unleavened bread (the host) that the priest, empowered with a special character through ordination, transformed by speaking the words "This is my body given for you," with which Christ established the perpetual memorial of his sacrifice for sin in sacramental form.[17]

Even the notion of sacrament seemed too weak to bespeak the power of this saving mystery, such that tests of orthodox faith pivoted on professing the "real presence" of Christ, the fully incarnate Son/Word of God, in the consecrated bread and wine. The eucharistic motif of *thanksgiving* (the very meaning of the Greek root behind "Eucharist") ceded to that of sacrifice, with the priest functioning "in the person of Christ" to effect, now on the altar, the immolated body of Christ. The character of eucharistic worship had shifted from praise and thanksgiving to sacrifice (sin offering) and adoration. By the beginning of the twelfth century, the people's act of adoration was enhanced by the priest, having softly recited the words of consecration in Latin, elevating the host high overhead. Bell ringing alerted the people to the miraculous moment. With the exception of a pious few, the laity rarely received holy Communion. Grace was received through witnessing the sacrifice, while the merits of Christ's death for sin in each Mass could be designated for the benefit of a deceased believer, for whose sins, mercifully forgiven, divine justice nonetheless required temporal punishment before entry into the blessed vision of heaven. The merits of Christ's death ("graces"), understood as produced in each Mass, led people to pay a stipend for a priest to offer the Mass for a deceased relative or friend, with the person requesting the Mass not even needing to be in attendance.[18]

Thus an element of Logos Christology that had come to the fore in the medieval West was that of a humanly unpayable debt to the all-powerful Di-

17. For an insightful analysis of these developments, including their interrelatedness due to Christology, see Mary Collins, "Critical Questions for Liturgical Studies," *Worship* 53, no. 4 (July 1979): 302–17.

18. See Paul F. Bradshaw and Maxwell E. Johnson, *The Eucharistic Liturgies: Their Evolution and Interpretation* (Collegeville, MN: Liturgical Press, 2012), 218–30.

vine. The catalytic figure of the Protestant Reformation, Martin Luther, was tormented over his inability, as a guilty sinner trapped in the devil's dominion, to orient his intentions of prayer, worship, and acts of satisfaction through sacramental penance so as to receive a share in the merits of Christ's suffering and death. Luther's imagination drew heavily on the notion of divine wrath. His breakthrough came in perceiving grace as God's free offer of life in the dominion of Christ, available through faith in him—a theology built on Paul's Letter to the Romans. Luther shaped his theology of worship accordingly.[19] The sacraments have no power in themselves, per the medieval transactional practice of them. Their power, rather, resides in the testament of the incarnate Word of God, whose words of promise (e.g., "This is my body . . ."), borne by signs, the faithful receive in grateful obedience and are thereby built up in their faith. Acts of worship are means of grace, not works producing merit. The sole merit was Christ's death, which Luther interpreted, classically, as release from the curse of debt.

Distinctive to the influential Protestant Reformer John Calvin's soteriology was a variation on classical Logos Christology's view of humanity's legal bind, figured not as indebtedness but as being found guilty of capital crime warranting death.[20] Noting the details of Jesus's criminal trial and execution, Calvin interpreted salvation as the Son of God substituting himself for guilty humanity at the bar of justice. The largesse of divine love is evident in Christ's expiatory self-sacrifice in satisfaction for the full measure of humanity's sin, taking on the severest degree of earthly punishment, while also descending into the torments of hell. Moreover, for Calvin the story of divine largesse did not stop with satisfaction for sin and death's defeat; rather, his theology laudably turns to the restorative power of Christ's resurrection and to the ongoing intercessory role of the Son, in his divinity *and* humanity, seated at the right hand of the Father.[21] In a theological move reflective of the sacramental theology of the early church fathers, Calvin taught that the divine power uniting Christ in heaven with humanity on earth is that of the Holy Spirit. The Spirit both communicates the presence of Christ in the Lord's Supper and instills the grace of faith in believers so that they are united spiritually with Christ in Word and sacrament.[22]

19. See William R. Crockett, *Eucharist: Symbol of Transformation* (Collegeville, MN: Liturgical Press, 1989), 130–35, 143–45.

20. For relevant quotations and treatment of Calvin's *Institutes of the Christian Religion* 2.16–22, see Ryan, *Jesus and Salvation*, 95–96.

21. For a critical discussion of the strengths and weaknesses of Calvin on this point, including the pneumatologic and eucharistic implications, see Douglas B. Farrow, *Ascension and Ecclesia: On the Significance of the Doctrine of the Ascension* (Grand Rapids: Eerdmans, 1999), 175–80.

22. See Crockett, *Eucharist*, 158–60.

Practical Implications for Worship

This survey could consider only highlights and a few key figures in the history of Logos Christology's relationship to the understanding and practice of worship. The intricacies, for example, of the heated debates and mutual condemnations among leaders in the Reformation period, within Protestantism and with Roman Catholicism, would require pages well exceeding those available here. Nonetheless, common to the significantly varied forms of worship and liturgy across all Western traditions to this day is a functional Christology of the Incarnate Word and his atoning, sacrificial death. Praise, thanks, and adoration of Christ, who suffered death for one's sins, for humans trapped in the dominion of death ("the enemy"), is the governing narrative across traditions, old and new, however much they differ in their ways of celebrating it in and as church.

Surely the medieval Logos Christology is the theological foundation to understand, for example, why in Roman Catholicism the words and gestures of consecration so predominate the Mass, and with it the fundamental identity of the priest in whose hands the host and chalice are consecrated. That foundation has proved to be firm. Some fifty years ago Vatican Council II set in motion a sweeping reform and renewal of the sacraments and liturgy, based on the principle of all the faithful participating together, as a priestly people, in the mystery of salvation in Christ. Henceforth, sacraments were not to be instrumentally administered but always situated in a liturgy of the Word, which in the case of the Sunday Mass now entails multiple biblical readings and a homily. Yet for the vast majority of clergy and people alike, in Catholic worship the primary ritual symbols, the climactic foci, persists specifically in the priest performing the words and gestures consecrating the host as Christ's body (signaled by bells ringing) and the people approaching the altar for holy Communion. Contemporary Catholics largely practice both as personal acts of adoration of Jesus, God's Son, who died for them. A crucifix (a cross with a figure of the dead Jesus) typically dominates the center wall of the sanctuary, often with a second, smaller crucifix centered on the altar table itself. In coming to Communion, many people bow or cross themselves as much toward the crucifix as to the sacred host they are about to receive.

In Protestantism, much of the energy in worship comes through sung music. Lutheranism has a heritage of hymns not only proclaiming the unmerited and free gift of salvation in Christ's suffering and victory but also, in more pietistic registers (as amplified in J. S. Bach's chorales), addressing praise, thanks, and adoration to Christ directly. Theology borne of hymns is similarly characteristic of traditions descended from Charles and John

Wesley.[23] The particular history of African Americans has generated worship music with the added dimensions of strength for perseverance and promise of deliverance.[24] Contemporary praise music in nondenominational evangelical churches likewise constantly feature adoration of the Son, who took on the human condition and redeemed worshipers by the blood of his cross. Much of the preaching in such free-style churches centers on acceptance of Christ, surrender to the mighty one who surrendered all "for me."

In the accelerating globalized, market-driven, technologically mediated social context, perhaps one of the greatest dangers in the current intersection of Christology and worship is an entrenched individualism. At least two problems follow from this. First, the ethical response, which can slip into moralistic behavior motivated by what Christ has endured "for me" or by dreadful imagery of the fate of those living in sin's deadly dominion. Despite insistence on the free offer of grace, a sense of having to earn it or "make it up to Jesus" (for his sufferings) can creep in. The other danger is worship that solely seeks comfort, even in proclaiming the uncomfortable image of Christ crucified, by conforming the salvation story to the conventions of one's immediate circle. An in-group vision can distort both the challenge and the promise of the full biblical content of the faith, for which the poor (the materially destitute, socially denigrated, and/or spiritually despondent) are consistently the subject of God's favor (grace) and, indeed, Christ's promised occasion for truly knowing him (Matt. 25:35–40).

In the best of tradition, East and West, sacramental worship is the Spirit's incorporating believers into the mystery of what God is doing for humanity in Christ, which more often than not is a disruption of the perceptions we either create or, for some, have had mercilessly imposed on us. Liturgy, as participation in Christ's paschal mystery, is the ongoing work of the Spirit of the risen Crucified One in the real bodies of the assembled people. The assembly's action is a living sign (sacrament) of the salvation that God desires and so often, anonymously, is accomplishing throughout the world. By participating in that divine mystery, which is the believer's baptismal identity, the entire Christian life is worship of God. The church's ritual or liturgical worship is for the purpose of renewing and strengthening participants' lives as worship of God, which altogether constitutes their "reasonable" or "spiritual" worship (Rom. 12:1). Liturgy is encounter with Christ present in the

23. See Teresa Berger, *Theology in Hymns? A Study of the Relationship of Doxology and Theology according to a Collection of Hymns for the Use of the People Called Methodist (1780)*, trans. Timothy E. Kimbrough (Nashville: Kingswood, 1995), chap. 3.

24. See Melva Costen, *African American Christian Worship*, 2nd ed. (Nashville: Abingdon, 1994), 79–103.

assembly of the baptized, the proclaimed Word in Scripture and homily, and shared sacramental signs, of which the Sunday table is paramount.[25] God is glorified by people's participating in the mutual service-oriented love of Christ, across the entire scope of their lives, drawing hope from faith renewed through Word and sacrament, the nourishing foretaste of the heavenly banquet, the empowerment of the slain Lamb's victory.

For Further Reading

Goizueta, Roberto S. *Caminemos con Jesús: Toward a Hispanic/Latino Theology of Accompaniment*. Maryknoll, NY: Orbis Books, 1995.

Larson-Miller, Lizette. *Sacramentality Renewed: Contemporary Conversations in Sacramental Theology*. Collegeville, MN: Liturgical Press, 2016.

Morrill, Bruce T. *Encountering Christ in the Eucharist: The Paschal Mystery in People, Word, and Sacrament*. New York: Paulist Press, 2012.

Ryan, Robin. *Jesus and Salvation: Soundings in the Christian Tradition and Contemporary Theology*. Collegeville, MN: Liturgical Press, 2015.

Schmemann, Alexander. *For the Life of the World: Sacraments and Orthodoxy*. Crestwood, NY: St. Vladimir's Seminary Press, 1982.

25. See World Council of Churches, *Baptism, Eucharist and Ministry*, Faith and Order Paper No. 111 (Geneva: WCC, 1982), nos. 29, 31.

— 7 —

Pneumatology and Worship

Khalia J. Williams

Growing up in the Black church tradition in the United States, my faith and spiritual practices have always encompassed a high appreciation for the work and presence of the Holy Spirit in the Christian life. Being immersed in charismatic faith communities, this appreciation was normal and almost expected; yet I cannot say that as a child I fully understood the concept of "the work of the Holy Spirit." What is that work exactly? How do we know it? When can we pinpoint the Spirit's activity? In most cases it was manifested through forms of ecstatic behavior or response in worship, most of which I witnessed rather than personally experienced in my youth. Over time, I have found that this childhood ambiguity I experienced is familiar to many. While the particulars of faith communities and manifestations of the presence and activity of the Holy Spirit are different, I find that this ambiguity regarding the Spirit at work is often paired with a surety of the fact that the Spirit *is* at work in the Christian life. This tends to lead us on personal journeys of discovering God's Spirit in dynamic manifestations throughout our faith lives.

The longer I have journeyed with seminary students, church members, youth, and even my own thoughts, I find in myself deepening notions of the Spirit at work in our lives. As the one who leads the worship life of a theological institution, I cannot help but consistently seek to identify how the Spirit is at work in our community and in our worship. Therefore, I write this chapter while knowing that I cannot give a full examination of the Holy

Spirit's dynamic activity in Christian life and worship, but I hope to scratch the surface enough so that it sparks the passion of inquiry for all who read this. With that in mind, I have chosen to explore some of the classic theologies of the Holy Spirit as a foundation for further inquiry.

Theological Overview

Pneumatology is the theological pursuit of understanding the presence of the Holy Spirit in the Christian life. Within the past three decades, we have found a renaissance in the theological discourse regarding the Holy Spirit and have seen a turn to the doctrine of the Spirit as a resource for renewing specific understandings of faith. Historic and contemporary theological discourse around pneumatology can be found in three spaces: in Scripture, in charismatic renewal movements that have swept across denominations over the past thirty years, and in ecumenical conversations moving toward reconciliation of Western Christianity with Eastern Orthodoxy.[1] For the sake of this chapter, we will begin by briefly examining these sites of pneumatological discourse.

The Bible teaches about the Spirit through symbols and stories, emphasizing the spirituality or the work of the Spirit. Even though there is no one "doctrine" of the Spirit in the Bible, there is a common core.[2] Scripture presents images of how God's spirit is at work in creation and human life. In the Old Testament, the term "holy spirit" occurs only twice, in Psalm 51:11 and Isaiah 63:10–11, but these occurrences do not carry a New Testament understanding of God's Spirit; the faithful in the Old Testament did not yet have a fully developed understanding of the Holy Spirit. Therefore, what we see prevalent in the Old Testament is the representation of the spirit through the Hebrew term *rûaḥ* (breath, spirit, wind). This term *rûaḥ* carries with it the basic meaning of some kind of moving air, from which we get a more developed notion of who a person is—in this case God's own spirit; the term when attributed to God is speaking of God's life-giving breath. The use of this term can been seen when the Scripture is naming a wind sent by God (Exod. 14:21) and also when there is a quasi-personal entity or influence represented that directs people and circumstances (Num. 5:14; 11:17; Judg. 9:23; 2 Kings 2:9). The term "spirit" is used to describe the life force of a person or as a way of characterizing people (Pss. 31:5; 32:2).

---

1. Serene Jones and Paul Lakeland, eds., *Constructive Theology: A Contemporary Approach to Classical Themes* (Minneapolis: Fortress, 2005), 241–42.
2. Veli-Matti Kärkkäinen, *Pneumatology* (Grand Rapids: Baker Academic, 2002), 36.

When we turn to understanding God's *rûaḥ* in the Old Testament, we are given a positive depiction of the relationship between humanity and God. God's spirit is involved in creation and maintenance of life (Gen. 1:1–2; Ps. 104:29–30), and there is an intimate connection between God and humanity, so much so that God's breath brings about the breath of humanity. This presents a theological conversation of humanity's dependence on God, one in which we should be careful not to come dangerously close to blurring the lines between humanity and God. These representations of God's spirit are in association with creation and the giving of life.

The spirit of God is also an empowering spirit in giving outstanding gifts of interpretation, artistry, and wisdom. In the Genesis 41:38–39 account, we see not only the gift of dream interpretations; the spirit also empowers policy making during this dream interpretation. Exodus 31:1–6 presents the divine spirit (*rûaḥ Elohim*) giving this gift of artistry through enabling individuals to design and build. We see the gifts of understanding (Job 32:8) and empowerment in several accounts where "the spirit of the LORD" came upon great leaders and empowered them for mighty acts of leadership (Judg. 3:10; 6:34; 11:29; 13:25). The spirit of God is also present in prophecy: Micah writes about being filled with "the spirit of the LORD" (3:8), and Ezekiel expresses a similar notion of the spirit coming upon (or entering into) him and empowering him to speak (2:1–2; 3:12; 8:3; 11:1; 37:1). God's *rûaḥ* empowers great gifts.

Other places that have sparked theological inquiry into the presence of God's spirit (which the New Testament calls "the Holy Spirit") in the Old Testament are through depictions of the work of the spirit (Ezek. 37 is a great example of this work) and the association of a future hope for the people of Israel (Isa. 11:1–2; 42:1–4; 61:1–4). There is also a prominent focus on God's presence or "dwelling" with the people (e.g., Exod. 13:21–22; 24:15–17; 33:9–10). Images of God's spirit related to *fire* (Isa. 4:4) provide background for the New Testament accounts of John's preaching and the Pentecost narrative. We also see images of *water* (Isa. 32:15), which present the spirit as being poured upon the people, bringing life to them and the thirsty land (making early connections to baptism and water rituals). In this short and fast overview, we can see these themes of God's spirit as the creative, life-giving, and empowering spirit.

In the New Testament we see the Holy Spirit as a gift, as empowerment, and as a guide. The evidence of the Spirit in the New Testament is often depicted through the Greek word *pneuma*, with the basic meaning of air and breathing. This term is also associated with life, like the Hebrew term *rûaḥ* in the Old Testament. Other images of the Holy Spirit in the New Testament are wind, tongues of fire, individuals speaking in other tongues, and empowered speech. The various New Testament Scriptures, particularly Acts, give evidence of the Spirit in the subtleties of life transformation, conversion, and baptism. In Matthew 3:7–12, we see John the Baptist presented as a "prophet of judgment" who proclaims that "the coming Messiah would baptize in the Holy Spirit and fire."[3] In Luke 4:18–19, Jesus's ministry in the Spirit is one of "eschatological blessing: good news, freedom, healing."[4] In the Gospels, Jesus was anointed with the Spirit at the time of his baptism (Matt. 3:16–17; Mark 1:10–11; Luke 3:22; John 1:32–33), and this is representative of his ministry, made effective by the Spirit. The Holy Spirit empowers Jesus in times of temptation (Matt. 4:1), in performing miracles (Matt. 12:28), in fulfilling prophecy and the ministry of justice (Luke 4:18), and in his acts of healing and deeds of power (Acts 10:38).

There is also a clear presentation of the interrelated nature of Jesus and the Holy Spirit: we see that Jesus will send the Spirit and baptize with the Spirit (Matt. 3:11–12). In John's Gospel we are introduced to the Holy Spirit as the Paraclete, the Advocate who is sent by the Father at Jesus's request (14:16, 26), "to be with you forever." John also presents a contrast between spirit and flesh (3:6; 6:63). The Holy Spirit is sent by Jesus and abides within, teaching everything and guiding Jesus's followers. Also, the Holy Spirit effects the giving and renewing of life (3:5; 6:63).

In Acts, the church's birth and ministry by the Holy Spirit's power and guidance is compared to the birth and ministry of Jesus;[5] the transforming nature of the Holy Spirit is evident at the beginning of the Christian church, as seen through the vivid work of the Spirit at Pentecost. Acts 2 connects the Holy Spirit with the sound of wind and the image of fire. The Spirit enables people to speak in other tongues; the Spirit empowers Peter's preaching and inspires young and old to prophesy; the Spirit draws people to repent, be baptized, and "receive the gift of the Holy Spirit" (2:38). The reception of the Holy Spirit is recognized by several visible or audible signs, and the Spirit gives extraordinary power (Acts 9:17; 11:15–18; 19:1–7), inspired speech (4:25), and boldness (4:31). The Spirit empowers people and gives them courage; we see the signs through bold speech, speaking in tongues (10:44–46), and prophecy. The primary depiction of the relationship between the Holy Spirit and the church is the Spirit as abiding within the community. Even though the Spirit intervenes in the community at different moments, there is no suggestion that the Spirit ever leaves the community.

3. Kärkkäinen, *Pneumatology*, 29.
4. Kärkkäinen, *Pneumatology*, 30.
5. Kärkkäinen, *Pneumatology*, 30.

Other New Testament portraits of the Spirit include the Spirit as "a down payment" of the glory to come (2 Cor. 1:22);[6] the Spirit of fellowship, or *koinōnia* (1 Cor. 12:13; Eph. 4:3); and the Spirit of prophecy (1 Pet. 1:11). The Spirit is the mediator and gives charismatic gifts (Acts 1:16; 3:18; 4:25; 1 Cor. 12; Gal. 3:5). Later the Spirit's relationship with the church becomes more formalized, with the Spirit now more closely connected within the church and its leaders and structure (1 Tim. 4:14; 2 Tim. 1:6). Throughout the New Testament we witness a shift from the Old Testament understanding of the Spirit abiding from creation toward an understanding of the Spirit as a later endowment, a belief that the good gifts of God come only through a filling by the Holy Spirit. There is an expansive expression of the Holy Spirit through scriptural manifestations that lead us to further contemplate ways in which we experience the Holy Spirit in liturgy.

One cannot pursue and understand the Holy Spirit in Christian worship apart from engaging the early Christian trinitarian theology; therefore, we will explore some of the early Christian understandings of the Trinity and the Holy Spirit's role and relationship within the Trinity through the theology of Basil of Caesarea (330–79) and Athanasius of Alexandria (ca. 297–373). Basil's theological claim is that the Holy Spirit is fully God, though he is cautious never to name the Spirit as God. His understanding is that if one denies the divinity of the Holy Spirit, one denies the experience of baptism. By starting with the liturgical practice of baptism, Basil infers that the Holy Spirit is at work within the primary liturgical practices. For Basil, the work of the Holy Spirit demonstrates the Spirit's full divinity, particularly in salvation and sanctification. Basil writes, "As he who grasps one end of the chain pulls along with it the other end to himself, so he [the believer] who draws the Spirit draws both the Son and the Father along with it."[7] This brings out Basil's truly trinitarian outlook in that "the role of the Holy Spirit according to this understanding makes the 'first contact,' which is followed by the revelation of the Son and, through him, the Father."[8] In other words, God accomplishes all things by the Son through the Spirit.

The full divinity of the Holy Spirit is a focus that is also shared by Athanasius, bishop of Alexandria. Athanasius understands that through the Spirit we are made partakers of God. He concludes that the Spirit must be fully divine in order to unite us with God because only God can unite us with God's self. For Athanasius, it is the Spirit's divinity that connects us to God, and the

6. Kärkkäinen, *Pneumatology*, 33.
7. Kärkkäinen, *Pneumatology*, 68–69.
8. Kärkkäinen, *Pneumatology*, 69.

Spirit must be fully divine in order to make that connection. In other words, the Spirit is the power that unites us with God, assuring our salvation. This understanding of the Spirit as connecting us to God is a primary basis for the Eastern Orthodox emphasis on the Spirit's role in the church and in the sacraments. Basil asserts, "Christ comes, the Spirit goes before. He is present in the flesh, and the Spirit is inseparable from him."[9] This theological statement anchors Christ's work in the church via the economy of the Spirit.[10] In the act of worship, the church is brought into communion with God through the divine Spirit.

Intersection: How Pneumatology Correlates with Worship

Exploring Basil's and Athanasius's theological understanding of the Holy Spirit leads me to take another look at the Holy Spirit in relation to trinitarian theology. Jürgen Moltmann writes about the Holy Spirit relating to believers in worship. In *Spirit of Life*, Moltmann, a Protestant theologian, focuses the Holy Spirit in relation to the Eucharist. He states, "The eucharistic concept of the Trinity is the logical consequence of the monarchical form of the Trinity (economy of grace), for the experience of grace arouses gratitude, and where God is known in his works, creation's song of praise awakens."[11]

Moltmann's eucharistic understanding of the Trinity is based on the actions of thanksgiving and gratitude that come to an individual through an experience of God's grace through the Holy Spirit. According to Moltmann, these acts of thanksgiving and praise "proceed from the energies of the Spirit."[12] These acts are directed and empowered by the Holy Spirit, who dwells within worshipers, and the thanksgiving goes through the Son to the Father. Moltmann's eucharistic concept of the Trinity is situated in the human life through "the celebration of the Eucharist and the life which itself becomes a feast because it has been filled with grace and happiness."[13] In particular liturgical practices, specifically in the Eucharist, we acknowledge and remember the suffering of Christ. Moltmann asserts that in the eucharistic concept of the Trinity, "God's suffering history in Christ's passion serves the history of God's joy in the Spirit over the homecoming of human beings and all other creatures into the kingdom of God."[14] Therefore, the

9. Kärkkäinen, *Pneumatology*, 70.
10. Kärkkäinen, *Pneumatology*, 70.
11. Jürgen Moltmann, *The Spirit of Life* (Minneapolis: Fortress, 2001), 298.
12. Moltmann, *The Spirit of Life*, 298.
13. Moltmann, *The Spirit of Life*, 298.
14. Moltmann, *The Spirit of Life*, 299.

work of the Holy Spirit in the celebration of the Eucharist is the revelation of God's love, which is received through the Eucharist and adds to our understanding of the Trinity. This experience then brings praise, thanksgiving, and adoration to the human life, all of which proceed from the Spirit. In short, Moltmann's eucharistic concept of the Trinity is based on an understanding of the Triune God, who receives the thanksgiving and praises of believers. Instead of approaching the Trinity as actively giving, Moltmann explores the Trinity as actively receiving. He connects this concept to the Eucharist by showing that in this liturgical act, the community of believers, empowered by the energies of the Holy Spirit, comes together in the remembrance of God's suffering through Christ. Then in the Eucharist believers offer thanksgiving and praise to God. This is a concept amid human life and manifested in worship.

I use Moltmann's pneumatology to highlight the all-encompassing nature of the Spirit in Christian worship. He also makes clear that in order to have this conversation about the Holy Spirit, we must understand the Spirit in relationship with trinitarian theology (which we cannot explore in depth here). The presence of the Holy Spirit in Christian life inevitably contributes to understanding the Spirit's presence and activity in worship, a presence that empowers and shapes who and how we are in worship and in life.

Different Approaches in Understanding Pneumatology

One of the most exciting aspects of pneumatology is the myriad of ways to engage the Spirit's ministry. Even though there is only one Spirit of God, the Spirit's activity in the Christian life can be expressed in varied ways, according to the particularities of churches, cultures, and lived experiences. This section gives a brief survey of approaches in understanding pneumatology in the main Christian traditions through the specific celebration of the Eucharist, a practice shared in most churches. Our exploration gives a focal point (the Eucharist) to help us in understanding the diverse expressions of the Holy Spirit in this special service.

From the Eastern Orthodox tradition we can find understandings of the Holy Spirit and the Eucharist as explained by Alexander Schmemann. He believes the Eucharist to be the center and the source of the whole life of the Christian church. Schmemann sees the Eucharist as the fulfillment and continuation of our participation in the life of the Trinity. He claims that the Eucharist is "entirely, from beginning to end, an epiclesis, an invocation of the Holy Spirit, who transfigures everything done in it, each solemn rite, into that which it manifests and reveals to us."[15] In other words, it is through the Holy Spirit that every aspect of the liturgical practice—the elements, prayers, and people assembled—becomes that which we believe it to be: the body and blood of Christ, communion with God, and the body of Christ to the world. "But this conversion remains invisible, for it is accomplished by the Holy Spirit, in the new time, and is only certified by faith."[16] For Schmemann, the work of the Holy Spirit is in this epiclesis. He states that this "unites 'all those things which have come to pass for us,' the entire mystery of salvation accomplished, the mystery of Christ's love, which embraces the whole world and has been granted to us." It is the power of the Holy Spirit that brings about this unity. In addition, the power of the Holy Spirit in the Eucharist unites the gathered assembly, as seen in the prayer of Basil of Caesarea: "And unite all of us to one another who become partakers of the one Bread and Cup in the communion of the Holy Spirit."[17]

Roman Catholic theologian Kevin Irwin speaks of the work of the Eucharist as drawing us closer to God through Christ and through the power of the Holy Spirit. He identifies the ways in which the role of the Holy Spirit in the Eucharist brings about greater appreciation for what the Eucharist means and what it does. Through the work of the Holy Spirit in the Eucharist, we experience deepened faith and heightened service unto God and to each other. This faith and service is from our own doing but is the work of the Spirit. Here is the essence of Christian spirituality, seen in the celebration of the Eucharist through the work of the Spirit. In the invocation of the Holy Spirit at the eucharistic celebration, our *lex orandi*[18] "should influence our *lex credendi*[19] and *lex vivendi* (how we live our lives)."[20] In this statement, Irwin is asserting that what the church believes and the church's lived experiences are shaped through the prayer (and scriptural beliefs) of the church. I assert that this relationship is not static or a one-way link from prayer to belief and life, but rather the *lex orandi*, *lex credendi*, and *lex vivendi* mutually impact each other. The converted life of the Christian is guided by the power of the Holy Spirit, and the participation in the Eucharist (and worship in general) is also led by the power of the Holy Spirit. Any performance that takes place during the ritual act of eucharistic celebration is fully empowered

15. Alexander Schmemann, *The Eucharist: Sacrament of the Kingdom* (Crestwood, NY: St. Vladimir's Seminary Press, 1988), 222.

16. Schmemann, *The Eucharist*, 222.

17. Schmemann, *The Eucharist*, 225.

18. *Lex orandi* is Latin for "the law of prayer."

19. *Lex credendi* is Latin for "the law of belief."

20. Kevin Irwin, *Context and Text: A Method for Liturgical Theology* (Collegeville, MN: Liturgical Press, 2018), 286.

by the Holy Spirit. It is the Spirit who prompts us to assemble, who leads us into remembrance of the saving work of Christ, and who unites us with Christ and the community in that very moment. Everything that we do in the eucharistic practice is really done through the power of the Holy Spirit, not through our own power.

An example of a Reformed tradition's approach to pneumatology through the Eucharist comes from John Calvin. For Calvin, the Holy Spirit is the power by which we experience the spiritual presence of Christ. Essentially, in the Eucharist Calvin sees the spiritual real presence of Christ through the power of the Holy Spirit. He states, "Even though it seems unbelievable that Christ's flesh, separated from us by such great distance, penetrates to us, so that it becomes our food, let us remember how far the secret power of the Holy Spirit towers above all our senses, and how foolish it is to wish to measure his immeasurableness by our measure. What, then, our mind does not comprehend, let faith conceive: that the Spirit truly unites things separated in space."[21] Calvin expresses his understanding of the mystery of the sacrament experienced through the activity of the Holy Spirit. He admits that what happens in the Eucharist is too much for the human mind to conceive and thus is an experience that is received by faith, not by intellect. The Holy Spirit's work in the Eucharist unites us with Christ's body, a supernatural union that goes beyond our human understanding. Calvin understands this union to occur not through Jesus's coming down to earth but through our mystically ascending into heaven. In the Eucharist, we ascend to where Christ is through the numinous union with the Holy Spirit.

For Calvin, this life-giving experience of the Eucharist comes only through the Holy Spirit. In the experience of the Eucharist and this mystical union, our faith grows. The Holy Spirit works within the Eucharist to increase our faith; in this increased faith we can have communion with the total person of Christ, including his broken body and shed blood, through the power of the Holy Spirit. According to Calvin's understanding of the Holy Spirit's work in the Eucharist, one can infer that the Holy Spirit's role, through the miracle and mystery of the incarnation, allows us to commune with the humanity of Christ while enabling our communion with the divinity of Christ. From a trinitarian perspective, this communion with the divinity of Christ then enables us to commune with the Godhead, the source of all spiritual life, thus bringing about a truly life-giving experience in the liturgical practice of the Eucharist, through the power of the Holy Spirit.

21. John Calvin, *Institutes of the Christian Religion* (1559), 2 vols., ed. John T. McNeill, trans. Ford Lewis Battles (Philadelphia: Westminster, 1960), 1:1370.

Finally, I cannot write about pneumatology and not include an approach from the Pentecostal tradition. I will divert from my pattern a bit and not focus specifically on the Eucharist but pursue a broad understanding of the Holy Spirit. For Pentecostals, worship is synonymous with the presence of God. With a mix of expressions in worship, the presence of the Spirit is manifested through jubilation and celebration, evoking ecstatic responses, and even resting gently in the midst of a community while holding and supporting them in lament. This type of worship is often accompanied by a mixture of spontaneity and the display of spiritual gifts, including speaking in tongues and rituals of healing. In Pentecostal worship, it is understood that the Spirit empowers and shapes humanity in worship. The people are empowered by the Spirit for witnessing and service, and this shows up in the most dynamic expression of worship—one that is audible, dialogical, and tangible. There is a shared experience of the Holy Spirit in Pentecostal worship, marked by Spirit baptism.

As we see, there are unique ways in which different traditions understand pneumatology; in some cases, certain similarities appear across traditions. This survey does not account for all the main Christian traditions, and it does not dive deeply into the diversity that is present within each tradition. In addition, exploring pneumatology along the lines of constructive theologies would be extremely important to expand the preliminary work that has been shared in this chapter. There is indeed more to discover regarding the work of the Holy Spirit.

Practical Implications for Worship

So what does all this mean for the community gathered in worship? The key point to take away from this examination is that through the work of the Holy Spirit in worship, we experience deepened faith and heightened service unto God and to each other. This faith and service are not a function of our own doing but are the work of the Holy Spirit. This is the essence of Christian spirituality, seen in the gathered assembly in worship, through the work of the Spirit. In the invocation of the Holy Spirit in worship, what the church believes and the church's lived experiences are shaped through the prayer (and scriptural beliefs) of the church. This is not a static line drawn from prayer to belief and life; rather, each mutually impacts the other. The converted life of the believer is guided by the power of the Holy Spirit, and the participation in worship is also led by the power of the Holy Spirit. Any performance that takes place during worship is fully empowered by the Holy Spirit. The

Spirit prompts us to assemble, leads us into remembrance of the saving work of Christ, and unites us with Christ and the community in the worship moments. Everything that we do is done through the power of the Holy Spirit, not through our own power.

In its centrality to the faith, public worship impacts and eradicates traditional boundaries, becomes a unifying agent of the Christian church, and unites the church with God through liturgical ritual. All this happens by the power of the Holy Spirit. In this power, the Holy Spirit inspires a core understanding of worship: the body of Christ joins in the shared experience of the celebration, praise, lament, and reverence to God. Through the power of the Spirit, the worshiping body becomes a united body of believers. Christian worship is a shared experience: the people work together in the celebration of God. In this communal participation, unity is created and is made possible only through the work of the Holy Spirit. In worship, we are invited by God, through the Holy Spirit, into a fellowship in which we exist not so much as individuals but as community; a fellowship that, if only for that moment, urges us to look beyond ourselves, our struggles, our differences, and our traditions, and to connect around a shared faith through liturgical practice. It is in this practice that we become one, a united body.

In addition to being an agent of community in worship, the Holy Spirit unites us with Christ. When we come together in worship, we come already connected by Jesus Christ, as members of his united body. Jesus Christ, the one who overcomes "transgressions against divine and social justice in the world,"[22] brings us courage and hope; in worship that collective courage and hope are empowered by the Holy Spirit. We as humanity are incapable of connecting to the divine Savior on our own; it is in the liturgical acts of baptism and the Eucharist that the Holy Spirit connects us with the humanity and divinity of Christ, thus putting us in communion with God. Here is an amazing act of the Holy Spirit. This perspective of the Holy Spirit's activity in worship also redirects our conception of the primary agent in liturgical practice. When we see the work of the Spirit as uniting us with God, it shifts the focus off what we are doing, or giving, and forces us to realize and admit that in worship there is something beyond our human ability taking place, something deeply spiritual. In the Eucharist, for example, Christ is made present, not by coming down to us, but by the Holy Spirit taking us up to Christ. This transcends our understanding and strips us of any power in this miraculous work of the Spirit in the Eucharist.

22. Karen Baker-Fletcher, *Dancing with God: The Trinity from a Womanist Perspective* (St. Louis: Chalice, 2006), 19.

Finally, the Holy Spirit works in and through worship, empowering the church to live a eucharistic life. In the Eucharist, we are given strength and courage to live what we have celebrated through the power of the Holy Spirit. The Holy Spirit equips us to encounter a true connection between real-life experiences and the hope that is anticipated and expressed at the eucharistic celebration. This eucharistic life is based on the foundation of thanksgiving and praise to God for the salvation and sanctification received through Christ. Such a life is guided by the Spirit; humanity is not able to live in a constant state of remembrance, thanksgiving, and praise without the power of the Spirit. With this theological thought, I conclude this exploration of pneumatology and worship, praying that we are strengthened in our worship to work with God, through the power of the Holy Spirit.

For Further Reading

Baker-Fletcher, Karen, *Dancing with God: The Trinity from a Womanist Perspective*. St. Louis: Chalice, 2006.

————. "More than Suffering: The Healing and Resurrecting Spirit of God." In *Womanist Theological Ethics: A Reader*. Louisville: Westminster John Knox, 2011.

Berger, Teresa, and Bryan D. Spinks, eds. *The Spirit in Worship, Worship in the Spirit*. Collegeville, MN: Liturgical Press, 2009.

Johnson, Elizabeth A. *She Who Is: The Mystery of God in Feminist Theological Discourse*. New York: Crossroad, 2002.

Kärkkäinen, Veli-Matti, *Pneumatology: The Holy Spirit in Ecumenical, International, and Contextual Perspective*. Grand Rapids: Baker Academic, 2002.

Moltmann, Jürgen. *The Spirit of Life: A Universal Affirmation*. Minneapolis: Fortress, 2001.

— 8 —

Eschatology and Worship

Maurice Lee

Theological Overview

There are several interesting and potentially fruitful ways to think theologically about worship. One important approach was exemplified in the twentieth century by Roman Catholic liturgical scholar Aidan Kavanagh. At the end of chapter 7 in his 1984 book *On Liturgical Theology*, Kavanagh summarizes:

> [This] chapter claimed that the true primary theologian in the Church is the liturgical assembly in each and every one of its members; that this primary theology is festive, ordered, steeped in the arts, canonical, and eschatological; [and] that this primary discourse is what produces the body of basic faith perceptions upon which secondary theology is nurtured in its normal and healthy state. . . . *Lex credendi* is at root not merely something which is done exclusively by secondary theologians in their studies, as opposed to *lex supplicandi* done by nontheologians indulging in religious worship elsewhere. . . . The liturgy of faithful Christians is the primary theological act of the Church itself.[1]

Kavanagh comments on the famous statement of Prosper of Aquitaine in the fifth century: *ut legem credendi lex statuat supplicandi*, "[so] that the law of supplication might establish the law of believing." To be precise, fame

---

1. Aidan Kavanagh, *On Liturgical Theology* (Collegeville, MN: Liturgical Press, 1984), 150.

mostly attaches to a different and more aphoristic version, not originating from Prosper: *lex orandi, lex credendi,* "the law of praying is the law of believing." Kavanagh thus characterizes the worship of the Christian assembly as theology, and indeed as *primary* theology, the *basic* kind of theology done by Christians. In this interpretation of Prosper's saying, the law of supplication, or law of praying—the ordered and repeated patterns of speech and action in which the assembly receives and experiences its communal relation to God—is fundamental to the law of believing. Then the more-or-less articulable and articulated deliberations, expressions, and formulas form the *secondary* theology, which represents the believing community's truth-claims concerning God and the world. By no means, of course, do thinkers of only one ecclesial tradition have a monopoly on this insight. Thus Lutheran liturgical scholar Maxwell Johnson observes in his 2015 book *The Church in Act*:

> An ancient Christian principle, often summarized by the Latin phrase, *lex orandi . . . lex credendi,* states that the "rule of praying establishes the rule of believing." That is, the faith of the church is both constituted and expressed by the prayer of the church. Indeed, the liturgy is not only the "school for prayer," but also the "school for faith." . . . It was the liturgy—baptismal and eucharistic—that assisted in forming orthodox Christian teaching. That is, orthodox trinitarian and christological doctrine developed, in large part, from the church at prayer, as the baptismal-credal profession of faith gave rise to the official creeds themselves.[2]

Kavanagh's and Johnson's explanations would be misunderstood if they were read as giving the church's worship a role something like that of "raw sensory data," uninterpreted and incommunicable until taken over and worked out by the "higher processing center" of academic, or at least reflective and critical, theology. Christian worship *itself* is the assembly, the people gathered, speaking of God, *theo-logia.* Admittedly, this theology expressed in worship is not in the form of a systematic treatise or a list of anathemas, but, as Kavanagh describes it, "in the vastly complex vocabulary of experiences had, prayers said, sights seen, smells smelled, words said and heard and responded to, emotions controlled and released, sins committed and repented, children born and loved ones buried, and in many other ways no one can count or always account for."[3]

This does not mean that all Christian worship is per se good theology—or indeed, per se good worship. But if the characterization of worship as theology

---

2. Maxwell E. Johnson, *The Church in Act: Lutheran Liturgical Theology in Ecumenical Conversation* (Minneapolis: Fortress, 2015), 8.

3. Kavanagh, *On Liturgical Theology,* 147.

has any substance, then insofar as judgment on "goodness" is to be rendered at all, the first principle of judgment cannot be found from answers to any questions like these: Is this (particular way of worshiping) useful for some organizational or personal purpose? Is this contextualized so as to be respectful of the culture(s) within which it is done? Does this promote social justice in a manner in keeping with contemporary urgencies? Instead, we must ask, at some level that does not involve the assimilation of worship to scholarly theological discourse, but at the same time does not encourage the assumption that worship is purely subjective and exempt from public standards of any kind: Is the true God being spoken of truly, in accordance with God's own Word? Even before that, we must ask: What is being said by this theology?

What Is Eschatology?

Kavanagh claims—and he is far from alone—that Christian worship is *eschatological*. What could be meant by this? The particular "specialization" within Christian theology indicated by the term *eschatological* is notoriously multivalent, not to mention divisive. That eschatology has to do with "last things" is etymologically true and universally agreed. But what those last things are; when they, or even their precursors, will happen; how and why they can be known or studied; what can or should be stated and taught about them—these have all been disputed, one is tempted to say, to no end! Even to summarize the disputes would require much more than this chapter. (Nor will I pretend to analyze Kavanagh's own conception of eschatology in what follows.)

The Christian claim is that the specific story involving Israel, Jesus, and the church is indeed the true story of the whole world. In the Christian Bible, it is at least clear that "the end of the story," the goal or telos toward which the entire complex narrative is moving, is yet never something that could simply be extrapolated or derived by some sort of internal ("immanent") necessity from what went before. The paradigmatic events of salvation history are repeatedly taken to give clues indicating what to hope for in the future. These primal events are Israel's exodus and Jesus's resurrection. Yet these are as much and more distinguished by radical *discontinuity*, by the confounding of creaturely expectations and the surpassing of creaturely possibilities by God's unforced and sovereign agency. These paradigmatic events are tied to created history by continuities of space, time, and person. Salvation, an eschatological concept in the Bible, comes from God, not as the result of the machinations and ambitions of human beings or any other creatures.

For just this reason, a *Christian* eschatology will find in *Jesus Christ*, the God-man, not only the "end [*telos*] of the law" (Rom. 10:4) but also, or rather just so, the one in whom "all the promises of God find their Yes" (2 Cor. 1:20). Christian eschatology recognizes Jesus Christ as the one who "is coming with the clouds" (Rev. 1:7) to "deliver the kingdom to God the Father after destroying every rule and every authority and power," "that God may be all in all" (1 Cor. 15:24, 28).

This is true of Christian eschatology whatever its hermeneutical strategy with regard to the visions of Revelation; whether it sanctions or repudiates universalism; whether or not it draws ethical conclusions concerning care of the nonhuman creation; in other words, however it negotiates the numberless fascinating issues under dispute. That does not mean that those other questions are unimportant, but that they can be addressed *only* in the light of the theological assertion that Jesus Christ, crucified and risen, is the goal of all God's ways and works and the personal reality of God's kingdom. It means that in Christ, the incarnate Son of God, is to be seen a glimpse, a preview, of the final destiny of all God's creation. It means that through this Israelite, the Messiah, God is fulfilling his ancient promises to bless the families and nations of the earth.

A Christian eschatology, in other words, will resonate (perhaps smilingly) with Lutheran theologian Robert Jenson's provocative formulation in his *Systematic Theology*: "Pietist ethicists of the simpler sort used to ask such questions as 'Could you invite Jesus into a bar with you?' Whatever the answer to that question, . . . they had a right idea in eschatological context. It is indeed a limitation of our fantasy: Could you invite Jesus into your envisioned Fulfillment? Or rather, Can you imagine Jesus taking you with him into it?"[4] Precisely in thus attending to Jesus Christ, eschatology explores what it means for Christians to know themselves as those on whom "the end of the ages has come" (1 Cor. 10:11)[5] and to whom "in these last days God has spoken by his Son" (Heb. 1:2). At the same time, Christians know that "what we will be has not yet appeared" (1 John 3:2) and that "if we hope for what we do not see, then we wait for it with patience" (Rom. 8:25).

Taking Christology in this way as its central and critical principle, a Christian eschatology will find itself having to do with—one might say, will find itself both assuming and putting questions to—the doctrine of God, the doctrine of creation, soteriology, anthropology, pneumatology, ecclesiology,

---

4. Robert W. Jenson, *Systematic Theology*, vol. 2, *The Works of God* (Oxford: Oxford University Press, 1999), chap. 31, §IV, Kindle location 5354.
5. In this chapter Scripture quotations are from the English Standard Version.

and indeed, every other "department" of doctrine. This is not only because theology is in some sense a seamlessly interconnected whole, but more basically because the inaugurated and still-coming rule of God in Jesus Christ does not intend to leave anything—any item of investigation, any corner of the universe—untouched. Therefore eschatology is a kind of capstone or summation of all Christian theology, as many suggest. For example, Lutheran theologian Wolfhart Pannenberg declares in his 1998 *Systematic Theology*: "Eschatology is not just the subject of a single chapter in dogmatics; it determines the perspective of Christian doctrine as a whole."[6]

We are thus led to ask if and how the church's worship, as primary theology, expresses or interprets eschatology. The concern is not so much whether the threat of final judgment must be held over congregants' heads, or whether or not any earthly liturgy is to be regarded as an icon of the life of heaven as revealed in Revelation 4–5, or in what ways biblical prophecies should be expounded in relation to current events. A reasonable case could be made for paying theological attention to all these matters and others. However, our concern is much more to understand how Jesus Christ—the one in whom "all things" are to be gathered, "things in heaven and things on earth" (Eph. 1:10), for the glory of the Father and in the Spirit of their love—gives meaning, form, and purpose to worship.

Eschatology *and* a Worship Practice

One way to ask the question would be to take a "deep dive" into specific practices and texts used in Christian worship, exploring these for eschatological presuppositions, themes, and ramifications. This makes sense because worship anything like the picture that the Bible paints is communal (not sheerly individual), embodied (not merely mental), and verbal (not completely silent). Worshiping people sense, sing, and do things together. (I am not proposing an *exhaustive* definition of worship but trying to say something *accurate* about worship.) Through the centuries, Christian worship in almost every tradition has organized the things sensed, sung, and done, by the commands and promises of Scripture, along the axes of Word and sacrament. Looking at a specific practice of a sacrament and considering its history with an "eschatological eye" is instructive.

Something along these lines is attempted by Methodist theologian Geoffrey Wainwright in his book *Eucharist and Eschatology*. Wainwright's project

---

6. Wolfhart Pannenberg, *Systematic Theology*, trans. Geoffrey W. Bromiley (Grand Rapids: Eerdmans, 1998), 3:531.

involves reflecting on the biblical descriptions of the Eucharist and on the developments and debates regarding those descriptions in the history of Christian thought. He does this under three headings: the Eucharist as meal anticipating the great future banquet, "Antepast of Heaven"; the Eucharist as remembrance of Christ's death until he comes, "Maranatha"; and the Eucharist as the sign of God's final transformation of his creation, "The Firstfruits of the Kingdom."

Ranging over liturgies from East and West, Wainwright elaborates a theological account of the Eucharist as the memorial (*anamnēsis*) of Christ: "The church recalls before the Father, with thanksgiving, the first coming of Christ and the work of salvation which he then began. Understanding that first coming as a promise and earnest of yet greater things, the church also prays the Father, in hope and expectation, that he will complete the bringing in of his kingdom by even now sending the one and the same messiah again, for the accomplishing of his final work."[7] In the Eucharist, Christian worshipers "proclaim the Lord's death until he comes" (1 Cor. 11:26). This liturgical proclamation points in two temporal "directions" simultaneously: toward Jesus's once-for-all sacrifice and resurrection in the past, and toward his coming-for-all final appearing (*parousia*) in the future.

The Eucharist is found to be shot through, top to bottom, with eschatological significance. Wainwright's rich findings concerning the eschatological "dimension" of the Eucharist allow him to draw out the "Ecclesiological Consequences" for the church's witness, preaching, mission, and unity. This last topic is especially neuralgic and pressing, given that the one church's terrible fragments and fissures are most obvious precisely when it comes to eucharistic fellowship.

For example, Wainwright suggests that differences in doctrine should not by themselves be enough to separate Christians and churches from one another at the Lord's Table:

> It might be argued from the eschatological perspective that the eucharist is more important for what it makes of us than for what it expresses as being already true of us. . . . Common participation in the one eucharist . . . will be the occasion for the Lord to exercise the three eschatological functions of casting out from us in judgment what is amiss in us, of uniting us closer to himself in divine fellowship, and of joining us together in common enjoyment of his presence and gifts.[8]

7. Geoffrey Wainwright, *Eucharist and Eschatology* (1971; repr., Akron: OSL Publications, 2002), 115.
8. Wainwright, *Eucharist and Eschatology*, 177.

Wainwright's conclusions might well be (and have been) disputed. He asks, What does the eschatology inherent in the Eucharist—as a worship practice, and so theology—entail for churches' actual practice of this sacrament? His example surely points to one of the things eschatology is for.

Standing church policies seem to prevent the Methodist Wainwright from being able to commune with Greek Orthodox theologian John Zizioulas. Even Zizioulas, in his 2011 book *The Eucharistic Communion and the World* (as well as in other texts), reaches parallel results concerning the Eucharist. For example:

> While the Passover meal is a family event, the Last Supper is an event that concerns a group of friends with Christ presiding. . . . This fundamental difference . . . reveals clearly the eschatological character of the Last Supper. . . . Inasmuch as the Last Supper is not an event of familial life but an event for "the friends of the Lamb," the Supper marks an eschatological "inbreaking" in the natural course of historical life. . . . By making the Twelve the sole participants at the Last Supper, Christ made the Eucharist an eschatological reality arising in the history of the people of God.[9]

Zizioulas goes on to say, "The 'memorial' of the Last Supper has several dimensions: through it, in the present, the past becomes a new reality, but the future becomes a reality that is already. . . . To understand the remembrance in this way makes the Eucharist not only a re-presentation of the sacrifice and resurrection of Christ, but also *a foretaste of the Kingdom to come.*"[10]

There is no doubt that there are significant differences in the theological traditions that formed these two authors. Agreement that the Eucharist is thoroughly eschatological is not agreement on the Eucharist as a whole, not to mention on the doctrines of church and salvation embedded in the theologies of the Eucharist in question. Yet such theological investigations—and even partial theological convergences—may be appropriate and incrementally helpful accompaniments to Jesus's prayer offered so fervently on behalf of his disciples, "that they may all be one" (John 17:21).

More generally, one great value of an approach such as Wainwright's or Zizioulas's is the seriousness with which it takes traditional liturgies, texts, and the reflection devoted to them by Christian leaders and thinkers over many centuries. Even over great distances in time and space, we can study practices like those associated with the Eucharist, not only but certainly in

---

9. John D. Zizioulas, *The Eucharistic Communion and the World*, ed. Luke Ben Tallon (London: T&T Clark, 2011), 3–4.

10. Zizioulas, *Eucharistic Communion*, 6, emphasis original.

part to discern and to assess their specifically eschatological content and intention. This opens us to an increasing familiarity with and appreciation for the ways of thinking and believing that have animated those practices and for the liturgies to which they have contributed.

Eschatology and Worship Overall

Another way—not an alternative, as if one had to choose between them—to ask the question about the relationship between worship and eschatology would be to investigate the nature of Christian worship itself. This makes sense because worship anything like the picture that the Bible paints is not a miscellaneous, "thrown together" collection of actions and rubrics, each perhaps with its own inner logic and perhaps appealing to some subgroup, but with the aggregate lacking overall direction or continuity. It also is not a merely instrumental set of methods to generate certain emotions or put people into certain moods. Some circles strangely regiment the term "worship" to mean "the music preceding the sermon" and thus are unintentionally vulnerable to this sort of misunderstanding. An overconcentration on the ritual or pragmatic aspects of worship—and there are plenty of those—runs the risk of reducing thinking about worship as a kind of religiously tinged anthropology. But worship is finally "about" *God*.

Something along these lines is attempted by Reformed theologian James Torrance in his 1996 book *Worship, Community, and the Triune God of Grace*. Torrance's project is, as he puts it, "to recover [the] New Testament understanding of worship which recognizes that the real agent in all true worship is Jesus Christ. He is our great High Priest and ascended Lord, the one true worshipper who unites us to himself by the Spirit in an act of memory and in a life of communion, as he lifts us up by Word and sacrament into the very triune life of God."[11] Torrance identifies what he calls the "unitarian" view of worship, "that worship is something which we, religious people, do," which "means that the only priesthood is our priesthood, the only offering our offering, the only intercessions our intercessions."[12] Throughout the book, Torrance contrasts that view with the "trinitarian" view, that Jesus Christ is given "to us as the Son living a life of union and communion with the Father in the Spirit, presenting himself in our humanity through the eternal Spirit to the Father on behalf of humankind." "By

11. James B. Torrance, *Worship, Community, and the Triune God of Grace* (Downers Grove, IL: IVP Academic, 1996), 17.
12. Torrance, *Worship, Community*, 20.

his Spirit [Christ] draws men and women to participate both in his life of worship and communion with the Father and in his mission from the Father to the world."[13]

Torrance places considerable emphasis on the biblical depiction of the high priesthood of Jesus, who makes the all-sufficient and final sacrifice that puts the human relationship with God in the condition that the Creator intended from the beginning. He stresses the biblical implication that, by virtue of Jesus's representative humanity, other human beings now have access to God. They can know God, love God, and worship God by being united to that high priest, by being made members of Christ's body.

> The fact that Jesus Christ is the leader of our worship, the High Priest who forgives us our sins and leads us into the holy presence of the Father, is the central theme of the Epistle to the Hebrews. . . . As Paul expounds justification by faith by contrasting life in the Spirit—the way of grace—with false self-confidence in the flesh, so . . . Hebrews contrasts two forms of worship: [1] true worship . . . means reposing on and participating in the self-offering of Christ[,] who alone can lead us into "the Holy of Holies"—the holy presence of the Father—and [2] false worship with its false reliance on what we do by following our own devices or the traditions of men.[14]

Torrance's basic characterization (developed in a great variety of ways) of worship—an activity involving created human agents!—is in terms of *God's* initiative, *God's* abundance, *God's* giving: "In worship . . . we are given the gift of participating through the Spirit in the incarnate Son's communion with the Father, in the trinitarian life of God."[15] Here he assumes the opposite of a "projection" theory of God, which would make the reality of God nothing more than an arbitrary construct of human imaginations and human (felt) needs. Yet he does not deny the reality of human persons, human worshipers, relating to God. The notion of *participation*, enthusiastically deployed by Torrance (following a long Christian tradition), presupposes the joint reality, both of those who share (participate) in worship and of that which is shared (participated in). Along the way, Torrance detects implications for the Christian view of persons, individuals, and community; for the practice of prayer; for the doctrine of Christ's vicarious humanity; for baptism and the Eucharist; and for the ways Christians think about gender and sexuality as they impinge on the language used for God.

13. Torrance, *Worship, Community*, 30–31.
14. Torrance, *Worship, Community*, 57, 59.
15. Torrance, *Worship, Community*, 39.

One might wonder if, given such a strong emphasis on worship as participation *now* (the present tense is pervasive) in God's eternal triune life, there would correspondingly little room for the *not yet*, the "through a glass, darkly" (1 Cor. 13:12 KJV) of the eschatological perspective. It is true that the future aspect is not a prominent theme in Torrance's treatment. He certainly does not *deny* that God's reign has yet to be fully consummated, that the creation has yet to be fully renewed. Speaking of the Lord's Supper (Eucharist), for example, Torrance remarks, in words reminiscent of Wainwright and Zizioulas: "[Christ] brings his passion to our remembrance and draws us into wonderful communion—Holy Communion—with the Father, with himself and with one another, proleptic of our life in the kingdom of God, nourishing our faith 'till he come.'"[16] But it is the idea of participation itself, within the context of the Christian identification of God as Trinity, that points toward the eschatology inherent in worship, even if Torrance does not take pains to highlight it. Participation is given by the Holy Spirit, who for worshipers is the *arrabōn*, the down payment or firstfruits, of what is to come (cf. 2 Cor. 1:22; 5:5; Eph. 1:14). In this sense Christian worship is participation—again, real participation, not playacting or private mental projection—in God's life precisely as a taste or glimpse of, but not full entrance into or possession of, the promised fulfillment.

From his Protestant ecclesial situation, Torrance insists on the priority of the category of *grace*—understood in an irreducibly trinitarian and incarnational manner—for rightly describing the reality of Christian worship. He has distinguished company in the person of Roman Catholic theologian Avery Cardinal Dulles. In the first of eight concluding theses in his 1998 article "The Ways We Worship," Dulles writes: "Liturgy is God's gift before it is a human response. It is not something we freely construct according to our own ideas and preferences. . . . It derives from the activity of God through Christ and the apostles. In the liturgy God turns to us, and we receive what he is pleased to give."[17] Dulles's third thesis in the series is as follows: "In order to bring about interior union with the mystery being celebrated in it, liturgy should prayerfully invoke the Holy Spirit. Where this invocation is omitted, a false impression of human autonomy can easily arise."[18]

Indeed, Torrance's main polemical target is precisely the (often subconscious) idea of worship as arising primarily from human initiative and agency, such that it could presumably be "aimed" in whatever "direction" was

---

16. Torrance, *Worship, Community*, 74.
17. Avery Cardinal Dulles, "The Ways We Worship," *First Things* (March 1998): 48, https://www.firstthings.com/article/1998/03/the-ways-we-worship.
18. Dulles, "Ways We Worship," 50.

regarded as best at any given time. What is remarkable about Torrance's approach is its characterization of worship, not in a generically theistic manner that could in principle be "tweaked" to fit any of a variety of conceptions of the God being worshiped, but in a deliberately trinitarian manner, "discovering" the church's worship within the life always already shared by Father, Son, and Holy Spirit. This opens the door to deeper exploration of the nature of worship as gift, of the asymmetrical determination of what worship is and how it "works" first and foremost by God-to-human giving, and then only dependently and contingently by human-to-God responding.

Practical Implications for Worship

Worship is fundamentally a gift from the Triune God, not produced, initiated, or actuated by human effort or creativity. Worship is fundamentally the gracious taking of worshipers into a story authored and directed by the Triune God, not a set of stratagems for manipulating or wheedling God into doing what humans want. Yet it is still true that such matters as posture, formality (or lack of it), musical selections, and topics for preaching and prayer (areas of human action, shaped by human choices and cultures, subject to human interpretation) are loci where the reality of worship may be displayed and communicated more or less well. The quality of this communication, the *fidelity* of humanly enacted practices of worship to the underlying divinely given reality of worship, is by no means easy to adjudicate. There is no simple or even complex formula to determine (putting the question another way) to what extent the church's worship at a particular place and time has been taken captive to the often militantly non-Christian presuppositions and pieties of the secular culture, rather than to the Word of God made known definitively in Jesus Christ. For example, the lines do not run neatly between "traditional" and "contemporary" styles. Some may say, "If a congregation recites the Nicene Creed, then it is in the thrall of vain repetition, and repetition of something other than Scripture to boot," or "If a congregation sings trendy 'praise' music, then it has sold its liturgical birthright for a mess of ear-splitting, content-poor pottage." Such simplistic conclusions evade the true and difficult issue.

Yet disputes over such things as which way the presiding minister should face at the eucharistic table—toward or away from the people—are not disputes over nothing. They cannot be dismissed by saying, "Just do whatever makes you feel comfortable," or, "If you don't like it, then just go to another church." If worship is theology, then there are theological truths at stake.

Hence these matters must be argued theologically. Reformed philosopher James K. A. Smith, in his Cultural Liturgies trilogy (*Desiring the Kingdom, Imagining the Kingdom, Awaiting the King*),[19] exemplifies a way of arguing about these matters that pays attention to how people are formed. Their hidden assumptions about God and the world are partly shaped and regulated by repeated, pervasive, and culturally specific practices. Pre-reflectively, it all may seem plausible, obvious, and desirable to them. Nevertheless, the things they do certainly communicate what they believe. One might question the specific points at which Smith finds irreconcilable conflicts between Christian faith (and so Christian worship) and, say, consumer behavior or national pride. Yet it should be possible to argue intelligently over whether certain worship practices, otherwise thought to be neutral, might be usable for either good or bad purposes. Perhaps these practices are actually communicating, against worshipers' intention, that true happiness is found in possessing things rather than in obeying God, or that allegiance to an ethnic group or political system may rightly eclipse citizenship in God's kingdom.

This suggests that it is not only possible but also important to consider carefully what the Christian community's worship—its primary theology—is indeed saying via its forms, orientations, and practices. What does this worship actually communicate about God and about the world in relation to God, including the world's final fulfillment in and from God? This is not in the service of a mere theological "recital" (as it were). In the Christian tradition, eschatology is far from being a set of abstract facts, much less a timetable of future catastrophes or a secret religious decoder ring. Instead, eschatology offers substance and shape to the specifically "theological" virtue of hope. There are many definitions of hope and ways to hope, and not all of them have as their basis the Word of the God revealed through Jesus Christ in the power of the Holy Spirit. Pannenberg points out that "Christians do not hope just for themselves. . . . In Christ they share in a universal hope for humanity. . . . By faith Christians are snatched out of bondage to their egotistical striving for happiness and find the fulfillment of their personal life precisely in the fellowship of the body of Christ and in work for the future of humanity in the kingdom of God."[20]

In his 1978 book *Visible Words*, Robert Jenson describes the traditional task of catechesis, which is not identical to worship, yet neither is it independent.

19. James K. A. Smith, *Desiring the Kingdom: Worship, Worldview, and Cultural Formation* (Grand Rapids: Baker Academic, 2009); Smith, *Imagining the Kingdom: How Worship Works* (Grand Rapids: Baker Academic, 2013); Smith, *Awaiting the King: Reforming Public Theology* (Grand Rapids: Baker Academic, 2017).
20. Pannenberg, *Systematic Theology*, 3:177.

Jenson proposes: "Most groups now require theological instruction for those joining the church; what must be added is instruction in the moral dissensus between late modernity and the gospel: between consumer humanity and loving humanity, between self-realization and joint realization, between trust in weapons and trust in God. Such instruction is meaningless outside the practice of prayer and reflection."[21] The sanctuary is not a Christian classroom, and yet worship expresses, develops, and upholds the same way of thinking, the same specification of trust.

The church's Christian worship, in all the variety of its eschatological spirit and because the gift of the eschatological Spirit is being poured out, will be a training in hope. Believers hope not for an escape from this world, not for retribution against enemies, not for victory in the rat race for temporal goods, but for God's promised reign over all that is. This "training" will involve repeated refamiliarization with biblical language, thought patterns, and narratives; grateful knowledge of the community, extending across space and time, to which each individual worshiper belongs; sacramental imagination; reception and appreciation of the actual paths by which God lifts believers into participation in the triune life; and above all, the continual turning—more accurately, the being-turned—of human persons to know, love, obey, and serve the one true and living God.

For Further Reading

Jenson, Robert W. *Visible Words: The Interpretation and Practice of Christian Sacraments*. Philadelphia: Fortress, 1978.

Schmemann, Alexander. *The Eucharist: Sacrament of the Kingdom*. Translated by Paul Kachur. Crestwood, NY: St. Vladimir's Seminary Press, 2003.

Senn, Frank C. *Christian Liturgy: Catholic and Evangelical*. Minneapolis: Fortress, 1997.

Smith, James K. A. *Imagining the Kingdom: How Worship Works*. Grand Rapids: Baker Academic, 2013.

Wolterstorff, Nicholas. *Acting Liturgically: Philosophical Reflections on Religious Practice*. Oxford: Oxford University Press, 2018.

21. Robert W. Jenson, *Visible Words: The Interpretation and Practice of Christian Sacraments* (Philadelphia: Fortress, 1978), 167.

— 9 —

Ecclesiology and Worship

Rhodora E. Beaton

When my students ask how I became interested in the study of theology, I tell them that when I was a little girl, growing up in rural New Hampshire, I was fascinated by the worship practices of my small Roman Catholic parish. When my family went to church, we saw our neighbors, our friends, and our relatives. Our parish priest beamed at us from his chair as the lector proclaimed the readings from Scripture. From the coveted row of folding chairs that were right up against the rail of the balcony, I could look down over our assembly racing our way through the Creed. We believed "in one God, the Father almighty, maker of heaven and earth." We believed in our Lord Jesus Christ, who, somehow, was "God from God, Light from Light, true God from true God." We also believed in "one, holy, catholic and apostolic Church," and "one baptism for the forgiveness of sins."[1] After the Creed, we rounded the corner into the Liturgy of the Eucharist, recalling how Jesus shared a last meal with his disciples before he was betrayed. In our prayer, somehow, we participated in that meal and in his sacrifice. Maybe we even felt the guilt of the betrayal before we advanced in the swaying lines of the Communion procession, to kneel at the altar rail and hear the words "the body of Christ" proclaimed as we were served Communion. Then we climbed back upstairs to the balcony, with Communion melting on our tongues.

1. From the United States Conference of Bishops (Catholic version), https://www.usccb.org /beliefs-and-teachings/what-we-believe.

As I grew up, I began to wonder about how *our* church was part of *the* church, about why we all stood up and recited things about believing in "one baptism for the forgiveness of sins," and about why the phrase "the body of Christ" was used for both Holy Communion and for the church. Questions like these are questions of worship and ecclesiology. They emerged out of a specific experience of the liturgy as it was celebrated in the Roman Catholic Church in the late twentieth century, in a nearly forgotten corner of the Diocese of Manchester, New Hampshire. They also point to related issues of what it means to be part of the universal church. Although I did not know it at the time, my experience of worshiping was shaping what I would later recognize as an ecclesiology. Answers to ecclesiological questions can be found in Christian history, through a careful look at the ways Christians worship, and in ecumenical dialogue between Christians of different denominations. In this brief essay, we will first consider the field of ecclesiology in itself. Then we will turn to some of the differences in the ways modern-day Christians think about themselves as church. This will lead us to an analysis of some historical and contemporary worship practices that can illuminate an understanding of what it means to be church. Finally, we will consider some ways worship leaders can analyze and respond to prevailing ecclesiologies in their local communities.

Theological Overview

Ecclesiology is the theological study of the church. To study the church theologically, as opposed to sociologically, politically, or even historically, one considers the church from the perspective of "faith seeking understanding."[2] This view presumes certain personal and denominational beliefs about the church in its relationship to God, yet seeks to understand such beliefs more deeply. In this section we will consider some key issues in the study of ecclesiology. We will begin by looking at the etymology of the word and its biblical foundations. Then we will examine some contemporary approaches to this field of study.

The word "ecclesiology" comes from the Greek word *ekklēsia*, which means the community of those who have been called by God. The Septuagint uses it to translate the Hebrew word *qāhāl*, meaning "the gathered assembly."[3] It is

---

2. Anselm of Canterbury offered this famous description of theological method as the original title of what would eventually be known as his *Proslogion*. See Benedicta Ward, ed., *The Prayers and Meditations of St. Anselm with the Proslogion* (Harmondsworth, UK: Penguin Classics, 1973), 239. Ward translates this phrase as "faith in search of understanding."

3. K. L. Schmidt, "ἐκκλησία," in *Theological Dictionary of the New Testament*, ed. G. Kittel and G. Friedrich, trans. and ed. G. W. Bromiley (Grand Rapids: Eerdmans: 1965), 3:527.

important to understand that the church is thus a *response* to God's initial call to humanity. This sense of call is indicated in many passages from the New Testament that are associated with the beginnings of the Christian church. Among these are the following: Jesus's calling of the first disciples to follow him after his baptism in the Jordan; his declaration to Peter, "Upon this Rock I will build my church" (Matt. 16:18 NASB); and the early community's later response to Peter's preaching and their subsequent way of life together as described in the second chapter of the book of Acts. Each of these biblical accounts sheds light on the Christian church's earliest self-understanding.

Jesus's baptism in the Jordan River is included at the beginning of each of the Synoptic Gospels. The baptism includes a trinitarian theophany, a revelation of God. The Holy Spirit descends on Jesus, and a voice from the heavens identifies Jesus as "my beloved Son" (Matt. 3:17; Mark 1:11; Luke 3:22). It is an event that marks the beginning of Jesus's public ministry and is broadly understood as a model for Christians to follow. Soon after this baptism, Jesus calls the first disciples to leave their occupations and former ways of life to come and follow him (Matt. 4:19). These first followers, while not yet formally "church," set the example for what would become the Christian practice of discipleship. They join their lives to that of Jesus, following him as friends and companions while he preaches the good news of the kingdom of God and leads them on his journey to Jerusalem and the cross. When Jesus adds that these professional fishermen will now seek people instead of fish (Matt. 4:19), he is indicating the evangelical mission of the church to proclaim the kingdom of God to all people.

One of the few mentions of the word *ekklēsia*, or "church," in the Gospels is found in the Gospel of Matthew: Simon Peter, with the help of divine revelation, recognizes that Jesus is the "Messiah, the Son of the living God" (Matt. 16:16).[4] In this conversation, Jesus plays on Simon Peter's nickname (*Kephā'*, meaning "rock" in Aramaic),[5] saying, "You are Peter, and upon this rock I will build my church" (Matt. 16:18). His statement to Peter has been interpreted in several ways. Many Christians understand it as a declaration of Peter's leadership in the church that will emerge after Jesus's death and resurrection. An ecclesiological difference is found between Christians who emphasize the

4. The other reference in the Gospels is in Matt. 18:17: "If he refused to listen to them, tell the church. If he refuses to listen even to the church, then treat him as you would a Gentile or tax collector" (ESV).

5. "In Matt. 10:2 Simon is said to have been called 'Peter.' In Greek there is a play on the name *Petros* and the word *petra* ('rock'). In Aramaic, the play is more perfect on *kephā'*. Peter/ Cephas may not have been a proper name but rather a nickname, which perhaps had some connection with Peter's personal characteristics ('Rocky')." Daniel J. Harrington, *The Gospel of Matthew*, Sacra Pagina, Series 1 (Collegeville, MN: Liturgical Press, 1991), 247–48.

person of Peter as the rock on which the church will be built and Christians who emphasize the *faith* of Peter as the rock on which the church will be built. Roman Catholics, for example, understand later bishops at Rome, also known as popes, to be the successors of Peter and the primary leaders of the church. This understanding has shaped Roman Catholic ecclesiology. Some other Christians acknowledge Peter's special leadership, or primacy, but do not believe that the primacy applies to his successors throughout Christian history. Still others understand Peter as one leader among many in the early church and emphasize his significance as a flawed and yet effective leader. Questions of church structure and organization are important to the study of ecclesiology.[6]

However Peter's leadership may be understood, it is clear that when Jesus spoke to Peter about the foundation of the church, he spoke of a future event. Most scholars place the beginnings of the church itself at the first Pentecost after Jesus's death and resurrection, when the early community is gathered in the courtyard of the Jerusalem temple or nearby. They hear Peter preach, and each understands what is said their own language (Acts 2:1–11). Peter's call to "repent and be baptized every one of you in the name of Jesus Christ for the forgiveness of your sins, and you will receive the gift of the Holy Spirit" (Acts 2:38 ESV) marks a liturgical beginning to the church in which communal repentance, baptism, and reception of the Holy Spirit lead directly into a communal life devoted to "the apostles' teaching and the fellowship, to the breaking of the bread and the prayers" of praise to God (Acts 2:42–46 ESV). Although perhaps idealized, these communal values of the Christian life have provided the model for later believers to follow.

In contemporary Christian theological discourse, ecclesiology falls into the field of systematic theology. Here it is studied in conversation with other doctrinal approaches like Christology, pneumatology, eschatology, and theological anthropology. We can understand this by realizing that what we believe about Christ (Christology), about the Holy Spirit (pneumatology), about the end of the world (eschatology), and about what it means to be a human being in relationship with God (theological anthropology) are all related to what we believe about the church.

For example, for most Christians the church is not simply a group of human beings who share something in common and gather on Sunday mornings.

---

6. For an overview of some of the differences in the structures and organizations of Christian churches, particularly those rooted in disagreements over the meaning or significance of apostolic succession, see World Council of Churches, *Baptism, Eucharist, and Ministry*, Faith and Order Paper No. 111 (Geneva: WCC, 1982), nos. 33–38. See also World Council of Churches, *The Church: Towards a Common Vision*, Faith and Order Paper No. 214 (Geneva: WCC, 2013), nos. 44–57.

Christians believe that effective preaching and worship are possible because of the presence of the Holy Spirit, who works through the ministers and the people in liturgical celebration and also guides the church in belief and practice. The presence of the Holy Spirit, experienced diversely in sacramental rites, altar calls, and laying on of hands, is what differentiates the church from other human gatherings. While the church is visibly human, it is also intimately related to the trinitarian life of God. Some Christians emphasize the visible church; others emphasize that only God knows who truly is part of the church. Many Christians also acknowledge that the church of God extends beyond the boundaries of those Christians who are alive at any given point, including the holy ones who have died in faith. There is thus an eschatological dimension to ecclesiology. Beliefs about the church can affect our understanding of these other fields of theological inquiry.

Since this volume is concerned with public worship by Christians, it is important to consider the relationship between ecclesiology and liturgical prayer. From the early centuries of the church, the relationship between liturgy and doctrine has been recognized. In the fifth century, Prosper of Aquitaine, a bishop and theologian, advanced a doctrinal argument on the basis of liturgical evidence.[7] Taking a side in a theological dispute about whether or not Christians needed God's grace in order to do good, Prosper argued that because the church prayed for specific groups of people in the Good Friday liturgy, it must be true that these people needed God's grace to help them in their lives. If they did not need God's grace, then the church would not be praying for such a thing. Prosper's famous phrase in Latin, *ut legem credendi lex statuat supplicandi*, is usually translated, "[so] that the law of prayer might establish the law of belief." It is sometimes abbreviated to "*lex orandi, lex credendi*," which functions as a shorthand way of remembering that prayer and belief are closely linked. It is important that our public prayers are in accord with our professed beliefs. It is also often the case, although not always, that our most important beliefs are preserved and proclaimed in public prayer. The Lord's Prayer, rooted in the biblical text and frequently prayed communally in Christian worship, offers one example. This prayer of praise and petition also includes faith claims about the doctrine of God, theological anthropology, eschatology, and even ecclesiology, since it is always prayed in the first-person plural (we, us, our).

7. For example, see Paul De Clerck, "*'Lex orandi, lex credendi*': Original Sense and Historical Avatars of an Equivocal Age," *Studia Liturgica* 24 (1994): 178–200. See also Martha Moore-Keish, "Interreligious Ritual Participation: Insights from Inter-Christian Ritual Participation," in *Ritual Participation and Interreligious Dialogue: Boundaries, Transgressions and Innovations*, ed. Marianne Moyaert and Joris Geldhof (New York: Bloomsbury Academic, 2015), 70–74.

To more clearly map beliefs about the church in relationship to belief in other doctrines, Christians have developed many images or "models" of the church through the centuries. These images can help us to picture and better understand the diverse expressions of Christianity that exist and have existed. Theologian Avery Dulles, for example, describes some of the many ways that Christians, past and present, have thought about the church. In his now-classic book,[8] Dulles describes the following models of the church: as an institution that is visible and has an organizational structure; as an experience of mystical communion among Christians and between Christians and the God who calls them; as a sacrament, or visible and effective sign of God's transformative presence in the world; as a herald preaching the good news of Jesus Christ; as servant of the world, following the model of Jesus, who came to heal and reconcile; and as the community of disciples responding to the call of Jesus. Dulles himself believes that this last model is the most comprehensive.[9]

Each of these examples offers a guiding image for thinking about the ways that Christians seek to live in relationship with God, with one another, and with the world. Some of these images put greater emphasis on the preaching of the Word of God, some on Christian action to help others in the world, and some on the intimate bond between Christians in their union with God. Some of them are anthropomorphic in that they portray the church as a person. Others present the church as a type of organization or action. Christians from different denominations may find that different models best fit their understanding of the church. Even within denominations, different models may appeal to different individuals. New models can also be developed from biblical, doctrinal, and liturgical sources.

Different Approaches in Understanding Ecclesiology

While different methodological approaches are often necessary and helpful to the theological tradition, extreme differences in ecclesiology have, throughout the centuries, divided Christianity into many smaller subgroups. Some Christians see this fracture as a scandal and work diligently for a restoration of Christian unity. Other Christians are more focused on their local churches and are less disturbed by theological and denominational differences in ecclesiology. To examine these approaches, we turn to a recent text produced by the

8. Avery Dulles, *Models of the Church,* expanded ed. (New York: Random House, 2000).
9. Dulles, *Models of the Church,* 198.

World Council of Churches (WCC), an organization dedicated to ecumenical dialogue and Christian unity.[10]

As a recent WCC document titled *The Church: Towards a Common Vision* explains, the very different approaches that Christians take for understanding the word "church" indicate the difficulties of ecclesial agreement around related topics.

> Currently some identify the church of Christ exclusively with their own community, while others would acknowledge in communities other than their own a real but incomplete presence of the elements which make up the church. Others have joined into various types of covenant relationships which sometimes include the sharing of worship. Some believe that the church of Christ is located in all communities that present a convincing claim to be Christian, while others maintain that Christ's church is invisible and cannot be adequately identified during this earthly pilgrimage.[11]

In addition to these struggles, Christians do not agree on common criteria to distinguish legitimate and illegitimate diversity.[12] As Christians struggle to understand their community in relationship to other Christian communities, this document suggests that they consider the following questions: "'How can we identify the church which the creed calls one, holy, catholic, and apostolic?' 'What is God's will for the unity of this church?' 'What do we need to do to put God's will into practice?'"[13]

To engage these questions, the authors suggest several starting points, many of which overlap to some degree with the models that Dulles provides. They include consideration of the missionary nature of the church, the church as Communion, the church "as the pilgrim people moving towards the kingdom

10. The World Council of Churches, an organization dedicated to the realization of Christian unity, fosters ecumenical dialogue on a variety of topics of difference among Christian churches. It describes itself as "a community of churches on the way to visible unity in one faith and one eucharistic fellowship, expressed in worship and in common life in Christ. It seeks to advance towards this unity, as Jesus prayed for his followers, 'so that the world may believe' (John 17:21)." World Council of Churches, https://www.oikoumene.org/en/about-us. The WCC is thus not itself a church, but rather an organization that helps Christians of various denominations to speak frankly about their differences in doctrine and in practice in order to seek greater unity. This practice of ecumenical dialogue, or dialogue between Christians of different denominations, is distinct from interreligious dialogue that takes place between people of different religions, such as between Christians and Hindus. Ecumenical dialogue builds on a shared religious tradition and seeks to advance understanding of Christian doctrine and practice through conversation and, most often, with a goal of greater unity.
11. WCC, *Common Vision*, par. 10.
12. WCC, *Common Vision*, par. 30.
13. WCC, *Common Vision*, par. 10.

of God," and the "ways in which the church relates to the world as a sign and agent of God's love, such as proclaiming Christ within an interreligious context, witnessing to the moral values of the Gospel, and responding to human suffering and need."[14] Communities might ask which image fits them most naturally, which image they would like to strive to embody, or which image they see most clearly reflected in other communities around them.

Intersection: How Ecclesiology Correlates with Worship Practice

Theological conversations about liturgy and ecclesiology most often take place in connection with the images of church as communion or of church as a sign and instrument of God's love proclaiming Christ. Some of the earliest Christian liturgical documents point to the early significance of an understanding of the church as communion. Throughout Christian history, theologians have asked and answered questions about the relationship between the church gathered for worship and the church operative in the world. In the contemporary context, the prayers and practices that some churches use regularly in worship can also shed light on a community's or denomination's self-understanding.

In the *Didache*, a church order that scholars date to late first- or early second-century Syria,[15] an early liturgical prayer sets up the comparison between bread that is blessed and the grains of wheat that contribute to it. This ancient text says, "As this fragment of bread [broken bread] was scattered upon the mountains and was gathered to become one, so may your church be gathered together from the ends of the earth into your kingdom. . . . Let no one eat or drink from your thanksgiving meal unless they have been baptized in the name of the Lord" (*Did.* 9:4–5).[16] The communion of the church is of central importance here. We do not know exactly how the authors of this text envisioned "your church," and yet it is clear that they are thinking beyond themselves to "the ends of the earth." In the liturgical celebration, the unity of the scattered church is compared to the unity of the one loaf of bread, made from many grains, that will be broken and shared among the people gathered.

14. WCC, *Common Vision*, par. 2. As a convergence document, the text recognizes that, while most denominations can agree that each of these approaches has something to contribute to the ecclesiological conversation, there will be similarities and differences in the aspects that they emphasize.

15. Maxwell Johnson, *The Rites of Christian Initiation*, rev. ed. (Collegeville, MN: Liturgical Press, 2007), 43–47.

16. Bart D. Ehrman, "Didache," in *Lost Scriptures: Books That Did Not Make It into the New Testament* (New York: Oxford University Press, 2003), 215.

The meaning of baptism is not discussed in detail in this text, but this discussion of the Eucharist seems to reflect a right for those baptized to participate.

This requirement, which continues to be applied in many, but not all, Christian churches today, can be understood via the metaphor of the body of Christ as discussed in the First Letter to the Corinthians. Through baptism one becomes a member, or "part" of the body of Christ. Paul describes baptism "into one body" in the Spirit (1 Cor. 12:13), concluding, "Now you are the body of Christ, and individually members of it. And God has appointed in the church first apostles, second prophets, third teachers; then deeds of power, then gifts of healing, forms of assistance, forms of leadership, various kinds of tongues" (12:27–28). There is thus a link between baptism, the eucharistic Communion, the image of Communion in church as the body of Christ, and the various roles and responsibilities that individuals take up in the church. In our contemporary context, these roles are reflected in the value that different types of Christians place on evangelization, prophetic speech or actions, teaching, health care, administration, and charismatic gifts such as speaking in tongues.

Another quite early liturgical text that emphasizes the link between the liturgical assembly and the larger Christian community is found in Justin Martyr's *First Apology*, which dates to Rome in the middle of the second century AD. Justin describes the liturgical celebration that is held on Sunday, explaining that after the leader has offered "up prayers and thanksgivings to the best of his ability, and the people assent, saying the Amen, . . . the distribution and the partaking of the eucharistized elements is to each, and to those who are absent a portion is sent by the deacons."[17] The *Didache* emphasizes that the eucharistic Communion is like the church scattered over the hillsides. Justin emphasizes that those who are scattered and not able to be present should be sent a portion so that they can share in Communion with those who have gathered. There is also evidence that some early Christians exchanged consecrated bread between communities as a sign of their unity.[18]

Over the centuries, many theologians (of different denominations and with different starting points) have reflected on the meaning of the church in light of the liturgical practices and prayer of Christians.[19] In the contemporary theo-

---

17. Justin Martyr, *First Apology*, in *St. Justin Martyr: The First and Second Apologies*, trans. and ed. Leslie William Barnard (Mahwah, NJ: Paulist Press, 1997), par. 67.

18. Michael Fahey notes that "Eusebius records this practice in citing a letter from Irenaeus to Victor concerning an Easter controversy." "Church," in *Systematic Theology: Roman Catholic Perspectives*, ed. Francis Schüssler Fiorenza and John P. Galvin (Minneapolis: Fortress, 1991), 26.

19. For example, Martin Luther understood the church as "the communion of those who hear the gospel and believe in it." See Dorothea Wendebourg, "The Church in the Magisterial Reformers," in *The Oxford Handbook of Ecclesiology* (Oxford: Oxford University Press, 2018),

logical conversation, Wolfhart Pannenberg links eschatology and sacrament, declaring that "the church's most authentic way to be an eschatological sign is thus to worship God in its liturgical life, because through the proclamation of the gospel in Word and sacrament the church points most clearly to its future goal and hope in God's kingdom."[20] This approach offers a way of linking an eschatological understanding of the kingdom of God to the Sunday worship of a community. Ecclesiologist Richard McBrien links liturgy and Christian service as ways that Christians "acknowledge the Lordship of Jesus . . . and, through the power of the Holy Spirit . . . collaborate with Jesus' historic mission for the sake of the Kingdom of God."[21] Liturgical actions thus link past and future, worship and service, for the sake of the kingdom of God.

The liturgy also serves to ground and inform Christian understandings of church in the worshiping community. Indicators of liturgical ecclesiology can be found in the Creed (as was my childhood experience), in the intercessions, in the eucharistic prayers, and in communal song. In the Creed, Christians profess faith in the one, holy, catholic, and apostolic church. These "marks" of the church date back to the early centuries of Christianity.[22] Christians affirm that the church is one, emphasizing the importance of Christian unity even when denominations differ doctrinally. They also affirm that the church is holy, even though members of the church are known to do sinful things. When the Creed speaks of the church as "catholic," it does not mean that the whole church is *Roman* Catholic or *Coptic* Catholic or *Byzantine* Catholic. Instead, it refers to an ancient Christian understanding of the universal church, or the church spread throughout the world. Finally, the Creed indicates that the church is apostolic. It was founded by the apostles and has been handed on to us today. While some Christians emphasize the importance of apostolic succession or the ability to trace the ordination of bishops all the way back to the apostles, other Christians accept a more general understanding of the church's apostolic origins and are less concerned about the exact succession.

---

219. John Calvin's ecclesiology was also rooted in a liturgical understanding: "Wherever we see the Word of God purely preached and heard, and the sacraments administered according to Christ's institution, there it is not to be doubted, a church of God exists." *Institutes of the Christian Religion*, trans. John Allen, 7th American ed., 2 vols. (Philadelphia: Presbyterian Board of Christian Education, 1936), 4.1.9.

20. Friederike Nüssel, "Wolfhart Pannenberg," in *The Oxford Handbook of Ecclesiology* (Oxford: Oxford University Press, 2018), 488–89.

21. Richard P. McBrien, *The Church: The Evolution of Catholicism* (New York: Harper-Collins, 2008), 3.

22. William Madges, "An Historical Overview," in *The Many Marks of the Church*, ed. William Madges and Michael J. Daley (New London, CT: Twenty-Third Publications, 2006), 9. See also WCC, *Common Vision*, par. 22.

In addition to the proclamation of the Creed, denominations that use a set format for the "Universal Prayers" or "General Intercessions" usually begin with a petition for the church. The petitions proceed from universal to local, with prayers for the church followed by prayers for the world (or specifically for the earth), for governments, for local leaders and issues, and then to petitions for the specific community itself. Such petitions often include prayers for members of the community who are absent due to illness or travel. Some communities also offer prayers for the dead or for those who mourn. Sequentially, the church is thus presented as *more* universal than any other group; yet subsequent petitions might be for individuals and groups that do not necessarily share the Christian faith of those gathered.

In modern liturgies the church is also mentioned explicitly or implicitly in the Eucharistic Prayer, following the words of institution and the memorial in what is sometimes known as the second epiclesis. In Rite II of the Episcopal Church's Book of Common Prayer, for example, we find the following:

> Recalling his death,
> resurrection, and ascension, we offer you these gifts.
> Sanctify them by your Holy Spirit to be for your people the
> Body and Blood of your Son, the holy food and drink of new
> and unending life in him. Sanctify us also that we may faithfully
> receive this holy Sacrament, and serve you in unity, constancy,
> and peace; and at the last day bring us with all your saints
> into the joy of your eternal kingdom.[23]

This prayer links the "gifts" and "your people," asking that the community be made holy to both receive the sacrament and to serve God in unity until the end of time. The Roman Catholic church's Eucharistic Prayer II follows a similar structure:

> Humbly we pray
> That, partaking of the Body and Blood of Christ,
> We may be gathered into one by the Holy Spirit.
> Remember, Lord, your church,
> Spread throughout the world,
> And bring her to the fullness of charity
> Together with N. our Pope, and N. our Bishop
> And all the clergy.[24]

23. "Holy Eucharist II," in *The Book of Common Prayer* (New York: Church Hymnal, 1979), 362.

24. "Eucharistic Prayer II," in *The Roman Missal: English Translation according to the Third Typical Edition*, trans. International Commission on English in the Liturgy, study ed.

In this latter case, although the explicit mention of "church" might seem to be the more significant ecclesiological moment in the prayer, the petition that both prayers include for the Holy Spirit to "sanctify . . . that we may serve you in unity" or that "we may be gathered into one by the Holy Spirit" are of greater theological significance. Asking God to "remember" the church is one indication of universality, but praying for the Holy Spirit to unite us in the Communion of the body and blood of Christ speaks to a deeper form of unity than the structural unity symbolized by the mention of church leaders. This sense of unity is also evident in denominations that value extemporaneous and nonscripted prayer[25] as itself evidence for the unifying presence of the Holy Spirit.

Finally, liturgical actions such as communal song, sometimes accompanied by procession or gesture, also evoke a community's understanding of itself as church. This might happen through use of songs or hymns that depict particular images of church or understandings of mission.[26] Congregational songs and hymns that are not explicitly ecclesiological also form communities as expressions of praise, worship, thanksgiving, and intercession that are deeply personal and at the same time deeply communal.[27] Through repetition and shared movement, worshipers are formed into a unity that is physical, psychological, and spiritual. In the case of the many hymns that are shared across denominations, such communal singing also becomes a sign and cause of the depths of Christian unity even where doctrinal differences exist.

Implications for Leading and Worship

Everyone has an ecclesiology. Many people do not know that they have one, nor do they know that others around them might have a different operative ecclesiology. Often liturgical disagreements, even within communities that share the same denominational commitments, are rooted in ecclesiological disagreements. A pastoral minister who understands the operative ecclesiologies can help a community to recognize and address the foundational issues

---

(Collegeville, MN: Liturgical Press, 2011), par. 105. Permission for inclusion of this excerpt was obtained from the English translation of The Roman Missal © 2010, International Commission on English in the Liturgy Corporation. All rights reserved.

25. See, e.g., Ruth Duck, *Worship for the Whole People: Vital Worship for the 21st Century* (Louisville: Westminster John Knox, 2013), 198.

26. Judith Kubicki, "Images of Church in Classic Hymnody," *Worship* 84.5 (2010): 432–52.

27. For nonliturgical churches, praise-and-worship music plays an especially important role in forming ecclesial unity. See, e.g., "CCLI Top Songs," SongSelect by CCLI, https://songselect .ccli.com/.

of the disagreement and to move toward a richer understanding of themselves as church. Often this richer understanding will draw from more than one of the ecclesiological images that we have discussed in this essay.

For example, we might think of two neighboring churches of different denominations. One embraces Dulles's servant model and is dedicated to helping the city's poor and suffering. The church hall has been turned into a soup kitchen, and the sanctuary space relies on temporary furniture and folding chairs so that it can easily be converted into a sleeping area on cold winter nights. Members of this church are very politically involved. They can be found protesting on street corners or traveling on mission trips. They are often short on money and have not had a music director in several years. Down the street is another church that emphasizes the communion model. This community puts its resources into facilitating the relationship between God and humanity through their worship. The music and the worship space are uplifting and transcendent. As visitors leave, they talk about how the service left them feeling like they were in heaven. Bible studies and small faith communities support individuals as they forge relationships with one another and learn more about their faith. This community also places a high value on its relationship with other communities in its denomination.

Within both communities, some individuals might find themselves uncomfortable with the dominant ecclesiological model. One longtime member of the first community tries to raise money to redecorate the sanctuary space to make it feel more sacred. She thinks that it would be good to hire a staff member with administrative experience to bring a stronger sense of organization to the church. She would like to be able to share resources more efficiently with other churches in the denomination. Some new members of the second community fear that their church is too inwardly focused; they would like to see a more outward focus on the proclamation of the kingdom of God to their neighbors. They try to organize more opportunities for seekers to engage with the established community, and they have petitioned the pastor to allow one corner of the church hall to be used for a weekly clothing distribution center. Some in their community are concerned that this emphasis on "social justice" is a distraction from the mission of the church.

In each of these somewhat stereotypical examples, it is easy to identify a prevailing ecclesiology. The ecclesiologies influence the worship choices of the community; in turn, these worship choices can bolster the prevailing ecclesiology. It is also clear that in each case the prevailing ecclesiology, while strengthening some aspects of the mission, also has the potential to stifle a deeper understanding of what it means to be church. The first community might neglect the worship life that should be nurturing it as members pour themselves out in service to others. The second community might prize its beautiful worship to the degree that they neglect their other Christian obligations to serve the kingdom of God. Neither choice is necessary.

A thoughtful liturgical leader has many options for helping communities move toward a more integrated ecclesiology and communal life of worship. Such a leader might first reflect, perhaps in conversation with members of the community, on the ways that this specific community thinks about itself as church. Is this self-understanding consistent within the community and in relationship to the doctrine of the denomination (if that question is applicable)? Are there ways the community might grow in its understanding of what it means to be church?

In the specifically liturgical context, communal growth might take place in several ways. Music leaders might consider an analysis of the prevailing ecclesiology of their repertoire. Is greater diversity needed? How are music, lyrics, and participation shaping the community's self-understanding? Liturgical leaders who manage the worship space might consider how the positioning and movement of ministers and assembly support or suppress certain ecclesiologies.

There are also many opportunities for preachers to engage the community regarding its ecclesiology. Some preachers might find ways to connect the Scriptures to the ecclesiology of the Creed, the eucharistic prayers, or the intercessions. They might consider the relationship between the experience of liturgical communion and the communion that is fostered among members of the gathered assembly and even other members who are absent. On the feast or during the season of Pentecost, preachers and other liturgical ministers could deliberately foster reflection on what it means to be church today. The lectionary readings and collects offer a variety of images and models that can help to deepen an operative or unreflective ecclesiology. Celebrations of baptism, especially around the feasts of Epiphany or Easter or Pentecost, could gesture beyond the individual or family and toward the call to collective participation in the mission of Jesus, which began with his own baptism.

Finally, ecclesiologically aware approaches to worship invite the possibility of ecumenical liturgical celebrations that involve more than one denomination or worshiping community. Worshiping together with other Christians, to whatever degree is feasible, invites local communities to greater consciousness of their own beliefs and self-understanding and to a developing sense of the universal church.[28]

---

28. Ecumenical observances of events like the Week of Prayer for Christian Unity provide important opportunities for ecumenical worship and conversation.

For Further Reading

Duck, Ruth. *Worship for the Whole People: Vital Worship for the 21st Century*. Louisville: Westminster John Knox, 2013.

Dulles, Avery. *Models of the Church*. Expanded ed. New York: Random House, 2000.

Kubicki, Judith. "Images of Church in Classic Hymnody." *Worship* 84 (2010): 432–52.

Madges, William, and Michael J. Daley, eds. *The Many Marks of the Church*. New London, CT: Twenty-Third Publications, 2006.

Osiek, Carolyn, and Margaret McDonald. *A Woman's Place: House Churches in Earliest Christianity*. Minneapolis: Fortress, 2006.

World Council of Churches. *Baptism, Eucharist, and Ministry*. Faith and Order Paper No. 111. Geneva: WCC, 1982.

———. *The Church: Towards a Common Vision*, Faith and Order Paper No. 214. Geneva: WCC, 2013.

← 10 →

Mission and Worship

Eugene R. Schlesinger

Theological Overview

Mission occurs at the command of the risen Christ, who tells his disciples, "Go therefore and make disciples of all nations, baptizing them in the name of the Father and of the Son and of the Holy Spirit, and teaching them to obey everything that I have commanded you" (Matt. 28:19–20). Thus all who would claim to be Jesus's disciples must also be missionaries.[1]

Yet mission is more than a matter of mere obedience. It is not just something that the church does. Rather, it expresses what the church is. This understanding is clearly expressed by the Second Vatican Council's Decree on Mission, *Ad gentes*, which states, "The pilgrim church is of its very nature missionary, since it draws its origin from the mission of the Son and the

---

1. On the Great Commission, see, e.g., Craig S. Keener, "Matthew's Missiology: Making Disciples of the Nations (Matthew 28:19–20)," *Asian Journal of Pentecostal Studies* 12, no. 1 (2009): 3–20; David J. Bosch, "The Structure of Mission: An Exposition of Matthew 28:16–20," in *The Study of Evangelism: Exploring a Missional Practice of the Church*, ed. Paul W. Chilcote and Laceye C. Warner (Grand Rapids: Eerdmans, 2008), 73–92. The theme of missionary discipleship is a major emphasis of CELAM [Conselho Episcopal Latino-Americano], "Aparecida [Brazil]: Concluding Document," http://www.celam.org/aparecida/Ingles.pdf; Pope Francis, *Evangelii gaudium*, Nov. 24, 2013, http://w2.vatican.va/content/francesco/en/apost_exhortations/documents/papa-francesco_esortazione-ap_20131124_evangelii-gaudium.html.

mission of the holy Spirit, in accordance with the plan of God the Father."[2] This insight has been embraced by the majority of Christian traditions: in the time between Christ's comings, the church exists in a permanent state of mission.[3]

Mission, though, is a much broader reality than just the activity of the Christian church. As the quote above from *Ad gentes* implies, before mission is ever the act of any human being or community, it is the act of God. The idea of the *missio Dei*, or mission of God, revolutionized mission theology in the twentieth century and beyond.[4] The concept of *missio Dei* quite helpfully moves human endeavors out of the center stage; it recognizes that God is on a mission to redeem the world and that we are invited to share in this mission. Mission aims at the world, rather than stopping at the church, and it is not bound by any human community or institution (though the Christian community is an integral component of that mission).

2. Decree on Mission, *Ad gentes* (Dec. 7, 1965), no. 2; in *Decrees of the Ecumenical Councils*, ed. Norman Tanner (Washington, DC: Georgetown University Press, 1990), 2:1011; cf. http://www.vatican.va/archive/hist_councils/ii_vatican_council/documents/vat-ii_decree_19651207_ad-gentes_en.html.

3. For example, Darrell L. Guder, ed., *Missional Church: A Vision for the Sending of the Church in North America* (Grand Rapids: Eerdmans, 1998); Church of England, *Mission-Shaped Church* (London: Church House, 2004); Paul Avis, *A Ministry Shaped by Mission* (London: T&T Clark, 2005); Lesslie Newbigin, *The Gospel in a Pluralist Society* (Grand Rapids: Eerdmans, 1989), 116–40, 222–41; Ruth A. Meyers, *Missional Worship, Worshipful Mission: Gathering as God's People, Going Out in God's Name* (Grand Rapids: Eerdmans, 2014), 1–23; World Council of Churches, *The Nature and Mission of the Church: A Stage on the Way to a Common Statement*, Faith and Order Paper No. 198 (Geneva: WCC, 2005), nos. 35–47; Ross Hastings, *Missional God, Missional Church: Hope for Re-Evangelizing the West* (Downers Grove, IL: InterVarsity, 2012).

4. The touchstone was the International Missionary Conference held at Willingen in 1952: see *Missions under the Cross: Addresses Delivered at the Enlarged Meeting of the Committee of the International Missionary Council at Willingen, in Germany, 1952; with Statements Issued by the Meeting*, ed. Norman Goodall (London: Edinburgh House, 1953). Mission theology is also strongly developed in *Ad gentes*, nos. 2–5 (in Tanner, *Decrees*, 2:1011–14); Dogmatic Constitution on the Church, *Lumen gentium* (Nov. 21, 1964), nos. 2–4 (in Tanner, *Decrees*, 2:850); Pope John Paul II, *Redemptoris missio: On the Permanent Validity of the Church's Missionary Mandate*, Dec. 7, 1990, nos. 1–2, http://www.vatican.va/holy_father/john_paul_ii/encyclicals/documents/hf_jp-ii_enc_07121990_redemptoris-missio_en.html. See also Wilhelm Andersen, *Towards a Theology of Mission: A Study of the Encounter between the Missionary Enterprise and the Church and Its Theology*, trans. Stephen Neill (London: SCM, 1955); Georg F. Vicedom, *The Mission of God: An Introduction to a Theology of Mission*, trans. Gilbert A. Thiele and Dennis Hilgendorf (St. Louis: Concordia, 1965); Hastings, *Missional God, Missional Church*; Stephen B. Bevans and Roger P. Schroeder, *Constants in Context: A Theology of Mission for Today* (Maryknoll, NY: Orbis Books, 2004), 286–304; John G. Flett, *The Witness of God: The Trinity, Missio Dei, Karl Barth, and the Nature of Christian Community* (Grand Rapids: Eerdmans, 2010).

The idea of the mission of God is a trinitarian concept because the original missions are those of the Son and the Holy Spirit into the world.[5] In the Gospels, Jesus Christ is depicted as being on a mission from God. His Father has sent him, and he delights to do the Father's will (Matt. 10:5–16 par.; Luke 4:18; John 5:17–37; 6:37–59; 8:14–20, 26, 38; 10:14–38; 12:26–28, 49–50; 14–17). As his earthly mission draws to a close, Jesus promises that he and the Father will also send the Holy Spirit, who will lead the church into all truth and empower it to carry out its own mission, which will be analogous to and a continuation of Christ's own (John 14–16; 20:21–22). At the culmination of his mission, his death upon the cross, he announces, "It is finished," signaling that the work given to him by the Father has been completed (John 19:30). Risen from the dead, he breathes forth the Holy Spirit upon his apostles and tells them, "As the Father has sent me, so I send you" (John 20:21).

In the Acts of the Apostles, we read the record of the Christian church's initial expansion as the community pursued the mission entrusted to it by Christ in the power of the promised Holy Spirit. The various letters that comprise the rest of the New Testament are also artifacts of mission, addressed to churches near the Mediterranean, all of which existed as the outcome of missionary outreach. The church's subsequent history is one of continued missionary existence: with varying degrees of success and of faithfulness, the gospel has been preached throughout the world, and Christian communities have been established as outposts of continued mission.[6]

Decentering human activities and institutions, expanding our view beyond the narrow confines of the institutional church, and understanding mission in terms of the *missio Dei* also broaden our conception of what mission is.

5. This theme is developed from Augustine, *The Trinity*, ed. John E. Rotelle, trans. Edmund Hill, 2nd ed., in *The Works of Saint Augustine: A Translation for the 21st Century*, part 1, vol. 5 (Hyde Park, NY: New City Press, 2012); to Thomas Aquinas, *Summa Theologiæ* (Cambridge, UK: Blackfriars, 1964), 1:43. It receives a rather important articulation in Bernard J. F. Lonergan, *The Triune God: Systematics*, trans. Michael G. Shields from *De Deo Trino: Pars Systematica* (1964), ed. Robert M. Doran and H. Daniel Monsour, Collected Works of Bernard Lonergan 12 (Toronto: University of Toronto Press, 2007); and is also a major theme of Hans Urs von Balthasar's "multi-trilogy" of *The Glory of the Lord*, 7 vols.; *Theo-Drama*, 5 vols.; and *Theo-Logic*, 3 vols. (San Francisco: Ignatius, 1982–2004). I discuss it at length in Eugene R. Schlesinger, *Missa Est! A Missional Liturgical Ecclesiology* (Minneapolis: Fortress, 2017), 49–85; and Schlesinger, *Sacrificing the Church: Mass, Mission, and Ecumenism* (Lanham, MD: Lexington/Fortress Academic, 2019), 17–24.

6. See the historical treatments in David J. Bosch, *Transforming Mission: Paradigm Shifts in Theology of Mission* (Maryknoll, NY: Orbis Books, 2004); Stanley H. Skreslet, *Comprehending Mission: The Questions, Methods, Themes, Problems, and Prospects of Missiology* (Maryknoll, NY: Orbis Books, 2012); Michael W. Goheen, *Introducing Christian Mission Today: Scripture, History and Issues* (Downers Grove, IL: InterVarsity, 2014); Scott W. Sunquist, *Understanding Christian Mission: Participation in Suffering and Glory* (Grand Rapids: Baker Academic, 2013).

Because "mission" refers to all that God is doing to restore the world to himself, it is necessarily a holistic endeavor.[7] We cannot reduce it to mere evangelization or "saving souls" to the exclusion of correcting injustices, caring for the poor and marginalized, feeding the hungry, reconciling groups that are at enmity with each other, protecting and preserving the natural environment, and so on. The mission of God aims at the full flourishing of the human family, and indeed, the created order. Therefore, so must the church's mission aim.

Christ came announcing the reign of God (e.g., Matt. 4:17; Luke 4:43). His inaugural sermon in Nazareth was a manifesto of his mission. Quoting from Isaiah 61:1–2, Jesus reads: "The Spirit of the Lord is upon me, because he has anointed me to bring good news to the poor. He has sent me to proclaim release to the captives and recovery of sight to the blind, to let the oppressed go free, to proclaim the year of the Lord's favor." Then Jesus declares that this Scripture is fulfilled in himself (Luke 4:18–20). With these words, Jesus indicates that his mission will involve economic and political dimensions (the poor, release of the captives and the oppressed), physical health (sight for the blind), and spiritual realities (the Lord's favor). It is a holistic endeavor: leaving off any of these aspects amounts to engaging in something less than the mission Jesus undertook and into which he recruits his followers by commanding them to teach others to observe all that he has commanded (Matt. 28:18–20).

The church's mission has not always been conducted faithfully. At times it has been used as a tool of colonial expansion or an instrument of oppression. At times various Western and European values have been confused with the gospel and imposed upon indigenous peoples in the name of Christ. At times Christians have judged that the world was adequately evangelized and slowed their missionary activity to a trickle. But through it all, the mission of God has continued. The fact that a Christian is writing this chapter and there are other Christians to read it is a testament to that ongoing mission. As Jesus himself indicated in his Great Commission, this is an undertaking that will encompass the entire world and last until the end of time (Matt. 28:19–20).

7. This holistic understanding of mission is affirmed by Catholic, evangelical, and ecumenical statements. For Catholic statements, see Pope Paul VI, *Evangelii nuntiandi*, Dec. 8, 1975, http://www.vatican.va/holy_father/paul_vi/apost_exhortations/documents/hf_p-vi_exh_1975 1208_evangelii-nuntiandi_en.html; John Paul II, *Redemptoris missio*; Pope Francis, *Evangelii gaudium*. For an evangelical statement, see Lausanne Movement, "The Cape Town Commitment," 2010, http://www.lausanne.org/content/ctc/ctcommitment. For ecumenical statements, see World Council of Churches, "Mission and Evangelism in Unity Today," *International Review of Mission* 88 (1999): 109–27; World Council of Churches, "Together Towards Life: Mission and Evangelism in Changing Landscapes," Sept. 5, 2012, https://www.oikoumene.org/en/re sources/documents/commissions/mission-and-evangelism/together-towards-life-mission-and -evangelism-in-changing-landscapes.

Intersection: How Mission Correlates with Worship Practice

Worship and mission are joined by the most intimate of bonds, for they are both expressive of the same purpose: the return of creatures to the God who made them. They are, moreover, both perfectly accomplished by Jesus Christ, in whom the church's worship is acceptable to God and at whose command the church engages in its mission. Worship and mission, while distinguishable from each other, are mutually implicated realities. The church's worship depends upon a prior mission and necessarily leads its participants to engage in mission, yet without subordinating the one to the other.

As was noted above, the origin of all mission is the *missio Dei*, "mission of God," by which God moves beyond Godself and into the world he has created in order to bring that creation into union with himself. Through the missions of the Son and Holy Spirit, human creatures are caught up into the life of God, reconciled to our Creator, and elevated beyond what we would be capable of by nature, even if our nature had remained unfallen. Our sharing in the divine mission leads us at once into both worship and mission.

Jesus's mission reaches its culmination in his cry upon the cross, "It is finished." By this singular act, he has accomplished the mission given to him by the Father, reconciling humanity to God. This completion of Christ's mission is also a perfect act of worship, as attested in those traditions that understand Jesus's death as sacrificial (Rom. 3:25; 1 Cor. 5:7; Eph. 5:2; Hebrews; 1 John 2:2; 4:10) and in Jesus's own high-priestly prayer in John 17.

This unity of worship and mission can also be discerned in the Pauline letters, where Paul interprets his own apostolic mission, and support for it, in terms drawn from the world of the temple. It is a liturgy (service: Rom. 15:27; 2 Cor. 9:12; Phil. 2:25, 30), a libation (Phil. 2:17), and a sacrifice offered to God (Phil. 4:18). It aims at making acceptable the "offering of the Gentiles" (Rom. 15:16–17), suggesting that the objects of the church's mission are themselves the matter of a sacrifice offered to God. Indeed, the whole of the Christian life can be construed as a sacrifice (Rom. 12:1), with mission as one particular application of this principle.[8] That they are bound together is clear enough, but their precise relationship needs to be more clearly specified or we risk serious distortions.

---

8. See Robert Jewett, *Romans: A Commentary*, ed. Eldon Jay Epp, Hermeneia (Minneapolis: Fortress, 2007), 724–31, 906–8. This position is further refined by Augustine, *The City of God (I–X)*, ed. Boniface Ramsey, trans. William Babcock, *Works of Saint Augustine*, part 1, vol. 6 (Hyde Park, NY: New City Press, 2012), 10.3–6. Once more, I discuss this at length in Schlesinger, *Sacrificing the Church*, 38–44, 110–16.

Worship Depends on Mission

Every act of Christian worship is preceded by mission, and this can be seen in two primary ways. First, all Christian worship is preceded by mission because it is the result of the divine missions of the Son and Holy Spirit. The church is a creature of the divine missions, and only because of them is there a church to offer worship.[9] This leads us to the second way in which worship is preceded by mission: Christianity is not a natural state but rather a supernatural gift of God. The Christian community, which offers God worship, receives its competency to do so through the sacrament of baptism, which both empowers and obliges its recipients to offer worship to God through Christ.

Baptism points us to the centrality of conversion for the Christian life. This is especially evident when the person baptized is an adult convert to the faith, yet it is still the case when infant baptism is practiced. Baptism entails a turning away from sin and toward Christ, a radical new beginning, a passage from death into life in union with Christ (Acts 2:38; Rom. 6:3–14; Col. 2:11–13). This is given particularly strong expression in those traditions where baptism is celebrated with its traditional renunciations of sin and the devil's power, and with affirmations of faith in Christ, but this new beginning is also implicit in other manners of practicing baptism. To be baptized is to be converted, and this conversion is the outcome of mission. Only as the church proclaims the gospel of Christ are women and men converted, baptized, and brought to share in the worship of the church.

Worship Leads to Mission

Just as every act of worship is preceded by mission, so every act of worship leads back into mission. The Catholic Mass derives its name from this reality. The announcement "Go forth, the Mass is ended,"[10] translates the Latin phrase, *Ite, missa est*, which contains a command to go (*ite*) along with the recognition that this going is not just a departure but also a being sent

---

9. This is the outcome of the emphasis on the *missio Dei* and is clearly articulated in Vatican II's *Lumen gentium*, nos. 1–4 (in Tanner, *Decrees*, 2:849–52), which on this score reflects the mainstream of theological opinion.

10. *The Roman Missal: Renewed by Decree of the Most Holy Second Ecumenical Council of the Vatican, Promulgated by Authority of Pope Paul VI and Revised at the Direction of Pope John Paul II*, Third Typical Edition (Collegeville, MN: Liturgical Press, 2011), no. 144. See further Patrick Chukwudezie Chibuko, "*Ite Missa Est*—Go, the Mass Is Ended: Implications for Missionary Activities in the Third Millennium Church," *Questions Liturgiques* 86, no. 1 (2005): 57–82; Joseph C. Koechel, "'*Ite Missa Est*' and Catholic Action," *Orate Fratres* 11, no. 5 (March 21, 1937): 206–8; Gerald T. Chinchar, "The Missiology of the Concluding Rite of the Mass of the Roman Rite," *Liturgical Ministry* 11 (2002): 45–46, http://www.naal-liturgy.org /pav/docs/seminars/formation/chinchar2002.pdf.

on mission (*missa*). The specific vocabulary of the Catholic liturgy makes this dynamic especially evident, but it is also at work in other traditions and patterns of worship.

In worship, the Christian community enacts the outcome of mission, the return of creatures to the God who has both made them and redeemed them. This return to God, though, is not unidirectional, because it is the result of and shares in the *missio Dei*, which aims at the redemption of the entire world not just the church. Christ came forth from the Father and returned to him. His path of return to the Father was the way of his mission. The return to God is necessarily bidirectional. This is evident in the way in which Christ offers himself to the disciples at the Last Supper, "This is my body, . . . given for you" (Luke 22:19; cf. 1 Cor. 11:24), and to the Father upon the cross. These two self-offerings of Christ are not actually two, but one. It is precisely in giving himself to the disciples that Christ makes his return to the Father. It is precisely in his mission that he makes his return. As we return to God, united to Christ, the same will also be the case for us.[11]

Worship anticipates the consummation of all things. The book of Revelation is, rightly, associated with the end, for it closes with a vision of the resurrection of the dead, the final judgment, and the final perfected state of creation (Rev. 19–22). Yet crucially and fundamentally, Revelation is a book of worship, filled with visions of the heavenly liturgy, which punctuate and celebrate God's activity throughout the book (Rev. 4:8–11; 5:8–14; 7:9–12; 11:15–18; 14:1–5; 15:2–8; 19:1–8), and culminates in a vision in which the entire cosmos has become a temple of worship to God (Rev. 21:22–22:5). The church's celebration of the Eucharist "proclaim[s] the Lord's death until he comes" (1 Cor. 11:26). The eschaton and worship are intertwined because in the end all shall be worship. And this crucially connects us to mission.

When God's reign has arrived in its eschatological perfection, all will be reconciled to God. This refers, of course, to the restoration of women and men to a right relationship to God, but also to the righting of all wrongs. Salvation is holistic, pertaining to all aspects of humanity: spiritual and corporeal, personal and social.[12] So long as the present reality falls short of this perfection, the mission must continue. To celebrate one's reconciliation with

11. Schlesinger, *Missa Est!*, 145–49; Schlesinger, *Sacrificing the Church*, 104–10, 113–16.

12. As a classic expression of this view, see Henri de Lubac, *Catholicism: Christ and the Common Destiny of Man*, trans. Lancelot C. Sheppard and Elizabeth Englund (San Francisco: Ignatius, 1998). See also the way this insight about holistic salvation is developed by Gustavo Gutiérrez, *A Theology of Liberation: History, Politics, Salvation*, trans. Caridad Inda and John Eagleson, 15th anniv. ed. (Maryknoll, NY: Orbis Books, 1988); Ignacio Ellacuría, *Freedom Made Flesh: The Mission of Christ and His Church*, trans. John Drury (Maryknoll, NY: Orbis Books, 1976).

God in worship and then rest content with a state of affairs in which others remain alienated from him, or where injustices go unchallenged, is a performative contradiction. To share in Christ is to share in his mission.

Worship and Mission Should Not Be Confused

Given the close relationship between worship and mission we have discerned, it might seem as though worship and mission could be treated as synonyms. However, if we do this we run the very real risk of doing neither worship nor mission especially well (if at all). Stephen Neill put his finger on one aspect of this problem: "If everything is mission then nothing is mission."[13] For instance, consider a church that understands everything it does to be "mission." One might think that such a church would faithfully carry out the mission entrusted to it by God. Yet when anything and everything the church happens to be doing counts as mission, it is quite easy for key aspects of mission to fall by the wayside, ironically in the name of mission. For example, a church with a predilection for evangelistic proclamation might emphasize that but neglect matters of justice, which are also dimensions of the *missio Dei*. Or conversely, a justice-oriented church might do a fine job of advocating for and standing in solidarity with those at the margins, just as Jesus did, yet neglect the proclamation of his death and resurrection. Or a church might decide that its primary mission is to offer worship to God and/or formation to those who are already Christian. Each of these communities understands itself to be doing mission; none of them is carrying out that mission as fully as they ought. When everything is mission, though, it can be difficult to discern this. By distinguishing worship from mission, we avoid clutter and can better see the parameters of mission.

Similarly, when we fail to distinguish worship and mission, our practice of worship can become distorted. This could take the form of neglecting the church's liturgies (I use the term broadly to include all patterns of worship, even those of "nonliturgical" churches), because mission is itself a form of worship. Or it could take the form of repurposing the church's liturgies so that they do the work of mission. Although all worship has a missional dimension and should be undertaken with a sensitivity to the presence of non-Christians, to repurpose worship in this way runs the risk of idolatry, since worship is directed from its proper end of giving glory to God. To treat worship as a means to an end is deeply problematic because it reduces God to a means to some other end. Again, by differentiating between worship and mission, we are better able to engage in both.

13. Stephen Neill, *Creative Tension* (London: Edinburgh House, 1959), 81.

And so we ought to see worship and mission as intrinsically related, yet distinct from each other. By stating that they are intrinsically linked, we affirm that they are inseparable. An extrinsic relationship would allow us to have either worship or mission, or perhaps both, but without seeing any necessary relationship between the two. An intrinsic relationship recognizes the dynamic we have seen where mission leads to worship (because it aims at our restoration to God) and where worship leads to mission (because it anticipates a state of affairs that has not yet been fully realized). It moreover allows us to see a couple of especially pertinent points of contact.

Consider, for instance, the sacrament of baptism. On the one hand, it is an act of worship. It brings people into the church, involves prayer to God, and is among the church's sacraments. Most baptisms occur as part of the liturgy of worshiping communities. The exemplar of all Christian baptism, Christ's own baptism, gave expression to God's delight in Christ as his well-beloved Son, and the Son's own devotion to his Father, all of which lie at the heart of worship (Matt. 3; Luke 3).

At the same time, though, baptism is an aspect of the church's mission. In his Great Commission to the church, Jesus instructs us to carry out the mission of "mak[ing] disciples of all nations, [by] baptizing them" in the name of the Trinity (Matt. 28:19). The church's mission involves more than baptism, but the church cannot pursue this mission apart from baptism. As Christians proclaim the gospel and call women and men to repentance, baptism is the outcome. And so baptism, which belongs to both, is especially expressive of this intrinsic relationship between worship and mission.

Different Approaches to Understanding Mission

Even with these parameters about the importance of distinguishing between worship and mission while also upholding their intrinsic relationship, there is still a fairly wide range of ways in which churches might live out their relationship. For instance, one might view worship as an opportunity for mission. In such a case, one recognizes that at any given liturgy, some non-Christians may be present, and so believers lean into the liturgy's potential for evangelization. The way the church worships is, or should be, informed by the gospel that the church believes. The Scriptures read, sermons preached, music sung: all give expression to the saving work of Christ. The sacraments' celebration likewise is expressive of Jesus's death and resurrection (e.g., Rom. 6:3–5; 1 Cor. 11:26). In traditions that foreground an individual conversion experience, explicit invitations to make a Christian commitment might be regular features of worship services. Some churches promote inviting one's friends to church as an evangelistic strategy. By bringing friends, one ensures that they will hear the gospel and be invited to believe it.

Depending upon a given community's relationship to historical patterns of worship, such an understanding might take other forms as well. For instance, in a church where traditional liturgies are either highly valued or mandated, sensitivity to people for whom all this is new might lead them to provide explanations (written or verbal) of the meaning and purpose of various liturgical elements (e.g., the sign of the cross, Gospel procession, eucharistic prayers). In a church where historic liturgies are optional, or even looked upon with some suspicion, worship might take on other cultural forms (e.g., a concert), so as to be more familiar, allowing for fewer distractions from the evangelistic appeals that will be made.

Another common approach is to see the church's worship as a formative preparation for mission. Recognizing that the days are probably gone when curious non-Christians are likely to come to a church's liturgies in any significant numbers, a church might utilize its worship to equip its members to engage in mission in their neighborhoods, workplaces, and third spaces (coffee shops, bars, and the like). In such an approach, the instruction offered in sermons might emphasize the responsibilities of Christian disciples to engage the world for the better, and especially to do so in the name of Christ and with the gospel on their lips.

Depending upon a church's understanding of the nature of mission, these exhortations could include or emphasize different elements. Churches more oriented toward the concrete, social justice–oriented aspects of mission might promote organizations aligned with these priorities, or even initiatives of the church community itself. Churches more oriented toward the spiritual dimensions of mission might offer programs designed to make parishioners comfortable with initiating spiritual conversations or sharing and explaining the gospel to those who do not yet believe. Ideally, churches will emphasize both, because, as we have seen, the mission into which God invites his people is a holistic reality.

Still others might not make any explicit connection between the church's mission and its worship. This can happen either in the arena of worship or of mission. Christians might engage in mission without explicitly relating their mission back to the church's worshiping life. For instance, one might volunteer at a soup kitchen or build homes for Habitat for Humanity out of a sincere Christian conviction that this service is part of one's mission from Christ, yet not seek to connect those one serves to the life of the church. Or one might engage in evangelism, calling upon people to exercise faith in Christ, but have little concern for those people's ongoing Christian discipleship beyond their "getting saved."

Conversely, churches might engage in their liturgical life without ever explicitly mentioning their mission to the world. This is rather difficult to do in a church that follows traditional liturgies, for they all make some application to the missionary task in their prayers and biddings, but it is possible to make no more application beyond this. Such a lack of direct application may stem from a sense of antipathy toward mission, since some churches are increasingly uncomfortable about proselyting, but this is not necessarily the case. There might be an assumption (perhaps even accurate) that the mission is happening and that there is no need to belabor it in worship, which has a distinct purpose, after all.

These possibilities, of course, exist along a spectrum, and no doubt churches from all traditions can be found at various points within or between them. All of them are defensible in their own ways, so long as neither worship nor mission are neglected. However, some direct and explicit connection between the two is probably for the best, given their intrinsic connection. This is all the more important as the cultures of the Northern and Western hemispheres become decreasingly Christianized, making the missionary task all the more imperative and assumptions about anyone's Christian commitment tenuous.[14]

In all this, though, it is important to avoid an instrumentalized account of the relationship between liturgy and mission.[15] This is a particular danger in the first two approaches: worship as an opportunity for mission, and worship as formative preparation for mission. If one is not careful, such approaches could lead to a loss of worship's properly doxological end. Worship is offered for the glory of God and must not be relegated to the level of a means to some other end, even an end as important as mission, even an end as close to the priorities of God as mission. Therein lies idolatry. This does not suggest that such approaches are necessarily and inescapably idolatrous, but the worshiping community must be vigilant in guarding against any temptation toward a missionary idolatry within its worship.

14. Charles Taylor, *A Secular Age* (Cambridge, MA: Harvard University Press, 2007); John Milbank, *Theology and Social Theory: Beyond Secular Reason*, 2nd ed. (Oxford: Blackwell, 2006); Alasdair MacIntyre, *After Virtue: A Study in Moral Theory*, 3rd ed. (Notre Dame, IN: University of Notre Dame Press, 2007); Catherine Pickstock, *After Writing: On the Liturgical Consummation of Philosophy* (Oxford: Blackwell, 1998), 3–166.

15. See Nathan R. Kerr, *Christ, History and Apocalyptic: The Politics of Christian Mission*, Theopolitical Visions (Eugene, OR: Cascade Books, 2009).

Concern for the Community

When considering the relation between worship and mission, concern for the community takes on a twofold character because two overlapping communities are in view. Let us begin with the worshiping community, people beloved by God, created in his image, and redeemed by his Son. They have been brought into the Christian community as the outcome of its mission. For them, worship is to express their gratitude and love for God, to deepen their connection to him, to enact their return to him, and to anticipate the end when all shall be worship. Whatever missionary dimensions of worship one may wish to accentuate, it must not be at the expense of the proper worship, which is the right and the duty of the gathered community to offer.

At the same time, the people who make up the worshiping community have a missional responsibility. As disciples of Christ, they are called upon to engage the world in his name, to proclaim the gospel, and to work for the good. Oftentimes Christians would like to share their faith but are unsure how to do that. Exhortations to engage in mission are well and good, but they probably are not needed, at least not in the sense of informing Christians of a responsibility they did not know was theirs. Poorly done, such exhortations will amount to little more than "piling on," further troubling already troubled consciences. Instead, leaders may need to make more explicit connections between what occurs in worship and the mission to which Christians are called so the missionary task can be kept at the forefront without becoming an exercise in redundancy or a source of increased guilt. The church's worship rehearses and reinforces the truth of salvation. As Christians are helped to see the connection between their calling as missionaries and as worshipers, they can come to realize that they are better equipped for mission than they had previously suspected.

The other community to keep in view is the community beyond the church, which is likewise beloved by God, who has sent his Son to redeem it. Crucially, this community overlaps with the church. These two communities are not in tension or opposition. The church is part of the world and, as a missionary church, is called to be in service to the world. As the church engages in its mission, people are brought into its fellowship. This is not as an end in itself because the church's mission aims beyond the church to the reign of God, but it still is an aspect of how that mission unfolds: "Make disciples of all nations, baptizing them" (Matt. 28:19). This being the case, the church's worship should be offered with sensitivity to the surrounding community. Worship can and should be properly enculturated rather than simply reproducing the cultural forms of times and places that lack relevance to the community (whether they be ancient or modern, European or other).[16]

Enculturation can be done well or poorly. Done poorly, it can be little more than cultural appropriation; it can fail to adequately embody the new culture, or it can embrace the local culture while losing sight of Christian distinctives and so become little more than syncretism. Done well, it will resemble what Bernard Lonergan describes: "The Christian message is to be communicated to all nations. Such communication presupposes that preachers and teachers enlarge their horizons to include an accurate and intimate understanding of the culture and the language of the people they address. They must grasp the virtual resources of that culture and that language, and they must use those virtual resources creatively so that the Christian message becomes, not disruptive of the culture, not an alien patch superimposed upon it, but a line of development within the culture."[17] There is no ready-made form for inculturation. One must deeply inhabit both the Christian gospel and the culture in which it is to be given expression.

Practical Implications of Mission in Worship

From these theological and missiological considerations, we can draw two primary practical conclusions to guide worship leaders. First, we ought to be sensitive to the missionary task and be aware of the connection between worship and mission. The church has the twin purposes of worship and of mission. These purposes form a unity and should not be opposed to each other. Mission, among other things, leads to worship as God's redemptive work extends further into the world, and people are brought into the church as an outcome of mission. By the same token, worship leads to mission. As our priorities are realigned with God's, we cannot rest content but must join God in the mission he is already pursuing in the world. The Lord's Prayer, which appears in so many Christian liturgies, gives some expression to this: until God's kingdom comes in its fulness, until God's will is done on earth as it is in heaven, the church's mission continues. What we pray for in worship, we must enact in mission.

Therefore, worship leaders should seek to make this connection visible. Most Christians have a sense that what they do in worship should inform

16. Lamin Sanneh, *Translating the Message: The Missionary Impact on Culture*, 2nd ed. (Maryknoll, NY: Orbis Books, 2009); Stephan B. Bevans, *Models of Contextual Theology* (Maryknoll, NY: Orbis Books, 1992).

17. Bernard J. F. Lonergan, *Method in Theology* (Toronto: University of Toronto Press, 1971), 362, emphasis added.

their lives for the other 167 hours each week. Leaders should help them to see that missionary engagement is among the ways worship should impinge upon "real life." This can take the form of giving a missionary application to elements of worship (such as I have done with the Lord's Prayer, above), or exhortations to the effect that what the Christian community celebrates in its worship is news worth sharing and embodying in the world. At the same time, worship leaders should be careful not to force this connection or to guilt-trip parishioners. There are enough natural points of contact that we do not need to make tendentious connections. The goal is to make visible what is already there.

Above, I noted different ways in which churches might adapt their worship to be more hospitable to newcomers and outsiders. In doing this, we should remember that all worship, however enculturated and contextualized, will be somewhat foreign to non-Christians. Christianity is not anyone's natural state. Instead, we must convert to be Christians. Thus we need not fear that our liturgies may be unfamiliar or strange to those outside our community. Nothing we do can avoid this. Instead, we should strive to be welcoming and be ready to explain what we are doing and why we do it.

Second, we should let worship be worship and mission be mission. Though they are inseparably united, these are two distinct realities. If we try to make worship do the work that properly belongs to mission, we will lose sight of its true purpose, the glory of God, and will wind up doing neither mission nor worship very well. Waiting for people to show up at church before we engage in mission is a singularly ineffective approach; making worship's purpose to be mission relegates God to a subsidiary role. Instead, trust that worship is a worthy goal. It is, in fact, the worthiest of goals. As we plan worship and offer worship to God, and as we make the connections between worship and mission clear, trust that God is already more committed to his own mission than we ever possibly could be. He desires to recruit us to share in this mission. And he will do so. As Jesus said, "The harvest truly is plenteous, but the labourers are few; pray ye therefore the Lord of the harvest, that he will send forth labourers into his harvest" (Matt. 9:37–38 KJV).

For Further Reading

Bevans, Stephen B., and Roger P. Schroeder. *Constants in Context: A Theology of Mission for Today*. Maryknoll, NY: Orbis Books, 2004.

Bosch, David J. *Transforming Mission: Paradigm Shifts in Theology of Mission*. Maryknoll, NY: Orbis Books, 2004.

Flett, John G. *The Witness of God: The Trinity,* Missio Dei, *Karl Barth, and the Nature of Christian Community.* Grand Rapids: Eerdmans, 2010.

Meyers, Ruth A. *Missional Worship, Worshipful Mission: Gathering as God's People, Going Out in God's Name.* Grand Rapids: Eerdmans, 2014.

Schlesinger, Eugene R. *Missa Est! A Missional Liturgical Ecclesiology.* Minneapolis: Fortress, 2017.

———. *Sacrificing the Church: Mass, Mission, and Ecumenism.* Lanham, MD: Lexington/Fortress Academic, 2019.

Smith, James K. A. *Imagining the Kingdom: How Worship Works.* Grand Rapids: Baker Academic, 2013.

— 11 —

Mystery and Worship

Ivana Noble

This chapter explores the relationship between worship and mystery. Thus, unlike some of the previous chapters, it does not seek to relate any specific Christian doctrine—such as Christology, pneumatology, ecclesiology, or eschatology—to the understanding of worship; rather, it focuses on what cannot fully pass into doctrinal expression.

When people speak of mystery in today's world, they often mean something exceptional, some challenge to our rational life in the here and now. Mystery books or mystery films, a genre so popular these days, operate precisely on this level. The Harry Potter or The Lord of the Rings series offer a mythical-epic fantasy, full of symbols and rituals that mediate between meaning shared by our broader culture and desires that are not and perhaps even cannot be realized in it. In this sense, the current use of the word "mystery" is not far from its ancient roots.

The word comes from the Greek μυστήριον (*mystērion*), where it means something hidden or secret, some secret knowledge, doctrine, or rite. Thus we can see two main strands of meaning, coming from two verbs: from μυέω (*mueō*, "I initiate") and from μύω (*myō*, "I close," e.g., close my eyes or mouth). The very concept had both a ritual meaning, signifying initiation into

This work has been supported by the Charles University Research Centre program No. 204052.

a secret knowledge and participation in the hidden, μυσταγωγία (*mystagōgia*); and also a mystical meaning, signifying an awareness and deep respect for what goes beyond one's possibilities to grasp and comprehend. The one initiated into the mystery was called μύστης (*mystēs*, "mystic"), and the one initiating others was called μυσταγωγός (*mystagōgos*, "mystagogue"). Both the immediate-experiential meaning and the ritual meaning of mystery were incorporated into Christian theology. However, it was not a borrowing without problems.

Examining the Scriptures and especially the Septuagint, the primary text of the Holy Scriptures for most early Christians, we find both attacks on and an influence from the mystery cults.[1] The polemics included a refusal of polytheism but also of the exclusivism of secret knowledge and of claims by the "initiated" to be able to have and to transmit a privileged access to transcendence and to holiness. The influence could be seen more in terms of a sensitivity toward the role of the initiation into and participation in the unknown, which was offered in religious symbols, rituals, or narratives. They are all part of liturgical action, of worship.[2]

One of the most influential Orthodox liturgical theologians of the last century, Alexander Schmemann, stated that in liturgy all our existence is included into the "all-embracing vision of life."[3] The things hidden since the foundation of the world, of which everybody has an intuitive knowledge, are revealed in liturgy. The mystery becomes epiphany.[4]

1. Mystery religions had a long history in the Greco-Roman world. It is an umbrella term for various cults, offering people who were dissatisfied with the public religion a way into elite groups claiming to have the key to secret knowledge and a more secure participation in the holy. The cults varied greatly. The best known are the cult of Dionysius, with its common meals, dances, and initiation into sexual practice; the Eleusinian mysteries, focusing on the rhythms of natural life and death and links with ancestors; the Orphic cult, offering a way out of sin and guilt through the liberation of the soul from the body; and the Pythagorean cult, similarly stressing the return of the soul to its celestial home. There were secular as well as religious cults, anti-intellectual ones as well as philosophically grounded ones, such as the Neoplatonism of Plotinus or Porphyry. See Reinhold Merkelbach, "Mystery Religion: Greco-Roman Religion," in *Encyclopaedia Britannica*, https://www.britannica.com/topic/mystery-religion/Mystery-religions-and-Christianity; more recently, see, e.g., Hugh Bowden, *Mystery Cults of the Ancient World* (Princeton: Princeton University Press, 2010).

2. I use "worship" and "liturgy" as synonymous.

3. See Alexander Schmemann, "Liturgy and Theology," in *Liturgy and Tradition: Theological Reflections of Alexander Schmemann*, ed. Thomas Fisch (Crestwood, NY: St. Vladimir's Seminary Press, 1990), 51–52.

4. Schmemann stresses that believers need to learn to understand the revelation in which they participate. See Alexander Schmemann, *Liturgy and Life: Christian Development through Liturgical Experience* (New York: Department of Religious Education, Orthodox Church in America, 1993), 13–14; Schmemann, *The Eucharist: Sacrament of the Kingdom* (Crestwood, NY: St. Vladimir's Seminary Press, 1987), 34.

This chapter starts with the scriptural and patristic notions of mystery and their relation to worship. Then I will move to the modern debate and look at how the exaggerated emphasis on rationality has sidelined the notion of mystery in different traditions and how that sense of mystery has been recovered. In the conclusion we will consider practical implications arising from the recovered meaning of mystery for Christian worship.

Mystery in Early Christian Thought

The Christian approach to mystery started with emphasizing what was specific, the experience of Christ, the gifts of the Holy Spirit, and gradually the theology spelling out human participation in the mystery of God with the help of a trinitarian economy.[5] In Jesus Christ the hidden God was recognized and "the mysteries of the kingdom of Heaven" (Matt. 13:11 NJB) revealed. The Holy Spirit was seen as a great Mystagogue[6] since the Spirit was the one who explores and examines everything, including the depth of God, and who initiated Christians into the divine wisdom.[7] Through Christ and in the Spirit, the mystery of the Father came near. People were healed and transformed. Yet the trinitarian God who acted that way did not cease to be mystery for them. Those who had the experience of Christ and were given the Spirit participated also in the mystagogic ministry by initiating others into the mystery of salvation,[8] related both to Israel[9] and to the church.[10] The emphasis on things unknown was strengthened by the book of Revelation, which makes a strong distinction between the present time and the period when the end of the times will be announced by God's angels, and "the mystery of God will be fulfilled" (10:7).

Since the second coming of Christ had not happened as soon as expected, Christians had to change their time prospects and adjust to living in the world for an uncertain number of generations; hence, the notion of mystery was more and more interpreted to account for this uncertainty. The Christocentric

5. For more detail, see Boris Bobrinskoy, *The Mystery of the Holy Trinity: Trinitarian Experience and Vision in the Biblical and Patristic Tradition* (Crestwood, NY: St. Vladimir's Seminary Press, 1999), esp. 63–100.
6. See Rom. 11:25; 1 Cor. 2:1; cf. with the broader Pauline tradition in Eph. 3:9; Col. 1:26–27; 2:2.
7. See 1 Cor. 2:6–10.
8. See Eph. 3:1–10; the Epistles also speak about "the mystery of the gospel" (Eph. 6:19), "the mystery of the faith" (1 Tim. 3:9), or "the mystery of our religion" (3:16).
9. See Rom. 11:1–35, esp. v. 25.
10. See Eph. 5:32, where the relationship between Christ and the church is compared to the communion of love between a husband and a wife.

focus and the implicitly early and explicitly later trinitarian orientation of the central mystery of their lives remained, and so did the emphasis on mystagogy.[11] But other meanings returned, and the meanings of mystery and mysticism later joined. For Christians, mysticism represented that type of religious ecstasy that leads toward union with God, experienced here and now. Mystical experiences were identified as gifts of the Holy Spirit, were often modeled on Christ's union with the Father, and included the darkness of the cross as bringing light and life. Mystics had a direct knowledge of God and of the world in God, coming from participation with God, for which they had to be purified.[12] At their best they presented the beating heart of Christian theology. The darkness they experienced, however, did not always lead to light. The illumination could be illusory or, in its effects, sectarian.

In the Septuagint, the early Hellenistic Christians found again the notion of the "dark" (*skoteinos*) as a synonym for the hidden mystery of God, mystery that could bring life, but also judgment.[13] The lack of understanding was not an excuse[14] but rather a symptom of being alienated from God, and often it came along with other symptoms, such as idolatry.[15] The polemics with the mystery cults were clear. The mystery that people try to work out in their own ways could lead them into further harm, whether expressed by means of orgies or of human sacrifices.[16]

11. "Mystagogy" in the early church referred to the last stage of the preparation for a full Christian life. The newly baptized (neophytes) received further instruction in faith, seeing it already from inside the church. A mystagogue was the guide explaining to them the mysteries of Christian life. Thus several patristic works bear the title *Mystagogical Catecheses*.

12. There has been a diversity of approaches toward mysticism in Christianity, ranging from the ascetic experiences of ecstasy documented by the Desert Fathers, to attempts at understanding the limits of human understanding when faced with the divine darkness, such as Pseudo-Dionysius the Aeropagite (ca. 650–ca. 725) in his *Mystical Theology*, deeply influenced by Neoplatonism. Others tried to spell out their life in Christ, experiences of the gifts of the Spirit, insights into what they named as ultimate reality: spiritual truth, overwhelming beauty, or goodness. They often operated at the limits of what any language could mediate and were eclectic in borrowing terms from the Scriptures, philosophy, theology, love poetry, or other religious or esoteric traditions.

13. God's light was counted as a special gift, not given to everybody, but, e.g., to the faithful servant Daniel, who risked his life because of his faith in the true God. Daniel, who was given the content and the understanding of the dream that disturbed King Nebuchadnezzar, recognized God as the Revealer of mysteries. See Dan. 2:22, 24, 29, 47.

14. In the book of Wisdom it was promised that no mysteries will remain unexplained regarding Wisdom's way of truth. See Wis. 6:22.

15. An example is posed: when a father mourns the untimely death of his child, which he cannot explain, he starts worshiping the dead body; thus "to what yesterday was only a corpse, [the father is] handing on mysteries and ceremonies to his people" (Wis. 14:15 NJB).

16. The book of Wisdom raises the accusation of "occult mysteries, or their frenzied orgies with outlandish customs" (Wis. 14:23 NJB).

Persecuted Christians knew the impact of religious imagination going mad, people drunk with power, and violent ritualized abuse. Yet at the same time, the early generations of the church already experienced divisions from within. There also the concept of mystery had a negative meaning, emphasizing that evil things could not be fully explained either, that they had a mysterious character.[17] The fact that something or someone was mysterious, that there was something hidden in them, some inner inexplicable secret, could thus be good or bad. Therefore, discernment was needed. A generation after the persecutions ended, Augustine of Hippo pondered the difference between a direct but also naive engagement with the mystery, on the one hand, and the knowledge of God that was safe, on the other. He said, "For if I do not know you [God], I may call upon someone other rather than you."[18] The initiation into the mystery was needed; according to him, such initiation involved both the experience within, understood through the gift of faith, and the ministry of a reliable preacher.[19]

The early Christian tradition differed on whether people can reach something genuine of the divine mystery when they seek for transcending goodness, for truth, or for beauty. In the second century, Justin Martyr assumed that God was so sovereign that no other power could take away people who were seeking.[20] The seed of Logos was given to all nations and cultures, and thus at least a partial relationship with the divine mystery was possible without the explicit knowledge of the full Logos, Christ. God gave people the power to contemplate, to think and discern, and to act justly, and God cooperated with these powers.[21] Tertullian was more skeptical regarding the possibility of a good and genuine relationship with the mystery when people did not know God. Right faith was central; without it, people could relate to their fantasies or to powers other than God.[22] The relationship with the mystery

17. For example, 2 Thessalonians speaks of "the mystery of wickedness" (2:7 NJB).

18. Augustine, Confessions, trans. Henry Chadwick, Oxford World Classics (Oxford: Oxford University Press, 2008), 1.1.1.

19. "My faith calls upon you, O Lord, the faith which you have given me, which you have breathed into me through the humanity of your Son, through the ministry of your preacher." Augustine, Confessions 1.1.1.

20. Justin even claimed that there was nothing outside God, nothing "secular for God," because God created everything. See Justin Martyr, The Resurrection of the Flesh 5.

21. See Justin, First Apology 28; Justin, Second Apology 8; 10.

22. Tertullian was skeptical regarding philosophical speculation, as his famous statement that there is nothing in common between Athens and Jerusalem illustrates. See Tertullian, Prescription against Heretics 7.3. He drew on the tradition of Roman law, however, and with its help was able to defend Christianity as a trustworthy religion among other religions in the empire. For more detail, see Denisa Červenková, Jak se křesťanství stalo náboženstvím: Recepce pojmu religio v Tertuliánově Apologetiku (Praha, SK: Karolinum, 2012).

was safeguarded by the rule of faith, on which the authority of the church was based.[23] Positions closer to that of Justin or closer to that of Tertullian have continued to influence the relationship between mystery and worship throughout Christian history.

The languages in which people were embedded had an impact on understanding the mystery. Tertullian was a good linguist, and due to him we have translations of much theological terminology from Greek into Latin. But every translation is also an interpretation. We gain a new access, and we lose some of the spectrum of previous meanings. He translated the Greek term *mystērion* into Latin as *sacramentum*,[24] which in the fourth century passed to some of the texts in the Vulgate, and then, most importantly, to Latin sacramental theology. When *mystērion* became *sacramentum*, it signified, as Ernest Evans sums up, "the whole sacred act in which material things are used for spiritual purposes."[25] The proximity of *mystērion—mystic—mystagogue* was lost in the translation.[26] We still need to be careful not to project the medieval Latin teaching on sacraments back into Tertullian. He did not work with a definite number of sacraments, and even at times he used the word *scramentum* in a more general sense, of "any religious or symbolic act or type."[27] Yet the preference for the mediated, church-guarded experience of God over against a journey toward a direct encounter with the mystery was clear.

In the Eastern Church a richer sense of mystery remained. Sacraments were called the holy mysteries; liturgy held together the unity of a profound experience of the transcendent and the sacred. The liturgical and the mystical approach to the mystery found a much more balanced way in the seventh-century

23. According to Tertullian, if people accepted the authority of the church and embraced the simplicity of their hearts, they could learn that the very nature of their soul was Christian. See Tertullian, *Apology* 17. The church for him has the right authority because "one Lord God does she acknowledge, the Creator of the universe, and Christ Jesus [born] of the Virgin Mary, the Son of God the Creator; and the Resurrection of the flesh; the law and the prophets she unites in one volume with the writings of evangelists and apostles, from which she drinks in her faith. This she seals with the water [of baptism], arrays with the Holy Ghost, feeds with the Eucharist, cheers with martyrdom, and against such a discipline thus (maintained) she admits no gainsayer." Tertullian, *Prescription against Heretics* 36. See also chaps. 21 and 13, where Tertullian paraphrases Irenaeus, *Against Praxeas* 2.

24. See Tertullian, *Baptism* 1 or 3 or 5 or 12. For an analysis of the shift of meaning, see Ernest Evans, "Introduction," in *Tertullian's Homily on Baptism: The Text Edited with an Introduction, Translation, and Commentary* (Eugene, OR: Wipf & Stock, 2013), ix–xl, here xxxviii–xl.

25. Evans, "Introduction," xxxix.

26. This was noted already in 1909 by G. G. Findlay. He also said that the passages in the Vulgate that "replaced *mystērium* by the alien rendering *sacramentum* (the soldier's oath of allegiance)" brought modifications. See G. G. Findlay, "Mystery," in James Hastings, *Dictionary of the Bible* (1909), https://www.studylight.org/dictionaries/hdb/m/mystery.html.

27. See Evans, "Introduction," xl.

Byzantine theologian Maximus the Confessor. His integrative approach was somewhat akin to that of Justin, but more developed.[28] According to him, the different strands of Christian experience—the liturgical, the ascetic, and the contemplative—not only belonged together but also shed light on each other, transformed each other, and thus served the movement in which the broken world was healed and brought back to God. Thus the world was deified. How? Through the mystery of Christ's hypostatic union with the created world, people were able to participate in the divine nature and to mediate this participation throughout creation. In celebrating the liturgy, the church could then be recognized as a symbol of this incarnational mystery,[29] the mystery of love.

Like Gregory of Nazianzus, when he emphasized the goodness of God as the bond with as well as within the creation,[30] Maximus ascribed such a bonding role to divine love. Love moves people to mediate between the five divisions in the universe: (1) the female—the male; (2) paradise—the inhabited world; (3) the earth—the heaven (sky); (4) the material world—the spiritual world; (5) the creation—God, or the created—the uncreated.[31] Being united to Christ makes this mediation possible. Mysticism in Maximus is nothing other than a contemplative knowledge of God's love. But before people are made capable of seeing that love in its pure form, they need to be purified.

Liturgy is a good teacher of purification since in it the entire church is included in the movement of supplication: receive us on our way to the kingdom; show us the way toward salvation, as you have bestowed on us the revelation of the heavenly mysteries.[32] Maximus draws on the liturgical tradition in which coming close to God is like coming close to a fire. Consuming the gifts of God means a risk that one can be consumed by the fire if one receives the gifts unworthily.[33] This does not mean that people should become

28. Maximus drew on the ascetic tradition, especially drawing from Evagrios, and as George Bertold says, he reinterpreted the Dionysian mysticism in a way much more at home with the Orthodox tradition. See George Bertold, "Introduction," in *Maximus the Confessor: Selected Writings* (Mahwah, NJ: Paulist Press, 1985), 1–13, here 6–7.

29. See Maximus the Confessor, *Ambigua* 23–71; David C. Scott, *Re-Envisioning Transformation: Toward a Theology of the Christian Life* (Eugene, OR: Wipf & Stock, 2018), 82, 89.

30. See Gregory of Nazianzus, *Oration* 38.9.

31. See Maximus the Confessor, *Ambigua* 41. See also Lars Thunberg, *Microcosm and Mediator: The Theological Anthropology of Maximus Confessor* (Chicago: Open Court, 1995), 373–429; Nonna Verna Harrison, *God's Many-Splendored Image: Theological Anthropology* (Grand Rapids: Baker Academic, 2010), 131–38.

32. For more on this, see Maximus, *Mystagogia* 8 and 16.

33. In the Divine Liturgy of John Chrysostom, there is a prayer to go with coming near to receive Holy Communion: "Behold, I approach for Holy Communion. O Creator, burn me not as I partake, For Thou art Fire which burns the unworthy, Wherefore do thou cleanse me from

scrupulously afraid of God, but rather that they need to remain on the way of transformation with their whole being, with the entire church, and with the whole of creation. This is how the cosmic movement toward union with God happens, and this is also how it can be contemplated as the fullness of the eschatological mystery.

The Modern Primacy of Reason and the Quest to Reconnect Mystery and Worship

In premodern thought, mystery could be experienced "beyond but not necessarily apart from rational thought."[34] The modern emphasis on rationality as the supreme expression of human existence could not coexist easily with the otherness challenging the limits of human reason and reminding people that the ultimate cannot be controlled by science or by technology, however far these will progress. Besides the secular rejection of mystery, there were milder Christian forms of doing away with the reminders of the incomplete knowledge of God or the impact of the direct experiences of the divine and the holy.

In Roman Catholic worship and theology, the emphasis on the transcendent and the sacred remained, but the two came too close together. Using Maximus's language, there was unity, but often not distinction. Both were subject to an overgrown controlling role of the church, seen as the sole mediatrix of the divine revelation, divine order, divine grace. Mystics did not cease to exist but were often seen as dangerous for the stability of the developed system.

In Protestantism the transcendent and the sacred were often divorced. Transcendence was upheld, but in a bare form; the emphasis on the divine majesty could be so strong that it excluded everything else, including love, goodness, or beauty. Truth remained a guiding value joined to the power of the word, the dominant and at times the only mediation of the divine revelation. The desire to purify worship of anything to do with superstition or magic was guided on principles not dissimilar to secular rationalism. Evangelical churches worked more with the experiential reality, with feelings or even sentiments, but shared a similar suspicion toward the sacred as though it were idolatrous.

In Orthodoxy there was a division between liturgy, deeply embedded in a premodern world, and largely westernized theology. Before the patristic,

---

every stain." See *The Divine Liturgy Explained: A Guide for Orthodox Christian Worshippers* (Athens: Papadimitriou, 2005), 293; http://orthodoxcheyenne.org/daily-prayers-for-orthodox -christians/post-communion-prayers.

34. Scott, *Re-Envisioning Transformation*, 91.

liturgical, and hesychast[35] renewals in the last century, priests who were to lead worship were educated in a neo-scholastic theology; hence the experience coming from worship and the tools for articulating that experience theologically did not match each other very well.

When, to paraphrase Paul Ricoeur, the children of reason came with the help of reason to the appreciation of the limits of reason,[36] the emphasis on mystery returned in different ways. The first way was through the liturgical and patristic renewal. One of the most influential early figures, Dom Odo Casel, was a Benedictine monk from Maria Laach Abbey in the Rhineland, an important center of the renewal early in the twentieth century. Casel based his liturgical theology on recovering the sense of mystery.[37] Opposing reduction of worship to an anthropocentric exercise of extrapolation of doctrine and institutional discipline, he called on the church to rediscover the eschatological orientation of worship. He emphasized that we live in "the time between" Christ's earthly life and the parousia; in other words, with Christ we are experiencing the suffering in the world and looking for the coming of Christ in the full strength of his glory.[38] Meanwhile the Lord is still hidden. We could say that the manner of his presence bears features of his absence.[39] In this time between, the church "lives by faith and in the mysteries of Christ's worship."[40] By "mysteries" (plural), he means the redeeming work of the risen Christ in the church in liturgical action. "Mystery" (singular) refers to Christ, who acts, who holds the church together as his mystical body. Casel's emphasis on the mystery in the present inspired others, most prominently

35. Hesychasm refers to the spiritual tradition stemming from the Desert Fathers. The word comes from the Greek ἡσυχία (hēsychia, "stillness, silence, peace"). Hesychasts sought a life of prayer and attention to God in silence, embraced specific physical and mental ways of uniting all their powers focused in the heart as center of the human person, and were invoking the name of Jesus while journeying toward full union with God. This type of spirituality appeared in Syria, Palestine, and Egypt in the fourth century. It experienced a revival in Byzantium in the eleventh century and in the first half of the fourteenth century, when its name "hesychasm" originated from monks on Mount Athos. Hesychast teaching and practice were systematized and defended by the monk and later bishop of Thessalonica, Gregory Palamas (ca. 1296–1359).

36. See Paul Ricoeur, Symbolism of Evil (Boston: Beacon, 1967), 350–52.

37. Among Odo Casel's works in German on recovering the notion of mystery, we find these: Die Liturgie als Mysterienfeier (1922); Das christliche Kult-Mysterium (1932); Das christliche Festmysterium (1941); Glaube, Gnosis, Mysterium (1941); then postmortem: Mysterium des Kommenden (1952); Mysterium des Kreuzes (1954); and Mysterium der Ekklesia: Von der Gemeinschaft aller Erlösten in Christus Jesus; Aus Schriften und Vorträgen (1961).

38. Odo Casel, The Mystery of Christian Worship (New York: Herder & Herder, 1962), 27–28.

39. The dynamics between the presence and the absence of the Lord was further developed much later by Louis Marie Chauvet in his book Symbol and Sacrament: A Sacramental Reinterpretation of Christian Existence (Collegeville, MN: Liturgical Press, 1995).

40. Casel, Mystery of Christian Worship, 27.

Edward Schillebeeckx, and more recently Aidan Kavanagh.[41] They spelled out the theological consequences of the return of mystery as the lost heart of worship.

The Russian émigré theologian Alexander Schmemann had the strongest impact on joining liturgy and theology together in twentieth-century Orthodoxy. Schmemann lived in the West, first in Paris, then near New York, and thus he was embedded in modern Western culture. At the same time, he participated in the liturgical life of the Orthodox Church. Thus he had access to the premodern sense of the mystery, alive and active. He saw this mystery as descending from the realm of God, as giving dignity even to those who lost everything after the Bolshevik Revolution and taking them along the transformative way.[42] Modern culture and premodern ritual were thus brought into conversation by Schmemann. The dialogue was not always easy. He was critical of modern anthropocentrism and rationalism, and yet, culturally, he was also a child of the very traditions of thought that he criticized.

Along with other Orthodox theologians—such as Vladimir Lossky, John Meyendorff, and Metropolitan John Zizioulas[43]—Schmemann opposed the isolation of theological knowledge from mystery. He stated, "Theology is not only related to the '*mystērion*' but has in its source the condition of its very possibility. Theology as proper words and knowledge *about* God is the result of the knowledge *of* God—and in Him of all reality."[44] Schmemann emphasized that in liturgy the celebrating church can be grasped by the mystery of God moving toward us, revealing a passage from this world toward the kingdom of God.[45] The worshiping community participates in the

---

41. See Joris Geldhof, "Paschal Joy Continued: Exploring Leo the Great's Theology of Christ's Ascension into Heaven," in *Preaching after Easter: Mid-Pentecost, Ascension, and Pentecost in Late Antiquity*, by Richard W. Bishop, Johan Leemans, Hajnalka Tamas et al. (Leiden: Brill, 2016), 386–404.

42. Here I draw on my earlier study: Ivana Noble, "From Sacramentality of the Church to the Sacramentality of the World: An Exploration of the Theology of Alexander Schmemann and Louis-Marie Chauvet," in *Charting Churches in Changing Europe: Charta Oecumenica and the Process of Ecumenical Encounter*, ed. Martien Brinkman et al. (Amsterdam: Rodopi, 2006), 165–200.

43. See, e.g., Vladimir Lossky, *The Mystical Theology of the Eastern Church* (London: James Clarke & Co., 1957); John Meyendorff, *Byzantine Theology: Historical Trends and Doctrinal Themes* (New York: Fordham University Press, 1979); John D. Zizioulas, *Being as Communion: Studies in Personhood and the Church* (Crestwood, NY: St. Vladimir's Seminary Press, 1997).

44. Alexander Schmemann, *For the Life of the World: Sacraments and Orthodoxy* (Crestwood, NY: St. Vladimir's Seminary Press, 1998), 141.

45. Schmemann articulates the relation between the world, the church, and the kingdom in the following way. The church is rooted in the world. It bears all the positives and the negatives of this rootedness. Its history is bound up with the history of the world. Yet it is also instituted as a passage to the new creation. "The church, as visible society and organization, belongs to

mystery of God through the revelatory symbols. Through them the mystery became epiphany. Liturgy did not create a new reality; it celebrated what was there, yet hidden. Schmemann recovered the relation between knowing and celebrating.[46] Celebrating allowed for participation. It drew on the intuitive knowledge, expanded it, and deepened it. The business-minded rationality was, for Schmemann, not only a wrong starting point but also a wrong end. He said: "Feast means *joy*. Yet, if there is something that we—the serious adult and frustrated Christians of the twentieth century—look at with suspicion, it is certainly joy. How can one be joyful when so many people suffer? When so many things need to be done? How can one indulge in festivals and celebrations when people expect from us 'serious' answers to their problems? Consciously or subconsciously, Christians have accepted the whole ethos of our joyless and business-minded culture."[47] The mystery of God did not primarily mean the darkness of unknowing, but rather the light of being overwhelmed by meaning and by joy. This was the great paradox, that amid our suffering in the world the goodness of God could be found, and the passage to God's kingdom was open. Symbols allowed the paradoxical nature of God's engagement with what we could see as reality to be preserved. By means of them we could speak of "the visibility of the invisible *as* invisible, the knowledge of the unknowable *as* unknowable, the presence of the future *as* future."[48]

For Schmemann, there is a symbolic unity between the world and Christ.[49] The world featured in Schmemann in a double way—positively as cosmos, the created sacrament,[50] and negatively as *polis*, which he characterized as broken-

this world," says Schmemann. The church is vulnerable and struggles with the same problems as the rest of the world, yet "she is 'instituted' to . . . stand for the world" and to "assume . . . all the natural forms of human existence in the world, . . . in order to reveal and manifest the true meaning of creation as fulfillment in Christ, to announce to the world its end and the inauguration of the Kingdom." Alexander Schmemann, "Ecclesiological Notes," *St. Vladimir's Theological Quarterly* 1 (1967): 35–39, note 3.

46. Schmemann interprets the relation between theology and liturgy on the basis of the Latin connection between *lex orandi* and *lex credendi*. See Schmemann, *Liturgy and Life*, 22; see also Bruce T. Morrill, *Anamnesis as Dangerous Memory: Political and Liturgical Theology in Dialogue* (Collegeville, MN: Liturgical Press, 2000), 83, 90.

47. Schmemann, *Life of the World*, 53.

48. Schmemann, *Life of the World*, 141.

49. According to Schmemann, the world is symbolical; it belongs to its ontology. See Schmemann, *Life of the World*, 139–40.

50. Schmemann says that natural symbolism is used and transfigured to witness and celebrate Christ and his kingdom. Water, fire, oil, milk, honey, bread, and wine participate in this celebration. They are not a reality of a lower rank compared to the "supranatural" reality. The world is the first symbol, and Schmemann would go as far as saying that we could speak of it even in terms of the first sacrament, because it makes all other sacraments possible. The world

ness.[51] A Christian understanding of mystery, according to him, united three fundamental truths: (1) the world is good; (2) the world is fallen; (3) the world is redeemed.[52] Schmemann taught that the church "stands for the world": it is here to "assume . . . all the natural forms of human existence in the world, . . . in order to reveal and manifest the true meaning of creation as fulfillment in Christ, to announce to the world its end and the inauguration of the Kingdom."[53]

In later generations Schmemann has been criticized, partly justly, for operating at a meta-level he himself disliked, rather than with the actual liturgical rites; or for transposing the Western search for "the true liturgical *ordo*," doing so to the degree of "undermining the very liturgy he knew and experienced."[54] Yet now we can recognize lasting value in his work: his rehabilitation of the centrality of the mystery, and with it the participatory knowledge of God, plus the power of symbols holding together the world, the church, and the kingdom.

In Protestantism the recovery of mystery also went hand in hand with a renewed appreciation of the power of symbols. The two most important influences have been Paul Tillich and Paul Ricoeur.[55] Tillich drew on the Byzantine understanding of symbols as gates to the mystery of God and, in it, of the ultimate reality.[56] He believed that it was possible, through a symbol, to "express the divine ground of all things" in which we participated, without venerating the human as though the human were divine.[57] Tillich spoke of

---

is created through Logos to have its eschatological fulfillment in the Logos, when all things will be gathered in Christ. See Schmemann, *Life of the World*, 143.

51. Here he speaks about the continuity between the world and Christ, being marked by the discontinuity caused by sin. Although Schmemann does not use the fall as an interpretative key for understanding the world, he does not minimize its effects. This meaning comes to use when he says that the church bears on itself all the weaknesses of the world. See Schmemann, "Ecclesiological Notes," note 3.

52. See Alexander Schmemann, "Between Utopia and Escape" (lecture, Mar. 22, 1981), http://www.schmemann.org/byhim/betweenutopiaandescape.html; Schmemann, "Ecclesiological Notes," note 2.

53. Schmemann, "Ecclesiological Notes," note 3.

54. Andrew Louth, foreword to *Liturgical Theology after Schmemann: An Orthodox Reading of Paul Ricoeur*, by Brian A. Butcher (New York: Fordham University Press, 2018), ix–xi, here ix.

55. See Ivana Noble, "The Symbolic Nature of a Christian Existence according to Ricoeur and Chauvet," *Communio Viatorum* 43.1 (2001): 39–59; Noble, "The Tension between an Eschatological and a Utopic Understanding of Tradition in Three Twentieth-Century Theologians: Tillich, Florovsky, and Congar," *Harvard Theological Review* 109 (2016): 400–421.

56. Tillich writes: "This is the principle of Byzantine culture, namely[,] to transform reality into something which points to the eternal, not to *change* reality as in the Western world." Paul Tillich, *A History of Christian Thought*, ed. Carl E. Braaten (New York: Harper & Row, 1968), 95–96.

57. Tillich, *History of Christian Thought*, 96; on 89–90, he analyzes the relation between the veneration of icons and christological dogma.

the transparency of symbols, which was not the same as their idealization.[58] Symbols could not be invented, but only discovered. They were born, but they could also die if they lost openness toward the human condition and the existential questions that stem from that condition.[59] For Tillich, it was not possible to separate symbols from the ambiguity of our existence, and yet they mediated that which transcended history. In the symbols, "the eternal now" was fully transparent; the past and the future met in the present. Tillich stated, "In this way, *eschaton* becomes a matter of present experience without losing its futuristic dimension: we stand *now* in face of the eternal."[60]

Ricoeur radicalized and further developed Tillich's insights. Like Tillich, he was interested in the integration of modern critical thinking and the immediacy of mystery as testified in premodern religious cultures. He sketched a journey from a "first *naïveté*," the precritical immediacy of meaning, through a "hermeneutics of suspicion," to the "second *naïveté*," which he saw as the "postcritical equivalent of the precritical hierophany."[61] Thus a hermeneutical circle was completed: "We must understand in order to believe, but we must believe in order to understand."[62] The mature understanding involved a sense of what is not and cannot be understood by reason, yet without abandoning critical thinking. Like Maximus the Confessor many centuries ago, Ricoeur sought for integration of the opposites, allowing them to form a unity with distinctions.

In his work *Interpretation Theory*, he then elaborated on why symbols overflow with meaning, and he integrated the transcendent and the sacred to the very core of religious symbols, as he identified them, and within the symbols he found both verbal and nonverbal double meaning.[63] The semantic

---

58. In Byzantine icons and mosaics, we do not find Jesus portrayed as the contemporary ideal of beauty; the divine majesty, however, is visible throughout. Tillich suggests that in this way "the Eastern Church represents something that we have lost." See Tillich, *History of Christian Thought*, 96–97.

59. See Paul Tillich, "The Dynamics of Faith (1957)," in *Main Works*, vol. 5, *Writings on Religion*, ed. Robert P. Scharlemann (Berlin: de Gruyter, 1988), 231–90; Tillich, "The Religious Symbol / Symbol and Knowledge (1940–41)," in *Main Works*, vol. 4, *Writings in the Philosophy of Religion*, ed. John Clayton (Berlin: de Gruyter, 1987), 253–72; Tillich, "Philosophical Background of My Theology (1960)," in *Main Works*, vol. 1, *Philosophical Writings*, ed. Gunther Wenz (Berlin: de Gruyter, 1989), 411–20, esp. 414–15; Tillich, *Systematic Theology*, vol. 2, *Existence and the Christ* (Chicago: University of Chicago Press, 1957), 33–34.

60. Paul Tillich, *Systematic Theology*, vol. 3, *Life and the Spirit: History and the Kingdom of God* (Chicago: University of Chicago Press, 1963), 396.

61. Paul Ricoeur, *Symbolism of Evil* (Boston: Beacon, 1967), 352.

62. Ricoeur, *Symbolism of Evil*, 351.

63. Since "within the symbol . . . is something non-semantic as well as something semantic, it follows that a better hypothesis would be to approach the symbol in terms of a structure of double-meaning, which is not a purely semantic structure, which, as we shall see is the case with

moment in symbol, according to Ricoeur, bore literal as well as figurative meaning. The non-semantic moment represented the power, which did not pass over completely into the articulation of meaning. He would not use the language of mystery, but as we will see, greatly aided a recovery of the meaning of mystery. Religious symbols, according to Ricoeur, signified and referred to the divine transcendence, on one hand, and, on the other hand, to the sacred attested by everything that is.

Ricoeur thus identified the fact that God transcends every attempt of our grasp for the numinous, and he reconciled that with the religious person's vision of the world, where the sacred is present in the fertility of the soil, the vegetative exuberance, the flourishing of the flock or fertility of the maternal womb.[64] Similarly, Ricoeur explored the role of myth, the power of metaphor and narrative, investigating the conflict of interpretations and the role of time, memory, and forgetting.[65] He used mainly philosophical tools to examine religious themes. His complex analysis of the rational and the nonrational dimensions of meaning were extremely helpful for finding healthy, rooted, and contemporary approaches to mystery. Thus it is not surprising that his influence reached far beyond Protestant circles.[66]

These different examples of recovering a rich meaning of mystery, each embedded in a distinct confessional background, will now accompany us in the final exercise: spelling out the practical implications for avoiding distortions and seeking a healthy role of mystery in worship.

Practical Implications for Worship

The modern Christian rehabilitation of mystery focused largely, but not only, on its specific Christian meaning. The return to the eschatological orientation of worship, in which the church lives by the mysteries springing from

---

metaphor. . . . The symbol will allow us to extend our theory of signification by allowing us to include within it, not only verbal double-meaning, but non-verbal double-meaning as well." Paul Ricoeur, *Interpretation Theory: Discourse and the Surplus of Meaning* (Fort Worth: Texas Christian University Press, 1976), 45–46.

64. Paul Ricoeur, *Time and Narrative* (Chicago: University of Chicago Press, 1984), 70.

65. Also see other works by Paul Ricoeur: *The Conflict of Interpretations: Essays in Hermeneutics* (1974); *The Rule of Metaphor: Multidisciplinary Studies of the Creation and Meaning in Language* (1977); *Time and Narrative* (1983–85); *Figuring the Sacred: Religion, Narrative, and Imagination* (1992); or *Memory, History, Forgetting* (2004).

66. Brian A. Butcher considers Ricoeur's thought as addressing "almost every aspect of how *meaning* is made, communicated and received," and as such offering Orthodox liturgical theology "a plethora of resources," helping it to counterbalance the weaknesses of Schmemann's approach. See Brian A. Butcher, *Liturgical Theology after Schmemann: An Orthodox Reading of Paul Ricoeur* (New York: Fordham University Press, 2018), 2.

the central mystery of Christ, was accompanied by the need to understand "the time between." Worship was to teach Christians how to hold together the relationship between the world, the church, and the kingdom of God. This was to prevent them from avoiding either a temptation to emigrate to an other-worldly construction, or an enticement to reduce the goodness, the truth, or the beauty of God to human businesslike projections and plans. In what was seen as anthropocentric reduction of worship—or in other words, idolatry—the transformative power of worship was at stake.

Paradoxically, the anthropomorphic ideas about how God is and works prevented people from taking into worship all their human experience, and then to take from the worship the joy of the genuinely new possibilities of life. The search for a prerational, postrational, but not nonrational grasp of "the ultimate reality" was joined to the new appreciation of the role and the power of symbols. Symbols employed in liturgy were understood as mediators of the mystery of God without becoming that mystery's replacement. Indeed, symbols could be abused or killed, but in their pure iconicity they made people participate in what they symbolized. The emphasis on participation was one of the most important premodern insights into mystery that needed to be regained. Participation in God was mirrored by participation in the world. Symbols carrying the transcendent and the sacred dimensions of life moved this double participation from the intuitive knowledge to the light of revelation and the movement of celebration.

In our time, there are new challenges facing worshiping communities, and we could say that one of the expressions of these challenges is the popularity of the hidden, secret knowledge or even of such rituals. In this aspect the postmodern culture is not that different from the Hellenistic culture, where various mystery cults operated. In current "liquid societies"[67] the religious "agenda" no longer predominantly includes the life of one or another world religion, but it does have many different attempts to engage with the "mysterious." The quickly changing plurality of religious and semi-religious positions often operate on post-truth principles and lack criteria for discerning between healthy and unhealthy religiosity. And yet the desire for a greater depth and for human wholeness has not disappeared.[68] People who gather to celebrate liturgy are also part of this liquid culture, and their problems, hopes, or aspirations are rooted both in their religious tradition

67. I borrow this concept of "liquid" from Zygmunt Bauman, *Liquid Times: Living in an Age of Uncertainty* (Cambridge, UK: Polity, 2007).

68. I have dealt with this issue in more detail in Ivana Noble, "Contemporary Religiosity and the Absence of Solidarity with Those in Need," *Journal of Nationalism, Memory & Language Politics* 13, no. 2 (2019): 224–38.

and in the liquid culture. We need to be aware of the implications of this double participation.

Some of the practical problems in worship emerge out of reducing either one or the other side of the mystery—participation in God or participation in the world—or when the transformational movement of the kingdom of God is exchanged for something else. Let us now briefly explore these three problems.

When participation in the mystery of God is reduced, the worship becomes anthropocentric, governed either by concern for the world, as Schmemann criticized, or by a compulsion to entertain people. The otherness and transcendence of God is bracketed or lost, and people (whether clergy or the celebrating community) place themselves into the positions of being the secretaries of God.[69] But the human representation is more like a human caricature of the mystery of God. It is painful to take part in the type of service that feels like the enacted plan of an activist group or a party where one should have good fun. Sometimes it is made still worse by an assumption that as people are the children of God, they should be made infantile. Without a genuine participation in the mystery of God, the transformation that takes place is more like a group conformity or alienation.

The other problem emerges when "vertical theocentrism" is pushed to its limits and thus deprives worship "of its properly human significance."[70] When participation in the mystery of the world is reduced, services become emotionally cold, become suspect of the contributions of human reason and critical thinking in particular, and become detached from the realm of experience, investing all in a particular dualist image of God and God's reign. There can be a disproportionate emphasis on the role of human will to bring all other human capacities into a numb submission to the dominating vision of the will of God. Different confessional families would use different language for that submission, but the effect is very similar, whether one ought to accept the infallibility of a local preacher interpreting particular sections of the Bible or of a priest insisting on definitive knowledge of the right and only way of ritual, following canonical or doctrinal rules. What is missing in either case is a healthy, Spirit-inspired hermeneutics of suspicion. And as in the previous case, the transformation that takes place may have nothing to do with the living God, the lover of his creatures.

Either of these two distortions is rarely found in its pure form, but even elements of them do harm to people and to the transformative movement

69. This can be based on the wrong understanding of what being "ambassadors for Christ" (2 Cor. 5:20) means.

70. See Chauvet, *Symbol and Sacrament*, 412, where he quotes Antoine Vergote, *Interprétation du language religieux* (Paris: Seuil, 1974), 201.

of creation, salvation, and deification, in which people are grasped by and grasp the relation between the world, God, and the kingdom of God. Here transformative movement is vital. If there is a worship that is well-balanced between the two participations, in God and in the world, but that does not bring transformation, it is dead. It could be like a visiting a museum with interesting and well-intentioned exhibits, but not a house where new life happens with the beauty of tradition and the messiness of the unknown.

There are other dangers, such as the instrumentalization of imbalanced participatory worship, making individualist or collectivist distortions of it. In one service the structured collective response is everything; in the other "the celebrating community . . . fades into the background," and a human response confuses "authenticity with human sincerity and runs the risk of elitism, rigorism, or anti-institutional hostility towards the Church."[71]

Good practices of worship in current cultures hold together the specific and the general understandings of mystery. The how may differ from tradition to tradition, from community to community. The mystagogue and the mystic, however, need to have a place in each. The church needs to integrate some forms of liturgical, ascetic, and contemplative strands of its life with what is going on around and in the lives of the people who come to worship. Where Christian worship does not create a ghetto mentality, the general human notions of goodness, truth, or beauty *and* the tradition safeguarding the mystery of faith continue to communicate with each other.

For Further Reading

Casel, Odo. *Mystery of Christian Worship*. New York: Herder & Herder, 1962.

Saint Maximus the Confessor. *On the Ecclesiastical Mystagogy: A Theological Vision of the Liturgy by St. Maximus the Confessor*. Translated by Jonathan J. Armstrong. Popular Patristics 59. Yonkers, NY: St. Vladimir's Seminary Press, 2019.

Ricoeur, Paul. *The Conflict of Interpretations: Essays in Hermeneutics*. Evanston, IL: Northwestern University Press, 1974.

———. *Symbolism of Evil*. Boston: Beacon, 1967.

Schmemann, Alexander. *For the Life of the World: Sacraments and Orthodoxy*. Crestwood, NY: St. Vladimir's Seminary Press, 1998.

Tillich, Paul. "The Dynamics of Faith (1957)." In *Writings on Religion*, edited by Robert P. Scharlemann, 231–90. Vol. 5 of *Main Works*. Berlin: de Gruyter, 1988.

71. See Michael Kirwan, "The Word of God and the Idea of Sacrament: A Catholic Theological Perspective," in *Catholics and Shi'a in Dialogue: Studies in Theology and Spirituality*, ed. Anthony O'Mahony, Wulstan Petersbur, Mohamed Ali Shomali (London: Melisende, 2004), 266–67.

Sanctification and Worship

Lizette Larson-Miller

This chapter looks at theologies of sanctification and worship as essential elements of Christian living and salvation, first as separate dimensions of Christian life and practice, then in their intersection in forming a third articulation of Christian understanding. Following these theological reviews, this chapter turns to pastoral considerations of these theologies in the practice of Christian worship.

A Theology of Sanctification

If faith, an innate knowledge of God, is a pure gift from God, that gift is a constant reality. But theology, "faith seeking understanding,"[1] must always be changing. The understanding of sanctification is, therefore, a theology that develops and changes through centuries of Christians knowing, learning, experiencing, and reflecting on their relationship with God.

Sanctification is closely related to other biblical words because the Greek *hagiazō* (and to a lesser extent, the Hebrew *qādaš*) give rise to different translations and interpretations. This means (primarily in the New Testament) that we inherit a spectrum of interpretations circling around the concepts of holy,

---

1. "*Fides quaerens intellectum,*" in the words of Anselm of Canterbury, *Proslogion, or Discourse on the Existence of God*, books II–IV (1077–78), https://sourcebooks.fordham.edu/basis/anselm-proslogium.asp.

consecrated, dedicated, and hallowed. "Sanctification," therefore, often means "to make holy," generally understood as to set apart, to move people or places from former ways, and to be consecrated (dedicated) solely to God. Sanctification is God's gift (see 1 Thess. 5:23), either through the work of the Holy Spirit (1 Pet. 1:2) or of Christ, starting with the sanctity of the Triune God and extending outward to those who follow Christ (John 17:17, 19). This setting apart is a process, either as the fruit of a life being lived in Christ, or a progress from being of the world onward to being of God (Rom. 6:22; Phil. 1:25).

But in long Christian theological tradition, sanctification also develops from these New Testament ideas, circling around the terms *theōsis* and *deification*. Prominent throughout the writings of early theologians in the church, it remains a central theology for Eastern Christians, yet increasingly is being reintroduced in Western Christian theology as well.

In classical Christian theology, the terms "*theōsis*," "deification," and "divinization" are all developed from the New Testament teaching on sanctification joined to theologies of incarnation (God become flesh) and soteriology (the theology of salvation). The apostle Paul's writings provided one rich source for early Christian theology: "And all of us, with unveiled faces, seeing the glory of the Lord as though reflected in a mirror, are being transformed into the same image from one degree of glory to another; for this comes from the Lord, the Spirit" (2 Cor. 3:18). The gradual transformation into the "same image," meaning "the image of the Lord," is also a reflection of God's "ownership" of Paul: "I have been crucified with Christ; and it is no longer I who live, but it is Christ who lives in me" (Gal. 2:20). Beyond Pauline writing, the Letter to the Hebrews presents this partnership (or participation) in ways that have inspired centuries of theological reflections: "For we have become partners [*metochoi*] of Christ" (Heb. 3:14).

The theology of deification or divinization brings this participation and transformation together with the impact that the incarnation has on humanity. What is that impact? The incarnation changes everything.

> The Word became flesh and lived among us, and we have seen his glory, the glory as of a father's only son, full of grace and truth. (John 1:14)

> To all who received him, who believed in his name, he gave power to become children of God, who were born, not of blood or of the will of the flesh or of the will of man, but of God. (1:12–13)

Again and again, many Christian theologians have seen in the incarnation the means of transformation and a divine exchange: God becomes flesh so that we can move from image to likeness in God. This is not becoming the same *nature* as God, but rather a movement into God's energy and will. Thus Irenaeus, bishop of Lyon and martyr in 202, wrote, "The Word of God, our Lord Jesus Christ, Who did, through His transcendent love, become what we are, that He might bring us to be even what He is Himself."[2] Athanasius, bishop of Alexandria some years in the fourth century, summarized many theological reflections on the topic by writing: "For the Son of God became man so that we might become God."[3]

The most influential Western Christian voice in the early church, Augustine, bishop of Hippo (354–430), incorporated Athanasius's famous phrase into his own writing:

> The Word became flesh to make us "partakers of the divine nature:" For this is why the Word became man, and the Son of God became the Son of man: so that man, by entering into communion with the Word and thus receiving divine sonship, might become a son of God. . . . For the Son of God became man so that we might become God. . . . The only-begotten Son of God, wanting to make us sharers in his divinity, assumed our nature, so that he, made man, might make men gods.[4]

Two centuries later in Constantinople, Maximus the Confessor (580–662) developed Athanasius's theology as a theologian of the East.

> A sure warrant for looking forward with hope to deification of human nature is provided by the Incarnation of God, which makes man God to the same degree as God Himself became man. . . . Let us become the image of the one whole God, bearing nothing earthly in ourselves, so that we may consort with God and become gods, receiving from God our existence as gods. For it is clear that He Who became man without sin will divinize human nature without changing it into the Divine Nature and will raise it up for His Own sake to the same degree as He lowered Himself for man's sake. This is what St Paul teaches mystically when he says, "that in the ages to come he might display the overflowing richness of His grace."[5]

2. Irenaeus of Lyons, *Against Heresies*, book 5, Preface, in *Early Christian Writings*, http://www.earlychristianwritings.com/text/irenaeus-book5.html.

3. Athanasius, *On the Incarnation* 54, trans. and ed. Stephen R. Holmes and Shawn Bawulski (Oxfordshire: Routledge, 2014).

4. "*Deos facturus qui homines erant, homo factus est qui Deus erat,*" in *Sermo* 192.1, in *Patrologia Latina* 38:1012. Cited in Gerald Bonner, "Augustine's Conception of Deification," *Journal of Theological Studies* 37 (1986): 376.

5. Maximos the Confessor, *Philokalia*, vol. 2:62, on page 171 at https://archive.org/stream/Philokalia-TheCompleteText/Philokalia-Complete-Text_djvu.txt.

Such theology continues in both Eastern and Western theological reflection, including Thomas Aquinas (1225–74): "Now the gift of grace surpasses every capability of created nature, since it is nothing short of a partaking of the Divine Nature, which exceeds every other nature. And thus it is impossible that any creature should cause grace. For it is as necessary that God alone should deify, bestowing a partaking of the Divine Nature by a participated likeness, as it is impossible that anything save fire should enkindle."[6]

The Anglican theologian and bishop Lancelot Andrewes (1555–1626) preached on the Feast of Pentecost a similar theology in the early seventeenth century: "Whereby, as before He of ours, so now we of His are made partakers. He clothed with our flesh, and we invested with His Spirit. The great promise of the Old Testament accomplished, that He should partake our human nature; and the great and precious promise of the New, that we should be "*consortes divinae naturae*," "partakers of his divine nature, both are this day accomplished."[7] And finally, this approach carries through to the twentieth-century insights of C. S. Lewis (1898–1963):

> The command "Be ye perfect" is not idealistic gas. Nor is it a command to do the impossible. He is going to make us into creatures that can obey that command. He said (in the Bible) that we were "gods" and He is going to make good His words. If we let Him—for we can prevent Him, if we choose—He will make the feeblest and filthiest of us into a god or goddess, dazzling, radiant, immortal creature, pulsating all through with such energy and joy and wisdom and love as we cannot now imagine, a bright stainless mirror which reflects back to God perfectly (though, of course, on a smaller scale) His own boundless power and delight and goodness. The process will be long and in parts very painful; but that is what we are in for. Nothing less. He meant what He said.[8]

The long theological reflection throughout Christian theological writing points to sanctification as transformation, from one primary identification to another. Here the sacrament of baptism is essential since it begins a transformation of drawing near to God through sacramental means. But before joining sacrament, liturgy, and sanctification together, we move to a reflection on the other half of the equation, "Sanctification and Worship."

6. Thomas Aquinas, *Summa Theologiae*, First Part of the Second Part, Question 112: "The Cause of Grace," Article 1, http://www.newadvent.org/summa/2112.htm.

7. Lancelot Andrewes, "Of the Holy Ghost, Preached upon Whit-Sunday," in *Ninety-Six Sermons* (Oxford: Oxford University [Press], 1841), 3:109.

8. C. S. Lewis, *Mere Christianity* (New York: HarperCollins, 1953), 173–74.

A Theology of Worship

In contemporary conversations, liturgy and worship are often used interchangeably, but there is a difference, particularly in breadth. Liturgy is one way to worship; in other words, "worship" is the umbrella term, "liturgy" is a subset. "Worship" is a word inherited from early English (and found only in the English language). *Weoröscipe* appears in the ninth century, meaning "deserving of or being held in high esteem."[9] The use of the word seems to have been primarily directed to royalty and other individuals with rank and honor, but it eventually describes the honor due to God (and the places of worship where that honor was given to God).[10] Narrowing the breadth of ways in which humanity worships God to just ritual and liturgical actions obscures the richness of the meaning of worship as an all-encompassing stance in the life of a Christian. Andrew McGowan reminds us of the 1549 Book of Common Prayer's language of marriage as an articulation of this in a specific context. The groom gives a ring to the bride and says: "With this ring I thee wed; this gold and silver I thee give; with my body I thee worship; and withal my worldly goods I thee endow."[11] "This sharing of wealth was itself 'worship'—a ritual, but also a literal form of reverent service, the founding example of a set of acts and dispositions inherent in marriage rather than merely a sign pointing to them."[12] What McGowan and others are getting at is that "worship," as a specific act of ritual or type of corporate prayer, is only one manifestation of the broader meaning of the term. Worship is overall about "obedience or service, not gatherings, nor beliefs, nor song, nor ritual, except within that wider whole."[13] Worship then is "the orientation of all forms of human activity, including the liturgical or ritual, toward a particular allegiance."[14] Our lives as Christians are lives of worship, "embodied life and ethics,"[15] which encompass all aspects of how we live after death, having died in Christ (see, e.g., Rom. 6:8), rather than particular events or types of events that we might call "worship styles" in contemporary circles.

It might be helpful to reflect on another important word regarding the broader meaning of worship. Liturgy, as mentioned above, is a form of

9. See Louis Weil, "Worship," in *The Study of Liturgy and Worship*, ed. Juliette Day and Benjamin Gordon-Taylor (London: SPCK, 2013), 3.

10. Weil, "Worship," 3.

11. Online resource for early copies of the Book of Common Prayer can be found at http://justus.anglican.org/resources/bcp/1549/Marriage_1549.htm.

12. Andrew B. McGowan, *Ancient Christian Worship: Early Church Practices in Social, Historical, and Theological Perspective* (Grand Rapids: Baker Academic, 2014), 3.

13. McGowan, *Ancient Christian Worship*, 3.

14. McGowan, *Ancient Christian Worship*, 4.

15. McGowan, *Ancient Christian Worship*, 4.

worship, an activity within a lifestyle of worship. Drawing from the Greek in the New Testament itself, as well as early patristic writings, *leitourgia* often refers to the actions of Christ himself as high priest or to "the cultic celebration of the Christians who 'made liturgy to the Lord,'" such as in Acts 13:2.[16] In the excitement of the ecumenical liturgical renewal (the second half of the twentieth century), the Greek term *leitourgia* was often translated as "the work of the people."[17] Drawn from etymology, this theology supported and encouraged the return of liturgical action as something that everyone present did together, not simply the clergy for the laity. A return to a less politically charged and more correct etymology, however, has tempered that translation with the reality that its original usage, at the time of the developing Christian ritual and in the New Testament evidence, is more likely referring to official civic activities "done on *behalf of* the people."[18] This is, in the end, more consistent with the theology of liturgical action as intrinsically linked to ethical action, which is explored in the next section.

Above all, the richer breadth of the meaning of worship as an all-encompassing living of Christian life, a spirituality or rule of life, is worth reclaiming and reemphasizing, rather than limiting the term to a specific cultic (liturgical) event. A life of worship—a worshipful life—is an active and conscious way of being before God.

Sanctification and Worship

Putting sanctification (both the meaning of dedication to God and the transformative movement into union with God) and worship (in both of its meanings: a life of worship and the specificity of liturgical action) together brings us to the contexts and practices of liturgy as well as their theological meanings. The field of liturgical theology continues to expand in the breadth of multiple disciplines brought to bear on understanding at the same time as it sinks roots into heart of Christian theology. Looking back at a notable scholar such as Alexander Schmemann, writing on "the relationship between worship and theology" as "the theological agenda of our time,"[19] one can see a

---

16. See Anscar J. Chupungco, "A Definition of Liturgy," in *Handbook of Liturgical Studies*, vol. 1, *Introduction to the Liturgy* (Collegeville, MN: Liturgical Press, 1997), 3.

17. The emphasis on the liturgy as what all the participants were doing was used extensively, even as a book title. See, e.g., Frank C. Senn, *The People's Work: A Social History of the Liturgy* (Minneapolis: Augsburg Fortress, 2006), 1.

18. Senn, *People's Work*, 3–4.

19. Alexander Schmemann, "Theology and Liturgical Tradition," in *Worship in Scripture and Tradition*, ed. Massey H. Shepherd (New York: Oxford University Press, 1963), 165. The

renaissance of the same questions regarding the relationship between liturgy and theology being reshaped today. Does liturgy express or create theology, and in what mode(s) does it do this?[20]

Liturgy and Sanctification

In the second part of the twentieth century and now into the twenty-first century, scholars have been fascinated with the meaning and continued use of a fifth-century phrase, almost always taken out of context: *ut legem credendi lex statuat supplicandi*. This phrase is difficult to translate but is usually taken to mean "that the law of supplication establishes the law of belief." The phrase is drawn from the writings of Prosper of Aquitaine (in ca. 435–42) and is embedded in a letter responding to a query about the intercessions prayed on Good Friday.[21] Against Pelagianism, Prosper argues that these prayers of the church prove the necessity of grace for all people. In ancient times the phrase was recast as *lex orandi, lex credendi*. This version appears in conversations of the past fifty to sixty years and is usually interpreted to mean "the law of faith [equals] the law of prayer," or "we pray what we believe and believe what we pray."

For a focus on sanctification and worship, this "bumper-sticker" summary of much liturgical theology gets to the point of the relationship of theology and worship: they are intimately related in a circular (or spiraling) way, always mutually influencing each other. That is an essential part of the relationship of sanctification and worship in its narrower expression, focused on the celebration of liturgy and on the reason to establish the multiple meanings of sanctification and liturgy first.

Sanctification in and through Liturgical Practices

Drawing on writings of Western Christianity down through the centuries, Cyprian Vagaggini wrote that what this narrower dimension of a life of

ongoing influence of Schmemann is evident in the number of recent citations and studies revisiting his liturgical theology. See particularly *We Give Our Thanks unto Thee: Essays in Memory of Fr. Alexander Schmemann*, ed. Porter C. Taylor (Portland, OR: Pickwick, 2019).

20. To review the circle of primary and secondary theologies of the liturgy, see the earlier work of Kevin Irwin, which articulated a sharp difference between the two (primary and secondary), as in *Liturgical Theology: A Primer* (Collegeville, MN: Liturgical Press, 1990) and in his later work nuancing the relationship between theology and the articulation of faith in liturgy, *Context and Text: A Method for Liturgical Theology* (Collegeville, MN: Liturgical Press, 2018).

21. For a helpful presentation, see Maxwell E. Johnson, *Praying and Believing in Early Christianity: The Interplay between Christian Worship and Doctrine* (Collegeville, MN: Liturgical Press, 2013).

worship is actually about is a "complexus of the sensible, efficacious signs of the Church's sanctification and of her worship [of God]."[22] Contemporary theologian Brandon P. Otto describes this as "a mutual doxology," in which our worship of God—or, more commonly, the glorification of God—and our sanctification by God are the dual elements of any transformative liturgical event.[23]

In order for this articulation to make sense, however, the reflection on liturgical practice needed to move beyond the incorrect translation of *leitourgia* mentioned above.[24] The problem with saying liturgy is simply the "work of the people" is that it has often been interpreted to mean that liturgy is something we humans alone do, or worse, that we think of liturgy as the place in which we create liturgies that reflect our own agendas and needs. An ecumenical correction has emerged over the past twenty years. Roman Catholic, Anglican, Lutheran, and other theologians have reminded us that liturgy is not simply something we are doing but the space in which God acts on us also. Indeed, that pattern restores the biblical and theological pattern of all Christian living: God initiates and we respond. In the words of one of those theologians:

> Without a more organic reintegration of liturgy and theology, we have an ex-
> panded market of theological possibilities which, in turn, threaten to break
> apart and leave us with either a fundamentalist monism on the one hand or a
> pluralism of individualistic religious randomness on the other. . . . [The solu-
> tion is to] recover the awareness of the divine initiative in liturgical events. . . .
> Liturgical questions and liturgical matters are . . . theological because their
> object is God and they are seen with their origin and orientation towards God.[25]

God initiates, we respond, and in ritual worship of God via liturgy, that response continues as a dialogue between our worship, our glorification of God, and God's response in sanctification, transforming us as the church.

A substantial part of how liturgy transforms us is often part of the conversation around sacramental worship. Christian communities articulate the meaning of "sacrament" differently,[26] but perhaps the comprehensive work

---

22. Cyprian Vagaggini, *Theological Dimensions of the Liturgy: A General Treatise on the Theology of the Liturgy*, trans. Leonard J. Doyle and W. A. Jurgens (Collegeville, MN: Liturgical Press, 1976), 27.

23. Brendon P. Otto, "The Dialectic of Mutual Glorification," *Homiletic and Pastoral Review*, Nov. 4, 2016, https://www.hprweb.com/2016/11/the-dialectic-of-mutual-glorification/.

24. See above, under the heading "A Theology of Worship."

25. Michael Aune, "Liturgy and Theology: Rethinking the Relationship," *Worship* 81 (2007): 152, 155.

26. The rather straightforward articulation in the Episcopal catechism is useful to many Christian communities: "The sacraments are outward and visible signs of inward and spiritual

of the World Council of Churches may be helpful. In their 1982 Faith and Order Document, *Baptism, Eucharist, and Ministry*,[27] and in the responses and study guides since its publication, an amazing ecumenical agreement has arisen about the "sacramental" nature of baptism and the Eucharist, with various articulations (although less agreement) on the liturgical rites of reconciliation, healing, and ordination as important to the life of the church overall. The agreement on the two primary (or dominical) sacraments is based on their being rooted in Christ's actions and commandments, their essential character of shaping (or transforming) Christians individually and corporately, and their eschatological telos in practice and theology. A brief look at the first of these two sacramental actions, baptism, may exemplify this transformational character.

Baptism

How is baptism both worship and sanctification? Baptism is imitation of Christ. All four of the canonical Gospels include a description of or a reflection on the baptism of Jesus. His baptism was a moment when one of the primary manifestations of "God become flesh" in various combinations of sight and sound and action marked a turning point in Jesus's earthly life and all who would follow Christ through the waters of new birth. As early as AD 197, Tertullian wrote that "Christians are made, not born" and that this creation begins in the waters of baptism.[28] Ephrem the Syrian, writing in the fourth century, poetically expresses the connection between Jesus's baptism and our sanctification:

> The Father has signed Baptism, to exalt it!
> and the Son has espoused it to glorify it.
> and the Spirit with threefold seal has stamped it,
> and it has shone in holiness.

---

grace, given by Christ as sure and certain means by which we receive that grace." "An outline of the Faith: Commonly Called the Catechism," in *The Book of Common Prayer and Administration of the Sacraments and Other Rites and Ceremonies of the Church, Together with the Psalter or Psalms of David, according to the Use of the Episcopal Church* (New York: Church House, 1979), 857.

27. World Council of Churches, *Baptism, Eucharist, and Ministry*, Faith and Order Paper No. 111 (Geneva: WCC, 1982), also known as the "Lima Document," is most readily available online through the World Council of Churches, https://www.oikoumene.org/en/resources/do cuments/commissions/faith-and-order/i-unity-the-church-and-its-mission/baptism-eucharist -and-ministry-faith-and-order-paper-no-111-the-lima-text.

28. "*Fiunt non nascuntur christiani*": Tertullian, *The Apology*," in *Early Christian Writings*, http://www.earlychristianwritings.com/text/tertullian01.html.

Blessed be He that has mercy on all!
The Trinity that is unsearchable has laid up treasures in baptism.
Descend, ye poor, to its fountain! and be enriched from it, ye needy!
Blessed be He that has mercy on all![29]

By at least the third century the church gave ritual expression to being "christed" through immersion in water and anointing with oil (the etymological and symbolic link to *Christos*). This rebirth was a new beginning, a turning away from what was, from practices and settings that stood between the individual and God and the worship of other gods (sin), to the worship of the Triune God revealed in Jesus the Christ.

But there is another set of images for the baptismal journey in Christ as imitation and sanctification, the transformative journey through death and resurrection so revered by the apostle Paul. "Do you not know that all of us who have been baptized into Christ Jesus were baptized into his death? Therefore we have been buried with him by baptism into death, so that, just as Christ was raised from the dead by the glory of the Father, so we too might walk in newness of life" (Rom. 6:3–4). Here the imitation of Christ is not first and foremost an imitation of Jesus's own baptism but rather an imitation of Christ's dying and rising. In the Pauline theology the transformative movement is through death to the old life, signified by "drowning" in the waters of baptism; and then new life, a resurrected life, symbolized by being pulled out of the font. We know that these two ancient symbolic systems (birth and death) are both rooted in Scripture and tradition, and both emphasize change—the sanctification and transformation of the individual and the community. We also know that the preference for one set of images would predominate in Eastern Christianity (the model of Jesus's own baptism) versus the Pauline dying and rising dominating in Western Christian baptismal theology.

These theologies and ritual expressions of baptism are about the means of sanctification and transformation, and both of these are also worship of God. To glorify God is to imitate, to follow, to obey the *mandatum novum* of Jesus, not just in verbal profession but also in actions: "So if I, your Lord and Teacher, have washed your feet, you also ought to wash one another's feet. For I have set you an example, that you also should do as I have done to

29. Ephrem the Syrian, *Hymns on the Epiphany* 12.6–7. Ephrem also wrote of the firstfruits of Jesus's baptism: "Our Lord opened up Baptism in the midst of Jordan the blessed river. The height and the depth rejoiced in Him; He brings forth the first fruits of His peace from the water, for they are first fruits, the fruits of Baptism. The good God in His compassion will bring to pass that His peace shall be first fruits on earth." *Hymns on the Epiphany* 11.2. See translation by A. E. Johnston, in *Nicene and Post-Nicene Fathers*, ed. A. Robertson, Second Series, vol. 13, *Gregory the Great, Ephraim Syrus, Aphrahat* (Oxford: Parker, 1898, many reprints), 250–62.

you" (John 13:14–15). "I give you a new commandment, that you love one another. Just as I have loved you, you also should love one another" (13:34). And here, baptism turns us to the larger context of worship, a worshipful life, an all-encompassing rule of life that is liturgical and extra-liturgical, rooted in baptism.

Worship as Life

The ecclesial traditions of preparation for baptism were historically an apprenticeship in living life as a follower of Christ. Depending on when and where, it could take from one to three years to be made a Christian in the waters of baptism, in the oil of salvation, and in the breaking of the bread. One "discipled," or developed a muscle memory, of how to act as a Christian by practicing charity, visiting the sick and those in prison, feeding others, visiting the widows and orphans, changing patterns of living that were destructive to oneself or misleading to others, perhaps changing from careers that earlier obliged one to go against the teachings of the church, and learning the narratives of the body of Christ. It was a laboratory in living (Matt. 25:31–46). But learning the stories of Jesus, the practices of the church, and memorizing the summaries of Christian faith (the Lord's Prayer and the Creed) also meant becoming part of that story, to the point of being willing to die for one's faith. The arrangement of early North African churches was striking in that catechumens (hearers of the Word and called to baptism) often had to walk over the graves of martyrs on the way to the baptistry, a tangible reminder of the potential cost of baptism and of those whose imitation of Christ was a very physical dying and rising in Christ.[30]

Baptism is the beginning of a life of worship, both in the liturgical sense of offering the sacrifice of praise and thanksgiving in all the liturgies of the church and in the broadest sense of a life of worship—a stance before God. It is also the gateway to another articulation of the relationship between liturgy and life, liturgy and ethics.

For too long in the teaching of liturgy, the integral relationship between the worship of God and the living of Christian life was de-emphasized. In recent decades, this essential connection has been revisited and revitalized as an unbreakable bond. The more accurate translation of the Greek word *leitourgia* has helped, with its stress on an action done *on behalf of* others. This could, however, remain narrowly internal if interpreted as a clerical act

---

30. See Robin Margaret Jensen, "Baptismal Practices at North African Martyrs' Shrines," in *Ablution, Initiation, and Baptism: Late Antiquity, Early Judaism, and Early Christianity*, ed. David Hellholm (Berlin: de Gruyter, 2010), 3:1673–95.

done on behalf of the gathered lay community. It is far better to understand this as a directive that all the baptized should offer the sacrifice of praise and thanksgiving for the sake of the world and understand the multiple acts of worship as one continuum.

The theology of real absence in liturgy is fundamentally eschatological. No liturgy, particularly the eucharistic liturgy, is complete in this world, but it always anticipates, even while participating, in the fullness of the God's reign to come. Every liturgy then is a "pre-presentation of the Parousia."[31] Real absence, therefore, is essential in that it contributes both to our understanding of the necessity of God's gift of desire in us and to the "unease" with the way things are, spurring us to act on the commandment of Jesus to "love one another." Desiring God is a gift from God that draws us from the spiritual, intellectual, emotional, and social dimensions of living in the incomplete present to the fullness of the heavenly banquet. The teleology is clear in an ongoing dynamic of divine call and faithful human response to all that God loves. In the late fourth century John Chrysostom already gave warning that liturgy and charity are to be thought of as a unity:

> Do you wish to honor the body of Christ? Do not ignore him when he is naked. Do not pay him homage in the temple clad in silk, only then to neglect him outside where he is cold and ill-clad. He who said: "This is my body" is the same who said: "You saw me hungry and you gave me no food," and "Whatever you did to the least of my brothers, you did also to me." What good is it if the eucharistic table is overloaded with golden chalices when your brother is dying of hunger? Start by satisfying his hunger, and then with what is left you may adorn the altar as well.[32]

Regarding the eucharistic liturgy, one of the most important contemporary advocates of the unity of liturgy and ethical action has been Louis-Marie Chauvet. He has argued that Scripture, liturgy, and ethics are bound together and that from this foundation "an intrinsic connection between liturgical memorial and ethical life"[33] follows. For Chauvet, Scripture represents "everything

31. Donald Gray, "The Real Absence," in *Living Bread, Saving Cup: Readings on the Eucharist*, ed. R. Kevin Seasoltz (Collegeville, MN: Liturgical Press, 1982), 194.

32. John Chrysostom, *Homily 50* on Matt. 14, modern translation adapted from *Nicene and Post-Nicene Fathers*, ed. P. Schaff, First Series, vol. 10 (New York: Christian Literature, 1888), available at https://en.wikisource.org/wiki/Nicene_and_Post-Nicene_Fathers:_Series_I/Volume_X/The_Homilies_of_St._John_Chrysostom/Homily_50.

33. Bruce Morrill, "Time, Absence and Otherness: Divine-Human Paradoxes Bonding Liturgy and Ethics," in *Sacraments: Revelations of the Humanity of God; Engaging the Fundamental Theology of Louis-Marie Chauvet*, ed. Philippe Bordeyne and Bruce T. Morrill (Collegeville, MN: Liturgical Press, 2008), 140.

that pertains to the *knowledge* of God's mystery revealed in Jesus Christ." The Bible is the foundation of "all the theological discourse of yesterday and today."[34] The sacraments, and liturgy in general, include all "the *various forms of celebration* which the church performs in memory of Jesus' death and resurrection," essentially "everything that pertains to the thankfulness which the church expresses to God."[35] The third, "*ethical* conduct," is "the mark . . . by which Christians testify to the gospel by their actions."[36] These three, "knowledge, gratitude, and action,"[37] or "believing (*kerygma*), celebrating (*leitourgia*), and loving (ethics-*diakonia*),"[38] form the essence of what it is to be Christian. At the heart of Chauvet's scheme is a theological version of the popular cultural phrase "pay it forward." God gives us salvation and eternal life; our response is not to try to give something equivalent back to God, which is impossible, but rather to receive and acknowledge that embodied love and give it to others in our actions of loving service to all. This is worship, our lives as Christians in "embodied life and ethics,"[39] which encompasses all aspects of how we live for others after dying in Christ.

Practical Implications for Liturgy Today

Revisiting the theology of sanctification and worship together raises questions of pastoral practice in our churches today. A primary theological challenge is how to address two related inculturation issues: we live in an era when the "subjectification of reality"[40] is rampant, and the cultural assumption that everything is entertainment deeply affects the doing of liturgy in worshiping communities. What do these have to do with sanctification and worship? The first, well articulated by M. Francis Mannion, is that there is a philosophically shaped cultural reality tied to the cult of the individual: there is no greater reality than "me," a worldview at odds with Christianity as a "we" religion. Contemporary Christians struggle with understanding the communal nature of the body of Christ as something real. That is compounded with the

34. Louis-Marie Chauvet, *The Sacraments: The Word of God at the Mercy of the Body* (Collegeville, MN: Liturgical Press, 2001), 29.

35. Chauvet, *Sacraments*, 30.

36. Chauvet, *Sacraments*, 31.

37. Chauvet, *Sacraments*, 31.

38. Kristiaan Depoortere, "From Sacramentality to Sacraments and Vice-Versa," in *Contemporary Contours of a God Incarnate* (Leuven: Peeters, 2001), 57.

39. McGowan, *Ancient Christian Worship*, 4.

40. See M. Francis Mannion, "Liturgy and the Present Crisis of Culture," *Worship* 62 (1989): 98–123; reprinted in *Liturgy and Spirituality in Context*, ed. Eleanor Bernstein (Collegeville, MN: Liturgical Press, 1990), 1–26.

assumption that everything is entertainment.[41] Even when we attend a concert or a film that deeply touches us, it is still primarily an event external to us. There is me (in my insular reality), and there is this event that remains outside of me. The problem is, as baptized members of the body of Christ, we are participating ontologically and by will. It is interesting that evangelical Christians entering into the conversations on sacramental theology have turned to the metaphysical language of the Middle Ages to talk about the reality of participation by using the term "ontology" (a state of being).[42] They are particularly concerned with the assumption that the affective alone is considered real: "If I don't feel it, it isn't real." Transformation as sanctification is not simply about feeling; instead, it is about an intrinsic change in us. To be baptized is to be in a different relationship with our Triune God; in a different relationship with the church, the body of Christ; and thus to be a transformed person. A baptized person cannot *not* participate in God: it is not a metaphysical option.[43] How do we find ways to catechize, in words and actions, this reality that "church" is something quite different than the local theater?

Another pastoral challenge is countering the misunderstanding that sacraments are static and onetime events. Baptism, along with the other rites of initiation, happens once, but it takes a lifetime (and perhaps more) for baptism to unfold. Sacramental worship is part of a dynamic lifelong journey into God: we are never "done." The "fruits" of corporate prayer, of sacramental liturgy, of a life of worship—these fruits are always moving and growing, drawing us into the heart of God, which is salvation. How do we always point baptism and the Eucharist forward through real absence to eschatological fulfillment?

Finally, the often pastorally invisible links between our communal liturgy and ethics is one that continues to need catechesis in parish life. The closing of a liturgical eucharistic liturgy, "Go in peace to love and serve the Lord," is often the least understood line we will say in the liturgy, but at the same time one of the most important. It should shape everything we say and do as we head out the door; it is rooted in rituals such as the kiss of peace, the reconciliation that the Eucharist itself effects, our intercessions for the church and the world, and our corporate sense that we all celebrate these liturgies together for the good of the world. How do we understand our participation

---

41. The Canadian Catholic Bishops (*National Bulletin on Liturgy*) wrote on the insidious and often invisible inculturation of liturgy, particularly the North American desire to be entertained.

42. See esp. Hans Boersma, *Heavenly Participation: The Weaving of a Sacramental Tapestry* (Grand Rapids: Eerdmans, 2011), 9–11.

43. See Mark Searle, *Called to Participate: Theological, Ritual, and Social Perspectives*, ed. Barbara Searle and Anne Y. Koester (Collegeville, MN: Liturgical Press, 2006), 30.

in the dying and rising of Christ, our "christing," as doing the work of Christ in the world? How can we keep our celebration of the Eucharist from coming across as simply about something long ago and far away, but as a reality now and still to be fully realized?

Our liturgical celebrations, transformative here and now and over the long pilgrimage of life (the *kairos* and *chronos* of Christian life)[44] change us and the world, they confirm transformation, they are the means of sanctifying grace. They also call us to turn, to pray for kenosis (*kenōsis*) so that we can be filled with the Holy Spirit (for a discussion of kenosis see the epilogue at the end of this book). By our participation in these realities, we worship the living God in whose image we are made, into whose likeness we grow, and in whom "we live and move and have our being" (Acts 17:28).

For Further Reading

Belcher, Kimberly Hope. *Efficacious Engagement: Sacramental Participation in the Trinitarian Mystery*. Collegeville, MN: Liturgical Press, 2011.

Boersma, Hans. *Heavenly Participation: The Weaving of a Sacramental Tapestry*. Oxford: Oxford University Press, 2015.

Johnson, Maxwell E. *Praying and Believing in Early Christianity: The Interplay between Christian Worship and Doctrine*. Collegeville, MN: Liturgical Press, 2013.

Larson-Miller, Lizette. *Sacramentality Renewed: Contemporary Conversations in Sacramental Theology*. Collegeville, MN: Liturgical Press, 2016.

McGowan, Andrew B. *Ancient Christian Worship: Early Church Practices in Social, Historical, and Theological Perspective*. Grand Rapids: Baker Academic, 2014.

Searle, Mark. *Called to Participate: Theological, Ritual, and Social Perspectives*. Edited by Barbara Searle and Anne Y. Koester. Collegeville, MN: Liturgical Press, 2006.

---

44. Using both of the Greek terms for time, *kairos*, a moment in time, and *chronos*, ongoing or chronological time.

PART 3

Cultural Possibilities for Worship

Practical and Apologetical Theology

— 13 —

Cultural Considerations and Sacred Significance of Time in Worship

Anne McGowan

In the beginning God created, launching a narrative of salvation with a beginning, middle, and end. God gave all creatures the opportunity to receive their existence as gift, but humans are uniquely poised to praise and petition God in time and community while conceiving of a remote past and a distant future framing their own temporal span. With the incarnation, God entered time, and Jesus Christ—through his life and death and resurrection—radically reshaped human possibilities for engaging God in time and beyond time. Incorporated into Christ's dying and rising by their baptism, Christians already live in the future they still await, when they hope to share further in God's eternal life. Meanwhile, humans experience time mediated by culture and overlaid with myriad complementary ways of honoring cycles of the natural world and human labor and of celebrating singular historical events and ongoing realities that shape the identities of individuals, families, peoples, and nations.

Christian worship sustains conditions for communal encounter with God in time, in which the Spirit leads God's people to live into the fullness of time in Christ. Time as a universal factor impinging on all human lives is presented in the Christian tradition, and its worship is irrevocably animated by God's saving will for the world manifested most profoundly in Christ and continued on earth between Pentecost and the parousia in the life and mission of the church. Through the language, symbols, and rituals of worship, Christians rehearse their new relationship with God in Christ in ways that recombine and reorient their perceptions of past, present, and future, thus revisioning their experience of time in ways that may corroborate and/or challenge the worldview held by the prevailing culture. Distinctively Christian ways of punctuating the week, the year, and the day with worship often surface challenges and opportunities for churches committed both to continuity with Christian tradition and to evangelizing cultures as an ongoing incarnation of the church's mission.

Time as Invitation to Cooperate in God's Creative Work

Through the ages, humans have channeled their awareness of time toward developing theories about time[1] and modes of measuring time.[2] Natural aspects of time apparent in the sun's daily rising and setting, the moon's monthly orbit of the earth, and the earth's yearly journey around the sun underscore a cyclical dimension of time that concerns many of God's creatures. Humans also can conceive of time as a linear progression from a primordial past to a far-flung future.[3] Many calculations of time superimpose these two patterns into a spiral, "plot[ting] the relentlessness of time's forward movement against the inevitable recurrence of observable patterns."[4] While cosmic measures of time have a "givenness" about them regardless of one's faith commitments, other aspects of time, like the seven-day week, could have been arranged otherwise.[5]

1. See Dan Falk, *In Search of Time: The History, Physics, and Philosophy of Time* (New York: Thomas Dunne, 2008); and Adrian Bardon, *A Brief History of the Philosophy of Time* (Oxford: Oxford University Press, 2013).

2. Accessible overviews include Leofranc Holford-Strevens, *The History of Time: A Very Short Introduction* (Oxford: Oxford University Press, 2005); Jo Ellen Barnett, *Time's Pendulum: From Sundials to Atomic Clocks, the Fascinating History of Timekeeping and How Our Discoveries Changed the World* (San Diego: Harcourt Brace, 1999).

3. Psychologists and neurologists propose that abilities to ponder the past and foresee future possibilities seem to be closely related aspects intrinsic to the human capacity to relate meaningfully to time. Some theological implications are discussed in David Hogue, *Remembering the Future, Imagining the Past: Story, Ritual, and the Human Brain* (Cleveland: Pilgrim, 2003).

4. J. Neil Alexander, *Celebrating Liturgical Time: Days, Weeks, and Seasons* (New York: Church Publishing, 2014), 3.

5. Once established as a religious framework, however, attempts to reframe the seven-day week to loosen the attachment of the people to Christianity and its weekly cycle generally have

The opening chapters of Genesis present God's creation, ordering, and hallowing of time, including the seven-day week, as a matter of divine revelation (Gen. 1:1–2:3). "In the beginning when God created the heavens and the earth" (1:1), God started a time-bounded story in which the experience of present possibilities for Jews and Christians was informed by both collective recall of God's wondrous deeds worked in the past and shared anticipation for what God would yet accomplish in time.[6] Henceforth, the progression of time unfolds for God's chosen people who live between memory and eschatological hope. The passage of time and events that occur in time are imbued with spiritual meaning, making all time potentially revelatory while *some* times are explicitly experienced as moments of God's ongoing creative and redemptive love—sometimes retroactively in chronological time.[7] Time itself becomes a gift of God's grace, time in which God acts and God's people can respond.

With the incarnation, God entered time, making a radically new mode of encounter with God possible in time. Jesus Christ enfleshed past hopes of God's saving presence with people. His human words and actions in time and space were simultaneously the sayings and doings of the eternal God. Through his salvific life, death, and resurrection—often designated by the shorthand term "paschal mystery"—Jesus Christ redeemed and fulfilled all creation. He made it possible for people to share in his relationship with God as adopted sons and daughters who have already "passed over" from death to new life in Christ through the Spirit in baptism. After Jesus's bodily ascension into heaven and the sending of the Spirit at Pentecost, Christians continue to enjoy saving contact with Christ's glorified body in time because the risen, glorified One who now resides beyond the confines of time and space is still present in the body of Christ, which is the church.[8] Realized

---

been met with resistance. See Martin Connell, *Eternity Today: On the Liturgical Year* (New York: Continuum, 2006), 1:37–40, for some short-lived calendar experiments implemented after the French Revolution in the eighteenth century and the Russian Revolution in the twentieth century.

6. The sense of communal religious experience in time, especially as experienced in worship, is explored extensively in Emma O'Donnell, *Remembering the Future: The Experience of Time in Jewish and Christian Liturgy* (Collegeville, MN: Liturgical Press, 2015).

7. The ancient Greeks had two words available to denote time, both used in the New Testament. *Chronos*, the more generic term, designated time in general that could be calculated according to discrete units of measurement. *Kairos*, in contrast, is time with a depth dimension exceeding the bounds of its chronology; it is used in passages such as 2 Cor. 6:2: "See, now is the acceptable time; see, now is the day of salvation!"

8. Some traditional metaphors for the church make more sense as temporal constructs than as spatial ones. Paul's understanding of the church as the body of Christ (e.g., 1 Cor. 12:12–27; Rom. 12:4–5) implies an entity that grows and changes over time as new members are incorporated. The primary reference of *ekklēsia* is to the assembly, to the ones God has called out who

already on one level, the fullness of God's divine plan has yet to be *fully* realized in created time.

The church awaits this fullness, especially in its worship, which happens in time but fuses conventional distinctions between past, present, and future. Contemporary philosophers and neuroscientists readily admit to the possibility of perceiving the past as present; indeed, perceiving the *actual* present is strictly impossible, given the delay (on the scale of milliseconds) between sensory appropriation and the brain's processing of information through the nervous system.[9] Humans can likewise use their memory to imagine events in the future. The claim of Christian worship, however, is that the fullness of future salvific reality is *already* here—and that the church experiences this in its cycles of worship through days, weeks, seasons, and years overlaid upon the ongoing progression of historical time until Christ comes again and God will be "all in all" (1 Cor. 15:28). Christians are invited to "remember the future" that has become their present saving reality in a way that is just as real as their capacity to remember God's mighty deeds of old. This informs the task of worship as the church's cocreative response to labor with God on the pilgrimage through time. In the words of Adrien Nocent: "In our liturgical experience of God, we are always constructing a future. We are not simply being drawn toward a future; we are building it together with Christ, who is present through us. The entire world has the task of reconstructing itself in view of a future until God's plan is perfectly fulfilled and Christ comes to gather in the mature fruit of his entire work of paschal reconciliation."[10] In Christ, time is revealed—now more fully—as a vehicle of grace and medium of God's transforming work.[11] The resurrection recalibrates believers' understanding of the past, present, and the future, and regular participation in worship reinforces this sensibility as believers are drawn more deeply into new life in Christ.

---

have now gathered, rather than to the space where the church meets. See John Allyn Melloh, "Liturgical Time, Theology of," in *The New Dictionary of Sacramental Worship*, ed. Peter E. Fink (Collegeville, MN: Liturgical Press, 1990), 733.

9. Thus, there is a distinction between "perceiving the present and perceiving something *as* present." Robin Le Poidevin, "The Experience and Perception of Time," *The Stanford Encyclopedia of Philosophy*, ed. Edward N. Zalta (Summer 2019 Edition), emphasis original, https://plato.stanford.edu/archives/sum2019/entries/time-experience/.

10. Adrien Nocent, *The Liturgical Year*, vol. 1, *Advent, Christmas, Epiphany*, trans. Matthew J. O'Connell, annotated by Paul Turner (Collegeville, MN: Liturgical Press, 2013), 16. The terms "worship" and "liturgy" will be used synonymously herein. For distinctions among various terms used for Christian worship, see James F. White, *Introduction to Christian Worship*, 3rd ed. (Nashville: Abingdon, 2001), 25–30.

11. Laurence Hull Stookey, *Calendar: Christ's Time for the Church* (Nashville: Abingdon, 1996), 37.

Remembering the Future in the Church's Present Worship

Whenever the church gathers for worship, God's saving work on behalf of humanity becomes visible in the world through the people who in proper temporal order first receive what God offers them and then respond with praise and thanksgiving. From the human side, worship becomes a revitalizing encounter, with the eternal God accompanying us in time. Such encounter is possible since actualizing a singular past event or anticipating a future one in history through the mode of "mystery" or "sacrament" is no obstacle for God. As God's work with people continues, the church's collective experience of past-present and future-present time converging in worship is mediated through the social, ethnic, and ecclesial "cultures" of the many local communities that comprise it. People who live out of a liturgically formed vision of time will find future hopes real enough to enliven present living and thus contribute to the ongoing tradition of the church journeying toward its final future in Christ.[12]

Worship channels time on multiple scales. Patterns of syllables and silence give meaning to speech—and notes and pauses make music. A deliberate movement once initiated eventually ends somewhere else so that this hand might be raised in blessing, this bread and wine might reach the altar, this body of a beloved daughter of God might be borne from the church to her final resting place in the cemetery. All these actions take a certain amount of time in a sequence where the passing away of one element makes way for the next to arise in sequence.

Like salvation history, every worship service has a beginning, middle, and end. How these are structured varies among denominations and among worship events with the words, actions, music, symbols, and silence prescribed to greater or lesser degrees. Regardless, some things tend to happen first, second, and third in a recognizable deep structure that plays out over time. This is obvious in churches whose worship unfolds in relation to a denominationally mandated or authorized ritual framework. Even in churches with a flexible order of worship, however, some temporal necessities inherently apply. It is impossible for the community to be sent on mission, for example, before it has gathered and worshiped well. Furthermore, since ritual thrives on repetition, at least a loose structure coordinating the community's regular occasions for worship together will inherently develop and evolve.[13] Even in denominations

12. See O'Donnell, *Remembering the Future*, 37.
13. This is illustrated well by a video parody of contemporary American megachurch worship, where a worship set features an opening song with "lights and big drums," followed by "the song that everyone knows," and then the "new song . . . nobody knows" (yet). See "Learning

that worship "by the [ritual] book," local congregations develop their own particular culture around aspects of worship like beginning the service, sharing a sign of peace, and negotiating the transition between the church's time of worship and time for mission in the wider world.[14]

The pattern of worship as encounter with the risen Christ on the journey to Emmaus (Luke 24:13–35) presents a fourfold paradigm for worship as encounter with the risen Christ, still discernable in most instances of the church's official public prayer. First, the community gathers in Christ's presence. Then the Scriptures are proclaimed and preached, inspired by the Spirit. Next, the community engages in some form of faith-filled response to God's Word (which can take many forms).[15] Finally, the community is dismissed to continue serving God by loving and serving others in the world. In each of these ritual subunits of the worship service, we can find appropriations of a theology of God's presence in time enfleshed in the worship life of the community. We can also observe differences in ecclesial culture that will nuance how the worshiping community experiences time in their individual and collective life of faith.

Worship begins several times. There is the official ritualized beginning, spoken or sung, formal or informal. Before that, people must gather—a movement begun already when hospitality ministers arrive to prepare the place for God's holy people to gather. Still earlier, however, *God* has called all these unlikely people together, a point made memorably by the Russian Orthodox theologian Alexander Schmemann: "The journey begins when Christians leave their homes and beds . . . on their way to *constitute the Church*, or to be more exact, to be transformed into the Church of God."[16]

The local community's implicit or explicit "culture" around worship and community life will characterize the contours of gathering upon arrival at the place of worship and the appropriate procedures (and time scale) for transitioning from welcome to worship. Does worship begin promptly at the appointed hour? Or does worship begin when everyone is *present* and *ready*—even if the service begins much later than "scheduled" or even must be postponed

---

from a Parody on Contemporary Worship," RenewingWorship, https://www.renewingworship nc.org/a-parody-on-contemporary-worship/.

14. The series of anonymous "Mystery Worshiper" reports curated at http://www.ship-of -fools.com/mystery/ offers an interesting collection of anecdotal evidence for such variations in "culture" at the congregational level.

15. A Sunday service, e.g., might encompass profession of faith, prayer for the needs of the church and the world, the celebration of the Lord's Supper/Eucharist and/or other spoken, sung, or enacted rituals involving the community in embodied praise and thanksgiving.

16. Alexander Schmemann, *For the Life of the World: Sacraments and Orthodoxy*, 2nd ed. (Crestwood, NY: St. Vladimir's Seminary Press, 2000), 27.

to accommodate the needs of the worshipers to prepare well?[17] Does a sonic signal like ringing bells demarcate time before and during worship?[18]

When they gather for worship, Christians hear and reflect on the Scriptures to remember their identity in Christ, strengthen their hope for God's final fulfillment of all things, and appropriate God's saving action on humanity's behalf in the present. Foundational sacred stories, replete with references to God's saving work in time, are proclaimed anew in the assembly of the church, and the movement of the Spirit unfolds their ongoing relevance through preaching and the community's prayer. Meanwhile, a negotiation of time transpires as these stories are received by communities of worshipers shaped individually and collectively by their ecclesial tradition and cultural communities[19] For churches that use a lectionary (a book of readings excerpted from the Bible and arranged to be read in conjunction with days, seasons, and worship occasions), the "narratives proclaimed in the taxonomy of the calendar are a gift wrought by the inspiration of the Holy Spirit and realized in the Church's vocation to bring the people of God together."[20] Other churches might experience the immediate presence of Christ in his Word most profoundly through the Spirit-inspired selection of Scripture passages and preaching that engage the most timely concerns of worshipers and their local communities.

As the worshiping community responds to God's Word, the ritual tendency to focus on the "liturgical present" becomes especially prominent in the church's prayers (although it is not absent earlier).[21] Christmas prayers insist that *today* Christ is born for us. Easter Vigil proclamations exult "*This*

17. An extreme example is the practice of a congregational council meeting in some branches of the Anabaptist tradition to discern the community's readiness to hold Communion services; if members are not "at peace" with one another, Communion will be postponed until differences causing rifts are resolved. This is described in Donald B. Kraybill, *The Riddle of Amish Culture* (Baltimore: Johns Hopkins University Press, 1989), 107–9.

18. In some traditions, bells may also sound at significant moments *during* a worship service. For examples, see Jennifer L. Lord, "Their Proclamation Has Gone Out into All the Earth: An Account of the Aural Iconography of Orthodox Church Bells," *Proceedings of the North American Academy of Liturgy* (2017): 11–31, https://issuu.com/naal-proceedings/docs/17-naal_proceedings2017_fnlweb.

19. Fritz West proposes that most Catholic (and Orthodox and other Eastern) Christians and most Protestant Christians read Scripture out of two different operative paradigms. The Catholic liturgical paradigm situates Scripture within the church's communal memory conveyed through sacramental ritual and the liturgical calendar. In contrast, the Protestant liturgical paradigm relies on the biblical text and its narrative framework "to structure the selection of Scripture and to proclaim the memory of the salvation of God in Jesus Christ." *Scripture and Memory: The Ecumenical Hermeneutic of the Three-Year Lectionaries* (Collegeville, MN: Liturgical Press, 1997), 42–70, quote from 68.

20. Connell, *Eternity Today*, 1:4.

21. See O'Donnell, *Remembering the Future*, 4. For some parallel reflections from a philosopher's perspective, see Nicholas Wolterstorff, *Acting Liturgically: Philosophical Reflections*

is the night" when Christ passed over from death to life.[22] The present prayer in response to God's offer of salvation is patterned on how God has acted in the past and what God has promised for our future—which inform hope of how God might be likely to act *now*. The Lord's Prayer, which figures frequently in the worship service's third movement, draws together eschatological longing ("Thy kingdom come, Thy will be done on earth as it is in heaven"), present need ("Give us this day our daily bread, . . . forgive us, . . . deliver us from evil"), and active remembrance of Christ, who taught us to boldly pray this way (Matt. 6:9–13 KJV; Luke 11:2–4).[23] Remembrance of the future is sometimes expressed quite bluntly, as in Eastern eucharistic prayers that remember Christ's "second and glorious coming," a future event that has already transpired in God's eternity but not yet in our time.[24]

Dismissal rites tend to be brief. As the community is sent from worship to mission, Christ's ecclesial body is commissioned to embody his self-sacrificing love in the world. God's holy people emerge from but remain formed by liturgical time, characterized by "a certain disengagement from measured time, a focus on eternity present in time" made possible by the commingling of past, present, and future time from the vantage point of faith.[25] The end point of their service is unspecified, for it will find its fulfillment only in the eternal love of God.

Since it is difficult to completely disengage from worldly time while worshiping, those who prepare and lead worship would wisely attend to the "temporal culture" of the congregations they serve. Are church members held hostage

---

on Religious Practice (Oxford: Oxford University Press, 2018), esp. chap. 9, "The Liturgical Present Tense."

22. The paschal proclamation belongs to the extended introductory rites of the Easter Vigil and is a paradigmatic example of this past-present temporality in liturgical prayer. For two versions, see (1) the Paschal Proclamation (Exsultet) in the *Roman Missal*, 3rd typical ed., for use in the dioceses of the United States of America (Collegeville, MN: Liturgical Press, 2011), Proper of Time, The Easter Vigil in the Holy Night; reproduced online with accompanying audio at https://npm.org/wp-content/uploads/2017/08/exsultet.pdf; and (2) the Exsultet in the Episcopal *Book of Common Prayer* (New York: Seabury, 1979), Proper Liturgies for Special Days, The Great Vigil of Easter, https://www.bcponline.org.

23. Bob Hurd, *Compassionate Christ, Compassionate People: Liturgical Foundations of Christian Spirituality* (Collegeville, MN: Liturgical Press, 2019), 91.

24. From the Anaphora of St. John Chrysostom; in context this prayer reads: "We therefore, remembering this saving commandment [to eat the blessed bread and drink from the cup of the new covenant] and all the things that were done for us: the cross, the tomb, the resurrection on the third day, the ascension into heaven, the session at the right hand, the second and glorious coming . . ." English translation from Ronald Claud Dudley Jasper and G. J. Cuming, *Prayers of the Eucharist: Early and Reformed; Texts Translated and Edited with Introductions*, ed. Paul F. Bradshaw and Maxwell E. Johnson, 4th ed., Alcuin Club Collections (Collegeville, MN: Liturgical Press, 2019), 169.

25. Melloh, "Liturgical Time," 733.

hourly, driven by clocks and calendars and conscious or unconscious expecta-tions to fill time with productive activities, fitting worship into their schedules as they can? Or do many worshipers suffer injustice even in relation to time—a rare resource allotted equally to all—from the need, perhaps, to work multiple low-wage jobs with unpredictable schedules that make it difficult to find time for rest and renewal in the church's worship or to nurture important relation-ships? Are conflicting sensibilities around how to spend time in community, in worship, or in service to God causing tension in multigenerational or mul-ticultural congregations? How might churches address warped dimensions of time-tending, take time to worship fully, and preach the hope of living in *God's* good time?

The Worship of People in Weeks, Years, and Days

Worshiping in time over the course of days, weeks, and years is commonly understood in Jewish and Christian tradition as a means of remembering that *all* time is holy, through consciously setting aside *some* time for public wor-ship and private prayer. At first glance this may seem to run counter to Paul's critique of the Galatians for "observing special days, and months, and seasons, and years" (Gal. 4:10), yet Christian communities nevertheless adopted such practices quite early. Although living already in salvation's "end times" and no longer compelled to time-bound worship, "it is normal that a certain recur-rence and repetition should enable [Christians] to enter more deeply into their own joy and to unite themselves more fully to the deliverance bestowed upon them" in Christ.[26] Thus the real orientation of prayer in time is for the glory of God and the sanctification of *people* since time has already been redeemed by Christ.[27] Worship does not convert secular time to sacred time but "creates an experience of time which communicates the divine mystery" such that any time potentially becomes participation in God, who is holy.[28] Advocating for more widespread adoption of "Christian-year spirituality" in evangeli-cal circles, Robert Webber classifies disciplines of Christian connection with time reshaped by Christ's death and resurrection as a subjective faith response that can intensify a Christian's baptismal calling to live *with* Christ and *in* Christ (see, e.g., Rom. 6:3–11; Gal. 2:19–20; Eph. 2:5–6).[29] The remainder of

26. Nocent, *Liturgical Year*, 1:10.
27. See Melloh, "Liturgical Time," 738; and O'Donnell, *Remembering the Future*, 177.
28. O'Donnell, *Remembering the Future*, 144.
29. Robert Webber, *Ancient-Future Time: Forming Spirituality through the Christian Year* (Grand Rapids: Baker Books, 2004), 20–21.

this section explores theological principles underpinning weekly, yearly, and daily cycles of worship, along with cultural challenges and opportunities for embodying this theology through communal worship practices in our own times.

Sanctifying the Church on Sunday

All four Gospel accounts received by the church testify that Jesus's followers began to experience his ongoing presence with them after his death on the first day of the week, initially through the disturbing *absence* of the corpse they expected to find in his tomb (Mark 16:1–2, 6; Matt. 28:1, 6; Luke 24:1–2, 5; John 20:1–2, 5–7) and then through encounters that same day with the Christ who was raised from the dead (Mark 16:9–20 [the longer ending]; Matt. 28:9–10; Luke 24:13–53; John 20:11–23). Early Christian theological reflection connected Jesus's resurrection, on the day beginning the new week, to God's radical act of inaugurating a new creation on the "eighth day" after the ultimate Sabbath rest of God's Son in the tomb. Sunday become "the day of the Lord," a designation it still bears in contemporary Romance languages such as Spanish, French, and Italian (as Day of God = Domingo, Dimanche, Domenica).

Within a few generations of Jesus's death, Christians were gathering on Sunday to celebrate the Eucharist (Lord's Supper), a meal with both memorial and eschatological components. However, the primary impetus in early Christianity for selecting Sunday as the preeminent day for gathering the assembly of God's people renewed in Christ through the Spirit seemingly was motivated less by viewing the day as a weekly memorial of Christ's resurrection and more as embodying most intensely the eschatological expectation proper to the eighth day, which should guide Christian life at *all* times.[30] On Sundays, the eighth day, the *ekklēsia* (assembly) and the Eucharist converged. Sunday becomes a day for Christians to "remember" the future they share in Christ as people incorporated into his death and resurrection through baptism, sustained by the continual outpouring of the Spirit and the regular celebration of the Eucharist, and committed to a life of discipleship that will endure into eternity.

Most Christians have quite strongly maintained the practice of gathering as the church of Christ on Sundays, even if not all Christian traditions have historically emphasized a consistent connection between the Lord's Day and the Lord's Supper. Cultures that valorize individual freedom and choice, however,

---

30. Paul F. Bradshaw, *The Origins of Feasts, Fasts, and Seasons in Early Christianity*, Alcuin Club Collections (London: SPCK; Collegeville, MN: Liturgical Press), 13.

will likely find Sunday as a day *of* the church a tough sell. The decision to go to church at all (or not)—let alone *which* church to attend—is more easily situated within the realm of personal initiative in response to nurturing one's own relationship with God than conceived as a divine calling to "re-member" the body of Christ by bringing one's body to worship with other people at a particular time. Church leaders and members could ponder how worship might more fully become a high point of the week, celebrating what God is accomplishing *for us* as a church (at the universal and local levels) that includes but also transcends significant ways God is working in the lives of individual church members. Cultivating a collective communal vision of what it means to *be* the worshiping church could also overflow into the church's mission. This sense of Sunday as festive, freeing time in Christ *in community* experiences can influence worship forms and convey the vision of what the church could be in and for the world.

The encroachment of work into the "weekend," the blurring of the division between work and leisure, and the "work" of self-development and self-fulfillment also compete with prioritizing Sunday worship, even for committed Christians.[31] Worship becomes another activity that needs to fit into the calendar around paid and volunteer work, family commitments, errands, and other activities. Some churches have responded to the reality that Sundays are busy and demographics are shifting by offering alternative Sunday-style worship services on different days (beyond later in the day on Saturday, a time span already assimilated to Sunday through the Jewish custom of marking days from sundown to sundown and a mode of timekeeping retained at least for major feasts in many branches of the Christian tradition). Although trends like "Thursday is the new Sunday" represent well-intentioned attempts to make worship (and the gospel) widely accessible, promoting worship on other days as a straightforward substitution for Sunday worship is theologically problematic for the reasons discussed above. If Sunday is *the* day for weekly remembrance (*anamnēsis*) of the paschal mystery continued in the life and witness of the church, a temporal substitution is inadequate. "Since the weekly anamnesis is bound to Sunday, no other day of the week can replace this day. The adoption of a day other than Sunday, possibly because of the special significance it has in a people's culture, like Friday in predominantly Muslim countries, does not meet the requirement of weekly anamnesis."[32]

---

31. Melloh, "Liturgical Time," 738–39.
32. Anscar J. Chupungco, *Liturgies of the Future: The Process and Methods of Inculturation* (Mahwah, NJ: Paulist Press, 1989), 166.

The Christian tradition itself lends perspective to this contemporary time bind. Sunday is a day of joy but need not be a day devoted *exclusively* to rest and worship. This would not have been possible for most Christians before the fourth century, when Constantine declared it a day of public rest, and still is impossible for Christians today in places where Sunday is part of the standard workweek.[33] If Christians find their ultimate fulfillment in Christ, how might Christians today bring the experience of the church's worship to people where they are on Sundays? Churches might experiment with abbreviated opportunities for Sunday worship that nonetheless give dignity to the day and strive to connect absent church members to the Sunday assembly in some way.[34] All Christians might consider how their observance of Sundays as individuals, families, and local church communities might become a countercultural witness, especially in cultures gripped by consumerism; such Sundays all Christians could "bear in comportment, company, and conversation, in their habits of rest, leisure, and social cohesion."[35]

Celebrating Christ through the Year

Most Christian traditions celebrate at least Christmas Day (or Epiphany) and Easter Sunday every year as annual observances of Christ's incarnation and resurrection, respectively. Some also have preparatory and celebratory seasons extending backward and forward from these days: Advent and Christmas/ Epiphany on the one hand, and Lent and Easter on the other. Some churches describe their observance of the liturgical year in highly sacramental terms; it is one mode of the liturgical presence of Christ the Lord, who continues to celebrate his paschal mystery in the Spirit with the church and for the glory of God.[36] Other denominations might be more comfortable beginning with the biblical text and ending with ethical implications to convey the same reality. Through "non-identical repetitions" of ecclesial engagement with the core

33. Although some Christians have promoted Sunday as the Christian equivalent of the Jewish Sabbath in terms of injunctions to rest, avoid unnecessary servile work and commercial pursuits, and center the day around worship of God in fidelity to God's commandment to keep the Sabbath holy, enforcing this strictly at the level of civil legislation tended to be a fairly late development. See Susan J. White, *Foundations of Christian Worship* (Louisville: Westminster John Knox, 2006), 59; and Connell, *Eternity Today*, 2:18–25.

34. One prominent option in the tradition is to bring eucharistic Communion to those absent from the ecclesial communion of the church gathered for prayer. Justin Martyr (d. ca. 165) refers to this practice in his *First Apology* 67: the "things over which thanks have been given" are "sent to those not present through the deacons." English translation from Jasper and Cuming, *Prayers of the Eucharist*, 27.

35. Connell, *Eternity Today*, 2:25.

36. This is a close reproduction of a concept expressed in Nocent, *Liturgical Year*, 1:16.

Gospel narratives of salvation won for us in Christ, the church led by Christ is effectively "re-inhabiting them, making them present in the church's worship in such a way that they challenge individuals and the community to discern how to act in the future."[37]

Easter anchors the church's year analogous to the way Sunday grounds the week. Properly speaking, Sunday is not a "little Easter"; rather, Easter is a *very big* Sunday.[38] Easter also provides an apt illustration of some cultural-ecclesial tensions that apply more broadly to the ways many contemporary churches keep the church's annual feasts in general.[39] First, overemphasizing anticipation and preparation in advance can shortchange the prolonged celebration of the feast—and the challenge for Christian life that more frequently comes from dwelling with the further observance. For example, many churches have robust seasonal offerings for Lent, liturgical and otherwise, but nearly nothing "extra" between Easter and Pentecost to help the congregation live more fully into the open-ended eschatological commitment of being the church in the world until Christ comes again.[40] Second, there is a temptation among worship planners to overlay the liturgical seasons with unique yearly "themes." This risks "intellectualizing" worship and thereby attenuating the experiential and emotional impact of the scriptural texts and liturgical symbols of the central seasons and feasts (e.g., baptismal water for the Easter season); worshipers' imaginations are less free to appropriate Scriptures and symbols in manifold ways that connect with how Christ is working now in their own lives. Third, the tendency to celebrate major feasts as historical commemorations of events in Christ's life (such as making a dramatic reenactment of the Gospel story a focal point of worship) promotes remembrance of what is *past* for the historical Jesus rather than what is *present* for us.[41]

The diverse cultures where Christianity has taken root have their own times of sacred and secular significance, including annual cycles honoring the earth's seasons and human labor and days dedicated to rest, thanksgiving, and festivity. Nations honor anniversaries of their founding or independence

37. Scott Waalkes, *The Fullness of Time in a Flat World: Globalization and the Liturgical Year*, Theopolitical Visions (Eugene, OR: Cascade Books, 2010), 12.

38. See Stookey, *Calendar*, 54–55; and Alexander, *Celebrating Liturgical Time*, 14.

39. The three points below are drawn from Melloh, "Liturgical Time," 739.

40. For further reflections on this point, see Bruce T. Morrill, "Faith's Unfinished Business: Can the Easter Season's Mysticism Empower Ethical Praxis?," *Proceedings of the North American Academy of Liturgy* (2019): 5–18; https://issuu.com/naal-proceedings/docs/proceedings_2019_web.

41. For example, John Allyn Melloh observes that a better question for Good Friday than "Were you there when they crucified my Lord?" would be "How is the passion, death and resurrection of Jesus as *present* reality . . . experienced among God's people today?" Melloh, "Liturgical Time," 739, emphasis added.

and the ideals embodied by significant citizens. The addition of new feasts to the Christian calendar, even if they are celebrated only on a local or regional level, "could bear witness to the desire to locate the proclamation of the Gospel solidly in the setting of the traditions to which each human group has been long attached."[42] Anscar Chupungco, a pioneer in the field of liturgical inculturation, offers advice for discerning the institution of new Christian liturgical feasts to complement civic and cultural festivities. First, avoid far-fetched biblical typology. Second, strive for nobility and beauty in language and ritual to foster genuine prayer. Finally and most important, always center the new feast, even if secular in origin, in relation to how it leads Christians more deeply into some aspect of the paschal mystery.[43] Several Christian traditions, for example, have developed worship services for the Lunar New Year holiday, adapting traditional aspects of the festival to pray for God's blessing in Christ on the year ahead and to honor the memory of ancestors. Christian communities in their worship might also reemphasize the Christian underpinnings of holidays widely embraced as secular celebrations, including Valentine's Day, Mardi Gras, St. Patrick's Day, and Halloween.

Some annual celebrations of secular origin, such as Mother's Day and Father's Day, have already migrated into Christian worship to some extent. Congregations ignore such secularly significant occasions at their peril, yet acknowledging various groups within worship does not demand making them the primary focus of worship. Christian groups generate a plethora of such observances as well, including a Season of Creation, a Week of Prayer for Christian Unity, and special Sundays honoring missionaries, vocations, and religious education ministries. When the values of these ideological celebrations too often and too intensively overlay the community's worship, the proper focus of every Sunday and season on Christ's death and resurrection and the community's consequent new life in Christ risks dilution and disintegration.

Even nature itself can pose problems for worshipers when the symbols and imagery of the church's common prayer are out of sync with the surroundings. The church's year developed amid theological reflection at the intersection of cosmic cycles and the historical salvation narrative in the northern hemisphere. Therefore, many of the traditional texts and hymns for Christmas and Easter liturgies give the impression that these are winter and spring celebrations, respectively, prompting considerable cognitive dissonance for

42. Irénée Henri Dalmais, "Time in the Liturgy," in *The Church at Prayer: An Introduction to the Liturgy*, ed. Aimé Georges Martimort (Collegeville, MN: Liturgical Press, 1986), 4:7.
43. Chupungco, *Liturgies of the Future*, 203.

communities in the southern hemisphere, with its inverse cycle of seasons.[44] Presuming the priority of Christians worldwide keeping a common festal calendar, Christians in the global south might search the Scriptures and the "book" of nature for a festal theology that resonates readily with the church's tradition while helping them apprehend manifestations of Christ's mystery in their own seasonal experience.[45]

Praying Daily with the Church

Drawing on daily experience, Christians have connected creation and the re-creation of Christ's resurrection to prayer alongside the morning's rising sun. They saw the light of Christ, which no darkness can overcome, attending their evening prayer. They prayed for the peace of God's presence as nighttime and the inevitable hour of death approached. Admittedly, daily public prayer at these major turning points of the day is a worship opportunity that "the great majority of Christians neither practice nor miss."[46] After daily public prayer flourished among God's people for a brief period in late antiquity, Eastern and Western Christian monastic communities preserved this tradition most strongly through the Middle Ages until today. Among churches flowing from the Western Reformations, some maintained strong connections to daily prayer practices (e.g., Anglicans and Episcopalians); others adapted the daily prayer concept to occasional midweek prayer gatherings and/or promoted daily domestic worship.[47] Many current denominational worship books—such as the Episcopal Church's *Book of Common Prayer* (1979), *Evangelical Lutheran Worship* (2006), and the Presbyterian Church (USA)'s *Book of Common Worship, Daily Prayer* (2018)—provide models for daily prayer.[48] These exist alongside less official initiatives to revive interest in daily prayer practices so that individuals and groups might experience solidarity

44. Carmel Pilcher, "Poinsettia: Christmas or Pentecost—Celebrating Liturgy in the Great South Land That Is Australia," *Worship* 81, no. 6 (November 2007): 508–20.

45. See Benjamin M. Stewart, *A Watered Garden: Christian Worship and Earth's Ecology*, Worship Matters (Minneapolis: Augsburg Fortress, 2011), 44–45; and Chupungco, *Liturgies of the Future*, 201.

46. White, *Introduction to Christian Worship*, 146. On the tradition of daily prayer more broadly, see George Guiver, *Company of Voices: Daily Prayer and the People of God*, rev. ed. (Norwich, UK: Canterbury, 2001).

47. White, *Introduction to Christian Worship*, 143–46.

48. Episcopal Church, *Book of Common Prayer* (New York: Seabury, 1979); Evangelical Lutheran Church in America / Evangelical Lutheran Church in Canada, *Evangelical Lutheran Worship* (Minneapolis: Augsburg Fortress, 2006); Presbyterian Church (USA), *Book of Common Worship, Daily Prayer* (Louisville: Westminster John Knox, 2018).

in prayer with the wider Christian community at pivotal times of day.[49] The typical disconnect between people in technologized societies and the daily cosmic rhythms of light and darkness, coupled with the pragmatic view of time in numerous cultures, make it quite difficult for many Christians today to easily appropriate daily prayer practices.[50] However, delighting daily in God's time with praise and prayer is yet another way to receive God's time as gift. Such prayer transcends worshipers' individual needs and connects them, at day's beginning and end, to the diffuse community of the church, continuing at prayer throughout time and space.

Cultural and sacred considerations of time interpenetrate for Christians formed by worship in ways that significantly shape their overall experience of liturgy and life. Since time is among the first creations of a holy God, humans have the capacity to cocreate with God insofar as they receive time as gift and as medium of their transformation. In the community's worship, salvation history, running backward and forward from creation to consummation in Christ's coming again, is taken up into *the* mystery of Christ's life now living in us through the Spirit as we await the final fulfillment of God's kingdom. Distinctively Christian ways of engaging Christ's paschal mystery are mediated through the church's worship: this daily, weekly, and yearly dying and rising with and in Christ overlap commitments on other calendars (civic, economic, academic, personal, etc.) that structure engagement with time in human communities. Time-related disruptions and disconnections might invite renewed participation in traditional forms of worship, prompt new ways of worshiping in a changing world, or inspire the incarnation of new aspects of human cultures in the church. In worship, Christians are drawn more deeply, in time and over time, to the life they hope to share with God forever by remembering the future in the liturgical present.

For Further Reading

Alexander, J. Neil. *Celebrating Liturgical Time: Days, Weeks, and Seasons.* New York: Church Publishing, 2014.

Connell, Martin. *Eternity Today: On the Liturgical Year.* 2 vols. New York: Continuum, 2006.

49. See Shane Claiborne, Jonathan Wilson-Hartgrove, and Enuma Okoro, *Common Prayer: A Liturgy for Ordinary Radicals* (Grand Rapids: Zondervan, 2010). This resource grew out of the "new monasticism" movement. Excerpts are available online (http://commonprayer.net) as models for group or individual prayer.

50. Melloh, "Liturgical Time," 739.

Dalmais, Irénée Henri, Pierre Jounel, and Aimé Georges Martimort. *The Church at Prayer: An Introduction to the Liturgy.* Vol. 4, *Liturgy and Time*, edited by Aimé Georges Martimort. New ed. Collegeville, MN: Liturgical Press, 1986.

Melloh, John Allyn. "Liturgical Time, Theology of." In *The New Dictionary of Sacramental Worship*, edited by Peter E. Fink, 733–40. Collegeville, MN: Liturgical Press, 1990.

O'Donnell, Emma. *Remembering the Future: The Experience of Time in Jewish and Christian Liturgy.* Collegeville, MN: Liturgical Press, 2015.

Stookey, Laurence Hull. *Calendar: Christ's Time for the Church.* Nashville: Abingdon, 1996.

Waalkes, Scott. *The Fullness of Time in a Flat World: Globalization and the Liturgical Year.* Theopolitical Visions 6. Eugene, OR: Cascade Books, 2010.

Webber, Robert. *Ancient-Future Time: Forming Spirituality through the Christian Year.* Ancient-Future Faith Series. Grand Rapids: Baker Books, 2004.

—14—

Ecology and Worship

Teresa Berger

What Does Christian Worship Have to Do with Ecology?

Given the relative newness of the subject "worship and ecology," it is worth beginning with the question of whether the two terms, "worship" and "ecology," can so easily be joined. Is a simple "and" enough to ground a link between practices of worship, on the one hand, and ecological concerns, on the other? The (relatively recent) link seems to sit uneasily with the long-standing image of Christian worship as a privileged site of encounter between God and human beings. Hence the question, What room is there to think about the cosmos, planet Earth, and the ecological emergency of our day as a foundational part of the worshipful encounter of human beings with the Triune God? One recent answer to this question has claimed "creation care" as a biblically rooted imperative for Christian living and thus for Christian worship too. The insistence on the importance of creation and its care has led to a surge of new worship practices and materials. These include creation-sensitive prayers, hymns and songs, sermon aids, intercessions, blessings, laments, and entire rituals—or even a whole new season in the Christian year dedicated to creation.[1] The latter begins with September 1, now designated as a Day of Prayer for Creation in

---

1. One place that has gathered many of these resources is the website of the Calvin Institute of Christian Worship; see Joan Huyser-Honig, "Worship Resources for Creation Care," June 14, 2017, https://worship.calvin.edu/resources/resource-library/worship-resources-for-creation-care/.

many Christian communities, and ends with October 4, the traditional feast day of St. Francis of Assisi. Creation-attentive worship materials have emerged within a broad network of environmental-activist, "green" congregations, and activist groups, which have embraced a wide range of issues, from land conservation to the protection of waterways, from fighting climate change to enhancing the lives of companion and farm animals, and so on.[2] Christian environmental activism has also produced its own version of a specialty Bible, *The Green Bible*, whose green-tinted texts foreground themes of creation care.[3]

The emergence of creation-attuned biblical and liturgical materials has also been nurtured by the work of theologians who have begun to carry the Christian tradition forward into this age of ecological emergency. They share notions of creation as a primordial sacrament, ideas of the world as the body of God, and visions of a "deep incarnation"[4] or a "cosmocentric sacramentality."[5] We find recent creation-themed publications from such prominent theologians as Elizabeth Johnson and Rowan Williams. Such voices are urgently speaking the Christian faith into the reality of a planet in peril.[6] These theological voices find echoes in statements from official ecclesial and ecumenical bodies, many of which have begun to foreground ecological concerns. In terms of ecumenical dialogues, for example, the World Council of Churches has long championed the "integrity of creation."[7] On a much smaller scale, the US Roman Catholic–United Methodist conversations produced a joint statement in 2012 on "The Eucharist and Stewardship of God's Creation," arguing that "Eucharistic renewal and environmental responsibility are intrinsically linked."[8] Individual churches, too, have embraced ecological

2. For specifics, see, e.g., the Ecumenical Water Network of the World Council of Churches, "About EWN," http://water.oikoumene.org/en/about; and the Project CreatureKind, which seeks to engage Christians with farm animals' welfare, at https://www.becreaturekind.org/.

3. *The Green Bible* is a version of the NRSV with green-tinted text that highlights creation-themed passages; it was released by HarperCollins in 2008. Compare the substantial review essay by Dennis Owen Frohlich, "Let There Be Highlights: A Framing Analysis of the Green Bible," *Journal for the Study of Religion, Nature and Culture* 7, no. 2 (June 2013): 208–30.

4. The term was coined by Danish theologian Niels Henrik Gregersen in 2002; see note 14 below.

5. Linda Gibler, *From the Beginning to Baptism: Scientific and Sacred Stories of Water, Oil, and Fire* (Collegeville, MN: Liturgical Press, 2010), see esp. chap. 4, "Cosmocentric Sacramentality," 111–29.

6. See Elizabeth A. Johnson, *Creation and the Cross: The Mercy of God for a Planet in Peril* (Maryknoll, NY: Orbis Books, 2018); Rowan Williams, *Christ the Heart of Creation* (London: Bloomsbury Continuum, 2018).

7. "Justice, Peace and the Integrity of Creation" became a program priority for the World Council of Churches in 1983.

8. The statement is available online: "Heaven and Earth are Full of Your Glory: A United Methodist and Roman Catholic Statement on the Eucharist and Ecology," United States Conference

concerns, the Orthodox Churches above all,[9] but also much smaller bodies such as the Presbyterian Church (USA).[10] Most comprehensive in its treatment and far-reaching in its reception has been the 2015 encyclical of Pope Francis, *Laudato Si': On Care for Our Common Home.*[11]

Rooting Worship in Creation

Beyond a biblically rooted call to creation care, it may not be immediately obvious how Christian convictions about the universe as created by God link directly to worship, so here is a sketch of what I consider to be the basics of this theological connection. My hope is that such a link will convincingly root the practice of worship in the primordial fact of createdness (for lack of a better word). The basic building blocks of this theological link are the following. First, for Christian faith, the universe is brought into existence not by chance but by the creative energy of God,[12] which means that everything that is—*as created*—has an inimitable relationship to God—namely, one of radical dependence upon the Creator. This Creator God alone, as the ultimate source of all that exists, is uncreated—that is, does not exist because of the creative energy of another.

Second, being created and called into existence is gift, and this gift of existence has flourishing as its telos. The primary and deepest response of everything that exists, therefore, is worship, understood here as turning to God, the Creator, in praise and adoration. Third, the Christian faith holds that creation, although deeply marred by sin, evil, and violence, is continuously God-sustained. God preserves the world in existence; that is, God can be found deeply within as well as beyond what God has called into being.

In particular, and this is the fourth point, God chose to enter the created order in deepest intimacy by taking on human form in Jesus of Nazareth,

---

of Catholic Bishops, issued April 20, 2012, http://www.usccb.org/beliefs-and-teachings /ecumenical-and-interreligious/ecumenical/methodist/upload/Heaven-and-Earth-are-Full-of -Your-Glory-Methodist-Catholic-Dialogue-Agreed-Statement-Round-Seven.pdf.

9. See the essay by Bert Groen, "The First of September: Environmental Care and Creation Day," in *Full of Your Glory: Liturgy, Cosmos, Creation*, ed. Teresa Berger (Collegeville, MN: Liturgical Press, 2019), 307–31.

10. See the "Affirmation of Creation," approved for distribution by the 222nd General Assembly of the PC(USA), June 22, 2016, http://fore.yale.edu/files/Affirmation_of_Creation_2016.pdf.

11. Pope Francis, *Laudato Si': On Care for Our Common Home* (Vatican City: Libreria Editrice Vaticana, 2015), http://w2.vatican.va/content/francesco/en/encyclicals/documents/papa -francesco_20150524_enciclica-laudato-si.html.

12. This is a faith claim that for me can cohabit with an astrophysicist's cosmology describing a big bang almost 15 billion years ago and/or with a biologist's theory of the evolution of living beings.

living and dying as a part of created reality. In Jesus's resurrection, God foreshadowed the final flourishing of all creation, thriving against all powers of destruction and evil. Fifth and finally, everything God has created is on a journey through time to its ultimate fulfillment in God, when the profoundest response of everything created, adoration and worship of God, will be all in all. This vision of the end is grounded not in any evolutionary optimism but in the faithfulness and mercy of God alone.[13]

Clearly, my sketch, although rooting creation from beginning to end in worship, does not find its focus in only earthly human beings. Rather, human beings are situated within the larger context of all other beings, created, sustained, and destined for flourishing by the Creator. At the same time, there is nothing in this sketch that denies the foundational Christian conviction that Jesus Christ is the key to the redemption of the cosmos. Danish theologian Niels Henrik Gregersen describes this in his notion of "deep incarnation": "In Jesus Christ, God became part of the nexus of the entire cosmos—around us and within ourselves. . . . As a human being he was also a material being. His body was composed of material particles coming from the explosion of stars. His blood was red due to the iron running in his veins. . . . Deep incarnation thus presupposes a radical embodiment of the Son of God that reaches into the roots (radices) of material and biological existence."[14] Sadly, today any Christian vision of the "createdness" of all that exists and of Godself entering into creation in a deep incarnation is challenged by developments that have put the very existence of life on our planetary home in peril. It is time to confront a Christian vision of creation with the environmental emergency that threatens planet Earth.

Christian Faith and Environmental Emergency

Profound questions have arisen in our time over the state of the natural world, the earth system, the web of life, the universe (or a possible multiverse), and most ominously, over the very sustainability of life on planet Earth. This list

---

13. Kathryn Tanner has recently summarized this powerfully: "That future state of the world to come . . . remains an absolutely other world in that only God [makes it possible] and nothing about the world's own tendencies and trajectories make it possible. Rather than being the realization of this world's own latent future possibilities, the power of God fully manifest in that future world is what presently pulls this one toward it." *Christianity and the New Spirit of Capitalism* (New Haven: Yale University Press, 2019), 165.

14. Niels Henrik Gregersen, "Deep Incarnation & the Cosmos: A Conversation with Niels Henrik Gregersen," interview by Ciara Reyes, *God and Nature Magazine*, Summer 2017, https://godandnature.asa3.org/interview-deep-incarnation--the-cosmos-a-conversation-with-niels-henrik-gregersen-by-ciara-reyes--niels-henrik-gregersen.html.

merely names some of the most prominent markers of the semantic terrain in question here. Other terms could easily be added: Mother Nature, the environment, the planetary community, the cosmos, or creation. But whatever linguistic markers one chooses (and none of them is simply "natural," innocent, or unmarked), Christian faith and worship are compelled to engage with this terrain. One basic reason for such engagement is simple enough: we live on a planet now clearly in peril. To cite a globally respected source as evidence, the 2018 Report by the United Nations' Intergovernmental Panel on Climate Change (IPCC) painted an alarming picture of the "unprecedented rate and global scale of impact of human influence on the Earth System."[15] In particular, the report warned of rising sea levels, increasingly extreme weather, mounting food shortages, worsening wildfires, escalating biodiversity loss, the mass die-off of coral reefs, and the shrinking of arctic ecosystems. Some of these developments were identified as potentially irreversible. To cite just one other source, the 2019 report by the Intergovernmental Science-Policy Platform on Biodiversity and Ecosystem Services (IPBES) included dire headlines such as "Nature's Dangerous Decline Unprecedented," "Species Extinction Rates Accelerating," and "Transformative Changes Needed to Restore and Protect Nature."[16]

With however many details and statistics one describes today's ecological emergency, this crisis has rapidly intensified in recent years and is now at the forefront of global concerns. And Christian theologians and activists have claimed that this emergency constitutes a moral imperative for the community of faith. Yet actions responding to this emergency by the major global players, especially the major polluters, have been much too slow. While Christian communities of faith have seen a rise of green Christian activism, many congregations have yet to move beyond a basic nod to creation in their worship life. Congregations have learned again to praise and thank God for the works of creation, and some are including ecological concerns in their prayers of intercession and lament. However, if being created is a basic feature of human existence that we share with all that exists, then much more than prayers of thanksgiving, or lament, or intercessions for creation should impel Christian worship. Here is why and how.

15. Valérie Masson-Delmotte et al., eds., *Global Warming of 1.5°C* (Geneva: IPCC, 2018), 54; search for "unprecedented rate" in chap. 1 at the website: https://www.ipcc.ch/sr15/. *Global Warming* describes itself as "an IPCC special report on the impacts of global warming of 1.5°C above pre-industrial levels and related global greenhouse gas emission pathways, in the context of strengthening the global response to the threat of climate change, sustainable development, and efforts to eradicate poverty."

16. IPBES, "Media Release," May 2019, https://ipbes.net/news/Media-Release-Global-Assessment.

Christian Worship in Communion with Everything Created

A glimpse of this deeper vision of how Christian worship and creation inter-twine comes from Rev. Stephen Blackmer, priest of the Church of the Woods in Canterbury, New Hampshire. This church is part of the Wild Church Network, a community of churches around the US whose members gather for worship outside and understand themselves to be part of a beloved web of life that encompasses all creation.[17] Here is how Blackmer describes his "congregational roll call":

> Barred owl, pileated woodpecker, short-tailed ermine.
> Bracken fern, sphagnum moss, princess pine.
> White pine, black birch, red maple, beech.
> Blueberry, winterberry, blackberry.
> Dragonfly, ant, mosquito, mayfly.
> Vernal pool and trickling stream.
> British soldier moss.
> Quartz and gneiss.
> Mud.
> . . .

And me, the lone human being this morning, as . . . liturgist and priest.[18]

In this congregational roll call, we catch a glimpse of worship as something infinitely larger than a group of human beings gathered in a church building. Instead, this congregational roll call projects a vision of a shared worship space—a communion, if you will—with all that exists. Worship here becomes visible as a posture or way of life of all creation, and by human beings as co-creatures and kin with all that exists. Obviously, this vision of worship puts pressure on what we usually think of as worship and going to church on a Sunday morning. But the fundamental question is whether such a seem-ingly novel vision of worship can be substantiated from within the Christian Scriptures and the history of worship throughout the centuries. My answer to this question is an emphatic *yes*.

To arrive at this affirmation, a fresh look at what we see as past practices of worship is essential to retrieve elements, which certainly do exist, of a deeply cosmic and creation-attuned vision of worship. This retrieval needs to unseat

17. For more, see the Wild Church Network's website, http://www.wildchurchnetwork.com.
18. Stephen Blackmer, "A Sacred Assembly of Pines, Plants, and People Too," in *Yale Divinity School Reflections* 106, no. 1 (Spring 2019): 37–39, https://reflections.yale.edu/article/crucified -creation-green-faith-rising/sacred-assembly-pines-plants-and-people-too. Copyright *Yale Di-vinity School Reflections* and Stephen Blackmer. Used with permission.

established images of the liturgical tradition as essentially interested in human worshipers alone. Such images, of a tradition largely unconcerned about cosmos and creation, were and continue to be in place. To cite just one example, an entry on "Creation Theology and Worship" in one of the standard dictionaries in liturgical studies states that "the created order has not been a conscious and consistent point of reference in worship."[19] Other dictionaries do not even have an entry dedicated to "creation" or "cosmos." The time is here *now* to put in place a more nuanced picture. This picture will reveal the liturgical tradition, when studied afresh, to be about much more than God and human beings alone. For starters, we now recognize that inhabitants of premodern worlds, including the authors of the biblical books, were acutely aware that they lived in interconnected ecological systems, even if they did not use our contemporary language of ecology or environment to describe this interconnectedness. Indeed, "many ancient texts display awareness of a complex relationship between human beings and the natural world."[20] We catch a glimpse of this in Psalm 148, to cite just one example. In this hymn of praise, the psalmist calls on everything created to worship the Creator. What becomes visible in this ancient poetic cosmology is a vast, antiphonal choir. One side of the choir is in the heavens, the other side on earth; their song is one shared hymn of praise:

> Praise the Lord! . . .
> Praise him, sun and moon;
>   praise him, all you shining stars!
> Praise him, you highest heavens,
>   and you waters above the heavens!
>
> Let them praise the name of the LORD,
>   for he commanded and they were created.
> He established them forever and ever;
>   he fixed their bounds, which cannot be passed.
>
> Praise the LORD from the earth,
>   you sea monsters and all deeps,
> fire and hail, snow and frost,
>   stormy wind fulfilling his command!

19. Theodore Runyon, "Creation Theology and Worship," in *The New Dictionary of Sacramental Worship*, ed. Peter E. Fink (Collegeville, MN: Liturgical Press, 1990), 299–302.

20. Ailsa Hunt and Hilary Marlow, introduction to *Ecology and Theology in the Ancient World: Cross-Disciplinary Perspectives*, ed. A. Hunt and H. Marlow (London: Bloomsbury Academic, 2019), 1–12, here 6. See also Virginia Burrus, *Ancient Christian Ecopoetics: Cosmologies, Saints, Things* (Philadelphia: University of Pennsylvania Press, 2019).

Mountains and all hills,
    fruit trees and all cedars!
Wild animals and all cattle,
    creeping things and flying birds!

Kings of the earth and all peoples,
    princes and all rulers of the earth!
Young men and women alike,
    old and young together!

Let them praise the name of the LORD,
    for his name alone is exalted;
    his glory is above earth and heaven. (Ps. 148:1, 3–13)

This psalm does not stand alone in the biblical witness. In recent years scholars have shown how deeply the natural environment and material world are intertwined in biblical faith.[21] They have also worked hard to reinterpret "dominion" language, instead foregrounding biblical notions of humans as "creatures within creation."[22] And importantly, the beginning and the end of the biblical witness have been linked again, in the shared images of creation and new creation. For example, think of Revelation's vision of worship that includes "every creature" praising God:

Then I heard every creature in heaven and on earth and under the earth and in the sea, and all that is in them, singing,

"To the one seated on the throne and to the Lamb
be blessing and honor and glory and might
forever and ever!" (5:13)

Such cosmic visions of worship do not break off with the biblical witness but continue through the centuries. Although later visions witness change and develop, always in some conversation with the cosmologies of their time, they also carry forward the older, biblical visions of cosmos and creation. Indeed, Christians and Jews today, in the twenty-first century, continue to sing and pray the psalms, although our current cosmology is light years away from the biblical ones.

Here is not the place to map the intervening millennia in any detail. Suffice it to say that there is much to discover about past visions of Christian worship,

21. See, e.g., Anathea Portier-Young's essay "'Bless the Lord, Fire and Heat': Reclaiming Daniel's Cosmic Liturgy for Contemporary Eco-Justice," in Berger, *Full of Your Glory*, 45–67.
22. See Meric Srokosz and Rebecca S. Watson, *Blue Planet, Blue God: The Bible and the Sea* (London: SCM, 2017).

visions that encompass much more than human earthlings standing before their divine Maker. And these expansive, even cosmic views of worship in the Christian tradition go much deeper and are much wider than the occasional pointers to such prominent "eco-sensitive" saints like Hildegard of Bingen or Francis of Assisi allow one to see. Indeed, Hildegard and Francis, rather than being startlingly unique voices, are part of a larger chorus within which they sound and to which they belong. This chorus reaches back to (but by no means begins with) Tertullian and his claim that every creature prays: "*Orat omnis creatura.*"[23] Tertullian spells out this insight at the conclusion of his treatise on prayer, no doubt with a view to calling his human audience into a deeper life of prayer: "The whole creation prays. Cattle and wild beasts pray, and bend their knees, and in coming forth from their stalls and lairs look up to heaven, their mouth not idle, making the spirit move in their own fashion. Moreover the birds now arising are lifting themselves up to heaven and instead of hands are spreading out the cross of their wings, while saying something which may be supposed to be a prayer. What more then of the obligation of prayer?"[24]

Similar themes appear in, for example, the Anaphora of St. James, the ancient eucharistic liturgy of Jerusalem, as well as in hymnic texts such as the "Phos Hilaron" in the Eastern church and the "Te Deum" and the "Gloria, Laus et Honor" in the Western church. The theme also appears in writings of mystics such as Henry Suso, Hildegard of Bingen, and Francis of Assisi. Moreover, it does not completely disappear with the advent of early modernity but continues, although submerged, especially among hymn writers who draw on the psalms or set to music Francis of Assisi's "Laudato Si' [Praise Be to You!]." Among English-language hymn writers, Henry Francis Lyte's (1793–1847) well-known hymn "Praise, My Soul, the King of Heaven" images, in verse 4, angelic and celestial realms adoring God, together with human worshipers:

> Angels, help us to adore him;
>   you behold him face to face.
> Sun and moon, bow down before him,
>   dwellers all in time and space.
> Alleluia, alleluia!
>   Praise with us the God of grace![25]

23. Tertullian, *De oratione* 29. Latin text with English translation in Ernest Evans, *Tertullian's Tract on the Prayer* (London: SPCK, 1953), 40–41.

24. Tertullian, *De oratione* 29, in Evans, *Tertullian's Tract*, 41.

25. The text is in many hymnals as well as online: e.g., https://hymnary.org/text/praise_my _soul_the_king_of_heaven.

Two early twentieth-century hymns also deserve mention. Henry van Dyke's (1853–1933) "Hymn to Joy" picks up on the creation story in Job 38–39 in its verse 4, envisioning human beings joining the "mighty chorus" begun at creation by the morning stars. Another early twentieth-century hymn, "All Creatures of Our God and King," by William Henry Draper (1855–1933), reprises Francis of Assisi's "Laudato Si'," calling all creation to praise and worship: "All creatures of our God and King, lift up your voice and with us sing."[26]

I applaud these creation-attuned elements in the Christian tradition. Yet I need to stress that a historical retrieval cannot merely be a facile celebration of past visions of creation in worship. The Christian tradition also exhibits profound ambiguities in how it relates to the natural world in worship. David Power has highlighted deep-seated fears of the natural world that were present in past liturgical practices, especially in the many apotropaic and exorcistic rites.[27] Such fears also underlie, for example, Rogation days, which in some circles today are revived primarily as creation-attuned celebrations. As Nathan Ristuccia has shown, however, the historical character of Rogation days was one of profound fears of the natural world.[28] This all goes to say that historical retrieval must not green-wash past practices of worship. Instead, historical retrieval needs to map the multifaceted, sometimes joyful, sometimes fearful engagement with the cosmos, creation, the earth, and nature that is a part of the Christian tradition. Even with such an acknowledgment of ambiguity, there still remains much that is startlingly creation-attuned. And whether joyful or fearful, themes of creation and cosmos clearly are no strangers to past practices of worship. This insight is important not least to undermine all-too-facile claims about the deep anthropocentrism of the Christian tradition. I am thinking here, for example, of Lynn White's sweeping, much-cited critique of medieval Christianity.[29] Inquiring into the past more deeply has the power to destabilize homogenous representations of the Christian tradition such as White's.

26. The text is available in many hymnals as well as online, e.g., at https://hymnary.org/text/all_creatures_of_our_god_and_king.

27. David Power, "Worship and Ecology," *Worship* 84, no. 4 (July 2010): 290–308, esp. 294–97.

28. Nathan J. Ristuccia, "Rogationtide and the Secular Imaginary," in Berger, *Full of Your Glory*, 165–85.

29. See Lynn White Jr., "The Historical Roots of Our Ecological Crisis," *Science* 155, no. 3767 (March 1967): 1203–7. For a recent, insightful critique of White's construal of "pagan animism," whose destruction by Christianity he lamented, see Ailsa Hunt, "Pagan Animism: A Modern Myth for a Green Age," in Hunt and Marlow, *Ecology and Theology*, 137–52.

Contemporary Developments

What about the present or more recent developments? We might conveniently begin with a text that follows nicely on the last two hymns quoted above. In 1937 the Anglican layperson Evelyn Underhill (1875–1941) opened her book *Worship* with these lines: "Worship, in all its grades and kinds, is the response of the creature to the Eternal: nor need we limit this definition to the human sphere. There is a sense in which we may think of the whole life of the Universe, seen and unseen, conscious and unconscious, as an act of worship, glorifying its Origin, Sustainer, and End."[30] This cosmic vision of worship, however, remained in the background in the Liturgical Movement of the time. That movement of liturgical renewal focused on the human-divine dialogue in worship, in particular the full, conscious, and active participation of the gathered assembly (of humans, that is). It was not until the second half of the twentieth century that more cosmic insights began to receive attention. Liturgical experimentations with a Cosmic or Planetary Mass, for example, emerge in the 1980s; they were preceded by the Earth Mass, created by saxophonist Paul Winter and first celebrated in 1981. The Earth Mass fused traditional Mass texts, contemporary music, and the sounds of animals, such as the howl of a tundra wolf in the "Kyrie," and the song of a humpback whale in the "Sanctus." The Earth Mass continues to be celebrated on the first Sunday in October every year at the (Episcopal) Cathedral of St. John the Divine in New York City. Earlier still than the Earth Mass, feminist liturgies were incorporating earth and eco-spiritual elements into their liturgical repertoire. Among more recent worship trends, the fascination with Celtic worship also foregrounds nature, since the Celtic tradition is thought to be deeply connected to the natural world.[31]

From within the field of liturgical studies, a somewhat different focus has emerged to strengthen the cosmic and earth-attuned orientation of Christian worship. Here I am thinking especially of newly composed eucharistic prayer texts such as those by Gail Ramshaw, Robert J. Daly, and Catherine Vincie.[32] These were preceded by the so-called Star Trek Prayer, a text from the early 1970s now in the Episcopal Book of Common Prayer as "Eucharistic Prayer C." The text got its nickname from a sentence that praises the vastness of

30. Evelyn Underhill, *Worship* (1937; repr., London: Aeterna, 2015), 7.

31. For a perceptive analysis, see Bryan D. Spinks, "What Is Celtic about Contemporary Celtic Worship?," in *The Worship Mall*, Alcuin Club Collections 85 (London: SPCK, 2010), 159–81.

32. See Gail Ramshaw, "Liturgical Considerations of the Myth of Eden," *Worship* 89, no. 1 (January 2015): 64–79, here 76–78; Robert J. Daly, "Ecological Euchology," *Worship* 89, no. 2 (March 2015): 166–72, here 170–71; Catherine Vincie, *Worship and the New Cosmology: Liturgical and Theological Challenges* (Collegeville, MN: Liturgical Press, 2014), 105–8.

God's creation: "At your command all things came to be: the vast expanse of
interstellar space, galaxies, suns, the planets in their courses, and this fragile
earth, our island home."[33] At the same time, boundaries between broader
practices of creation spirituality and Christian ritualizing are fluid, as some
of the eco-feminist rituals in the women's liturgical movement already made
clear. A more contemporary example of this fluidity is offered in Catherine
Vincie's "Evening Prayer for the Feast of the Birthing of the Cosmos."[34]

The various developments sketched above reveal how much has already
been done in terms of a renewed Christian vision of God's redemptive purpose for the whole cosmos. In several ways the field of liturgical studies has
played a part in these developments. "Ecology and Liturgy" as a concern was
already in view in 1997, when Lawrence Mick, a priest of the Archdiocese
of Cincinnati and a champion of pastoral-liturgical renewal, published his
little volume *Liturgy and Ecology in Dialogue*.[35] In the introduction, Mick
reported that he had written an article on the subject of ecology and worship
in 1972, a quarter century before his book appeared in print. In this earlier
article, Mick had sought to articulate some of the connections between the
liturgical renewal after Vatican II and the emerging ecological activism of
the time. These tenets are developed further in more recent work by scholars
of liturgy writing at the intersections of worship, ecology, and/or cosmology. Some foundational work has also been done in explorations around
liturgical theology (beyond the strong emphasis on theology and ecology in
Eastern churches). Of particular importance here is Gordon Lathrop's *Holy
Ground: A Liturgical Cosmology*.[36] In this book Lathrop seeks to break open
the central symbols of Christian liturgy in order to allow them to "orient us
anew in relationship to the universe."[37] Lathrop argues that the key symbols
of Christian worship—bath, table, prayer, and Word—have cosmological
significance because they are meant for the life of the world and therefore
invite us "to keep a wider company than we had thought."[38] With Benjamin
Stewart's important book *A Watered Garden: Christian Worship and Earth's
Ecology*, we move beyond a focus on worship as essentially a gathering of

33. "Eucharistic Prayer C," found in "The Holy Eucharist: Rite II," can be accessed online
through *The (Online) Book of Common Prayer* (New York: Church Hymnal, 1977), https://
www.bcponline.org/.

34. See Vincie, *Worship and the New Cosmology*, 113–19.

35. Lawrence E. Mick, *Liturgy and Ecology in Dialogue* (Collegeville, MN: Liturgical Press,
1997).

36. Gordon W. Lathrop, *Holy Ground: A Liturgical Cosmology* (Minneapolis: Fortress,
2003).

37. Lathrop, *Holy Ground*, 15.

38. Lathrop, *Holy Ground*, 228.

humans.[39] Stewart insists that Christian worship has always been an act of "joining the wider worship of the whole creation, a liturgy that began long before humans even existed."[40] He therefore can claim that "the horizon of concern in Christian worship extends outward to the entire universe."[41] One key question that arises with this expansive vision of worship relates to practical implications such a vision might have for congregational practices of worship. To this we now turn.

Practical Implications for Worship

The practical implications of ecological insights are often framed in terms of a response to the question, How can we green Christian worship? A plethora of suggestions and concrete worship materials are available now that respond to that question. I suggest, however, that we begin with a more foundational question: How might Christian worship become visible as a joining in the "wider worship of the whole creation, a liturgy that began long before humans even existed"?[42] Practical suggestions follow below, but I am convinced that these must be anchored in a reconfiguration of contemporary Christian communities' theological vision. This vision mostly continues to privilege an image of worship as something that happens between God and human beings alone (although animal blessings and related rituals have increased substantially in recent years).[43] Expanding this vision is a crucial component of all attempts to green the practices of Christian worship; it will also prevent these attempts from turning into a facile "green-washing" of worship.[44] If the fundamental self-understanding of Christians at worship can be expanded—to see what happens in church as entering into the wider worship of the whole of creation—then practical implications are grounded where they belong: in an overarching vision that reconceives the gathered assembly of worshipers. To put this challenge differently, what is needed is a rearticulation, for the twenty-first century, of the grand theological vision that claims, in the words of the "Te Deum," "All creation worships You."[45] Granted, such a rearticulation

39. Benjamin M. Stewart, *A Watered Garden: Christian Worship and Earth's Ecology*, Worship Matters (Minneapolis: Fortress, 2011).
40. Stewart, *Watered Garden*, 18.
41. Stewart, *Watered Garden*, 10.
42. Stewart, *Watered Garden*, 18.
43. For details, see Amelie A. Wilmer, "In the Sanctuary of Animals: Honoring God's Creatures through Ritual and Relationship," *Interpretation* 73, no. 3 (July 2019): 272–87.
44. Stewart, *Watered Garden*, 9.
45. The text is available in many print hymnals and online at, e.g., https://hymnary.org/text/you_are_god_we_praise_you. The original Latin text reads: "omnis terra veneratur."

cannot be found in the past alone and by retrieval (along the historical lines noted above), but needs to include forward-looking and constructive theological work. What if we theologians, scholars, and practitioners of worship, embedded Christian liturgy within a larger primordial act of worship as the response of everything that exists to being called into existence?

Following on the heels of this grandest of visions, here are some concrete, practical implications that grow out of such an expanded vision of worship. As already pointed out, there has been lively experimentation with creation-attuned worship materials in recent years, so numerous resources are available for prayers, intercessions, hymns, sermon preparation, lament, and entire rituals focused on creation and its care. One cautionary note to sound here is a concern flagged by Gail Ramshaw. She identifies a problem, particularly in hymns and prayers, with a preponderance of "nice nature" images that occlude what we today also know regarding, for example, perpetual extinctions and species violence. Ramshaw pleads for "a more factual and genuine picture of nature" in worship materials.[46] She offers her own composition of an "Earth Eucharistic Prayer," which does justice to her concern.[47] At the same time, and this is my cautionary note, the desire continuously to update public worship language to the most recent scientific readings of the cosmos and of nature carries two assumptions that are worth questioning. First, such an approach assumes that contemporary scientific insights do get the universe right; yet astrophysicists are currently hotly debating their understanding of the nature of the universe.[48] It seems questionable to assume that contemporary scientific and astrophysical definitions are stable and true and therefore should be acknowledged in worship; such an assumption sits on shifting sand. In addition, one may ask why Christian worship should privilege contemporary scientific insights over all others, when so many of our contemporaries positively delight in and indeed seek to inhabit more ancient worlds and fantasies. A second, related assumption worth questioning is that different visions of the cosmos cannot stand side by side, especially in poetic, biblical, devotional, and liturgical language. We already have three quite different biblical creation stories in the Hebrew Bible: Genesis 1 and 2 and Job 38. These three narratives cohabit with other cosmological narratives (e.g., Hildegard of Bingen's "cosmic egg") throughout Christian history. Why not also in worship today?

46. Ramshaw, "Liturgical Considerations," 75.
47. Ramshaw, "Liturgical Considerations," 77–78.
48. Adam G. Riess of Johns Hopkins University and the Space Telescope Science Institute explains that "everything, including phantom energy, is up for consideration." Dennis Overbye, "Have Dark Forces Been Messing with the Cosmos?," *New York Times*, Feb. 25, 2019, D6.

To return to specific practical implications for worship, we might conceive of different layers for this. One layer involves tweaking practices of worship: including more creation-themed prayers, hymns, and intercessions; preaching on creation and the environmental emergency of today; celebrating the season of creation in worship; and adding specific creation-themed worship services to a congregation's calendar.[49] In recent years came the remarkable proliferation of hymns that express an expansive communion of worshipers joining in praise of the Creator. Carl Daw's "Let All Creation Bless the Lord" is an excellent example; it takes its cue from Psalm 148. There is also a small but growing number of hymns that lament human environmental harm. Shirley Erena Murray's "The Garden of the World," a lament for the earth, is an example of that. Murray's text invokes the image of God's garden, now "dishonored and destroyed" by a "lifestyle such as ours."[50]

Another layer involves a deeper rethinking of all worship practices in the life of a congregation. After all, different liturgical practices demand quite different ways of rethinking creation attentiveness, as Benjamin Stewart's book demonstrates: water in baptism, Sunday morning worship, the Lord's Supper and the fruit of the earth, funerals,[51] the liturgical year, and so on.

Beyond the individual elements and materials used in worship, a third layer relates to the larger picture of the sustainability of congregational life and practices. This concern spans a whole host of issues, from air conditioning or heating of the sanctuary (Does it really need to be this cold or this hot?), to transportation (Do your congregants drive gas-guzzlers to worship? Have you ever preached about the importance of public transportation or about carpooling to come to church?), to the kind of materials used during coffee hours or in the soup kitchen. Green audits for sanctuaries are available!

Finally, as odd as this might seem, the heightening visibility of ever starker natural disasters and environmental degradation makes it easier and also imperative to render creation and all planetary life present again in all Christian worship. We can no longer afford to continue worshiping as if planet Earth, the universe, and all things other than human do not matter in the encounter between God and human earthlings.

---

49. A recent collection that contains rich materials for this is *God's Good Earth: Praise and Prayer for Creation*, comp. and ed. by Anne and Jeffery Rowthorn (Collegeville, MN: Liturgical Press, 2018).

50. Shirley Erena Murray, "The Garden of the World"; this text is available in, e.g., Huyser-Honig, "Worship Resources."

51. See Benjamin M. Stewart, "Wisdom's Buried Treasure: Ecological Cosmology in Funeral Rites," in Berger, *Full of Your Glory*, 353–76.

For Further Reading

Berger, Teresa, ed. *Full of Your Glory: Liturgy, Cosmos, Creation.* Collegeville, MN: Liturgical Press, 2019.

Hurd, Bob. "Every Creature Is Sister and Brother: Reading and Enacting Laudato Si' Liturgically." *Worship* 92, no. 2 (March 2018): 141–56.

"Liturgy and Ecology." Special issue, *Liturgy* 27, no. 2 (2012).

Rowthorn, Anne, and Jeffery Rowthorn, comps. and eds. *God's Good Earth: Praise and Prayer for Creation.* Collegeville, MN: Liturgical Press, 2018.

Stewart, Benjamin M. *A Watered Garden: Christian Worship and Earth's Ecology.* Worship Matters. Minneapolis: Fortress, 2011.

Vincie, Catherine. *Worship and the New Cosmology: Liturgical and Theological Challenges.* Collegeville, MN: Liturgical Press, 2014.

Further creation-attuned liturgical resources appear on the website of the Calvin Institute of Christian Worship: https://worship.calvin.edu/resources/resource -library/worship-resources-for-creation-care/.

— 15 —

Individualism and Community within Worship Practices

E. Byron (Ron) Anderson

Does it matter if, as an invitation to prayer, the worship leader begins by saying, "Let us pray," or by saying, "Pray with me"? In the greater scheme of things, perhaps not, but how we invite people to pray in community provides one indicator of the way we think about the relationship between the individual and the community in corporate worship. Both statements assume that there is a community being invited to pray. Whether that community is two or three gathered in the Lord's name or two or three thousand, we are not praying alone. "Let us pray" indicates a priority on the community, the "us" gathered in prayer and praying together. "Pray with me" suggests that the prayer is less our shared prayer and more our joining the prayer of a worship leader, the "me" who invites our participation. Because "Let us pray" is more common in worship traditions shaped and governed by authorized forms and traditions, and "Pray with me" more common in free-church/evangelical worship traditions, these two invitations also represent a perceived tension between the emphases given to ritual and spontaneity of expression that are characteristic of the two traditions. These two invitations point to different understandings of the relationship between the church and the individual believer, between corporate worship and personal piety, and between our shared and individual stories as Christian people.

To explore these concerns, I first consider a brief description of our North American social context and a consideration of the relationship between the individual and the church. Next, I briefly discuss the role of ritual in shaping individual and communal identity, our Protestant resistance to ritual, and the importance of ritual for developing a shared story and memory. What I intend to demonstrate throughout the chapter is that consideration of Christian worship always requires attention to the individual *and* the community, that Christian worship is always, perhaps even necessarily, "about *us* and for *me*."

The North American Social Context

The separation of the individual from the community in our understanding of worship is very much a "modern" concern, not limited to North American expressions of Christianity. Nevertheless, such separation is often expressed more strongly in this context because of the powerful culture-shaping traditions of "American individualism." Robert Bellah and his colleagues provided one of the most comprehensive studies of this tradition in relationship to religious commitment in their 1985 book *Habits of the Heart*. As they note, North Americans "believe in the dignity, indeed the sacredness of the individual. Anything that would violate our right to think for ourselves, judge for ourselves, make our own decisions, live our lives as we see fit, is not only morally wrong, it is sacrilegious." Their research led them to conclude that "some of our deepest problems both as individuals and as a society are also closely linked to our individualism."[1] They also noted a persisting tension: while "we deeply feel the emptiness of a life without sustaining social commitments, . . . we are hesitant to articulate our sense that we need one another as much as we need to stand alone."[2] One result of this tension is ambivalence about our need to regularly participate in practices such as corporate worship. We can "find God" anywhere, so we increasingly pray alone, engage in individualized spiritual practices, create our own virtual communities, and become more concerned with being "spiritual but not religious."

Sociologist Robert Wuthnow noted similar concerns in his book *After Heaven*, where he explores the changing understandings of spirituality, broadly conceived, in North America over the second half of the twentieth century. Although he does not focus explicitly on worship, Wuthnow does

1. Robert Bellah et al., *Habits of the Heart: Individualism and Commitment in American Life* (New York: Harper & Row, 1985), 142.
2. Bellah et al., *Habits of the Heart*, 151.

attend to the ways in which changing understandings of spirituality interact with and have been shaped by American individualism. He begins with a general claim: "The foundations of religious tradition seem to be less secure than in the past. Insisting that old phrases are cant [hypocritical or sanctimonious], many Americans struggle to invent new languages to describe their faith. As they do, their beliefs are becoming more eclectic, and their commitments are often becoming more private."[3] With this focus on individual practices and private beliefs, congregations become increasingly "suppliers of spiritual goods and services,"[4] and the individual believer becomes the one primarily responsible for shaping spiritual practice.[5] When this happens, social philosopher Charles Taylor states, "The individual has been taken out of a rich community life and now enters instead into a series of mobile, changing, revocable associations, often designed merely for highly specific ends. We end up relating to each other through a series of partial roles."[6] Our relationships become more and more transactional, concerned with what "I get out of it" rather than some shared good. Christian educator Paul Bramer echoes Taylor's concern with "changing revocable associations." The problem, Bramer notes, is not the question of psychological individuation, through which we become distinct "selves" in a "necessary element in human development," but the problem of individualism, which "assumes that the individual is prior to society and that the self is the fundamental unit of reality. In an individualistic approach, we try to create community with people who commit themselves to each other temporarily and partially and often primarily for the sake of one's own progress."[7] As a result, we lack the shared practices, communal memories, and worldviews that would normally bind us together (Latin: *religare*) in a community.

Although Bellah and his colleagues seem to have first identified the "spiritual but not religious" as a category of belief in their 1985 work,[8] it is only in more recent conversations that the "spiritual but not religious" have gained churches' and scholars' attention. In *Belief without Borders: Inside the Minds of the Spiritual but Not Religious*, Linda Mercadante provides one of the more substantive studies of "SBNR" persons, making clear connections to

3. Robert Wuthnow, *After Heaven: Spirituality in America since the 1950s* (Berkeley: University of California Press, 1999), 1.

4. Wuthnow, *After Heaven*, 15.

5. Wuthnow, *After Heaven*, 17.

6. Charles Taylor, *Sources of the Self: The Making of Modern Identity* (Cambridge, MA: Harvard University Press, 1989), 502.

7. Paul D. G. Bramer, "Christian Formation: Tweaking the Paradigm," *Christian Education Journal* 4, no. 2 (Fall 2007): 345.

8. Bellah et al., *Habits of the Heart*, 246.

the themes identified by Bellah and Wuthnow.[9] She documents and explores the ways in which references to the "spiritual" are increasingly focused on an individual's "interior life of faith," while references to "religion" are intended to refer to "the necessary communal and/or organizational component" of the religious/spiritual life.[10] Spirituality is seen to be about *me*; religion is understood to be about a community or institution, though such an institution is often treated as optional. Mercadante describes a process of "detraditioning" that emerges as people revoke "religious authority in favor of personal decision." The result, she argues, is an ethos that includes "an impersonalization of transcendence, a sacralization of the self, a focus on therapeutic rather than civic goals, and a self-needs orientation to community and commitment." This ethos, she argues, is not only "distinctly American and widespread" but also problematic.[11] As did Bellah and Wuthnow, she concludes that "the public influence of religion is waning, [and] a private sort of religion seems to be growing"; such private religion is drawing increasingly from a kind of "free market" of religious ideas, beliefs, and practices.[12] Mercadante affirms the many traditional theological themes that emerged from the interviews that form the core of her research: the Protestant emphasis on the "priesthood of believers," "the idea that God loves each person individually," a concern for the "inner testimony of the Holy Spirit or one's relationship with Jesus Christ," and an emphasis on personal salvation. She notes, however, that when these themes are separated from the life of a community of belief and practice, our pursuit of them creates a highly individualized spirituality characterized by "unmediated claims of personal revelation," "withdrawal from community," "a focus on personal experience as the touchstone of sacred power," and a distorted "focus on the self."[13] Worship becomes primarily about and for *me*.

What all these writers point to is the necessary relationship between the individual and the community in any consideration of Christian worship. The more we focus on "personalizing" worship, the harder it becomes to think of worship as a gathering of God's people in a common work of praise and prayer, as a place and time in which the diverse parts of the body of Christ are reunited and nourished. But worship "is intrinsically social and collective; it gives shape to the church as a 'visible organism.'"[14] Religious life (Christian

9. Linda A. Mercadante, *Belief without Borders: Inside the Minds of the Spiritual but Not Religious* (New York: Oxford University Press, 2014).

10. Mercadante, *Belief without Borders*, 5.

11. Mercadante, *Belief without Borders*, 231.

12. Mercadante, *Belief without Borders*, 241.

13. Mercadante, *Belief without Borders*, 254.

14. Joris Geldhof, *Liturgy and Secularism* (Collegeville, MN: Liturgical Press, 2018), 134.

as well as that of other religious traditions) is always concerned with the individual *and* the community, not the individual *or* the community; this "and" is, for Christians, of the essence of the church.

The Individual and the Church

What does it mean to claim that the individual and the community are together "of the essence of the church"? Several writers help us answer this question, particularly in the ways they speak from and to mainline and free-church Protestant traditions. We start with the work of Paul Waitman Hoon, one of the first "modern" Protestant liturgical theologians writing after the Second Vatican Council in the late 1960s and early 1970s. Hoon identifies several key concerns for how Protestants should think about worship, emphasizing, throughout his argument, the necessity of the "and" between the individual and communal aspects of worship. He makes four claims that are particularly relevant to our discussion.

First, Christian worship "theologically speaking is corporate by definition. . . . The 'Christian unit' is the Church, not the individual."[15] Christian worship is a gathering of the body of Christ, a body in which we are one by virtue of our baptism in Christ Jesus. While Hoon suggests that there may be some risk of overemphasizing that corporateness and denying the diverse gifts of individual members of the body, we are more at risk today of what he calls "an unhealthy individualism." As the apostle Paul reminded the churches in Corinth and Rome, we may be many in language, nationality/ethnicity, and gender, but we are one in Christ (Rom. 12:15; 1 Cor. 12:27; Gal. 3:23–29). We are Christians together and, as members of the body of Christ, we need each other.

Second, the community of faith "precedes what the individual worshipper does."[16] Just as a society and a family precede us and provide the contexts in which we develop psychosocially, so too the church precedes us as the context in which we develop in faith. For Hoon, this is both an ecclesiological and christological concern: "Because Christ's action first constitutes the Church, . . . worship is the Church's action before it is the individual's action. Because Christ is the true Celebrant, the Word can only be encountered by the individual through the Body of believers whom the Word has already encountered. Christ's service to his people precedes our service to him."[17]

---

15. Paul Waitman Hoon, *The Integrity of Worship: Ecumenical and Pastoral Studies in Liturgical Theology* (Nashville: Abingdon, 1971), 38.
16. Hoon, *Integrity of Worship*, 103.
17. Hoon, *Integrity of Worship*, 103.

Think, for example, of the ways in which the first disciples are called (esp. in John 1), or of Paul's dependence on the Christian community at the time of his call (Acts 9).

Third, worship is *about* us yet is *for* me. That is, while Christian worship is always concerned with the gathered community in its specific social context, what happens there must always also speak to the needs of the individual Christian. Another way to say this is that Christian worship is always public, corporate, and personal (about us, for me) rather than private, individual-ized, or impersonal.[18] Hoon therefore presses us to seek a necessary balance between the authoritative character of communal practices (liturgical books, sacramental rites) and "individual personhood" and piety. This balance, he argues, should avoid overemphasis on the corporate as much as it avoids an "overreaction against 'pietistic individualism.'"[19]

Finally, Hoon argues that there must be a balance between the objective quality of worship and the subjective character of worship.[20] He describes this balance in several ways. Hoon invites our attention to the balance between the outward and inward character of worship, which he describes as a bal-ance between the "objective" focus on "ethical concern and social reform" and the subjective concern for "the worshipper's inward emotional states." In my own United Methodist tradition, we often describe this as a balance between "works of mercy" and "works of piety," the two mutually informing each other as we mature in the Christian life. Thus we must attend *both* to the objective "celebration of the redemptive acts of God" and to our "subjective experience of these acts."[21] We experience and respond to God's redeeming work in the midst of the church, individually but *with* one another. One is not possible without the other.

A second voice helpful to our exploration of the individual and communal in worship is that of Miroslav Volf. In *After Our Likeness: The Church in the Image of the Trinity*, Volf provides one of the more extensive contemporary theological treatments of the relationship between individual and community

18. Hoon, *Integrity of Worship*, 49. This is extrapolation somewhat from Hoon. He devel-ops his claim with a quote from Karl Barth: "Without the *pro me* of the individual Christian there is no legitimate *pro nobis* of the faith of the Christian community." *Church Dogmatics*, vol. IV/1, *The Doctrine of Reconciliation*, trans. G. W. Bromiley, ed. T. F. Torrance (Edinburgh: T&T Clark, 1956), 755. While Barth was concerned to emphasize the importance of Christ's personal address to the individual as the foundation of Christian community, the heightened individualism of our current North American context seems to require a reversal of his claim. Without the community, there seems little possibility of the personal address.

19. Hoon, *Integrity of Worship*, 48.

20. Hoon, *Integrity of Worship*, 194.

21. Hoon, *Integrity of Worship*, 194.

in the church context, also exploring the consequences of this relationship for the mission of the church today.[22] As does Hoon, Volf makes several key points about the relationship between the individual and the community. Echoing the sociological studies I reviewed in the previous section, Volf states the problem this way: "In modern societies . . . the worm of modernity is slowly eating away at the root of this will to ecclesial community; faith lived ecclesially is being replaced by faith lived individualistically, a diffuse faith that includes within itself the elements of multiple forms of religiosity and is continually changing."[23] In response to the problem of "faith lived individualistically," which he also calls the risk of "ecclesiological individualism,"[24] Volf, like Hoon, argues that our individual identity as Christians depends on our relationship to the community of the church, that the church always precedes us, and that faith and belief are mediated to us through the church.

Although Volf's project is focused on the development of a trinitarian ecclesiology, he maintains that his ecclesiology is guided particularly by Matthew 18:20: "Where two or three are gathered in my name, I am there among them." That we have gathered and that we continue to gather, devoting ourselves to "the apostles' teaching and fellowship, to the breaking of bread and the prayers" (Acts 2:42), indicates we are not simply a flash mob gathered for one specific event. That we gather "in Christ's name" rather than in our own names or some organizational name (such as that of a company or service club) distinguishes us from all other associations. As Volf interprets this Scripture verse, he wants us to understand that "Christ's presence is promised not to the believing individual directly, but rather to the entire congregation, and only through the latter to the individual. This is why no one can come to faith alone and no one can live in faith alone."[25] The church precedes us before we are individually joined to it, just as do family, society, nation, and language. And if it precedes us, then its beliefs and practices also precede us; it is neither of our own making nor is it created to satisfy our individual needs and desires. Someone, some community, is there to tell the story, to invite us to discipleship and to the table, to pray for and with us, to nurture and care for us. As Volf writes, "That which a person believes is precisely that which the previously existing communion of believers has believed. By believing, a person appropriates the Spirit-infused confession of faith of all churches in time and space. There is no other way to believe unless one were to create one's

22. Miroslav Volf, *After Our Likeness: The Church in the Image of the Trinity* (Grand Rapids: Eerdmans, 1998).

23. Volf, *After Our Likeness*, 11.

24. Volf, *After Our Likeness*, 281.

25. Volf, *After Our Likeness*, 162.

own religion. It is from the church that one receives the content of faith, and it is in the church that one learns how faith is to be understood and lived."[26] For Volf, this also means that our relationship to Christ and the church is "mutually determinative," by which he means "the relation of individuals to the church depends on their relation to Christ, just as their relation to Christ depends on their relation to the church."[27] Another way of saying this is that we cannot be in relationship to Christ except through a relationship to the church. At the same time, we cannot be in relationship with the church except through our relationship to and with Christ.

A third contribution to this conversation comes from theologian Simon Chan, who draws together several of the concerns identified by Hoon and Volf in a discussion about our "active participation" in worship.[28] Describing such participation as the result of a "synergy" between the Spirit and the church, Chan argues that our active participation in Christian worship "requires the whole community of the faithful collectively, but also each member personally, to be engaged."[29] This does not mean, however, that we engage it primarily for personal benefit, for individual spiritual formation, or because of our personal feelings; it is not shaped into our image or reimagined to match our personal stories; there is no "personalized" liturgy (which would be an oxymoron). Rather, just as we are reborn into Christ through baptism, we are reshaped into Christ's image and nurtured in Christ's narrative through the ongoing practice of Christian worship. Chan argues, "As a member of the Body of Christ who has been incorporated into the Body by baptism, I place myself in the corporate life of the church. . . . One cooperates with others to carry out the 'work of the people of God' [one literal definition of "liturgy"]. When I place myself in the liturgy, rather than trying to apply the liturgy to myself, I am gradually formed as a member of the Body of Christ. My own feelings are not the primary consideration."[30] Note how, in this brief discussion, Chan pairs "community of the faithful" and "each member personally," "I" and "the people of God," "myself" and "the body of Christ." The church and its "public work of worship" (another definition of "liturgy") requires the individual *and* the community. Chan reminds us that "the church is the

---

26. Volf, *After Our Likeness*, 163.

27. Volf, *After Our Likeness*, 159.

28. "Active participation" became a significant theme in liturgical theology across many liturgical traditions following the Second Vatican Council. Simon Chan provides a concise summary of some of this discussion in *Liturgical Theology: The Church as Worshiping Community* (Downers Grove, IL: IVP Academic, 2006), 147–66.

29. Simon Chan, "The Liturgy as the Work of the Spirit," in *The Spirit in Worship—Worship in the Spirit*, ed. Teresa Berger and Bryan D. Spinks (Collegeville, MN: Liturgical Press, 2009), 55.

30. Chan, "Liturgy as the Work of the Spirit," 55. See also Chan's *Liturgical Theology*, 21–61.

people called out by God's Word to be the *congregation* [my emphasis] of God's people. What we call the liturgy is the people's *common* response to that word, their acceptance of the Word, which constitutes them as the covenant people."[31] When we separate the individual and the community, the result is either a private self-constructed spirituality or a closed and conformist community. By holding the individual and community together, we are through God formed in a common identity, in which we share equally God's loving regard and care for us.

Ritual Form and Personal Expression

In the opening question about "Let us pray" and "Pray with me," we noted that, generally speaking, "Let us pray" is more common in worship traditions shaped and governed by authorized forms and traditions, and "Pray with me" more common in free-church/evangelical worship traditions. While both expressions are forms of ritual practice, they represent a tension between the emphases given to ritual and spontaneity of personal expression that are characteristic of the two traditions. This tension is not new; it has shaped Protestant understandings of Christian worship for several centuries. The tension between ritual and spontaneity was especially prominent in the Reformation controversies about worship in sixteenth-century Europe and the prayer-book controversies in mid-seventeenth-century England; it continued to be prominent in the evangelical movements that emerged in the eighteenth century in England and the United States, and it continues in our churches today.[32] Lori Branch has traced some of this history in relationship to the prayer-book controversies in England, noting the ways in which ceremony and ritual "began to acquire negative connotations of hollowness and superstition" and the ways in which an emphasis on spontaneous, or free prayer, began to achieve prominence.[33] She describes how, in the period from 1660 to 1700, free prayer came to constitute "above all an emotionally compelling 'evidence and demonstration of the Spirit' and of grace," while liturgical prayer (such as the prayers of the Book of Common Prayer) came to be seen as "emotionally 'cold' or 'lukewarm,' mere 'lip-labor' born of 'custom and formality,'" and unable to evidence "emotional authenticity and

---

31. Chan, *Liturgical Theology*, 41.

32. For a general history of these movements in relationship to worship, see James White, *Protestant Worship: Traditions in Transition* (Louisville: Westminster John Knox, 1989).

33. Lori Branch, "The Rejection of Liturgy, the Rise of Free Prayer, and Modern Religious Subjectivity," *Restoration: Studies in English Literary Culture, 1660–1700* 29, no. 1 (Spring 2005): 2.

sincerity."[34] She also notes how, in this period, "words uttered spontaneously out of sincere emotional desires" came to be "the very ground for religious community in public prayer"[35] and how this emphasis on spontaneity began to create its own ritual forms. Yet her analysis misses some of the other ritual consequences of these developments. For example, while she attends to the criticisms of the ritual repetitions found in some of the prayers of the Book of Common Prayer, such as the repeated "Lord, have mercy" of the litany,[36] she does not notice how this development also led to the silencing of the congregation's voice in prayer and the elevation of a single voice—that of the pastor.[37] The seemingly "more sincere and authentic form" of spontaneous prayer becomes less communal in practice (less "our prayer") and increasingly individualistic ("pray with me"). In doing so, it risks becoming either an extension of the pastor's or worship leader's own desires and sometimes limited vision, or putting what is clearly an individual and personal prayer on the lips of the congregation. As we lose the *common* response that Chan argued is so essential to Christian worship, the individual voice is given priority over that of the church.

Branch's analysis of late seventeenth-century worship practices and the manuals that shaped them seem to provide a case study supporting the analysis of Protestant "anti-ritualism" that Mary Douglas provides in her now-classic anthropological work *Natural Symbols*. There Douglas notes how the word "ritual" has come "to mean empty symbols of conformity" and therefore to carry a negative connotation across various expressions of Protestantism. The strongest "anti-ritualists" argue that "ritual conformity is not a valid form of personal commitment and is not compatible with the full development of the personality."[38] Douglas, like Branch, describes the ways in which ritual conformity is understood to be incompatible with rational commitment and emotional sincerity, even to such an extent that some began to argue, "If Christianity is to be saved for future generations, ritualism must be rooted out, as if it were a weed choking the life of the spirit."[39] More important,

34. Branch, "Rejection of Liturgy," 9.

35. Branch, "Rejection of Liturgy," 15.

36. Contemporary forms of this litany are used by various churches: Episcopal, *The Book of Common Prayer* (New York: Church Hymnal, 1979), 383–85; *The United Methodist Book of Worship* (Nashville: United Methodist Publishing, 1992), 495; and the Presbyterian *Book of Common Worship* (Louisville: Westminster John Knox, 2018), 93–94, 99–101.

37. See Branch's discussion of the repetitions, in "Rejection of Liturgy," 12; and on 19, her discussion of the development of guidebooks for free prayer.

38. Mary Douglas, *Natural Symbols: Explorations in Cosmology* (New York: Pantheon, 1982), 4.

39. Douglas, *Natural Symbols*, 4.

she notes how "following in the footprints of the Protestant reformers," a set form of protest emerges, including "a denunciation not only of irrelevant rituals, but [even] of ritualism as such; exaltation of the inner experience and denigration of its standardized [and therefore communal] expressions; preference for intuitive and instant forms of knowledge; rejection of mediating institutions; rejection of any tendency to allow habit to provide the basis of a new symbolic system."[40] She also notes, however, that once the protest stage is past, a "need for organization" and "a coherent system of expression" are recognized, and a new ritual system begins to develop, much as has been the case in the "worship wars" of the late twentieth century and in the emergence of contemporary worship as its own ritual form.[41]

Taken together, Branch's historical work and Douglas's anthropological work help us see another level of the relationship between the individual and community. They show us some of the ways in which ritual patterns form individuals in belief and practice; how ritual/liturgical practices can both support and subvert our participation in communities and forms of shared life; and how those patterns and practices enable communities to persist (or prevent that persistence) over time. They remind us of the ways in which the ritual patterns of Christian worship shape our bodies and our minds, and also shape the ways in which we relate to one another, to the world, and to God; these rituals shape the stories we choose to tell about ourselves and our communities.

Our Story Is My Story

What's your story? All of us have been asked this question at some point in our lives. In telling our individual stories, it nevertheless becomes quickly evident that my story is never only *my* story but always also *our* story. Each family, each congregation, and each religious tradition has a story it tells about itself; these stories are woven into the rituals of our families and congregations. Individually, we are born into stories that preceded us—the stories of our parents and grandparents, the stories of nations and peoples, the stories of religious communities. In each context, as Bellah and others have reminded us, "the community maintains itself as a community of memory" through its stories.[42] In doing so, we discover that there is always a priority of the community over the individual, that there is a certain "givenness" to the community and its

40. Douglas, *Natural Symbols*, 19.
41. Douglas, *Natural Symbols*, 19.
42. Bellah et al., *Habits of the Heart*, 227.

traditions, and that "the community exists before the individual is born and will continue after his or her death."[43] We are not, sometimes to our surprise, self-made persons. The question will always be, Who will tell the community's story? Who will tell our story? Bellah notes that "people growing up in communities of memory not only hear the stories that tell how the community came to be, what its hopes and fears are, and how its ideals are exemplified in outstanding men and women [here we might think of the communion of saints]; they also participate in the practices—ritual, aesthetic, ethical—that define the community as a way of life." These practices, Bellah argues, "define the patterns of loyalty and obligation that keep the community alive."[44] They set out the hope and expectation that the communal story will become our individual story.

One way to think about this communal story is as one of several competing "social imaginaries" in which we live. Charles Taylor uses this concept of the "social imaginary" to describe the ways in which "people imagine their social existence" as it comes to be expressed in "images, stories, and legends" rather than in theoretical terms. In Taylor's understanding, the social imaginary is "shared by large groups of people" rather than a limited few and is a "common understanding that makes possible common practices and a widely shared sense of legitimacy."[45] It has a communal and public character. The social imaginary is both "factual and normative," providing a sense of "how things usually go" and "how they ought to go."[46] The social imaginary can be "full of self-serving fiction and suppression," leading to practices that are more death-giving than life-supporting (such as the ways in which Christians have used Scripture to support and continue practices of slavery and racial discrimination); yet "it is also an essential constituent of the real," shaping, conditioning, and organizing the way we live together and understand our world.[47] James K. A. Smith pursues these themes as he explores what he calls our "cultural liturgies" and the tensions between those cultural practices and our lives as Christians. Smith reminds us that "there are no private stories; every narrative draws upon tellings that have been handed down (*traditio*)." The social imaginary is "received from and shared with others" and becomes "a vision *of* and *for* social life."[48] Here Smith alludes to *tradition*, which

43. Bellah et al., *Habits of the Heart*, 227.
44. Bellah et al., *Habits of the Heart*, 154.
45. Charles Taylor, *Modern Social Imaginaries* (Durham, NC: Duke University Press, 2004), 23.
46. Taylor, *Modern Social Imaginaries*, 24.
47. Taylor, *Modern Social Imaginaries*, 183.
48. James K. A. Smith, *Desiring the Kingdom: Worship, Worldview, and Cultural Formation* (Grand Rapids: Baker Academic, 2009), 66.

concerns an active process of handing down or handing on and receiving that which has come before us. In Christian worship, a community gathers to "recall and renew, celebrate and ponder" its foundational story in God's saving work through Jesus Christ and the Holy Spirit. In worship, we remember, retell, and relive that story, "celebrating it with gratitude and praise."[49] In worship, we are "schooled in the beliefs, attitudes, and practices which constitute Christian identity and discipleship."[50]

In the context of individualism, so prominent in the United States, the relationship between the individual and communal often seem to be reversed, as if my individual story is determinative for a community; as if I am the primary mediator of a pattern of life rather than the community to which I belong; as if my private prayer should inform and shape the way we pray as a community of faith. What Smith and others show us is that a Christian way of being reverses each of these claims: the community of faith precedes us and is determinative for us. As Ruth Meyers asserts, "Public worship informs our personal prayer throughout the week, and personal prayer, even when we pray alone, is always offered in communion with other Christians and so draws us back into public worship."[51] Christian worship reminds us that it is not first our individual stories that we tell, but the story we have received and that we rehearse in the reading and interpreting of Scripture, in sacramental celebrations, and in the weekly rhythms of Christian worship.

Practical Implications for Worship

Susan White opens a chapter on the communal character of Christian worship with this quote from Cyprian of Carthage (third century): "Our prayer is public and common; and when we pray, we pray not for one, but for the whole people, because the whole people are one."[52] The quote comes from Cyprian's reflections on the Lord's Prayer: he reminds us that we do not pray "*My* Father . . . in heaven" or "Give *me* . . . my daily bread," but "*Our* Father . . . in heaven" and "Give *us* . . . our daily bread."[53] Perhaps we need no further

49. David Lonsdale, "The Church as Context for Christian Spirituality," in *The Blackwell Companion to Christian Spirituality*, ed. Arthur Holder (New York: Blackwell, 2005), 244.

50. Lonsdale, "Church as Context," 244.

51. Ruth Meyers, *Missional Worship, Worshipful Mission: Gathering as God's People, Going Out in God's Name* (Grand Rapids: Eerdmans, 2014), 45.

52. Susan J. White, *The Spirit of Worship: The Liturgical Tradition* (Maryknoll, NY: Orbis Books, 1999), 58.

53. Cyprian, "Treatise Four: On the Lord's Prayer," in *Ante-Nicene Fathers*, vol. 5, *Fathers of the Third Century*, ed. Alexander Roberts and James Donaldson (Buffalo: Christian Literature Publishing, 1885), par. 8, http://www.ccel.org/ccel/schaff/anf05.iv.v.iv.html.

example of how Christian worship is both communal and individual, *about us* and *for me*. As we have seen in Smith and Taylor, Christian worship is shaping (or is intended to shape) an image of how true human community "is intended by God to look and behave."[54] It does this, Susan White argues, as it provides us with the place in which to practice "courageous interaction with others," to ritualize "healthy and non-exploitive relationships," to learn and share words of joy and lament, and to be formed into a "pattern of feasting and fasting by which we are able to rejoice and to weep with others."[55] In many of our traditions we pray at the Lord's Table that the Spirit be "poured out on us gathered here that we may be the body of Christ." Yet still we come individually to that table with the reminder that this bread and cup are given "for you" and "for me."

As we attend to and practice this necessary balance between the individual and the community in Christian worship, we are given a resource that has the potential to address the extremes of North American individualism and reestablish us in communities of commitment and belief. In its ritualized patterns, Christian worship invites us to trust: on the one hand, to trust patterns of behavior that, while of human origin, are not of our own making; on the other hand, to trust that even in these patterns and practices, God is yet actively with us, present to us, gracing and gifting us. Through this very public work of worship ("liturgy"), we receive, are joined to, "rehearse," and hand on a story in which we are not the primary actors and yet in which we are personally involved. The very practical task today is to remember that Christian worship is about us and for me.

For Further Reading

Anderson, E. Byron. *Common Worship: Tradition, Formation, Mission*. Nashville: Foundery, 2017.

Chan, Simon. *Liturgical Theology: The Church as Worshiping Community*. Downers Grove, IL: InterVarsity, 2006.

Meyers, Ruth. *Missional Worship, Worshipful Mission: Gathering as God's People, Going Out in God's Name*. Grand Rapids: Eerdmans, 2014.

Smith, James K. A. *Desiring the Kingdom: Worship, Worldview, and Cultural Formation*. Grand Rapids: Baker Academic, 2009.

---

54. White, *Spirit of Worship*, 58; Smith, *Desiring the Kingdom*; Taylor, *Modern Social Imaginaries*.

55. White, *Spirit of Worship*, 74.

←16→

Secularization and Worship

James K. Wellman Jr.

This chapter offers a succinct history of what secularization is and what it means for Christian worship; how it has impacted us and how it impacts our desires and goals in life, both in our "secular" lives and in our "religious" lives; and why it makes such a difference in how we think and what we desire. We will then make sense of how and why megachurch worship works even in our secular society. Megachurches are a direct result of the modern secularization process, which seeks efficiency, demands results, streamlines costs, and seeks the largest payoff for one's money. Nearly half of American churchgoers attend megachurches of some kind, so this form and way of doing worship is the dominant way that Americans do religion, at least on the Protestant side. These concepts are applied to analyze how religion works more generally in our "modern, secular democratic economies," which largely function out of a secular and capitalist framework of cultural desires and goals. Christian worship, therefore, is now more a reflection of our modern forms of thinking than it is a function of whatever we might think of when we say, "the early church." Finally, we describe features of secularization and how it affects what religion is, what religion is supposed to do for us, how religion functions in megachurches in particular, and how megachurch worship pervades and dominates our thinking and practice more generally. This will give the reader a broad sense of why certain forms of religious ritual work and why they work in our present times.

232

Secularism and the Rise of Protestantism

Secularism and secularization can cause a great deal of confusion. For some, to be secular is to be rational and believe in universals; for many secularists, being rational by definition means one cannot be religious, since religion is prerational and particular. But all of this remains very much up for discussion. Are secularists really the only rational ones among us? Does the universalism of secularity solve all our present problems? The truth is that these either/or categories don't describe our modern lives: some are religious in private but secular in public; somewhat fewer others seek to be religious in both their private and public lives. Most commonly for those in the West, faith is lodged in our private life; it makes little or no difference in our secular societies and economies. So, in the West, how does one really tell whether a person is religious or secular? Most of us work in secular vocations and operate from a secular logic in our daily lives; our religion is maintained, more or less, for our private lives, at least for our lives with other believers. Thus we seem as secular as anyone, but to other believers we are religious. Yet this is not always true: in many Muslim countries, a different balance is kept, depending on where one lives and on how "advanced" one's economy is. Religion can be much more integral for Muslims in both their private and public lives than for many in the "Christian West."

For the most part, if we need to generalize, it is safe to say that the modern and secular economic forms and functions do dominate our lives; for most of us, the market shapes and determines how we live and what we do in our communities. Religion, if anything, has become a part of the background music in our lives, integral to many, but still not the first thing we think of or talk about. In today's Western world, which is increasingly global, a secular and capitalist ethos guides our action; one can be either religious or nonreligious, and often observers cannot tell one from the other. Thus the privatization of faith is a function of secular modernity: religion is separated from our public duties and economic and political decision-making. The modern world is secular: we act, speak, and most often look secular in public, and we speak from a secular perspective. But all of this has a history; it is a radical break with what humans have done in the past.

Before the Enlightenment, most countries were loyal to a specific religion, and that religion was a part of what it meant to be French, English, Egyptian, or even Chinese. Then secularism, as a part of the Enlightenment project, was intended to break the hold of religion over society, culture, and government. Following the European Wars of Religion in the sixteenth century, Enlightenment figures began to imagine a new world order, one in which religion no longer legitimated government or confirmed political leadership, where religion was displaced and reserved for the private lives of individuals. This was no simple process but the result of a period of endless wars, from which cultural and political leaders sought a way out. Their purpose was to free people to choose their governmental leaders separate from religious authorities so governments would become more impartial in governance, thus allowing all people, whether religious or not, to participate in their cultures and economies. To be sure, how power has been distributed in past and present history continues to be uneven at best; our past prejudices remain against women, minorities, and "others," whoever they might be. Nonetheless, religion is no longer *the* principle mechanism by which we determine who is in power and who is not.

We have come to call this the "privatization of religion," a pattern that separates religion from political and cultural power, freeing governments to rationalize their politics and economies based on the needs and desires for goods and services, regardless of a person's or group's affiliation with one religion or another. In this way, secularism creates the promise of universalism, where decisions and actions are separate and walled off from religious tests and the demands of religious leaders. It creates some ability for individuals to choose whether or not to participate in religion; people are given the freedom to refuse religious strictures and find their own identity in society and their own place in work and politics, regardless of whether they are religious or not. In fact, the term and category "religion" is a product of the secularization project. Before this time, one did not choose to be a Catholic: one was Catholic because that was the culture within which one was raised. To be French was to be Catholic; the two were synonymous. There were no religious choices or even the conception of choice. One's cultural religion was the air one breathed and the life one lived. One did not choose a religion; one was born into a religion.

The Reformation and the battles between Catholics and Protestants disrupted the old patterns, and for the first time Europeans could choose to which religion they would give their loyalty. Moreover, the wars between Catholics and Protestants in the sixteenth century, in which more than a third of Europe's people were killed, proved to many survivors that religion was more a source of conflict than communion. These conflicts and tensions motivated thinkers and activists to push religion out of politics and into the private sphere. Such change created a culture of choice in religion, something that was utterly new to human consciousness. This revolution developed rapidly over time, and in the nineteenth and twentieth centuries it evolved toward what we now call the "privatization of religion." One's religious affiliation was no longer part and parcel of one's culture and civilization; one's political affiliations were no longer tied to one's religion; the separation of religion from politics is a present ideal in our modern life. Yet this is far from universal: in many Muslim cultures and countries, to be an Afghan or Iranian or to be a Saudi Arabian is to be Muslim. To be sure, these patterns vary across the globe today. The rise of political religions is a potent recent reality. Politicians are using religion to rally populations. Narendra Modi, India's prime minister, uses his Hindutva party to control his country. Likewise, Turkey's President Erdoğan has reasserted a Turkish Muslim identity to dominate his state. And even in former communist countries like Russia, President Putin and the Orthodox Church are now once again using religion to rationalize political power. This is true even in the United States: presidential candidates have become "evangelicals," in part to appeal to the American evangelical vote in the United States. This voting block makes up 25 percent of the electoral population; evangelicals thus have real power in elections and have secured the election of recent modern presidents: Ronald Reagan, George W. Bush, and Donald J. Trump.[1]

How does all this relate to megachurch worship? What does it mean that megachurch worship has become secularized? Does this mean that megachurches are no longer religious? No, but it does mean that religion is tamed and at the mercy of politics and politicians. The Johnson amendment (1954) is supposed to keep churches from endorsing or opposing political candidates if they want to keep their nonprofit status. Some parts of the American church are politicized. As I have shown, higher percentages of evangelicals in megachurches vote for the Republican Party. Since the end of the Jimmy Carter administration and the 1980 election of Ronald Reagan, Republican activists have used the battle over abortion to convince white evangelicals that they should vote Republican to ban abortion.[2] Even here, evangelical voters are not allowed to politicize the pulpit, though they find ways to bypass this roadblock. Nevertheless, the separation between religion and politics remains, and secularization continues to rise. The newest generation of Americans are, by a large percentage, more secular than their previous cohorts, so America's status as the most highly religious developed country is in doubt in the near future—a trend that further marginalizes religion and ensures the continuing process of secularization of American religion in the future.[3] In this context,

1. See Andrew L. Whitehead and Samuel L. Perry, *Taking America Back for God: Christian Nationalism in the United States* (Oxford: Oxford University Press, 2020), 27–32.

2. See Randall Balmer, "The Real Origins of the Religious Right," *Politico Magazine*, May 27, 2014, https://www.politico.com/magazine/story/2014/05/religious-right-real-origins -107133.

3. See "In U.S., Decline of Christianity Continues at Rapid Pace," Pew Research Center: Religion and Public Life, Oct. 17, 2019, https://www.pewforum.org/2019/10/17/in-u-s-decline -of-christianity-continues-at-rapid-pace/.

we come to understand why American megachurches and their forms of worship are such an apt example of the American secularization of worship.

Why Megachurches Dominate the Worship Market

Because of secularization and to be relevant, religion must appeal to the subjective experience of the individual. Secularization sidelines religion primarily because it serves no purpose outside the confines of the private and subjective concerns of hope, desire, and love. Modern economies and democratic associations fill our needs for economic organization and political structure of power; thus the only place for religion is in the economy of the heart and the voluntary associations of service. We call this *the apotheosis of the privatization of religion*. "Privatization" means that if religion is to function at all, it must touch the emotions. Affectivity is the terrain of religion. Randall Collins has aptly labeled this function "interactive ritual chains," which are the corridors of emotional energy, whereby humans make their most intimate and powerful decisions. So religion is not only compartmentalized; it also does not belong in the political backrooms or in the boardrooms, or in our public life, but must offer something for our emotional lives. And it turns out, at least in the research of myself and my colleagues, megachurches function in critical and complex ways to serve these needs.[4]

Collins's work on *interactive ritual chains* helps to explain how *emotional energy* is produced in megachurches.[5] His contribution challenges postmodern theory in its description of how meaning is constructed in human beings and also, more important, in human groups. As opposed to a macro system of global capital hegemony or a framework of power that uses social controls to determine and shape human desire and activity, a microsociology of group interactions provides a more plausible explanation of how and why megachurch worship functions with such success, according to Collins. Often these theories are so abstract that it gives no real mechanism for how one might describe the actions of human beings as they are concretely acting and believing in their everyday lives. Collins's work is pragmatic and more empirical. It is informed by recent research on human emotion and evolutionary theory to make sense of how humans manage and negotiate their daily social and cultural interactions. Collins's approach fits well with

---

4. The following discussion draws from work done in collaboration with Katie E. Corcoran and Kate J. Stockly that is explored in much greater depth in our book *High on God: How Megachurches Won the Heart of America* (Oxford: Oxford University Press, 2020).

5. Randall Collins, *Interaction Ritual Chains* (Princeton: Princeton University Press, 2004).

our emphasis on radical empiricism, reflected also in the thinking of William James,[6] which examines how humans function in their actual circumstances, emotions, and events in their living; thus our aim is *the experience of bodies and emotions as they enact religiosity and are a part of megachurch worship.* We keep asking a commonsense question: Are the people in this study lying about the reasons they are involved in these churches? Are they practicing a form of false consciousness, only participating in these churches because they are prisoners of a capitalist economy that enflames a desire to consume even when it comes to church? This is a real question, but in this present volume we take at face value the answers that come from megachurch members; for them, their emotions lead them to invest in megachurches at a rate that we have found to be astonishing.

Furthermore, applying and extending Collins's work to our data, we can analyze and explain what moved megachurch members to become involved in megachurch worship. We argue that neither the seduction of postmodern capitalism nor pure rational choice leads our megachurch members to engage in such church; rather, what attracts members to these churches is a process of interaction and ritual chains that produce and evoke deep desires as well as the emotional energy created by collective effervescence. We suggest that rational choice does come into play, but only after humans first experience the affective pull of these megachurches. That is, the emotion and energy of megachurch practices are in the body *before* they are adjudicated in the mind. Then the overwhelming affective experience is so positive that rational choice is an ex post facto rationalization of just how good it feels to be in these institutions; this feeling often includes a review of the extraordinary benefits that accrue for these individuals and for their families. Affect, we argue, dominates their initial experience and produces a desire to be involved.

Emotion clearly leads, though a reflective choice follows. Thus we developed a theory of *embodied choice* to explain what we discovered. We argue that it is an embodied movement of experience that produces a choice and desire to participate in these megachurches. To be sure, the emotional energy convinces folks that the benefits of these churches far outweigh the costs. Thus rational choice is used to calculate a commitment to these churches, but emotional energy, created by the arc of activities that megachurches provide, drives these megachurch members into intense and satisfying relationships with their churches. The interaction ritual produces emotional energy through

---

6. William James, *Essays in Radical Empiricism* (Lincoln: University of Nebraska Press, 1996); Nancy Frankenberry, *Religion and Radical Empiricism* (Albany: State University of New York Press, 1987).

the microsociological interactions within megachurches; all the while these interactions stimulate a collective effervescence in these congregations, which draws so many to the megachurches.

In our research, after analyzing and considering all the data,[7] we enumerate *six core desires* that these megachurches evoke and meet: (1) Members feel *acceptance* immediately, which creates a feeling of *belonging*. (2) They experience a deep sense of *spiritual energy and stimulation*, in both the music and the atmosphere, which we name the *wow factor*. (3) They identify a *reliable leader* and describe the megachurch pastors in terms of their *charismatic leadership*. (4) They feel the exhilaration of *deliverance* and the promise of *certainty* produced by the altar calls or when mega-members describe "hundreds" coming down to "accept Jesus." (5) Megachurch members experience a sense of personal *purpose* in discovering their "gifts," which they use in *service* in the church as well as in their communities. (6) Their participation in small groups, which we define as a *re-membering process* (both as becoming promptly involved as well as confirming an affiliation) linked to the Sunday experience, gives members a bridge between their weekly worship services and creates a deep sense of *solidarity*, which becomes an extended primary community, as many of our informants report.

Megachurch worship creates a matrix within which these six desires are met. Our research shows how megachurch members are charged, how the cycles of emotional energy are produced, and the process by which collective effervescence creates an overwhelming connection of megachurch members to God, to each other, to their pastor, and to their communities. We connect this as well to Collins's four ritual ingredients of *copresence, a shared mood, a mutual focus of attention*, and *barriers to outsiders*. These ingredients produce what Collins outlines as ritual outcomes: (1) group solidarity in megachurch membership; (2) emotional energy in individuals, an energy that sustains participation; (3) symbols of social relationship or sacred objects (often charismatic pastors); and (4) standards of morality, ways in which megachurches pronounce rules and regulations for the moral lives of their members.[8] For an overview of what is to come in our discussion of the Megachurch Ritual Cycle, see figure 16.1.

Megachurches are total life systems: they seek to produce an experience that is all-enveloping, beginning with the ritual process of *copresence*. From websites, architecture, and aesthetic branding, to an ultra-friendly church welcome team, then to evangelism and outreach, being part a megachurch is

---

7. See appendix A in Wellman, Corcoran, and Stockly, *High on God*, 231–50.
8. Collins, *Interaction Ritual Chains*, 79–88.

6 DESIRES
1. Belonging/Acceptance
2. Wow/Hack the Happy
3. Reliable leader
4. Deliverance
5. Purpose in Service
6. Re-Member

SMALL GROUPS
Ritual Process Step 6:
small groups
intimate community, members support,
care for, and nurture each other, authentic,
groups reflect on the worship service
→ focus on **desire to re-member** →
leads to a sense of solidarity, the feeling
of family, intimacy, being seen, known,
loved, and supported, knowing that you
are looking out for each other

WELCOME
Ritual Process Step 1:
co-presence
Modern and inviting website, architecture,
asthetic, branding, welcome team, ultra-
friendliness, immediate handshakes/hugs
→ focus on **desire for acceptance** →
leads to feelings that one belongs, fits in,
and is welcomed home

SERVICE AND OUTREACH PROJECTS
Ritual Process Step 5:
service and outreach projects
Identifying and using spiritual gifts,
volunteering, outreach, service,
and evangelism, doing God's work
→ focus on **desire for purpose in service** →
leads to a sense of direction,
empowerment, and confidence that they
are doing the right things and following
their purpose/calling/vocation

WORSHIP
Ritual Process Step 2:
shared mood
Lighting, emotional songs, bodily
movements (hands raised, swaying, singing),
affective displays, spontaneous prayers
→ focus on **desire for wow** →
leads to awe, joy, amazement, presence of
God/Christ, intimacy with spiritual energy,
spark of collective effervescence

ALTAR CALL
Ritual Process Step 4:
barriers to outsiders
Getting saved, setting aside sinful
ways of the past, repentence, sharing
one's testimony, commitment to Christ,
joining the body of Christ
→ focus on **desire for deliverance** →
leads to a powerful sense of salvation,
liberation, certainty, purity, and release;
full inclusion in the community

SERMON
Ritual Process Step 3:
mutual focus of attention
Charisma of pastor, group symbols and
values, messages inspiring confidence,
healing, and transformation
→ focus on **desire for reliable leader** →
leads to a charismatic bond with
pastor, a sense of trust, being led,
having a reliable source of information
to understand God's will

Note: Although the ritual cycle is patterned, the ebbs and flows of desire and emotional energy
are much more fluid and unruly. For each step, one of the six affective desires is highlighted as a
primary focus, however, in reality the entire cycle is involved in creating and maintaining the affective pulse that meets each desire. Any and all of the six desires may be expressed and addressed
at any time throughout the cycle, even if there is a focus on one during each step.

Figure 16.1. Megachurch Ritual Cycle

James Wellman Jr., Katie Corcoran, and Kate Stockly, *High on God: How Megachurches Won
the Heart of America* (Oxford: Oxford University Press, 2020), 83. Used by permission.

in many ways like entering into a womb—a total system that seeks to communicate that "you" belong and that "you" are accepted. We know from our data that the experience can be quite electric and that it leads to a feeling of being comfortable, accepted, loved, and welcomed. Upon entering, people do not feel judged or looked down upon or conspicuous. They feel like they really "fit in." Normally, for many it is an overwhelming and jarring moment to enter a huge venue, to realize that they may not know anyone other than those who may have invited them. At that moment, then, the "need" to be accepted is at its most intense, and so for megachurches, the entrance, the first impression, becomes a critical moment in determining whether newcomers stay or leave. Megachurches leaders think intensely about how to welcome newcomers to their venues; they choose and train volunteers to greet with smiles and warm handshakes. The leaders labor to ensure that an excited sense of anticipation is triggered by signs and messaging both directing and reassuring the strangers that they are neither strange nor unwelcome. These experiences build on one another, intended to turn participants to Christ and, perhaps just as importantly, to bind them to the group and institution, making them feel that this is *their* place and this is *their* community. The thoughtfulness and intentionality of these churches is remarkable and often overlooked.

The second ritual ingredient is a shared mood. Of course, the mood is already initiated by a greeter, who is also one who guides and gives information. Coffee to one side, a place for children on the other, information for newcomers and for those who know what they want, and a friendly smiling face to give one a sense that in these churches the mood is "happy" and the greeters are happy to see newcomers. The lead into the worship service is also an "opportunity" for greeters and ushers to introduce newcomers to the lighting, songs, and bodily movements of worship. Seats are comfortable, the singing is upbeat, often accompanied by swaying, with hands raised, but nothing substantially different from what one would find at a subdued rock concert—at least not at first.

The leaders voice and show that they want "you" to be there; they welcome newcomers with announcements directed at those who are new and displaying the vitality and warmth of the community by offering prayers for those who are lonely or in need. The collective shared mood is one that speaks volumes about the desire to make one feel accepted, yet also suggests that this is a place where the moment of "wow" is experienced: people feel and express joy and want to share that mood of uplift with one another, or as one newcomer exclaimed, "I watched the Holy Spirit [move] like people doing the wave at a football game; . . . hundreds got saved!" In other words, the intentionality and focus that goes into creating a viable copresence intensifies and initiates a shared mood, and this is only the beginning of what is coming.

Collins's third ingredient in the ritual process is a *mutual focus of attention*, and this comes through with singers and song leaders, but the key focus is on the pastor or lead teacher, who is almost always male. Through both the music and the preaching, a desperate need is expressed, in that each person is, in some form, found wanting, a sinner. The minister is clear that he too stands in judgment, but that is quickly followed by the sense that while he's human and has many flaws, he also knows that in Christ the solution is found, that new life is available, that anyone can claim this life, and that the whole world is offered this free gift of grace. In other words, the worship service's messaging emphasizes and creates a sense of need, which is immediately followed by the redemptive inspiration that there is a way out, that relief is within reach, that one can be *delivered*, and that there is a *solution*. Thus the leader, who relates to you and knows where you have been, also offers you a way out, a solution to the grip of sin, guidance to the pattern of access to God, the Father who knows you, forgives you, and wants more than anything else to save you. So the focus of attention is the charismatic leader, the *reliable leader*, who, although human, has found a way through to the Father, who will never fail, the Father who is not like one's earthy father, but who will forgive you, release you, and send you out into the world a new woman or a new man, delivered and guided into a new life in Christ.

These churches create altar-call settings, in one form or another; here, after the buildup to the sense that one has a need and that that need can be remedied, the time for decision comes. There is relief from the despair of being separated from God the Father, and his Son, Jesus, who died and made the path open and free to the Father. This sense of deliverance through Christ ripples through these congregations and, without making it explicit, creates a *barrier to outsiders*. That is, all are welcome, but the true inner circle belongs to the saved, to those who have responded to the call for conversion. This is such a powerful process, by which one is welcomed, loved, accepted, called out for one's sin, offered a free pass to the "reliable Father," and can then go up to "touch" the pastor who wants to heal and accept you into deliverance from sin and separation. The movement of deliverance is a moment of liberation, of entrance into Christ, of purification, of being in the community of faith. The barriers to outsiders are real, though the constant hope and invitation are that you too, just like those you have witnessed, can come and be saved.

What follows are two ritual interaction links that highlight Collins's emphasis on the importance of understanding interaction rituals as existing in *chains*. In megachurches, worship is never understood as a once-a-week Sunday event. The invitation and expectation are not only to enter "into Christ" but also to enter into community, to mark oneself as a member of the family, and to discover one's strengths and purpose to serve others. The identity of evangelical Christians is inextricable from the call to serve the world in the name of Christ—to be Christ's body, his hands and feet, within their communities and throughout the world. In this process one not only takes on a new identity "in Christ" but one's gifts also are identified for the sake of serving the community and one's neighbor. Members are invited and encouraged to participate in all sorts of service projects aimed at enacting the identity of Christ's work within the wider community and world. As the "body of Christ," it is presented as a duty to serve, give, and spread the word. This has the dual effect of filling participants with a sense of purpose and direction, while also signaling, to themselves and the rest of the group, their devotion and loyalty to the gospel message and to the church community.

Last, the megachurch model is designed as a total life system: in the process of accepting God's grace, one is invited into small groups that underscore, develop, and reinforce one's new identity and that further solidify membership and commitment to the church. Small groups and opportunities to serve are vital ingredients for the *megachurch model* because they function to *enact* and *mobilize* what is learned (group symbols) and gained (emotional energy) during the worship service. These links channel and solidify the fleeting ener- gized experiences into transformed, cohesive personal *identities* and a vibrant, cooperative *community* (including subcommunities and small groups), which permeate the rest of their lives, both individually and communally. They also, in a pragmatic sense, create a bridge from Sunday to Sunday to keep the fire burning throughout the week.

Of course, both these chain links—service projects and small groups— are interaction rituals in and of themselves, even as they contribute to the larger chain initiated in the worship service. Our focus on these elements emphasizes the importance of what sociologists Edward Lawler, Shane Thye, and Jeongkoo Yoon call the "micro-to-macro process." They extend Lawler and Yoon's "relational cohesion theory" to explain how social interactions that include joint tasks, shared responsibility, and social unit attributions can accumulate to transform a network of individuals and pairs of indi- viduals into a cohesive, centralized group. That group, in turn, becomes an object of commitment, loyalty, and immense positive affect.[9] "In an in-

9. Edward J. Lawler and Jeongkoo Yoon, "Commitment in Exchange Relations," *American Sociological Review* 61, no. 1 (1996): 89–108; Edward J. Lawler, Shane R. Thye, and Jeongkoo

dividualized world," they explain, "group ties are self-generated from the bottom up. That is, they develop and are sustained through repeated social interactions that take place around joint tasks or activities, promoted and framed by the group unit . . . [and that] involve *affective sentiments* about the group itself."[10]

This is directly related to sociologist Émile Durkheim's concept of *homo duplex*: "How do individualized, privatized actors create and sustain affectively meaningful social ties to social units—relations, groups, organizations, communities, and nations?"[11] The answer: the micro-to-macro process. Megachurches—including each interaction during the worship services, small-group meetings, and outreach social-service activities—are complex collections of micro units that facilitate and enact macro impulses of devotion to the larger group. Through this process, the individual's commitment expands to motivate not only to service for the church but also to service for its surrounding community, the state, the nation, and even the world with the "life-changing" and "world-transforming" power of the message of Jesus Christ. Here it is not only a big-picture view that one is called to see but also a *process* by which members are first invited to "discover their gifts," then "develop their gifts," and ultimately to be called to "use their gifts" on behalf of Christ and others, to reach out and heal the world.

This micro-macro project resonates with a way to solve the tension that Durkheim outlines for *homo duplex*, where one is in-between, caught halfway between the self and the world, and the individual needs to be deeply invested in both, even at the same time. Megachurches understand that model and create a system that functions to do both: to develop individuals in their gifts, as well as to bind these folks together in a community, small and large, in which to find rest, strength, copresence, a shared mood, tools to develop oneself, and opportunities to help and serve the world. The genius of these institutions is that they meet the needs of individuals but also maintain a focus on their communal context. And when they serve, they do so in ways that use individual gifts to serve the person, the megachurch community, as well as the wider community and the global setting.

Yoon, *Social Commitments in a Depersonalized World* (New York: Russell Sage Foundation, 2009); Edward J. Lawler, Shane R. Thye, and Jeongkoo Yoon, "Emotions and Group Ties in Social Exchange," in *Handbook of the Sociology of Emotions*, ed. Jan E. Stets and Jonathan H. Turner (Dordrecht: Springer, 2014), 2:77–101.

10. Lawler, Thye, and Yoon, "Emotions and Group Ties," 79, emphasis original.

11. Lawler, Thye, and Yoon, "Emotions and Group Ties," 78. Durkheim discusses this concept in Émile Durkheim and Steven Lukes, *The Rules of Sociological Method and Selected Texts on Sociology and Its Method,* trans. W. D. Halls (New York: Macmillan, 1982), esp. chaps. 4 and 5.

Secularization in Early and Late Christendom

Did Jesus have megachurches in mind when he founded his movement? Hardly. He launched his ministry in a backward region of an obscure and faltering country. Rome dominated Jesus's world, and it can be argued that without the apostle Paul, the ministry of Jesus would not have spread. Paul's titanic conversion and drive to interpret the gospel of Jesus Christ into something that could be heard beyond the Jewish culture is the one the most remarkable cultural translations in the history of humankind. Paul made Christianity a faith for the whole world, infinitely translatable and marketable to the globe. The history of this translation is told in *High on God*, but for our purposes, what is critical is that the Christian faith was a religion of the heart from the beginning. Taking Jesus into one's heart could be translated into multiple languages and cultures; Christianity offered everyone a portable gift of freedom from sin and invited all to a new life. This transformative message achieved a universal appeal, regardless of language or custom. It remains one of the most remarkable transcultural ideas ever. "Come to Christ, and you are free to love, forgive, and live again." This simple argument can live in the cathedrals of Christendom and in the heart of a businessperson in any megacity of the twenty-first century. In some sense, then, secularism is not only Christianity's greatest enemy but also the frame by which the message can spread everywhere, as it does. Thus the secularization of worship is what the Jesus movement always had in mind, both its greatest vision and appeal but also it most potent temptation to accommodation. It remains to be seen which will win.

For Further Reading

Collins, Randall. *Interaction Ritual Chains*. Princeton: Princeton University Press, 2004.

Geldhof, Joris. *Liturgy and Secularism: Beyond the Divide*. Collegeville, MN: Liturgical Academic, 2018.

Jakobsen, Janet R., and Ann Pellegrini, eds. *Secularisms*. Chapel Hill, NC: Duke University Press, 2008.

Wellman, James, Jr., Katie Corcoran, and Kate Stockly. *High on God: How Megachurches Won the Heart of America*. Oxford: Oxford University Press, 2020.

Whitehead, Andrew L., and Samuel L. Perry. *Taking America Back for God: Christian Nationalism in the United States*. Oxford: Oxford University Press, 2020.

Christian Worship in the Context of Other World Religions

Peter C. Phan

This chapter focuses on what has been called "multifaith worship" and will not discuss ecumenical worship services—shared worship among different Christian denominations. There are, of course, multiple parallels between these two forms of religious sharing; multifaith worship has much to learn from the ecumenical scene, with which Christian churches have had extensive experience and on which there is abundant literature. I begin by defining what is meant by multifaith worship. Next, is an examination of the theological reasons that have been advanced to reject this form of religious sharing and, alternatively, to advocate its possibility and even necessity in the contemporary context of religious pluralism. Furthermore, the chapter spells out the essential conditions that must be fulfilled to make multifaith sharing of prayer and worship acceptable to all worshipers, Christians as well as believers of other religious traditions who participate in it. We conclude with reflections on worship sharing between Christianity and major world religions. The following reflections are done from the perspective of Christianity, and more specifically, Catholicism; followers of other religions may view multifaith worship differently, based on their beliefs and practices.[1]

1. As mentioned above, there are abundant studies on shared worship among different Christian churches and also on interreligious dialogue, yet works on multifaith worship are few and

What Is Multifaith Worship?

Usage of Terms

First, a plethora of terms are used to refer to the kind of religious sharing under consideration. In addition to "multifaith," other terms such as "interfaith," "interreligious," "faith-to-faith," and "inter-ritual" sharing are also used. These can be used interchangeably, without significant theological ambiguity. Because religious sharing can be done among more than two religions and because it poses serious challenges to personal faith and not simply to religious institutions and rituals, I prefer "multifaith." Furthermore, because "worship" in Christian theology has a very specific meaning—the cult of God, and more strictly, of the trinitarian God as Father, Son, and Spirit[2]—some think it should be replaced by more neutral terms such as "service," "observance," "celebration," "event," and "meditation," especially when religious sharing is done with followers of nontheistic and polytheistic religions. Since multifaith sharing is essentially religious and is most often understood as such by those who practice it, I prefer "worship," though I will note its analogical meaning when discussing religious sharing between Christianity and nontheistic and polytheistic religions.

Multifaith Prayer and Multifaith Worship

In interreligious sharing, it is important to distinguish between prayer and worship, especially in the case of the Christian churches that have sacra-

---

far between. The following are noteworthy: Marianne Moyaert and Joris Geldhof, eds., *Ritual Participation and Interreligious Dialogue: Boundaries, Transgressions and Innovations* (London: Bloomsbury, 2015); Michael Amaladoss, "Inter-Religious Worship," in *The Wiley-Blackwell Companion to Inter-Religious Dialogue*, ed. Catherine Cornille (Malden, MA: Wiley-Blackwell, 2013), 87–98; Pierre-François de Béthune, *Interreligious Hospitality: The Fulfillment of Dialogue*, trans. Robert Henrey (Collegeville, MN: Liturgical Press, 2010); British Council of Churches, *Multi-Faith Worship?* (London: Church House, 1992); British Council of Churches, *A Statement on Inter-Faith Services* (London: Church House, 1968); British Council of Churches, *Can We Pray Together? Guidelines on Worship in a Multi-Faith Society* (London: Church House, 1983); Marcus Braybrooks, ed., *Inter-Faith Worship: A Report of a Working Party* (London: Stainer & Bell, 1974); Peter R. Akehurst and R. W. F. Wootton, *Inter-Faith Worship?* (Bramcote, UK: Grove, 1977); Matt Sanders, *Interfaith Ministry Handbook: Prayers, Readings, and Other Resources for Pastoral Settings* (Berkeley: Apocryphile, 2016); Christopher Lewis and Dan Cohn-Sherbok, eds., *Interfaith Worship and Prayer* (London: Jessica Kingsley, 2019); Ted Brownstein, *The Interfaith Prayer Book* (Lake Worth, FL: Lake Worth Interfaith Network, 2014); Paul Puthanangady, ed., *Sharing Worship: Communicatio in Sacris* (Bangalore: National Biblical, Catechetical & Liturgical Centre, 1988). Other works will be cited throughout the chapter as appropriate.

2. Catholic theology distinguishes between *latreia* (adoration or worship), which is reserved for God alone; *doulia* (veneration), which is rendered to the saints; and *hyperdoulia* (higher veneration), which is reserved for Mary because of her special position as the Mother of God.

mental worship, often designated as "liturgy."[3] Sharing prayer with believers of other religions, especially with Judaism, whose psalms are recited by Christians in private and public prayers, is in principle noncontroversial for Christians. However, it does pose problems when Christians pray together with believers of nontheistic and polytheistic religions. By contrast, there is strong objection to multifaith worship not only between Christianity and other religions but also among Christian churches themselves—that is, ecumenical shared worship. The latter case is commonly referred to as *communicatio in sacris* (sharing in sacred things). Some churches, particularly the Catholic and Orthodox churches, discourage their members from taking part in other church services and especially receiving Communion by eating the bread and drinking the wine that are not believed to have been transubstantiated into the body and blood of Christ. Conversely, members of churches that do not have apostolic succession guaranteeing the validity of the Eucharist, or that do not believe in the "Real Presence" of Christ in the eucharistic elements of bread and wine, are generally excluded from receiving Communion.[4]

It goes without saying that this prohibition of shared worship among different Christian churches is all the more stringent in the case of multifaith worship, where there is no common faith in the trinitarian God as Father, Son, and Spirit and no common practice of Christian sacramental and liturgical worship. As a consequence, I will discuss multifaith prayer and multifaith worship separately as two different forms of interfaith sharing, each with a different set of conditions for the legitimacy of interreligious sharing.

3. In Catholic theology, "liturgy" (*leitourgia* literally means the work [*ergon*] of the people [*leitos*]) is the official, public, and communal worship of the church. This work is essentially God's work in Christ by the power of the Spirit, in which the church participates when it celebrates the liturgy with duly ordained ministers. Because the liturgy is God's work, it is said to be efficacious by itself (*ex opere operato*), in contrast to "popular devotions," which are not liturgical or sacramental and are efficacious, not *ex opere operato*, but only due to the spiritual condition of the one performing them (*ex opere operantis*). See *Catechism of the Catholic Church*, 2nd ed. (Vatican City: Libreria Editrice Vaticana, 1994), nos. 1066–109.

4. The Catholic Church and the Orthodox Church recognize the validity of each other's Eucharist, but the latter does not permit non-Orthodox Christians to receive Communion, whereas the former does permit its members to receive Communion in the Orthodox Church in case of urgency and necessity. Neither church permits members of churches that do not have apostolic succession—namely, churches that issued from the Reformation—to receive Communion in their churches. This applies to the Anglican/Episcopal Church, whose orders are not recognized by the Catholic Church. See William DeTucci, *Communicatio in Sacris: The Roman Catholic Church against Intercommunion with Non-Catholics* (Raleigh, NC: Lulu, 2012); Jeffrey VanderWilt, *Communion with Non-Catholic Christians: Risks, Challenges, and Opportunities* (Collegeville, MN: Liturgical Press, 2003).

Is Multifaith Worship a Theological Impossibility or a Religious Necessity?

Whether multifaith worship is a theological impossibility or a desideratum and even a necessity for our time depends on the specific theology of religion that is espoused. It is commonplace to classify this theology into three types: exclusivism, inclusivism, and pluralism.[5]

As far as multifaith worship is concerned, exclusivism, which holds that Jesus is the unique and universal Savior and that only Christianity is the true religion, logically regards multifaith worship not only as unnecessary but also as forbidden. Participation in multifaith worship would implicitly acknowledge that the religious rituals of non-Christian religions possess some salvific value and that Jesus is not the only Savior of all. Exclusivists maintain that religions other than Christianity are nothing more than humanity's sinful inventions and that their rituals are rank superstitions, which Christians must unconditionally condemn and not condone by taking part in them. Multifaith worship of any form is theologically unjustified, especially if the religions with which worship is shared either (1) do not mention God, even though they do not explicitly deny God, such as Buddhism, or (2) profess that there are many gods and goddesses, such as Hinduism. All mainline Christian churches have espoused exclusivism until approximately the second half of the twentieth century, when religious diversity severely challenged this traditional theology of religion.[6] This is particularly true of the Catholic Church, which made a significant turn toward what is today known as inclusivism only at the Second Vatican Council (1962–65). By contrast, all evangelical churches, including fundamentalist and Pentecostal churches—with the exception of a rare few of their theologians—continue to maintain exclusivism as their theological as well as missiological stance.[7]

5. The literature on the theology of religion is, by now, extremely vast, and each type has very articulate defenders. Furthermore, the dividing lines among the three types are quite porous, each type containing elements of the other two, especially in the case of inclusivism. One very helpful introduction is Paul Knitter, *Introducing Theologies of Religion* (Maryknoll, NY: Orbis Books, 2002). Knitter offers a more nuanced classification: replacement, fulfillment, mutuality, and acceptance models.

6. A representative advocate of exclusivism is the early Karl Barth, a Swiss Reformed theologian (1886–1968).

7. One Pentecostal theologian who is open to interreligious dialogue is the Malaysian-American Amos Yong (1965–), one of the most prolific and influential Pentecostal theologians of our time. True to his Pentecostal roots, Young develops a distinctive theology of religion from the perspective of pneumatology. My own theology of religious pluralism is akin to Yong's: see Peter C. Phan, *The Joy of Religious Pluralism: A Personal Journey* (Maryknoll, NY: Orbis Books, 2017).

On the opposite side of the spectrum, pluralism in its most radical form regards differences in religious beliefs and practices as essentially cultural, theologically equivalent, and mutually complementary interpretations of basically the same religious experience. Pluralists tend to downplay the particularity of all religions and emphasize their universality and similarity. Religions are like Joseph Jastrow's rabbit-duck representation, various ways of mapping the same terrain, and different paradigms to explain the same physical phenomenon—for example, light as a wave and as a particle.[8] Which alternative explanation should be accepted depends not on its alleged truth but on its usefulness for a particular task at hand. Religions may be regarded as equally valid paths to God or the "Real," John Hick's new name for God, to accommodate nontheistic religions.[9] The abilities to "see-that" and "to-see-as," to use Ludwig Wittgenstein's celebrated expressions, are not mutually contradictory but enrich each other and apply to religions as well.[10] For pluralists, consequently, multifaith worship is not only theologically possible but also highly desirable, even necessary, for our contemporary context of religious diversity, so that all religious traditions can be complemented and enriched by other religious traditions.[11]

In between these two theologies of religion stands inclusivism. On the one hand, like exclusivism, it maintains that Jesus and Christianity alone possess the fullness of truth and grace; on the other hand, like pluralism, it acknowledges that other religions do possess some elements of truth and grace or that believers of other religions may have formulated and/or practiced certain truths better than Christians.[12] Consequently, multifaith worship within the context of interreligious dialogue is a desideratum, even a necessity, but only under certain conditions that respect the truths about Jesus and the church for both multifaith prayer and multifaith worship.

It is hard to say which of these three theologies of religion carries the day with the most convincing arguments. Some theologians have called for a moratorium on the theological debate about their respective validity and suggested a new and allegedly more fruitful field of research—namely, comparative theology, in which theologians do a thick description and a detailed comparison between a particular text or ritual of one religion with those of

8. Jastrow's rabbit-duck figure can be easily located online.
9. John Hick, *God Has Many Names* (Louisville: Westminster John Knox, 1980).
10. See, e.g., https://www.phrases.org.uk/famous-last-words/ludwig-wittgenstein.html.
11. The best-known proponents of pluralism are the Scottish John Hick (1922–2012) and the American Paul Knitter (1939–). See Hick, *An Interpretation of Religion: Human Responses to the Transcendent*, 2nd ed. (New Haven: Yale University Press, 2005); Knitter, *No Other Name? A Critical Survey of Christian Attitudes toward the World Religions* (Maryknoll, NY: Orbis Books, 1985).
12. The most influential proponent of inclusivism is the German Karl Rahner (1904–84). See his *Foundations of Christian Faith: An Introduction to the Idea of Christianity*, trans. William Dych (New York: Herder & Herder, 1982).

another, with the sole goal of understanding better the text or ritual of one's own religion through the insights of those other religions.[13]

At the heart of the debate on multifaith worship is the question of Christian identity, which is seen by those opposing multifaith worship as being weakened or even betrayed by it, or by those supporting it as being enlarged and deepened. What is it and in what does it consist? In 1988 the Indian theologians gathered at the conference on "Worship Sharing" in Bangalore defined it as follows: "Our Christian identity is derived from Jesus Christ by our sharing in the experience of Jesus' relationship with the Father. An individual or a community participates in the paschal mystery by reliving the Resurrection-Pentecost event."[14] They go on to add that this Christian identity is indissolubly connected with the church as the visible community of Christ's disciples, the embodiment of his Spirit. But this church is far from being uniform, unchanging, and closed upon itself:

> This Christian identity and ecclesial reality have been incarnated and expressed in a variety of ways in different places and times, in diverse socio-cultural-religious milieux and as such they are called local Churches; the fellowship of these Churches is the universal Church. This localization and incarnation of the Church in different situations gives birth to a plurality of doctrine, formulations, forms of worship with symbols and rituals, community and social organizations, and forms of authority, law and government. These latter expressions are subject to change as history progresses and society evolves. The Christian identity and the ecclesial reality have to relate themselves afresh and respond adequately to the new exigencies and challenges of the pluri-cultural, multi-religious and unjust human situations in India by new and creative forms of open, wider and inclusive fellowship.[15]

One of these new exigencies and challenges is precisely multifaith worship. Its possibility depends on one's prior, explicit or implicit, theology of religion: exclusivism is most antagonistic to it, pluralism most favorable to it, and inclusivism open to it but only under certain conditions.

Urgent Demands for Multifaith Prayer and Worship

While a moratorium on discussing the theologies of religion may be advisable in the academy, everyday life presents many opportunities and demands

---

13. Two theologians who have made this suggestion are Francis Clooney (1950–) and James Fredericks (1951–), the former working on Hinduism, the latter on Buddhism.

14. Puthanangady, *Sharing Worship*, 788.

15. Puthanangady, *Sharing Worship*, 789.

for multifaith worship that cannot be ignored. Obviously, in countries in which believers of different religions live cheek by jowl, with Christianity as a minority religion, as in most countries of Asia, multifaith worship is an urgent issue requiring timely and appropriate solutions. It is no wonder that in places like India—the cradle of many religions, where believers of different religions live side by side and religious violence is a perpetual threat, to which political and religious leaders are not averse to exploiting for their advantage—multifaith worship is a topic of great relevance and vigorously disputed and fervently advocated.[16]

However, religious diversity is no longer confined to Asia but is now a fact of life in Europe and North America, where Christianity is still a majority religion.[17] Multifaith worship is an issue in many aspects of life. There are more than a few public religious celebrations, such as Thanksgiving and Christmas, in which all citizens, regardless of their faith allegiances, are expected to participate. In addition, public events of a political nature— such as the coronation of a king or a queen, the swearing-in of an elected politician to public office, community action after a natural disaster, and especially healing of religious violence—often call for prayers to be offered by ministers or chaplains of various religions. Furthermore, in institutions such as schools, hospitals, and prisons, where there are people of different faiths, religious services and chaplaincies are expected to cater to the spiritual needs of the students or inmates. Other private ceremonies—such as marriage between a Christian and a non-Christian, and funerals for families of different faiths—also require interfaith prayer and worship. Finally, there are hundreds of other mundane occasions in which people of diverse faiths are involved—such as sports competitions, social action volunteers' meetings, cultural activities, ethnic festivities, community meals, charitable services, business meetings, and environmental activities—where a multifaith prayer is not inappropriate. In our religiously diverse society, even in Christian-majority countries, multifaith prayer and multifaith worship are no longer a rare thing, restricted to a spiritual elite, but a new opportunity and challenge

16. See the 801-page and extremely rich volume containing the papers given at the conference on "Sharing Worship" convened at the National Biblical, Catechetical & Liturgical Centre in Bangalore, India, January 20–25, 1988: Puthanangady, *Sharing Worship*, cited above. See also "Findings of an Exploratory Consultation on Interreligious Prayer: Final Statement" (Bangalore, 1996), in *Pro Dialogo* 98, no. 2 (1998): 231–36; and Sela Raj and Corinne Dempsey, eds., *Popular Christianity in India: Riting between the Lines* (New York: University of New York Press, 2002).

17. See Diana L. Eck, *A New Religious America: How a "Christian Country" Has Become the World's Most Religiously Diverse Nation* (San Francisco: HarperSanFrancisco, 2002); and various recent polls on religious membership in the United States published by Pew Research Center, available online.

for believers of all religions to grow in mutual understanding and to extend hospitality to one another.

In our time, such opportunities for multifaith worship have increased significantly. Maryanne Moyaert enumerates five reasons for what she calls "interriting."[18] The first is an invitation by family members, friends, or colleagues who belong to religious traditions other than one's own to take part in their religious rituals such as birth, marriage, funerals, baptism, baby-naming, bar and bat mitzvahs, first Communion, confirmations, and other life-cycle events. This religious attendance, motivated mainly by family relationship or friendship, is often a one-off choice and does not normally involve a deep commitment to multifaith worship. However, it does afford attendees a useful entry into and experience of religious diversity and ritual variety in settings that prevent them from being a threat to their religious identity.

The second reason for multifaith worship is interfaith or mixed marriages, where the spouses are people practicing different faiths. Rather than an occasional opportunity, mixed marriages require multifaith worship to be constantly negotiated and practiced, not only by the spouses themselves but also, and more significantly, for their children. Different solutions are possible, ranging from attending worship services in different places by turn as a family, to worshiping individually in places of one's choice. Multifaith worship is also practiced daily in the family, from morning and evening prayers to blessings over meals; holy seasons such as Advent, Lent, and Ramadan; and religious festivals during the year. Furthermore, instead of making use of officially approved prayers, hymns, and rituals, the couple could compose their own to express common elements of their faiths.

The third reason is offered by the education environment with interfaith pedagogies. After careful preparation, students in courses on world religions may be given the choice to visit sacred places during the community's celebration of their religious rituals—for example, a Catholic church during the Mass, a Hindu temple during the puja ritual, a Jewish synagogue during the Seder or a bar mitzvah, a Muslim mosque during the Friday *Ṣalāt al-jumuʿah*, or a Buddhist sangha during its meditation. These visits convey to students not only an academic understanding of religion but also an experience of lived religion made up of a tightly connected web of doctrines, rituals, religious symbols, devotional practices, sacred art and architecture, spiritual songs, and dance. This embodied understanding of religion may lead students to adopt some religious practices that they may at first find strange or repugnant but eventually find to be spiritually enriching and transformative.

18. See Moyaert and Geldhof, *Ritual Participation and Interreligious Dialogue*, 3–5.

The fourth reason is that multifaith worship is a way to express solidarity with members of a particular religion that is being discriminated against. For example, to combat Islamophobia and to show support for Muslims, Christians may want to practice fasting with Muslims during Ramadan or to take part in the pilgrimage (*hajj*) to Mecca.

The fifth and last reason is the desire to grow spiritually by adopting certain spiritual practices of other religions. This is a lifelong and committed practice to follow a spiritual path taught by another religion while still maintaining and faithfully practicing the rituals and precepts of one's own faith. Sometimes this is referred to as multiple (dual) religious belonging or multiple religious participation.[19] Although the possibility of this multiple religious belonging—or at least practicing—continues to be debated in theological circles, there have been historical precedents of it among Christians. Famous names include French Benedictine Henri Le Saux, also known as Swami Abhishiktananda (1910–73), German-Japanese Jesuit Hugo M. Enomiya-Lassalle (1898–1990), American Cistercian Thomas Merton (1915–68), English Benedictine Bede Griffiths (1906–93), Spanish-Indian priest Raimon Panikkar (1918–2010), and more recently, Sri Lankan Jesuit Aloysius Pieris; Roger J. Corless; John P. Kennan; Ruben Habito and his wife, Maria Reis Habito; Sallie B. King; Paul Knitter; and a host of others.

Since there is not only the possibility but also the necessity of multifaith worship, especially in the context of the religious diversity in our time, what are the modes and conditions for its exercise?

Multifaith Prayer and Multifaith Worship

I mentioned above that a distinction should be made between multifaith prayer and multifaith worship since from the theological standpoint there is an essential difference between the two activities, between "veneration" and "adoration," each with a different set of church laws regulating them, conditions for implementation, varying degrees of frequency, and the number of participants.

Multifaith Prayer: Different Forms

Douglas Pratt sees interfaith prayer as rooted in interreligious dialogue and distinguishes four types or models of interfaith prayer, with ascending

19. On this practice, see Peter C. Phan, *Being Religious Interreligiously: Asian Perspectives on Interfaith Dialogue* (Maryknoll, NY: Orbis Books, 2004), 60–81; Rose Drew, *Buddhist and Christian? An Exploration into Dual Belonging* (London: Routledge, 2012); and Gideon Goosen, *Hyphenated Christians: Towards a Better Understanding of Dual Religious Belonging* (New York: Peter Lang, 2011).

degrees of intensity and difficulty.[20] The first is "shared multireligious act," in which believers of another religion are invited to be present at one's religious community. This form of interreligious prayer, if it can be called such at all, is not much more than "participant observation," even though it is religiously motivated and respectfully carried out.

The second is "contiguous multireligious act," where believers of different religions engage in their own prayer acts without the intermingling of acts of prayer. The most famous examples of this are the two World Days of Prayer for Peace convoked by Pope John Paul II in Assisi in 1986 and 2002 and the one by Pope Benedict XVI in 2011. It was explicitly stated that people of different faiths "come together to pray but not to pray together." This format of interreligious prayers *in series* in the same space and on the same day typically concludes with participants of all faiths gathering in a common place for silent prayer or meditation, but there is no praying vocally together by using some common formula.[21]

The third model, called "an intentional-combined religious act," is that in which common prayers are created out of the spiritual resources of several religious traditions by blending or combining them in such a way that the distinctive elements of each religion are left out and the lowest common denominator is maintained. This is usually done when those who participate in interreligious prayers come from theistic, nontheistic, monotheistic, and polytheistic religions. Most believers, especially religious leaders, would object to this form of interreligious prayer on the ground that it gives rise to syncretism and reductionism.

The fourth model, which Pratt calls "coherent-integrated interreligious prayer," is one in which prayers from different religious traditions are selected and interlinked around a theme, event, or need, thus providing "coherence" and "integration" to the "interreligious prayer," yet without changing their texts or combining them into another common prayer. As Pratt puts it, "There is no attempt to blend the rich diversity of contributions into a

---

20. Douglas Pratt, "Religion as Religion Does: Prayer as a Form of Ritual Participation," in Moyaert and Geldhof, *Ritual Participation and Interreligious Dialogue*, 53–66; cf. a quite helpful discussion of interreligious prayer, with a sample of prayers taken from different religions: Thomas Ryan, *Interreligious Prayer: A Christian Guide* (Mahwah, NJ: Paulist Press, 2008).

21. During the World Day of Prayer for Peace in 1986, Pope John Paul II gave instruction regarding three phases in this interreligious prayer: (1) separate praying by each religion in its own rite in separate places; (2) separate vocal and serial prayers by each religion in a common place; and (3) common prayer in this common place, not in verbal utterances but in silence. In this sense, the formula that is often used to describe the Assisi World Day of Prayer for Peace, "Come together to pray but not to pray together," is only partially correct: there *is* common praying, not in vocal utterances but in *silence*, often the most powerful and transformative form of prayer.

kind of spiritual porridge, nor is the outcome marked by the happy random-ness of a smorgasbord. No religious tradition is compromised, no reduction of essence or denial of religious self-identity of the participating traditions occurs."[22] Nevertheless, Pratt claims, there is "some sense of greater whole-ness, . . . an intuition of a larger context, a wider or deeper sphere wherein a unifying spirit is at work."[23]

All four models of interreligious prayer described above implicitly assume that authentic praying must be verbal and vocally uttered. The first model restricts it to participant *observation*, which, though labeled as "participant," by definition excludes praying on the part of the observer. The second model postulates that because praying demands verbalization, it can be legitimate only if it is said in *different locations* (or time slots) by each tradition. The third model attempts to compose a common verbal prayer by *combining verbal prayers* of different and at times self-contradictory religions, leading to syncretism and relativism. Even the fourth model, which Pratt seems to favor, is essentially similar to the second, since, as happened at the celebra-tions of the World Day of Prayer for World Peace at Assisi, there was a stage on which the various religious representatives gathered in a common space *after* their separate prayers, and then each recited aloud their own prayer se-riatim, to which the members of other religions *listened* with respect but did not internally appropriate as their own, as a prayer that might nourish and transform their spiritual lives. None of these models envisages the possibility and desirability of believers of one religion doing *all* of these actions: listen-ing to, receiving, appropriating internally and silently, integrating into their daily praying, and reciting jointly the prayers of another religious tradition. In this form of interreligious prayer, there is no verbal syncretistic blending of prayers and no denying and downplaying distinctive elements of religious self-identity. But there is no juxtaposition of the prayers of different religions side by side or seriatim either. Instead, there is the goal to appropriate some prayers of another religion and pray them *as one's own*, individually and as a community.

Of course, this kind of multifaith prayer is easier to achieve among the Abrahamic religions since these three religions possess extensive historical and doctrinal connections with each other. In fact, the psalms of Judaism are prayed daily by Christians, privately and liturgically. Furthermore, there should be no spiritual difficulty for the followers of the three religions to pray the Our Father, the Magnificat, St. Francis's Peace Prayer and the Canticle to

22. Pratt, "Religion as Religion Does," 59.
23. Pratt, "Religion as Religion Does," 59.

the Creatures, the Sura 1 (the Fatiha), the Litany of the Ninety-nine Names of God, just to give a few examples.[24] Moreover, common praying with the followers of the so-called Asian religions, which do not have common origins with the Abrahamic religions, is obviously more challenging but not impossible. Of course, the nontheistic and polytheistic elements in Buddhism and Hinduism must be recognized and carefully interpreted. A nontheistic religion is not necessarily anti-theistic or atheistic, and a polytheistic religion does not always deny the existence of one supreme God. Furthermore, not all Buddhist and Hindu prayers include these elements, just as not all Christian prayers invoke the Trinity and end "in the name of Jesus." Even Pope Paul VI prayed the Hindu prayer from Brihadaranyaka Upanishad 1.3.28 ("From the unreal lead me to the real; from darkness lead me to light; from death lead me to immortality") during his first visit to India in 1964. A careful and sensitive selection of prayers from the Asian religions for use of all believers is possible.[25]

Of course, interreligious prayer, whether among the Abrahamic religions or between these and Asian religions, must be preceded by a collaborative consultation to avoid anything that might hinder communion and offend religious sensibilities. Elements that should be discussed and agreed upon include the theme, the site, the day and time, the order and content of the service, the language used and translation, the choice of readings, the use of symbols and rituals, music and singing, silence and meditation, and the foods and drinks to be served at the end of the service.[26]

Multifaith Worship: A Possibility?

Finally, a brief consideration of multifaith worship in the strict sense of the term—that is, participation in another religion's rituals and sacraments, or *communicatio in sacris*. As mentioned earlier, multifaith sharing of the

24. There are three quite helpful collections of prayers of this type: Jean Potter and Marcus Braybrooke, eds., *All in Good Faith: A Resource Book for Multi-Faith Prayer* (Oxford: The World Congress of Faiths, 1997); Sanders, *Interfaith Ministry Handbook*; and Brownstein, *Interfaith Prayer Book*. Discussions of interreligious prayer with Muslims, Hinduism, Zen Buddhism, and Judaism are available in Moyaert and Geldhof, *Ritual Participation and Interreligious Dialogue*, 81–121 (for Islam), 126–37 (for Hinduism), 156–77 (for Zen Buddhism), and 181–223 (for Judaism).

25. The volume edited by Lewis and Cohn-Sherbok, *Interfaith Worship and Prayer*, discusses how interfaith prayer is possible and necessary, and the named religions include Hinduism, traditional African religions, Judaism, Jainism, Buddhism, Zoroastrianism, Shintoism, Christianity, Islam, Sikhism, Unitarianism, and the Baha'i faith. On prayer with nontheistic religions, see Michael Amaladoss, "Interreligious Worship," in Cornille, *Inter-Religious Dialogue*, 95–96.

26. See practical suggestions in Ryan, *Interreligious Prayer*, 41–46; and the British Council of Churches, *Multi-Faith Worship?*, 31–56.

sacraments and sacred rituals—not only prayers—of another religion is universally forbidden since it presumes that the participant has undergone an initiation ritual, such as baptism for Christians or taking refuge in the three jewels for Buddhists, and is a member in good standing of that religion. In addition, a religious organization may have further restrictions: for example, the Catholic Church restricts the reception of the body and blood of Christ under the species of bread and wine (Communion) only to its members and forbids them to receive Communion in a non-Catholic church. However, under exceptional cases, such as the danger of death, Catholic ministers can lawfully administer certain sacraments such as penance, Eucharist, and anointing of the sick to Orthodox Christians who are not in communion with Catholic Church, and Catholics can receive the same three sacraments from Orthodox ministers.[27] Of course, the prohibition of *communio in sacris* applies with greater force to non-Christians.

Some recent authors have attempted to make the case for *communio in sacris* not only for all Christians regardless of their denominations but, more significantly, even for non-Christians. Space limit allows me to consider only two cases. First, unsurprisingly, is a group of Indian theologians at the research seminar, already referred to above, at the National Biblical, Catechetical & Liturgical Centre in Bangalore in 1988; the theme of the seminar was "Sharing Worship." The *communio in sacris* under discussion includes both ecumenical and interreligious worship sharing. Regarding interreligious worship sharing, the "Final Statement" of the seminar mentions two issues: sharing the sacred scriptures and sharing the rituals of non-Christian religions. Regarding the first issue, the seminar says that "the liturgy is the most appropriate place to listen to and resonate with the promptings of the Spirit through the Scriptures of other religions."[28] Regarding the second issue, and more specifically, the sharing of the Eucharist with non-Christians, the seminar advocates its possibility on the basis of the common bond that unites Christians and believers of other religions: "Eucharistic hospitality to followers of other religions could be our expression of a common bond that exists *de facto* within the universal economy."[29] Taking into consideration the social condition of India, the seminar suggests that eucharistic Communion could be extended to "those who are committed to Christ but for some serious reason do not accept baptism[,] fearing alienation from their community," and to those who

---

27. For a detailed explanation of the Catholic Church's legislation on *communio in sacris*, see Puthanangady, *Sharing Worship*, 356–411. For the text of Canon 844 of the Code of Canon Law regulating *communio in sacris*, see VanderWilt, *Communion with Non-Catholic Christians*, 214.

28. Puthanangady, *Sharing Worship*, 792.

29. Puthanangady, *Sharing Worship*, 800.

are engaged in the work for "human liberation and solidarity with the poor, even if they might not have accepted Christ as their Lord."[30]

The second author arguing for *communicatio in sacris* with non-Christians is Richard Kearney, a professor of philosophy at Boston College. Kearny argues for what he calls "an Open Eucharist" by using the insights and practices of the Benedictine Henry Le Saux, also known as Abhishiktananda, and Teilhard de Chardin. Of the former, he cites his practice of eucharistic sharing in India and his startling saying: "A restricted Eucharist is false. . . . Whoever 'loves' his brother has a right to the Eucharist."[31] Of the latter, he expounds the theology of matter itself, especially the body, as the eucharistic body of Christ, of which all human beings are called to partake. Kearney urges extending the Eucharist to all, irrespective of religious belonging, and distinguishes four types of Eucharist, each successively enlarging the eucharistic circles: "Canonical Eucharist," "Interreligious Eucharist," "Fraternal Eucharist," and "Carnal Eucharist."[32]

Interfaith or multifaith worship, in the form of either sharing prayer or sacramental or ritual sharing, is becoming not only possible but also necessary, not only for the sake of the flourishing of Christianity and other religions, but also for the survival of our world and the cosmos itself, now under the threat of ecological disaster and extinction of biological species. Through interreligious dialogue by living a common life, collaborating with others for the common good, exchanging theological views, and even sharing spiritual experiences, religions can respond to the needs of humanity and build a just and peaceful world.

For Further Reading

British Council of Churches. *Multi-Faith Worship? Questions and Answers from the Inter-Faith Consultative Group.* London: Church House, 1992.

De Béthune, Pierre-François. *Interreligious Hospitality: The Fulfillment of Dialogue.* Collegeville, MN: Liturgical Press, 2010.

Lewis, Christopher, and Dan Cohn-Sherbok, eds. *Interfaith Worship and Prayer: We Must Pray Together.* London: Jessica Kingsley, 2019.

Moyaert, Marianne, and Joris Geldhof, eds. *Ritual Participation and Interreligious Dialogue: Boundaries, Transgressions and Innovations.* London: Bloomsbury, 2015.

30. Puthanangady, *Sharing Worship*, 800.
31. Ricard Kearney, "Toward an Open Eucharist," in Moyaert and Geldhof, *Ritual Participation and Interreligious Dialogue*, 138–55.
32. Kearney, "Toward an Open Eucharist," 153–55.

Phan, Peter C. *Being Religious Interreligiously: Asian Perspectives on Interfaith Dialogue.* Maryknoll, NY: Orbis Books, 2004.

————. *The Joy of Religious Pluralism: A Personal Journey.* Maryknoll, NY: Orbis Books, 2019.

Puthanangady, Paul. *Sharing Worship:* Communicatio in Sacris. Bangalore: National Biblical, Catechetical & Liturgical Centre, 1988.

Ryan, Thomas. *Interreligious Prayer: A Christian Guide.* Mahwah, NJ: Paulist Press, 2008.

Epilogue

Pursuing a Theology of Worship

Martyn Percy

Given that I spend a great deal of time in worship, I was nonetheless quite taken aback to be asked to write on my theology of worship. Like breathing, I had not really thought about it very much. Worship is just something that I do. I don't think about it very much. Like breathing, when I need to have conversations about it, the talk feels almost unnatural. I am the dean of an Oxford College and of a busy Anglican Cathedral—the Dean of Christ Church, Oxford, heads both. We have a world-famous choir, supported by a Cathedral Choristers' School that has been here for five hundred years, and helps us produce some of the most exquisite music on the planet.

Cathedral worship draws in people from just about everywhere: local, regional, national, and international. Some come for the predictability of the Daily Offices, with the fine intoned chanting of psalms and canticles. Others might be drawn to the "musical-mash" that one could encounter at a diocesan celebration or ordination—mixing contemporary praise songs with folk hymns, Taizé chants, and traditional choral fare. Others come for an occasional Jazz Mass, or Nine Lessons and Carols at Christmas, or an act of worship for a charity or civic occasion. There are baptisms, weddings, funerals, and memorial services. We are, literally, week by week, saturated in worship.

So, what is worship? What is a theology of worship supposed to tell you? You would need more than this epilogue to answer that, so what follows is a suggestive sketch of some theological lines you can trace and reflect on. Let me begin with some preliminaries.

First, if religion is anything, it is surrender. We are prepared to acknowledge and profess our awe, wonder, and incomprehension at revelation; rather than try to understand or deconstruct religious revelation, we submit. Vocations are a kind of double surrender—essentially preparing to admit that, since we have been overwhelmed by the grace and power of God, our lives are purposeless unless we are led into that purpose for which Christ calls us. Worship is a response to love that we did not initiate.

Second, worship accepts that we are always fundamentally struggling with the overwhelming abundance of God. Worship is a daily reminder of God's grace, love, tenderness, and mercy, which far exceeds anything we can desire, and it has nothing to do with what we think we deserve or might have earned. Worship is rooted in that other truth about the divine Presence, the infinite expansiveness of God, which is his wisdom. Worship is heart, head, mind, body, soul, spirit—because it cannot be contained and processed by feelings or rationality alone.

Third, worship is a relationship. It is a way of communing with God and one another. It requires others to share in it, even when we are solitary. Whether it is our prayers or our praises, any Christian theology of worship is, de facto, a recognition of the corporate nature of how we relate to God, and how God in turn relates to us. It is the expression of our social dependence on the Transcendent. It is inherently sacramental: a mediated point, time, and space of instrumentality in which the life of God meets the life of the world. In touching us like this, we are transformed, transcended, and transfixed. The burning bush, the still small voice, the gentle presence of the Spirit—all worship will change, comfort, consolidate, and console us at some level. It will discipline and disrupt us. It is personal, and it is corporate; it is pastoral and prescient. All worship has intrinsic socio-spiritual agency.

With these three preliminaries in place, we are now able to make some suggestions about certain other theological lines of inquiry that can be traced. Again, there are three to follow here: the corporate, spiritual, and dynamic.

Corporate

To some extent every denomination is, to borrow a phrase from John Caputo, an attempt to express the "mood of God."[1] Ecclesial life is, inevitably, the

---

1. See Gary Gutting, "Deconstructing God," *New York Times*, March 9, 2014, in an interview with John Caputo and discussing Caputo's book *The Prayers and Tears of Jacques Derrida:*

social reification of any group's theological priorities and spiritual proclivities. Class, ethnicity, gender, and various contextual factors all have a bearing on the shaping of denominational life, of course. But the mood of a denomination or congregation essentially captures and communicates what it thinks is the heart, mind, and nature of God. Emotions are an underappreciated dynamic in ecclesiology; in what follows, I outline why an anthropology of emotions and moods might be a helpful lens through which to refract a different kind of theological reflection. Namely, this is one that takes the "ideal emotional temperature" of a denomination or congregation seriously and understands that there is potential in this for perceiving new ways of configuring the theological repertoires of ecclesial communities.

A book that I often muse about penning, but am equally sure I will never write, would be titled *Weather Reports: Toward a Climatology of Denominations and Congregations*. The emotional repertoire and temperature of ecclesial communities has interested me for many years. I studied revivalism, and specifically the theme of power in the contemporary charismatic renewal.[2] The groups I looked at were within the "romantic negotiation," a term coined by James Hopewell in his groundbreaking (and rather eclectic) *Congregation: Stories and Structures*.[3] Hopewell's work draws on the anthropology of Clifford Geertz and his observation that religion is "a system of symbols which acts to establish powerful, pervasive and long-lasting moods and motivations in men by formulating conceptions of a general order of existence and clothing these conceptions with such an aura of factuality that the moods and motivations seem uniquely realistic."[4]

While it is true that all worship expresses a shared congregational or ecclesial mood and character, we should not lose sight of the observation that all ecclesiology flows from theology. Worship reflects who people think God is and what God is like. But is there anything that unites all theologies of worship? The answer to such a seemingly complex question is yes, and the theological key to this is far simpler than many might suppose. Essentially, a Christian theology of worship is rooted in the radical nature of gathering, which in turn was rooted in the revolutionary character of a theology that

---

Religion without Religion (Bloomington: Indiana University Press, 1997), https://opinionator.blogs.nytimes.com/2014/03/09/deconstructing-god/.

2. See Martyn Percy, *Words, Wonders and Powers: Understanding Contemporary Christian Fundamentalism and Revivalism* (London: SPCK, 1995); Percy, "The Morphology of Pilgrimage in the Toronto Blessing," *Religion* 28, no. 3 (July 1998): 281–89; Percy, "Adventure and Atrophy in a Charismatic Movement," in *Practicing the Faith: The Ritual Life of Pentecostal-Charismatic Christians*, ed. Martin Lindhardt (New York/Oxford: Berghahn Books, 2011), 152–78.

3. James Hopewell, *Congregation: Stories and Structures* (London: SCM, 1987).

4. Clifford Geertz, *The Interpretation of Cultures* (New York: Basic Books, 1973), 90.

believed in a God who called us to together to form a new community. But exactly how is this?

To make the point more sharply, we need to understand that long, long ago there were essentially two kinds of god.[5] The older and more primal gods are those that emerged out of communities, tribes, and nations; such gods consecrated their habits and forms of association as virtuous and sacred. The gods of the pagan world were of this kind, and they tended to reside in shrines and other specific places; unless visited or called upon, they did little to alter the day-to-day world of their followers. These gods looked like humans, lived and loved like humans; they could even be as fickle as humans.

The other kind of God does not live in a shrine. The second kind calls new communities into being. Every area of life is touched. God is infinite and beyond human thinking and emotions—indeed, beyond comprehension. This second kind of God is timeless and placeless; there can be no image for such a deity, save perhaps the one that the Gospel of John (1:14) gives us: "the Word made flesh." This kind of God is indescribable. All the words and images that convey the mystery and overwhelming reality are inherently insufficient.

And there are two kinds of religions.[6] The first is older and shrine-based. In ancient Rome, followers of the gods were much more like a clientele than a membership of worshipers. Clients came to temples with specific issues. But they patronized the temples and shrines; they did not belong to them. Thus, an average Roman in AD 30 might pay a visit to the temple of Zeus in the morning for one serious matter and, perhaps hoping for luck in love later in the day, might patronize the shrine of Aphrodite or Eros on the way home from work. The temples and shrines charged their clientele for prayers, feasts, services, and rituals. Many of these temples and shrines received financial support from the state as well. The gods who dwelt therein were appealing precisely because they were quite human in their virtues, faults, passions, and proclivities. They certainly supported the state—and the status quo.

The second kind of religion was more difficult to fathom. The religion of the monotheists made no sense to the modern world of the first-century Romans. A God who seemed distant and difficult to comprehend was one problem. But the larger problem for the first-century Romans was that monotheistic faiths tended to gather crowds, or congregations. The worshipers belonged to their God, and then to one another in worship and bonded fidelity. Moreover, to follow this one God necessarily meant that there was one kingdom—yet to be realized—that was greater than the state. To belong to

5. Rodney Stark, *The Triumph of Christianity* (New York: HarperOne, 2011), 9–31.
6. Stark, *Triumph of Christianity*, 9–31.

a faith that had one omnipotent ruler or God meant aligning oneself with a spiritual and political outlook that potentially placed the congregation above and certainly at odds with the state. The catholic ideal was, therefore, first and foremost a vision of faith that preceded the state and would finally triumph over temporal authority. The earthly kingdoms of the present were mere interludes.

Partly for this reason, the Romans persecuted the Zoroastrians and the Magi, who intentionally gathered for worship. They similarly suppressed the Bacchanalians, who also gathered as one. Isis inspired congregations too—and the Romans suppressed them as well. Just as the Romans also suppressed the Jews and then the Christians, both of whom formed congregations. There were good reasons for the Romans to be fearful of congregations. Every meeting was, potentially, a subversive political gathering; coming together for worship could not fail to make a sociopolitical statement.

There were other reasons to fear the new congregations rooted in monotheism. The old faiths dealt with the baser senses and were rooted in civic ceremonies, private petitions, and public feasts. The new faiths—of monotheism—touched the senses in quite different ways and were rooted in liberation, joy, and even ecstasy. There was talk of love for one another and of a God who loved creation and also humanity. No Roman seriously believed that Jupiter loved any human; their gods were fickle and to be feared. But monotheists did think that God loved them; and although God was to be feared, God was also a redeemer.

The new monotheistic faiths also stressed individualism and virtue. The gods of the state were to be set aside in favor of personal salvation. The monotheists believed that individuals could be saved; practices such as purification, prayer, baptism, and other practices emphasized this. The new faiths also had scriptures—something that most of the old faiths lacked. The emerging new faiths were, quite suddenly, written and therefore rational. They also became organized—not only with priests, deacons, and overseers but also as distinct bodies with memberships. Congregations came into existence. Romans were infrequent and irregular visitors to their temples and shrines. The new faiths gathered intentionally, purposefully, and regularly: "When you gather, . . . do this in remembrance of me" (cf. Luke 22:19; 1 Cor. 11:18, 24–25). And this is partly what made them such a threat to the Romans. This is indeed partly why the church, like the synagogues, was persecuted; the simple act of gathering was of itself revolutionary.

Churches rarely think about the origins of their identity in this radical way. They mostly go about their business, assuming their values, and implicitly imbibing these from one generation to the next. In a way, this is a pity, since valuable practices are often left to chance: inchoate by nature, they simply persist implicitly. Churches rarely think, for example, about how and why they welcome the strangers and aliens in their midst—mostly very easily, without fuss or further reflection. But welcome they do: not only giving to the stranger but also receiving from them. This is not merely an observation about how Christians engage with others who are not kith and kin; it is also a remark about the oft-hidden dynamic of reception, gift, and charity. So just how revolutionary is the church? Thomas Tweed observes that "[religions] are confluences of organic-cultural flows that intensify joy and confront suffering by drawing on human and supra-human (i.e., divine) forces to make homes and cross boundaries."[7] I am rather drawn to this definition of religion and, by extension, of churches. Churches, at their best—and one presumes a passionate real faith in a real God as a basis—know that good religion, when it comes together and gathers intentionally, performs four important transformative tasks.

First, they *intensify joy*. They take the ordinary and make it extraordinary. They know how to celebrate lives, love, and transitions. They bless what is good and raise hope, thanks, and expectation in prayer and praise. They lift an institution and individuals to a new plane of existence—one of blessing and thankfulness for what is and can be. And they not only move but also intensify. Just as a birth becomes even more significant in a baptism, so in mission and ministry does a ceremony become more with prayer and celebration. Second, *suffering is confronted*. Working with pain, bereavement, counseling, and consolation is familiar to all ministers and churches—providing the safe space and expertise that holds and slowly resolves the suffering that individuals and institutions carry inside them. Third, *the making of homes* is a profoundly analogical and literal reference to the function of faith. Our "faith homes" are places of both open hospitality and security: safe spaces of nourishment, well-being, maturity, diversity, and individuation. Fourth, faith helps us *to cross boundaries*—to move forward and over the challenges of life, on to new places. It can be crossing deserts to find promised lands or passing from darkness to light.

Religion never keeps us in one place; even with our homes, it moves us. It is in gathering that we meet the One who is present in bread and wine as we sit at table, who is there in the breaking of the bread, who makes our hearts burn as the Scriptures are read. Meeting together is where we encounter Jesus Christ more richly than we can on our own. In the radical act of our gatherings, we discover life-saving truths for the world.

7. Thomas Tweed, *Crossing and Dwelling* (Cambridge, MA: Harvard University Press, 2006), 12.

Spiritual

Any Christian theology of worship needs to begin with small words. One of the most significant yet overlooked words in the New Testament that is used about God is "with." Jesus chooses to be with us; Emmanuel is God-with-us. Jesus is the body language of God: seeing the unseen, hearing the unheard, touching the untouchable, embracing the marginalized and ostracized, and being "with" all those who are ignored by others. The Gospels also go further than this, seeming to suggest that one of the key words or ideas to help us understand the ministry of Jesus and the subsequent blueprint for the church is that of "abiding." The word is linked to another English word, "abode."

Thus, God abides with us. Christ bids us to abide in him, and he will abide in us. He bids us to make our home with him, as he has made his home with us. Christ tells us that there are many rooms in his Father's house. There are many places of gathering and meeting there. And central to the notion of an abode is the concept of abiding. To abide is to "wait patiently with." God has abided with us. He came to us in ordinary life, and he has sat with us, eaten with us, walked with us, and lived among us. That is why John ends his Gospel with Jesus doing ordinary things. Breaking bread with strangers; eating breakfast on the seashore. God continues to dwell with us. He was with us at the beginning, and he is with us at the end. He will not leave us. God wants his church to abide with the world—and especially to be with all those who have no one to be with them. The friendless, the forlorn, the forgotten—God wills us to abide with them and with each other. Fellowship is God's will for creation, not just for congregations. Worship is therefore "accommodating" God and a recognition that God accommodates us. In worship, God and humanity abide.

God is Emmanuel (God is with us), and a Christian theology of worship proceeds from this point. God made us for company with each other and for eternal company with him. God is with us in creation, in redemption, and finally, in heaven. "God with us" is how John's Prologue begins: the Word was with God; he was with us in the beginning. God is with us in the valley of the shadow of death; he is with us in light and dark, chaos and order, pain and passion. Though we may turn aside from God, God will not turn from us. In the resurrection, Jesus is again with us—more powerfully and intensely than ever. God is with us. That is the good news of the kingdom that Jesus proclaims. We will never be left or forsaken. Whatever befalls us personally or collectively, God will still be true to us and hold us. That is the question for the possibility of the church and is tested in worship week by week. As God is with us, can we be with each other? As God bears us all, can we bear each other? Can we truly bear the price of the church, which is togetherness, the price of not being alone? The possibility of the church is locked up in forsaking isolation from one another. Because togetherness—deep, abiding inclusiveness in worship, that we should not be alone—is part of our created and redeemed world.

This perhaps is why our spirituality of worship is something that sifts and sanctifies our desires and dreams. Similarly, in this poem George Herbert comprehends the mystery of prayer as a journey of the senses and soul, as it were:

> Prayer the church's banquet, angel's age,
> God's breath in man returning to his birth,
> The soul in paraphrase, heart in pilgrimage,
> . . . .
> A kind of tune, which all things hear and fear;
> Softness, and peace, and joy, and love, and bliss,
> Exalted manna, gladness of the best,
> Heaven in ordinary, man well drest,
> The milky way, the bird of Paradise,
> Church-bells beyond the stars heard, the soul's blood,
> The land of spices; something understood.[8]

In teaching his disciples to pray and worship, Jesus keeps the matter simple. God will answer prayers. God listens to persistence. We are to hallow the name of God, seek the coming of God's kingdom, name our needs (but note, *not* desires—God can *always* see what we *want*), ask forgiveness for our wrongdoings, forgive others, and pray for deliverance.

Worship is not the act of engaging a contract in which we are assured that God will answer our prayers directly or according to our (flawed and sinful) petitions and agendas. Rather, as the Scriptures attest, God is consistent and evenhandedly attentive, and God will always answer in love. No one who wants bread will get a stone; no one who wants a fish will get a scorpion. As the mystics say of worship: God does not know how to be absent. God does not know how to forget you or overlook you. God sees every sparrow that falls. God numbers the hairs of your head; God looks after one stray sheep, not just ninety-nine compliant ones.

God can give only good things. God can only bless; he does not curse. As the rabbis say, God rules by blessing. Christian theologies of worship are discerning: trying to develop a wisdom to see what God is giving in blessing. Worship, then, is attuning the person and congregation to God's heart and

---

8. George Herbert, "Prayer (1)," https://www.poetryfoundation.org/poems/44371/prayer-i.

mind, so that our own developing wisdom finds something of an echo with the wisdom that comes from above. Worship is not a vehicle for placing a list of demands before God. It is the self, placed before God, and surrendered in praise and submission, through which the needs and desires of the world and the individual can be set before the true light, which cleanses the thoughts of our hearts so that we can love and worship more perfectly.

I used to remark to students training for ordained ministry that they had no job and no profession to look forward to when the bishop laid hands upon them. What they were preparing for was a life that was an "occupation." Our priests are to be occupied with God and then to be preoccupied with all the people, places, and parishes that are given by God into our care: to dwell among, care for, and love those people and places as Christ himself would do.[9] Status has no value here. Moses led the Hebrews out of Egypt and to the promised land, and his humility was a sign of his godly strength and purpose, not weakness: "For Moses was a person of exceeding meekness above any that that dwelt upon the earth" (Num. 12:3). Surrender . . . awe, wonder . . . Jesus as the Praise of God. As the exquisite hymn in Philippians puts it, Jesus did not "cling to" or "grasp at" equality with God, "but emptied himself, taking the form of a slave. . . . And being found in human form, he humbled himself" (Phil. 2:7–8). From that place, it was a life of obedience, of blessing and gratitude, and of raising up those around him.

In view of this, where might we locate a Christian theology of worship? To be sure, no leader is remotely like Jesus, or ever could be. Here, I turn to kenosis—a term that generally refers to the "self-emptying" of Christ and is an aspect of the doctrine of the incarnation. It is expressed most succinctly in the (so-called) Christological Hymn found in Paul's Letter to the Philippians (2:6–11 ESV alt.):

> [Christ Jesus,] though he was in the form of God,
>   did not count equality with God a thing to be grasped,
> but emptied himself, by taking the form of a servant,
>   being born in human likeness.
>   And being found in human form,
> he humbled himself by becoming obedient to the point of death,
>   even death on a cross.
> Therefore, God has highly exalted him
>   and bestowed on him the name that is above every name,

9. See comments by Martyn Percy in Ian Tomlinson's work, *Clergy, Culture and Ministry: The Dynamics of Roles and Relations in Church and Society*, ed. M. Percy (London: SCM, 2017), vii–xvii, 165–75.

> so that at the name of Jesus every knee should bow,
>   in heaven and on earth and under the earth,
> and every tongue confess that Jesus Christ is Lord,
>   to the glory of God the Father.

Here we are faced with an incomparable sense of God's creative restraint that ends, as we have seen, in praise. Indeed, this call to humility and hope is rooted in the overwhelming abundance of God. The hymn follows a meditative exhortation from Paul on the nature of character in Christian leadership (Phil. 2:1–5 ESV):

> So if there is any encouragement in Christ, any comfort from love, any participation in the Spirit, any affection and sympathy, complete my joy by being of the same mind, having the same love, being in full accord and of one mind. Do nothing from selfish ambition or conceit, but in humility count others more significant than yourselves. Let each of you look not only to his own interests, but also to the interests of others. Have this mind among yourselves, which is yours in Christ Jesus.

Churches are, as Stanley Hauerwas notes, "communities of character."[10] In such communities, people are being *disciplined* by the grace of God into the new life that God, in Christ, has claimed them for. Such communities are not mere gatherings of groups with shared interests. Nor are they homogenous units. Rather, this is a "thick gathering" of those being consciously renewed by the salvific action of God in Christ. Such communities have to be called back, constantly, to the exposure of "all desires known," and so that "the thoughts of our hearts" might be cleansed by the inspiration—the very breath—of the Holy Spirit. This has an ontological depth to it, and it is kenotic in character. Only by following the one who "emptied himself" can one discover the foundation for humility, the space for joy in others, and for joy in God.

Dynamic

In one of the most remarkable theological meditations of the past fifty years, Daniel Hardy and David Ford reflect on how the ecology of praise, joy, and laughter is an essential component in facing evil, suffering, and death.[11] Hardy

10. Stanley Hauerwas, *A Community of Character: Toward a Constructive Christian Social Ethic* (South Bend, IN: University of Notre Dame, 1991).
11. Daniel W. Hardy and David F. Ford, *Jubilate: Theology in Praise* (London: Darton, Longman & Todd, 1984).

and Ford highlight the inadequacy of stoicism and call for a deeper theological response to the wickedness, malice, and horror that individuals and communities may face. They argue that joy and praise—rooted in our acknowledgment of the overwhelming abundance of God—can help us to face the darkness that threatens to envelope us and to address it with a different perspective. This means anticipating the flow of the Spirit of God in our lives, as uniquely embodied in the life of Jesus, which expresses the ultimate overflow of praise to God and brings the most manifest intensification of the good news of the kingdom. Jesus is, literally, the body language of God.

To some extent, the self-conscious kenosis of Christ anticipates this in the way of the cross. But "self-emptying" here is not a kind of resigned stoicism. It continues to be, in Jesus, a journey of praising, knowing, and joy; yet a journey that also faces evil and suffering. Golgotha is not for himself; it is for us. It is a kind of surrender, but not of stoicism and self-resignation; it is a surrender to God, into whose hands Jesus ultimately commits himself. The cross is therefore also an act of will and resistance too, for it refuses to abandon hope. Here humility remains the ground of wisdom; and it confounds and further infuriates others. So we must know and remember that others may want to humiliate those with vocations to leadership. This is part of the costly path to lead and to serve.

Hardy and Ford remind us, however, that while patience, endurance, and bravery are all important (in discipleship and leadership), this stoicism will not be sufficient as a proper theological response to the forces of evil that are sometimes faced and the suffering that results. Daringly, they argue that stoicism can prevent us from really facing the intensification of shame that sometimes grips institutions and communities, causing them to transfer their blame to others. Here, they suggest, "only joy can creatively oppose evil in all its perversion of both order and non-order; stoicism at best contains it, resists it and maintains order and dignity in the face of it."[12]

Therefore, they argue, it is only the overwhelming abundance of God—and the proper response of joy and praise to this—that can truly address the darkness that threatens to envelop. Moreover, there might need to be some recognition that the darkness itself contains some gift. By this, I do not mean to sacralize suffering and alienation. But it is worth remembering that the Old Testament sees the exile of the Israelites as a form of agency that both chastises and purifies God's people, even though this produces great sorrow (e.g., see Ps. 137). To enter into an understanding of God's ecology is to see that, in God, there is no darkness or light but only one equal light. Hence

12. Hardy and Ford, *Jubilate*, 141.

even some demanding difficulty and apparent loss can be transfigured.[13] This requires, however, a particular kind of faith, hope, and trust for what will be, and for what is: who we already are before God. It is this kind of kenosis—a self-emptying in order to be filled with the joy of the Spirit and with the overwhelming abundance of God—that makes the way of servant leadership so demanding and yet so very liberating. It is a kind of existence different from that of stoicism.[14]

Like most people in positions of institutional and religious leadership, I find myself more in tune with the Christian stoicism critiqued by Hardy and Ford, and less a creature of praise and joy.[15] So an ecology of grace (i.e., deeply comprehending God's full and unconditional love for the other), tempered by an appropriate and natural humility, might be the only way to cope with the projections and detriments done to us. For this reason, I admire Harry Smart's poem "Praise": "Praise be to God who pities wankers / and has mercy on miserable bastards."[16]

What this means in practice will vary across individuals, congregations, and communities. But what can be said is that all Christians are incorporated into Christ's perpetual oblation. In being part of the priesthood of all believers, everything that comes to us, or comes upon us, is returned to God in confession and intercession—and then offered up for sanctification and blessing, before being returned. Christians participate in the life of Christ; in our own self-emptying, willful descent and conscious path of humility, we are bound to an ecology of obedience rather than one of mere self-preserving resistance.[17]

There is, then, a paradox at the heart of kenosis. It is not a kind of weary resignation in the face of the malign forces of fate. It is, rather, an act of determination and resolve; an exercise of deep power from within that chooses—in the example of God in Christ—to limit power and knowledge but not to limit love, hope, joy, and peace. The path of leadership will be one of obedience, accepting that a conscious and deep form of humility will no longer privilege power and knowledge. Rather, these will be set aside in a continuous, willful, and generative life of humility, which will place others above the self.

13. My reflections on this have been greatly helped by John Hull, *In the Beginning There Was Darkness: A Blind Person's Conversations with the Bible* (London: SCM, 2010). Hull, who is blind, argues that as the darkness and light are all one to God, we need to "see" our challenges as disciples differently.

14. However, see also Margaret Whipp, *The Grace of Waiting* (Norwich, UK: Canterbury, 2017). Whipp argues for the virtue of watchful patience as one of the primary disciplines to be cultivated in addressing suffering, as well as discussing the shortcomings of stoicism.

15. Hardy and Ford, *Jubilate*, chap. 6.

16. Harry Smart, "Praise," in *A Fool's Pardon* (London: Faber & Faber, 1995), 7.

17. On this, see Jane Williams, *The Merciful Humility of God* (London: Bloomsbury, 2019).

These insights, I think, have some bearing on how we approach the practice of our worship. But such kenosis is, as I say, something of a paradox—because the love can be fierce, just as the passion is a willful act of determination, not resignation. Moreover, this love can contain anger and even make space for disruptive acts of prophetic leadership. It must make space for peace, joy, hope, patience, and kindness too—and so be formed by God's grace.

God's power is rooted in relinquishing and transforming. It is not kept or traded: it is given away, free. Human power and much leadership typically takes resources for its own ends, merely to maintain and grow itself. God's power—located on a foundation of sacrificial love, hospitality, and humility—builds up and is eternal. Human power, based on competition and dominance, is temporal and decays.

Small wonder then, that the formation of character is an area now receiving increasing attention from theologians. John Barton draws our gaze to how much of the Old Testament wisdom tradition emphasizes suffering and the apophatic as a key to our development.[18] But so is, equally, the concept of *disciplined attention*: watchful patience, moral sagacity, emotional intelligence, vicarious virtue-honed perception—all can be found in Proverbs, Ecclesiastes, Ecclesiasticus (Sirach), and Psalms.

Conclusion

The homiletic tone of this epilogue is intended to accomplish what we aspire for all sermons and homilies to do: prompt reflection, self-examination, and some soul-searching. At the same time, it may induct us into imaginative ways of thinking critically about the Scriptures and our Christian tradition, alongside the challenges we face in our daily lives and complex social existences.[19] Our concern has been to wrestle with some of the issues that leaders face, including the intensification of shame, and view these issues with humility, humiliation, and hope. We have commented on the need for these to be addressed through greater attention to praise and joy, and with the "self-emptying" kenosis that makes space for the abundant fruit of the Spirit (Gal. 5:22–23).

In closing, let me highlight kindness as something that flows naturally from a person's leadership because of their humility. Kindness is a rare quality, and it has been shown that modeling kindness and creating a culture of kindness

18. John Barton, "Character Formation in Biblical Wisdom," *Crucible: The Journal of Christian Social Ethics*, January 2019, 18–28.

19. See Simon Western, *Leadership: A Critical Text* (London: Sage, 2007).

can have a positive energizing effect, creating improved interpersonal relations and increasing commitment. Moreover, it is infectious. It is a named fruit of the Spirit (Gal. 5:22–23). Granted, kindness requires balance, because it cannot recuse the leaders from making difficult and costly decisions. However, kindness does express appropriate concern for others, and it communicates value and empathy in contexts that some can experience as alienating and marginalizing. However, it is both intriguing and concerning that the term "kindness" has been absent from leadership vocabulary. Many will perceive it to be a sign of weakness or possibly even manipulative. Yet when kindness flows from an authentic humility, it is energizing and enabling. Kindness is important as a "leadership behavior."[20] It is a fruit of the Spirit that becomes a gift to others.

Scott Cairns has written a poem on perspective in roles, taking the Beatitudes and extending them into the terrain over which we often find ourselves journeying as leaders: "Blessed are those who watch and pray, who seek and plead, / for they shall see, and shall be heard."[21]

In ending here, I simply invite all who lead to practice kindness, to be authentically humble, and to be charitable, even to those who might seek to humiliate you. Do not be afraid. There will be humiliations, naturally. But if we dare to wait in darkness, there will be light (Rom. 8:18–39). Indeed, it is often in the waiting, hoping, trusting, and kenosis that we are *refined*—formed anew to become those joyful, kind, patient, humble, gentle, and faithful leaders that God has called us to be.[22]

For Further Reading

Block, Daniel. *For the Glory of God: Recovering a Biblical Theology of Worship.* Grand Rapids: Baker Academic, 2016.

Hardy, Daniel, and David Ford. *Jubilate: Theology in Praise.* London: Darton, Longman & Todd, 1984.

Ingalls, Monique, and Amos Yong, eds. *The Spirit of Praise: Music and Worship in Global Pentecostal-Charismatic Christianity.* University Park: Pennsylvania State University Press, 2015.

20. See Gay Haskins, Lalit Johri, and Michael Thomas, *Kindness in Leadership and Its Many Manifestations* (London: Routledge, 2016).
21. See Scott Cairns, "Late Sayings," in *Slow Pilgrim: The Collected Poems* (Brewster, MA: Paraclete, 2015), 132; Mark Burrows, ed., *The Paraclete Poetry Anthology: 2005–2016* (Brewster, MA: Paraclete, 2017).
22. For further reading on waiting, see W. H. Vanstone, *The Stature of Waiting* (London: Darton, Longman & Todd, 1982); Whipp, *The Grace of Waiting.*

Lemons, Derrick, ed. *Theologically Engaged Anthropology*. Oxford: Oxford University Press, 2018.

Lync, Danielle Anne. *God in Sound and Silence: Music as Theology*. Eugene, OR: Pickwick, 2018.

Muers, Rachel. *Keeping God's Silence*. London: Blackwell-Wiley, 2004.

Acknowledgments

As Mark (Lamport) finished editing a three-volume book on "hymns and hymnology" (Cascade, 2019), he asked Lester Ruth, a leading scholar of worship studies at Duke Divinity School/Duke University, if, in his opinion, there were gaps in the academic field of worship and ministry studies for which additional textbooks should be created. His response has led directly to this series on "foundations of worship." Melanie Ross—one of the most important voices in liturgical studies today, in Mark's opinion, and a fabulous scholar at Yale Divinity School—also saw the opportunity to contribute in a meaningful way to her academic field and embraced the project by lending her credibility and massive network of the best scholars to partner with us in these volumes. One of our most pleasing moments was when Khalia J. Williams, a professor and assistant dean of worship at Candler School of Theology/Emory University, agreed to take on coediting duties for the "theology" book. She is a talented voice and passionate leader in worship and ministry studies.

We would also like to thank the following individuals who reviewed early drafts of our publishing proposal and offered sage advice: David Music, Michael Hawn, Paul Westermeyer, Robin Leaver, Byard Bennett, Bridget Nichols, Martin Tel, Corneliu Simut, Dan Sharp, Chris Bounds, Jim Samra, Jelle Creemers, Klaus Issler, Frank Senn, Dan Sharp, and Earl Waggoner. Our gratitude also goes to a stellar group of "editorial consultants" who handled the indexing: Ron J. Bigalke, Trent Hancock, Philip Bustrum, Mel Wilhoit, Benjamin Espinoza, Bryce Hantla, Jonathan Best, and Mark Eckel.

The brainstorming with our top-notch editorial advisory board (EAB) produced not only a rich conceptual framework for the series but also corralled leading academics and practitioners to write these chapters. See the names of the EAB on the masthead personnel page at the front of book.

Special appreciation goes to N. T. Wright and Nicholas Wolterstorff for endorsing the project by writing insightful and original introductions—Nick for the series, Tom for this book. They are some of our very favorite authors.

Finally, we credit Robert Hosack and the editorial board at Baker Academic for offering this two-volume contract. Bob's careful eye and the fabulous work of Brandy Scritchfield, Julie Zahm, and Sarah Gombis helped to shape our efforts and make the result even more coherent.

Contributors

Series Editors

Melanie C. Ross (PhD, University of Notre Dame; MA, Yale Divinity School/ Yale Institute of Sacred Music) is a professor of liturgical studies at Yale Divinity School. Her research lies at the intersection of ecumenical liturgical theology, North American evangelicalism, and the worship practices of contemporary congregations. Ross's most recent book is titled *Evangelical versus Liturgical? Defying a Dichotomy* (2014). She edited (with Simon Jones) *The Serious Business of Worship: Essays in Honour of Bryan D. Spinks* (2010). Her articles have appeared in *Liturgy, Scottish Journal of Theology, Pro Ecclesia*, and *Worship*. In 2014 she was awarded a Luce Fellowship by the Association of Theological Schools and a Sabbatical Grant for Researchers by the Louisville Institute in Louisville, enabling her to work on an ethnographic study titled "Varieties of Evangelical Worship: An American Mosaic." Ross is a member of the American Academy of Religion and the North American Academy of Liturgy.

Mark A. Lamport (PhD, Michigan State University; ThM, Princeton Theological Seminary) is professor of practical theology at graduate schools in Arizona, Colorado, Indiana, Virginia, Belgium, The Netherlands, and Portugal. He is coauthor of *Nurturing Faith: A Practical Theology for the Educational Mission of the Global Church* (2021), and editor of *Christianity in the Middle East* (2020); *Hymns and Hymnody: History and Theological Introductions* (3 vols., 2019); *Encyclopedia of Christianity in the Global South* (2 vols., 2018); *Encyclopedia of Martin Luther and the Reformation* (2 vols., 2017); *Encyclopedia of Christianity in the United States* (5 vols., 2016, named "Notable

Book of 2016" by *Christianity Today*); *Encyclopedia of Christian Education* (3 vols., 2015, winner as Booklist Editors' Choice: Adult Books).

Editors

Khalia J. Williams (PhD, Graduate Theological Union; MATS, Columbia Theological Seminary) is the assistant dean of worship and music, assistant professor in the practice of worship, and the codirector of Baptist studies at Emory University's Candler School of Theology. She conducts research focusing on womanist spirituality, embodiment, and worship.

Mark A. Lamport (see above, as a series editor).

Introducers

Nicholas Wolterstorff (PhD/MA, Harvard University) is retired from teaching philosophy for thirty years at Calvin College and for fifteen years at Yale University. He has been a visiting professor at Harvard, Princeton, Oxford, Notre Dame, the Free University of Amsterdam, and Temple; among other schools in Texas, Michigan, and Virginia. Among his more-recent book-length publications are *Hearing the Call: Liturgy, Justice, Church, and World*; *The God We Worship* (2011); and *Acting Liturgically* (2018).

N. T. (Tom) Wright is research professor of New Testament and early Christianity at St Andrews in Scotland, and senior research fellow at Wycliffe Hall in Oxford. The author of over eighty books, he earlier taught in Oxford, Cambridge, and McGill universities and held various positions in the Church of England, finally as Bishop of Durham (2003–10).

Chapter Authors

E. Byron (Ron) Anderson (PhD, Emory University; MDiv, Yale University Divinity School/Yale Institute of Sacred Music) is the Ernest and Bernice Styberg Professor of Worship and associate dean for Institutional and Educational Assessment at Garrett-Evangelical Theological Seminary in Evanston, Illinois.

Rhodora E. Beaton (PhD and MDiv, University of Notre Dame) is associate professor of liturgical and sacramental theology at the Oblate School of

Theology in San Antonio, Texas. Her research focuses on the sacramentality of the Word of God and human language.

Teresa Berger (Dr. Theol., Heidelberg; Dr. Theol. Habil., Münster) is professor of liturgical studies at the Yale Institute of Sacred Music and Yale Divinity School, where she also holds an appointment as the Thomas E. Golden Jr. Professor of Catholic Theology.

Andrew E. Hill (PhD, University of Michigan) is professor of Old Testament at Wheaton College and Graduate School. His current research and publications include topics of leadership, prayer, and the interface of positive psychology and Christian worship. Hill is also a faculty member of the Robert E. Webber Institute for Worship Studies, where he teaches the Biblical Foundations of Worship.

The Rev. Canon **Lizette Larson-Miller** (PhD, Graduate Theological Union) is an Anglican priest and the Huron Lawson Professor at Huron University College (University of Western Ontario, London, Ontario). Her degrees in music, liturgical studies, and sacramental theology are from the University of Southern California, St. John's University (Minnesota), and the Graduate Theological Union (Berkeley). Larson-Miller's most recent book is *Sacramentality Renewed* (2016).

Maurice Lee (PhD, Yale University; MA, Fuller Theological Seminary; MS, California Institute of Technology) is pastor of Prince of Peace Lutheran Church in Santa Barbara, California. He also teaches theology for the North American Lutheran Seminary in Ambridge, Pennsylvania.

Anne McGowan (PhD and MTS, University of Notre Dame) is assistant professor of liturgy at Catholic Theological Union in Chicago. She is the author of *Eucharistic Epicleses, Ancient and Modern* (2014) and coauthor (with Paul Bradshaw) of *The Pilgrimage of Egeria: A New Translation of the Itinerarium Egeriae with Introduction and Commentary* (2018).

Ronald T. Michener (Dr. Theol., D.E.S., Faculté Universitaire de Théologie Protestante de Bruxelles; MA, Western Seminary) is professor and chair of the Department of Systematic Theology, Evangelische Theologische Faculteit in Leuven, Belgium. His research focuses broadly on the interplay between postmodern philosophy and evangelical theology.

Bruce T. Morrill (PhD, Religion, Emory University) is the Edward A. Malloy Professor of Roman Catholic Studies at Vanderbilt University. He has published eight books and over a hundred journal articles, book chapters, and reviews in the areas of liturgical and systematic theology.

Ivana Noble (PhD, Heythrop College, University of London; MTh, Hussite Theological Faculty, Charles University, Prague) is a professor of ecumenical theology at Charles University in its Protestant Faculty, Prague, Czech Republic. She is a former president of Societas Oecumenica, and currently leads the project Theological Anthropology in Ecumenical Perspective.

The Very Reverend Professor **Martyn Percy** (PhD, King's College, University of London) is the forty-fifth Dean of Christ Church, Oxford, England, and a member of the faculty of theology at the University of Oxford. He writes and teaches in two interrelated arenas: contemporary ecclesiology (specializing in Anglicanism, fundamentalism, and new Christian movements); complemented by practical, pastoral, and contextual theology, with significant work on Christianity and contemporary culture. His recent books include *Anglicanism: Confidence, Commitment, Communion* (2013); *Thirty-Nine New Articles: An Anglican Landscape of Faith* (2013); *The Futures of Anglicanism: Contours, Currents, Charts* (2017); and he edited the *Oxford Handbook of Anglican Studies* (2015). Percy has the distinction of being the only living theologian mentioned and quoted in Dan Brown's *The Da Vinci Code* (chap. 55).

Pheme Perkins (PhD, New Testament and Christian Origins, Harvard University) is the Joseph Professor of Catholic Spirituality in the Theology Department of Boston College and an associate editor of the *New Oxford Annotated Bible*. She is the author of many books and articles, including *Gnosticism and the New Testament* (1993); *Introduction to the Synoptic Gospels* (2007); and *1 Corinthians* (2012). Perkins is a past president of the Catholic Biblical Association of America and chair of its executive board.

Peter C. Phan holds three earned doctorates (Pontificia Universitas Salesiana and University of London), is the author or editor of some forty books and over three hundred essays on theology, and is the inaugural holder of the Ignacio Ellacuria Chair of Catholic Social Thought at Georgetown University, Washington, DC. He is completing a manuscript on the theology of migration (Oxford University Press).

Don E. Saliers (PhD and BD, Yale University) is Canon Distinguished Professor of Theology and Worship, Emeritus, and Theologian-in-Residence, Emory University, and is widely published in liturgical theology, aesthetics, and music.

Eugene R. Schlesinger (PhD, Marquette University) is lecturer in the Department of Religious Studies at Santa Clara University. He specializes in systematic theology, focusing on ecclesiology, sacramental theology, and the relation between the church's worship and its mission. He is the author of *Missa Est! A Missional Liturgical Ecclesiology* (2017) and *Sacrificing the Church: Mass, Mission, and Ecumenism* (2019).

W. David O. Taylor (ThD, Duke Divinity School) is assistant professor of theology and culture at Fuller Theological Seminary. He is the author of *The Theater of God's Glory* (2017) and *Glimpses of the New Creation* (2019).

James K. Wellman Jr. is professor and chair of the Comparative Religion Program in the Jackson School of International Studies at the University of Washington. His books include *Evangelical vs. Liberal: The Clash of Christian Cultures in the Pacific Northwest* (2008), *Rob Bell and the New American Christianity* (2012), and (as coauthor) *High on God: How Megachurches Won the Heart of America* (2020).

Khalia J. Williams (see above, as an editor).

Index

Abraham, 6, 6n12, 7
Adonay-Yireh, 7
After Heaven (Wuthnow), 219
After Our Likeness (Volf), 223
American individualism, 219
Anaphora of St. James, 210
Anderson, Byron, 76
Andrewes, Lancelot, 170
Anselm, 54
Apocrypha, 16
apophatic theology, 56
apostolic succession, 129–30
ark of the covenant, 10–11
association regulations, 23
Augustine of Hippo, 40n26, 169
Augustus, 21

Baals, 9
Babylonia, 12, 12n21, 13
 exile, 13–14
Bacchanalians, 265
Bangalore (conference), 250, 257
baptism, 175–77
 into one body, 128, 142
 theologies of, 176
Bartholomew, Craig, 16
Barton, John, 273
Belief without Borders (Mercadante), 220
Bellah, Robert, 219, 220, 221, 228, 229
Benedict XVI (pope), 254
berakah, 61

Bernard of Clairvaux, 55
Bithynia, 28
blessing of animals, 49
body, 72–73
body of Christ. *See* Lord's Supper
Book of Common Prayer, 130, 226, 227
Bramer, Paul, 220
Branch, Lori, 226, 227, 228
Brown, Warren S., 72
Bush, George W., 235

Cairns, Scott, 274
Canaan, 9
Caputo, John, 262
Carter, Jimmy, 235
Catholicism, 245, 257
Catholic worship, 157
celebrations, 196–99
Chan, Simon, 72, 225, 227
charismatic renewal, xxv
Chauvet, Louis-Marie, 179
Christ Church, Oxford, 261
Christological Hymn, 269–70
collection of funds, 23
Collins, Randall, 236, 237, 238–42
communicatio in sacris, 247, 256–58
Communion, carrying the elements, 50
communities of character, 270
congregation, 226
Congregation: Stories and Structures (Hopewell), 263